Teaching Jung

AAR
AMERICAN ACADEMY OF RELIGION

Teaching Jung

Edited by

KELLY BULKELEY AND CLODAGH WELDON

OXFORD
UNIVERSITY PRESS

OXFORD
UNIVERSITY PRESS

Oxford University Press, Inc., publishes works that further
Oxford University's objective of excellence
in research, scholarship, and education.

Oxford   New York
Auckland   Cape Town   Dar es Salaam   Hong Kong   Karachi
Kuala Lumpur   Madrid   Melbourne   Mexico City   Nairobi
New Delhi   Shanghai   Taipei   Toronto

With offices in
Argentina   Austria   Brazil   Chile   Czech Republic   France   Greece
Guatemala   Hungary   Italy   Japan   Poland   Portugal   Singapore
South   Korea   Switzerland   Thailand   Turkey   Ukraine   Vietnam

Library of Congress Cataloging-in-Publication Data
Teaching Jung / edited by Kelly Bulkeley and Clodagh Weldon.
p.   cm.
Includes bibliographical references and index.
ISBN 978-0-19-973542-6
1. Psychology, Religious—Study and teaching.   2. Psychoanalysis and religion—Study and
teaching.   3. Jung, C. G. (Carl Gustav), 1875–1961.—Study and teaching.
I. Bulkeley, Kelly, 1962–   II. Weldon, Clodagh, 1970–
BL53.T43 2011
200.1'9—dc22   2010050964

9 8 7 6 5 4 3 2 1

Printed in the United States of America
on acid-free paper

Contents

Part III. Jung's Life, Work, and Critics

Part IV. Jungian Practices in the Classroom and Beyond

Contributors

John Beebe is a psychiatrist and Jungian analyst. A past President of the C. G. Jung Institute of San Francisco, where he is currently on the teaching faculty, Beebe is also a Distinguished Fellow of the American Psychiatric Association and Assistant and Clinical Professor of Psychiatry at the University of California Medical School, San Francisco. He is the author of *Integrity in Depth* (1992) and founding Editor of the *San Francisco Jung Institute Library Journal*.

Kelly Bulkeley is a Visiting Scholar at the Graduate Theological Union in Berkeley, California. He has written and edited several books on religion, psychology, and dreams, including *The Wilderness of Dreams* (1994), *An Introduction to the Psychology of Dreaming* (1997), *The Wondering Brain* (2004), and *Dreaming in the World's Religions* (2008).

Charlene P. E. Burns is Professor of Religion at the University of Wisconsin Eau-Claire. She is the author of *Divine Becoming* (2002), *More Moral Than God* (2008), and *Mis/Representing Evil* (2009).

John Haule is a Jungian analyst trained in Zurich and holds a doctorate in religious studies from Temple University. Haule is a training analyst at the C. G. Jung Institute of Boston. He is author of *The Love Cure* (1996), *Perils of the Soul* (1999), and *Divine Madness* (2010).

Laurel McCabe is Associate Professor of Psychology and Director of the M.A. program in Depth Psychology at Sonoma State University. Her teaching includes courses on dream work, art, and cross-cultural approaches to psychology.

David L. Miller is the Watson-Ledden Professor of Religion Emeritus at Syracuse University, and he has also taught seminars for trainees at the C. G. Jung Institute in Switzerland. His teaching and writing are in the areas of religion and myth, depth psychology, and literary theory. Miller is the recipient of the Outstanding Teacher Award from the Alumni Society of University College of Syracuse University in 1979–1980 and Syracuse University's Scholar-Teacher of the Year in 1980–1981. He is the author of *Gods and Games: Towards a Theology of Play* (1970), *The New Polytheism: Rebirth of the Gods and Goddesses* (1974), and *Christs: Archetypal Images in Christian Theology* (1981). Miller is also the editor of *Jung and the Interpretation of the Bible* (1995).

Christopher Ross is Associate Professor of Religion and Culture at Wilfred Laurier University, Canada. He is the author of several scholarly articles on Jung's theory of psychological types in relation to religion.

Susan Rowland was Professor of English and Jungian Studies at the University of Greenwich, London, UK. She is author of four books on C.G. Jung, gender and literary theory, a study of gender and detective fiction, editor of the essay collection, *Psyche and the Arts*, and author of the forthcoming monograph, *The Ecocritical Psyche* (Routledge, 2012).

Meredith Sabini is a Jungian scholar and licensed psychologist specializing in dream consultation. She is founder and director of the Dream Institute of Northern California, and editor of *The Earth Has a Soul: C. G. Jung on Nature, Technology & Modern Life* (2002).

Robert A. Segal is Professor at the University of Aberdeen, Scotland, where he holds the Sixth Century Chair in Religious Studies. He is the author of numerous books, including *The Gnostic Jung* (1992), *The Allure of Gnosticism: The Gnostic Experience in Jungian Psychology and Contemporary Culture* (1995), *Jung on Mythology* (1998), and *Myth: A Very Short Introduction* (2004).

Murray Stein is a former President of the International Association for Analytical Psychology, a founding member of the Inter-Regional Society of Jungian Analysts and the Chicago Society of Jungian Analysts, and currently Copresident and a training analyst at the International School for Analytical Psychology in Zurich, Switzerland. He is the author of *The Principle of Individuation, Jung's Map of the Soul, In Midlife*, and numerous books on Jung and religion, including *Jung's Treatment of Christianity: The Psychotherapy of a Religious Tradition* (1985). He is the senior editor of the *Jung-White Letters* (2007).

Bonnelle Strickling is a Jungian psychotherapist in private practice and a founding member of the Cathedral Centre for Spiritual Direction, where she is Senior Spiritual Director. She is also an instructor in philosophy at Langara College, Canada, and a clinical associate of the Department of Clinical Psychology at Simon Fraser University. She is the author of *Dreaming about the Divine* (2007).

David Tacey is Associate Professor of Psychoanalytic Studies and Reader in English in the School of Critical Enquiry, La Trobe University, Melbourne. He teaches courses on spirituality, Jungian psychology, and literature. He is the author of many books and articles on Jungian psychology, spirituality, and cultural studies. His most recent books include *How to Read Jung* (2006) and, as coeditor (with Ann Casement), *The Idea of the Numinous: Contemporary Jungian and Psychoanalytic Perspectives* (2006). Other recent books include *The Spirituality Revolution* (2004) and *Jung and the New Age* (2001).

Jeremy Taylor is an ordained Unitarian Universalist Minister. Founding member and past president of the International Association for the Study of Dreams, he is the author of *The Wisdom of Your Dreams* (2009) and *Dream Work* (1983). He has taught in the schools and seminaries of the Graduate Theological Union in Berkeley, California, for thirty years and continues to teach and travel widely throughout the United States, Europe, and Asia.

Ann Belford Ulanov is the Christiane Brooks Johnson Memorial Professor of Psychiatry and Religion at Union Theological Seminary in the City of New York. She is the author of numerous books on Jung, including *The Feminine in Christian Theology and in Jungian Psychology*, *Receiving Woman: Studies in the Psychology and Theology of the Feminine*, *Picturing God; The Wisdom of the Psyche*, *The Female Ancestors of Christ*, *The Functioning Transcendent*, *Religion and the Spiritual in Carl Jung*, and with her late husband, Barry Ulanov, *Religion and the Unconscious*, *Primary Speech: A Psychology of Prayer*, *Cinderella and Her Sisters: The Envied and the Envying*, *The Witch and The Clown: Two Archetypes of Human Sexuality*, *The Healing Imagination*, and *Transforming Sexuality: The Archetypal World of Anima and Animus*.

Clodagh Weldon is Associate Professor of Theology at Dominican University in Chicago and Visiting Research Scholar at Blackfriars Hall, University of Oxford. Recipient of Dominican University's 2005 Mother Evelyn Murphy Excellence in Teaching Award, Weldon is featured as a case study in highly effective undergraduate teaching in Barbara Walvoord's *Teaching and Learning in College Introductory Religion Courses* (2007). She is the author of *Fr Victor White OP: The Story of Jung's White Raven* (2007).

Teaching Jung

Introduction

Teaching with and against Jung

Kelly Bulkeley and Clodagh Weldon

Swiss analytical psychologist Carl Gustav Jung (1875–1961) made a major, though still contested, impact on the field of religious studies. Alternately revered and reviled, the subject of adoring memoirs and scathing exposés, Jung and his ideas have had at least as much influence on religious studies as have the psychoanalytic theories of his mentor, Sigmund Freud (1856–1939). Many of Jung's key psychological terms (*archetypes, collective unconscious, individuation, projection, synchronicity, extraversion,* and *introversion*) have become standard features of religious studies discourse. His extensive commentaries on various religious texts and traditions make it clear that Jung's psychology is, at one level, a significant contribution to the study of human religiosity. In works like *Symbols of Transformation* (1912), *Modern Man in Search of a Soul* (1933), *Psychology and Religion* (1938), *A Psychological Approach to the Trinity* (1942), *Transformation Symbolism in the Mass* (1942), *The Psychology of Eastern Meditation* (1943), *Aion* (1951), and *Answer to Job* (1952), Jung made pioneering efforts to explore the unconscious fantasies, fears, and desires underlying religious ideas and practices.

Furthermore, Jung's characterization of depth psychology as a fundamentally religious response to the secularizing power of modernity has left a lasting imprint on the relationship between religious studies and the psychological sciences. Just as he found protopsychological insights in the sacred texts of ancient religions, Jung identified essentially religious qualities in the modern scientific discipline of psychology. He not only used psychology to study religion but also used religion to study psychology. Of course, this opened him to strong criticism from both sides: from theologians who rejected any such attempt to apply psychological categories to religion and from scientists who rejected the equation of their rational, empirical work with the experiences of mystics and dreamers. Jung's whole career may be summed up as an effort to bridge that divide. As shown in Peter Homans's *Jung in Context: Modernity and the Making of a Psychology* (1979), Jung saw the secularization of modern Western culture in largely negative terms, as a rupture in humanity's connection with the instinctual wisdom of the collective unconscious and the natural world. Jung welcomed the declining significance of institutional religion insofar as it liberated people from the tyranny of stultifying dogma and abusive clerical authority, but he worried that without anything to replace religion as a source of meaning, many people would suffer psychological problems and become vulnerable to new forms of cultural tyranny because of their desperate yearning for a way to make sense of the world and find a meaningful place within it. The rise of psychology, in his view, represents a healthier transposition of religion into the modern world by providing a secular means of healing suffering, finding guidance through times of life transition, interpreting symbols, inspiring creativity, and making personal meaning of life experience. In this sense, Jung's psychology is both an *analysis* of religion in the modern world and an *example* of it.

Jung's ideas have filtered through the cultural awareness of the modern West to such a degree that the students who walk into today's classrooms are already Jungians in many important regards. The challenge for religious studies teachers is to help students become aware of their inchoate impressions and develop a more thoughtful and informed understanding of depth psychology as a resource for studying religion. A critical engagement with Jung is an excellent means of preparing students for the more general, and more complex, task of making sense of religious phenomena in the contemporary world. Psychoanalytically informed depth psychology has been one of the most fruitful perspectives in religious studies for more than a century, and it remains a vital theoretical tool for researchers, teachers, and students. In light of the increasing diversity we see in our classrooms, Jung's ideas about the psychological multiplicities of religion offer a stimulating resource for education that aspires to be interdisciplinary, personally relevant, and critically reflective.

Teaching Jung presents a collection of individually authored chapters that give several different perspectives on Jung's psychology and its relations with religion, theology, and contemporary culture. Written by experienced educators and scholars who teach courses in a variety of educational settings, the book provides a resource for anyone interested in the relationship between religious studies and Jungian psychology. The book's contributors describe their teaching of Jung in different academic contexts (universities, colleges, seminaries, psychology institutes), with special attention to the pedagogical and theoretical challenges that arise in their classrooms. A central theme running through all the chapters of *Teaching Jung* is the intensified self-reflexivity that students experience when they directly engage with Jung's ideas. As the contributors will show, this self-reflexivity can be further cultivated in the classroom in ways that enhance the analytic, interpretive, and critical thinking skills that characterize the best of religious studies scholarship.

The American Academy of Religion series on Teaching Religious Studies provides an ideal venue for scholars who work with Jung in these diverse academic, curricular, and pedagogical contexts and who want to engage in productive dialogue about how we teach Jung, what our learning goals are, how we integrate scholarly debates and concerns into our pedagogies, and how our teaching both reflects and influences the status of religious studies and theology in schools today. This book provides fresh perspectives on these issues by bringing together the ideas of well-respected scholars in religious studies, psychology, theology, and other disciplines whose teaching and research have explored the continuing relevance of Jung's ideas for the study of religion in the twenty-first century.

The book contains four main parts of four chapters each. The first part focuses on teaching Jung and religion in specific academic settings. These chapters lay out the pedagogical terrain, immediately alerting readers to the importance of institutional context in teaching Jung's work.

David Tacey, a professor of English, humanities, and the social sciences at La Trobe University, opens the book with an analysis of the conflict that may arise between Jung as an object of intellectual inquiry and Jung as an approach to the psyche. Such an imbalance, Tacey argues, not only misrepresents Jung but also leads to disastrous consequences for the learner (for example, an overemphasis on Jung as an approach to the psyche could lead to an inability to engage critically). In exploring the challenges of bringing Jung's ideas into the curriculum of contemporary universities, Tacey identifies four main approaches to teaching Jung (conforming, reforming, transforming, and informing), each with its own distinctive implications for the classroom. Readers will no doubt recognize aspects of these approaches to pedagogy in different chapters throughout the book.

Next, David L. Miller of Syracuse University reflects on forty years of experience of teaching Jung in a religious studies department. He discusses five major pedagogical pitfalls that can emerge when teaching Jung: a temptation to read Jungian thought in opposition to Freudian thought; a temptation to spiritualize Jung; a temptation to read Jung's notion of archetypes of the collective unconscious, as well as his views on anima and animus, as essentialist and essentializing; a temptation to view Jung's logic and rhetoric as "Gnostic"; and a temptation to read Jung's interpretations of art, religion, and culture as reductively psychologistic. In assessing these pitfalls, Miller argues that misreading Jung ultimately leads to misteaching Jung.

Ann Belford Ulanov, Christiane Brooks Johnson Memorial Professor of Psychiatry and Religion at Union Theological Seminary in New York City, considers the specific challenges involved in teaching Jung in a theological seminary and a graduate school of religion. Ulanov rejects the view that faith might be a drawback to effective teaching, a view common in secular settings and even in many departments of religion. Rather, she embraces faith as a resource in the study of the unconscious. Acknowledging that students of faith may experience fear of, as well as fascination with, the psyche, Ulanov describes how she creates a space in the classroom to explore Jung's ideas by teaching Jung in relation to other major schools and perspectives.

In the final chapter in this part, Murray Stein, a training analyst at the International School for Analytical Psychology in Zurich, draws on a wealth of teaching experience at analytical institutes on five continents to describe the educational methods used in preparing students for professional work as Jungian analysts. Offering unique insight into the Jungian training experience, Stein makes a passionate case for a slow, careful, and deep reading of primary texts over a long period of time as the key to understanding Jung's thought. Furthermore, Stein argues that Jungian psychology should be read not as the rigid doctrine of the master but as adventurous explorations in psychological thinking—explorations that often lead the students who learn about Jung to gain new perspectives on cross-cultural patterns in religious life and spiritual experience around the world.

The second part includes chapters on Jung's interpretation of particular religious texts, practices, and experiences. These chapters demonstrate several different ways of applying Jungian theory to religious phenomena, and the authors describe their most effective methods of teaching Jung's ideas to their students.

Robert Alan Segal, a religious studies professor at the University of Aberdeen, offers an in-depth exploration of Jung's ideas about myth. Segal's principal concern is to show that teaching Jung on myth involves correcting several misconceptions about myth—for example, the misconceptions that Jung's is the *only* theory of myth; that Jung's theory is the *only* alternative to a literal approach to myth; that applying Jung to myth means simply finding archetypes; that the more archetypes found, the better the application; that for Jung all myths mean the same thing; that for Jung, myths are interpretable without any knowledge of the people and cultural context that created them; and that for Jung, *everything* is mythic. Once these points have been clarified, Segal provides a more sophisticated framework for understanding mythology that makes effective but critically reflective use of Jung's ideas.

Charlene Burns teaches Jung's analysis of Christianity in her undergraduate religious studies courses at the University of Wisconsin, Eau-Claire. Many of the students come from conservative Christian backgrounds, so their encounter with Jung's ideas regularly elicits strong responses and sometimes surprising transformations. As her chapter explains, Burns has discovered that Jung's own methodological commitments provide the necessary tools for effective teaching in religious studies and other disciplines. In her classes, the students examine the epistemological, philosophical, and theological underpinnings of Jung's ideas, particularly in relation to Immanuel Kant's philosophy and Friedrich Schleiermacher's theology. This gives students a broader context in which to understand Jungian theory and their reactions to it. Burns draws attention to possible problems and pitfalls generated by the arousal of cognitive dissonance in educational experience, such as when a lifelong Christian first encounters a psychological analysis of religious belief, and she shares her methods for avoiding those problems and transforming students' personal reactions into a positive force in religious studies pedagogy.

Clodagh Weldon, a theologian at Dominican University in Chicago, focuses on the pedagogical challenges raised when teaching Jung's controversial and often vexing *Answer to Job* in an Old Testament theology course on Prophets and Wisdom Literature. Offering a detailed exposition of Jung's most theologically daring text, Weldon examines the educational process of a student's learning Jung's theories as he confronts the dark side of the biblical God. Weldon argues that *Answer to Job* provides a useful means of encouraging students to consider multiple perspectives and methodological approaches to scripture. Further, she discusses the necessity of a baptism by fire into analytical psychology and presents several suggestions for framing Jung's methodological approach to biblical texts. Finally, she offers a number of pedagogical strategies she has found to be very effective when teaching Jung.

Jung's theory of psychological types underlies the widely used Myers-Briggs personality test, but it has generally received less attention in the study of religion. Christopher Ross, of Wilfred Laurier University's Religious Studies Department, shows the potential value of Jung's psychological types for religious studies education. After summarizing the essentials of Jung's eight personality categories—determined by whether a person is (a) extraverted or introverted and (b) primarily oriented by feeling, thinking, intuition, or sensation—Ross argues that these ideas of Jung's help in the academic study of religious aspects of the life cycle, the psychology of religious differences, and religious responses to grief, loss, and death. While acknowledging the limits and potential abuses of Jung's theory of psychological types, Ross demonstrates from his own teaching career how these ideas can help educators achieve important pedagogical goals and enrich their students' learning experiences.

The third part of the book examines the relationship between Jung's life and work. He regarded his personal experiences as the raw material for his psychological research and theorizing. To understand Jung's psychology, one must know something about his personal life. And to know something about his personal life is to confront several controversial aspects of his character: his adultery and misbehavior with female analysands, his Eurocentrism, and rumors of his secret affinity for Nazism. Almost every chapter in this book addresses these issues to some extent. The chapters in this part look particularly closely at the interplay of personal experience and psychological theory in Jung's life by analyzing the available biographical information and assessing its significance for teaching Jung's ideas in contemporary classrooms.

John Haule, a Jungian analyst from C.G. Jung Institute of Boston, surveys the biographical landscape of Jung's life not only in terms of what his critics and disciples have said about him but also in relation to Jung's own criticism of his work and himself. Jung knew that his ideas and behavior were likely to prompt condemnation from many different directions, and Haule chronicles his efforts to respond to the charges while accounting for the irrational vehemence of some of his critics. Haule's chapter offers a detailed meta-analysis of biographical writings about Jung in which the controversies are highlighted as opportunities for a better understanding of Jung's psychology. Particularly on the subject of religion, which by all accounts fascinated him throughout his life, Jung diagnosed a spiritual malaise in modern society that angered religious and secular people alike. Haule's study of the multifaceted myths surrounding Jung's life reveals a man of his time, a figure who embodied many of the complex religious crosscurrents of modern society.

In Susan Rowland's chapter, the focus is on Jung's ideas about the anima archetype as a figure of the "inner feminine" in men. Rowland formerly, a reader in English and Jungian studies from the University of Greenwich, scrutinizes Jung's theory from a feminist perspective and finds much to question and critique in terms of reified gender stereotypes. The archetypes of anima and animus have long been attacked as Jung's own personal (and highly questionable) views of the proper roles of men and women cast in universalistic terms. Along with applying the necessary critique, Rowland also shows how Jungian psychology may be recruited as an ally in the feminist project of challenging patriarchal authority in religion, culture, and politics and also in the psychological sphere. Jung's call for a greater attention to the wisdom of nature and the deeper rhythms of instinctual life and his acute psychological diagnosis of the ailments of modern society correspond to major themes in feminist theory and practice over the past several decades. For teachers who hesitate to include Jung in their classes because of his views on gender, Rowland offers an articulate and creative response.

In recent years, Jung has attracted new attention for his environmentalist insights about the psychological dimensions of the human relationship with nature. Meredith Sabini, a Jungian psychotherapist and director of the Dream Institute of Northern California, looks at the full array of Jung's nature writings in conjunction with his deeply meaningful personal experiences with nature, starting with his pastoral childhood and rural upbringing in late-nineteenth-century Switzerland. Even though Jung himself might object, Sabini argues that Jung qualifies as a "nature mystic" in the basic meaning of that term, as a person who draws direct psychospiritual energy from, and feels an overwhelming kinship with, the whole of the natural world. Jung craved the purifying effect of immersing oneself in nature, and he expressed concern about the profoundly damaging psychological effects of the modern world's increasingly fast-paced, technologically driven, environmentally destructive ways.

Jeremy Taylor, a Unitarian-Universalist minister who has taught Jung's ideas about religion in many different educational settings, reflects on his efforts to educate students about the psychospiritual insights of Jungian psychology, as well as to discuss with them the criticism against Jung. In recent years, Taylor has taught in Korea, China, and other Asian settings, enabling him to offer particularly salient observations about the challenges and rewards of translating Jungian ideas in non-Western contexts. Taylor emphasizes the cross-cultural relevance of archetypal theory, not in a naive or simplistic way but rather as the ultimate psychological basis upon which humans recognize and relate to each other. Taylor's argument highlights the strong theological implications of Jung's theory of the collective unconscious, implications that Jung as a psychologist did not feel qualified to pursue but that strongly resonate in the present day with many liberal Christians.

The fourth and final part describes several practical methods for teaching students about Jung's views on psychology and religion. These chapters discuss practices of Jungian psychology that can help students, and ultimately anyone who gives the methods a try, recognize the unconscious roots of individual and collective problems.

Kelly Bulkeley, a psychologist of religion and visiting scholar at the Graduate Theological Union, describes Jung's method of dream interpretation and explains how contemporary teachers can apply his approach in different classroom settings. Bulkeley's chapter starts with a detailed reading of the newly published book *Children's Dreams: Notes from the Seminar Given in 1936–1940*, which contains the edited text from a series of classes Jung taught at a graduate school in Zurich on the subject of earliest remembered dreams from childhood. This book provides a fascinating window into Jung's own teaching methods, and it allows readers to hear his spontaneous personal voice more clearly than in his other writings. Following Jung's advice in these classes, Bulkeley outlines various ways of putting his dream interpretation methods into practice in present-day courses on religious studies, theology, psychology, and other disciplines. He addresses common concerns about bringing dreams into the classroom, concerns that can be allayed by a proper framing and more precise definition of what a Jungian dream interpretation can and cannot reveal.

Laurel McCabe, who directs a masters program in depth psychology at Sonoma State University, draws on the object-relations theory of D. W. Winnicott to explain her approach to teaching Jung. She argues that Winnicott's notion of a "holding space" between mother and infant applies not only to the analytic dyad but also to the atmosphere in a healthy classroom. A "good enough teacher" establishes secure psychological boundaries and principles of mutual respect to enable students to express themselves freely, raise questions, explore curiosities, and process new knowledge in highly efficient ways. Creating this kind of classroom environment is helpful in any discipline, but McCabe argues that it is essential for teaching Jung. Experiential methods like dream interpretation, artistic play, and active imagination are the teaching tools properly suited to the kind of psychological processes that Jungian theory addresses. The best way to employ these tools is to create a sufficiently strong holding space in the classroom for students to learn from their own experiments and discoveries.

As a Jungian psychotherapist, a philosophy teacher at Simon Fraser University, and a teacher of spiritual direction at Vancouver School of Theology, Bonnelle Strickling has had the opportunity to observe the impact of Jung's ideas on many different kinds of students. Her chapter takes this classroom impact as its main topic, examining what particular aspects of Jungian psychology stimulate certain kinds of interest and insight among various students. Strickling considers the ethical implications and educational responsibilities of teachers who bring Jung into the classroom, especially when the topic turns to the subject of Jung's misbehavior with his female clients. As a lifelong feminist, Strickling makes clear to her students where she thinks Jung went astray and violated the principles of his own theories and clinical advice. Along with these reflections, Strickling also evaluates Jung's ideas in their philosophical context, which she associates with the continental philosophy of Martin Heidegger and Karl Jaspers and, before them, with the lineage of Hegel, Spinoza, and Plato. This adds a new and important theme to consider in classroom discussions of Jung, for which Strickling offers a useful introductory guide.

The final chapter of the book, by John Beebe of the San Francisco Institute for Analytic Psychology, addresses the question of whether it is possible to practice a "science of the symbolic." Beebe acknowledges that many people question the status of Jung's ideas and psychological theory as science, given the highly subjective, irrational, unrepeatable phenomena it studies. But as Beebe shows in this chapter, the scientific integrity of Jung's approach derives from its self-reflective method of analyzing people's worldviews, enlarging their horizons, and healing them when they are broken. Beebe draws on the hermeneutic philosophy of Hans-Georg Gadamer, particularly his notion of truth as the unfolding product of open-ended dialogue, to argue that good teaching is like good analysis: both affirm the reality, autonomy, creativity, and purposefulness of the psyche. The spirit of scientific inquiry—that is, the discipline of observing reality, analyzing it, theorizing about it, and investigating its properties and processes—characterizes both endeavors.

Many of the chapters in *Teaching Jung* presume a high degree of familiarity with educational praxis and/or Jungian psychology. They speak to intermediate and advanced audiences of readers. Some chapters, however, provide excellent introductory surveys of Jung's basic ideas about myth (Segal, chapter 5), the Book of Job (Weldon, chapter 7), psychological types (Ross, chapter 8), nature (Sabini, chapter 11), and dream interpretation (Bulkeley, chapter 13). These chapters could serve as focal texts for students encountering Jung for the first time.

The recent publication of Jung's *Red Book* or *Liber Novus* potentially provides a pedagogical treasure for teaching religious studies. A magnificently illuminated manuscript, it chronicles Jung's "confrontation with the unconscious" from 1914 to 1930. Sonu Shamdasani, the book's editor, describes it as a deeply religious text: "The overall theme of the book is how Jung regains his soul and overcomes the contemporary malaise of spiritual alienation. This is ultimately achieved through enabling the rebirth of a new image of God in his soul and developing a new worldview in the form of a psychological and theological cosmogony." Though its pedagogical value in the religious studies classroom remains to be determined, it is a must read for anyone immersed in Jungian studies.

None of the contributors had sufficient time to read and process the voluminous material in *The Red Book* before completing their chapters. However, we suspect *The Red Book* may not be a good teaching resource for any but the most advanced students. The book's dense content, far-ranging network of personal and theoretical references, and otherworldly images and rhetorical style make it a difficult means of introductory access to Jungian psychology. Having said that, we also believe the publication of *The Red Book* marks an exciting watershed moment in the study of Jung. We hope the chapters of *Teaching Jung*, which represents hundreds of years of collective teaching experience (sixteen contributors with multiple decades working in the class-room), will provide the scholarly tools necessary to begin the process of ana-lyzing and evaluating the significance of *The Red Book*.

In today's world, where conflicts over religious identity and divine inspira-tion threaten to undermine the pillars of modern civilization, Jung's views on religion remain deeply relevant to the cultural and political debates of our time. Although *Teaching Jung* is written primarily for educators, we believe the book also speaks meaningfully to anyone seeking new insights into the always fasci-nating, sometimes violent nexus of religious, psychological, and cultural forces.

PART I

Different Educational Settings

I

The Challenge of Teaching Jung in the University

David Tacey

Perhaps it would not be too much to say that the most crucial
problems of the individual and society turn upon the way the psyche
functions in regard to spirit and matter.

—*Jung, Collected Works* 8:251

Jung in the Academy

Intellectual Culture and Experience

When I first tried to explore the exclusion of Jung from the universities in the 1970s, numerous Jungian analysts told me that Jung did
not belong in the university and is best not taught there. One of the
strongest advocates of this view was Marie-Louise von Franz, who
wrote to me that Jung in the university might degenerate into a "head
trip."[1] That is, he might become an object of purely intellectual study,
and the emotional and psychological process that makes Jung's work
meaningful—namely, one's own personal encounter with unconscious contents—would be missing. Effectively, this view maintained
that analytical psychology in its clinical practice *owned* Jung, and that
universities could not participate in this ownership, since they could
only view Jung externally and superficially and not from the inside.

Searching through the Jungian literature to find explicit statements about the clinical ownership of Jung is a difficult process and
yields few results. Mostly this problem is expressed in personal
remarks and letters, and not in the public domain. Andrew Samuels,
however, can always be relied on to be outspoken about what others do
not divulge. In his foreword to *Post-Jungian Criticism*, Samuels writes:

Certain analysts say that academics cannot really feel or suffer complex emotions because of their precocious intellectual development, which vitiates empathy and sensitivity. As this character assassination of the typical academic continues, she or he cannot really understand most of the concepts derived from Jungian psychology, because their provenance, and certainly their utility, are matters on which only practicing clinicians can rule.[2]

Samuels is an analyst and a clinical professor who is sticking up for academics, whereas I am an academic who wishes to support the analysts. I agree with Samuels that we cannot bracket out Jungian studies from the university curriculum on the grounds that the clinicians have exclusive ownership of this knowledge. However, I fully agree with analysts who object to the purely intellectual and therefore incomplete and inauthentic deployment of Jungian psychology in a university setting.

It seems to me that if Jung is to be used in the university, he should be used correctly, and this means teaching Jung in such a way that the whole self is engaged in this process, not simply the disembodied intellect with its reductive grasp of concepts. I agree with the analyst's typical objection that Jung's ideas are not really concepts to be taught but psychic images to be experienced.[3] Jung's psychology is a complex depth psychology in which archetypes are to be understood phenomenologically as elements of human experience or not at all. I agree with Jung that universities have been so preoccupied with a sterile "rationalism and intellectualism" that they have almost forfeited their right to appear as "disseminators of light."[4]

Testing Boundaries and Challenging Hegemonies

As a student, I found the Jungian criticism of the universities to be illuminating. It not only explained why Jung had been rejected by university knowledge but also accounted for why so many students find their university studies to be dull and boring, especially the academic study of psychology. A mind-numbing rationalism has conditioned and limited the discipline of psychology, and in this environment, it is understandable that a *depth* psychology based on experience has found itself confined to exclusive and elite institutes of analytical psychology. I am pleased that these private institutes have kept the candle burning for Jungian psychology and knowledge of archetypes, but surely the time has come to challenge both the hegemony of rationalism in the universities and the hegemony of the institutes in their "ownership" of Jung.

Although formal and expensive clinical analysis must remain a central element of Jungian psychology, I am concerned about several issues: (1) that the encounter with the unconscious has apparently been made synonymous with clinical practice, (2) that the professionalization of Jungian practice has served to strengthen and consolidate this fusion, (3) that Jungians have been unimaginative about finding other methods to impart their work beyond the clinical model, and (4) that this situation frequently boils down to the premise that only those who can afford to pay for therapy can embark on the complex journey of individuation. My social conscience rebels against these assumptions, yet it is clear that personal analysis is beneficial, and I have benefited from it myself.

Every year, I teach scores of students who have a desire to discover the life of the unconscious but cannot afford to go into expensive personal analysis. There must be other ways to encounter the unconscious apart from the clinical model, especially if, as Jung often claimed, individuation is a *natural* process.[5] In the past, there were numerous traditional methods to transcend the conscious realm and engage the unconscious, including religious belief and spiritual practice, ritual and dance, artwork and poetry, romance and relationship, music and dreams. In other words, any form of human activity that is creative, intuitive, or open to the nonrational side of experience is a potential site for the encounter with the unconscious. Of course, having that encounter monitored by someone with special knowledge is something that the clinical model has refined to an extraordinary degree with its sensitivity to transference and unconscious contents.

The increasingly rational nature of modern life has had a destructive impact on our traditional forms of transcendence. Typically, the modern person has little or no access to religion or spirituality, to ritual or poetry, and even romance and relationship have become attenuated, commercialized, and clichéd. Many of our nonrational outlets and avenues have been blocked, devalued, or destroyed. The question came to me in the late 1980s: How can I, as a university teacher, help my students approach the unconscious in a creative way?

An Experiment in Teaching

The idea of teaching Jungian psychology to students at my university was not mine. The notion came to me from my colleague in the philosophy department, Robert Farrell, who thought it would be a worthwhile venture for us to join forces and produce such a course. I was based in the English department, but we conducted our teaching experiment in a program called Interdisciplinary Studies. This seemed like an ideal place to teach Jung, whose work and vision encompass at least eight disciplines: psychology, classical studies, mythological studies, comparative religion, anthropology, sociology, philosophy, and the history of ideas.

Indeed, one of the reasons Jung is not taught in the modern university is that his work does not fit any specific academic discipline. Staff in psychology are likely to refer to it as religious studies, and lecturers in religious studies are likely to say that it is science and not religion. Philosophers regard the work of Jung as not squarely in the philosophical tradition, and of course, Jung himself often said that his work was not philosophy but empirical science. However, the empirical scientists on campus are likely to point to the highly speculative, intuitive, and philosophical nature of Jung's inquiry. As a doctoral candidate in Jungian studies, I was moved back and forth from English to anthropology, to psychology, and eventually back to English literature. The psychology professor referred to Jung as a "literary critic," and thus I incorporated the work into literary studies.

Jung's solitary confinement to the arts and humanities is, let us hope, temporary. It is an interesting place for him to be, but he cannot be confined to these disciplines. He is more than myth and literature; he is, or represents, an amalgam of mythos and logos, story and science. In truth, he does not belong to the arts faculty or in the science faculty; he belongs to both. He belongs to a university system that does not yet exist, one in which the whole of life is studied and taken seriously. Jung is the scientist and artist of life integration. His thinking is organic, holistic, literary, and scientific. As such, there is no available box or category for him. He is a scholar in the grand style, and his extraordinary breadth makes most academics feel humbled. Academics are often said to know more and more about less and less, but Jung works in reverse: his momentum is centrifugal, encompassing more fields in a desire to understand human reality.

There is always the grave danger, however, that such a colossal intellect, which seemingly fits everywhere, will be said to belong nowhere. Like God in creation, Jung in the academy can almost be said to be *felt everywhere* and *seen nowhere*. I think when integrative sciences finally emerge in our universities, which they must with the rise of ecological and organic thinking, we will find that Jung will eventually find his place in a new paradigm of knowledge that will appreciate his synthetic style and encompassing worldview.

Robert Farrell and I called our subject "Jungian psychology," but there was a protest from the psychology department that we were encroaching on their territory. I responded to this protest with a brief lecture on the etymology of the word *psychology*, pointing out its true meaning as the *logos of the psyche* or *soul* and suggesting to the psychology department that they had left *psyche* out of the study of human behavior. This protest was dropped, and we were free to develop our own subject, although it was noted that our students were frequently defecting from psychology to interdisciplinary studies. In due course, the psychology department dropped its antagonism and decided to include us in its range of subject choices, so that students majoring in psychology could study Jung as part of their behavioral science degree. We could not be defeated, and so we were incorporated.

As Robert and I designed our subject, we spoke about many things, including the objection of Marie-Louise von Franz: how could we do this so that it did not become a mere head trip that lost the value and intensity of Jung's vision? Obviously, we could not play the role of de facto therapists in the academic setting, and yet we both agreed that this subject would need to be *different*. Neither of us had the time, energy, or expertise to engage the student's interior process, and yet we agreed that we might be able to teach the subject in such a way that the nonrational dimension of life could be incorporated and assumed into the subject.

Robert Farrell and I have taught the Jung subject for nearly twenty years, and we feel that we have done so with reasonably good results. I am not talking about results in the narrow sense of high grades, but in the deeper and more important sense of having encouraged our students to engage the unconscious and to take the nonrational side of their experience seriously. We have concluded that the success or otherwise of this teaching depends on the way Jung is taught and the attitude of the teacher. A Jung subject has to be taught with *psychological* intelligence, and this may not be the same as intellectual intelligence. If the teacher can be open to the depths of the psyche and receptive to its autonomous and living reality, then a certain "reverence" toward the psyche can be found, which prevents the academic experience from falling into a head trip.

I believe there is a lot of *middle ground* to be explored between Jung as an object of intellectual inquiry and Jung as an approach to the psyche in therapy. I will later explore four approaches to teaching Jung that demonstrate the range of possible approaches to this academic challenge.

The Religious Factor

The academic teacher of Jung cannot engage the subjective or emotional process of every student. This is not possible, nor is it desirable. But my colleague and I have found that a form of therapy does indeed take place in the classroom when Jung is taught with passion and concern. As soon as the teacher conveys a convincing sense that he or she is open to the depths of the psyche, to its existence and its effects on us, something therapeutic happens in the classroom that is quite uncanny and moving. I have experienced this many times, and such moments are transformative for teachers and students who are open to such experiences. Other students find that such experiences wash over them and do not seem affected. In other words, such students are not ready for an experience of the autonomy of the psyche, and in this case no harm is done; an opportunity has been missed or deferred until later.

There is, of course, a *religious* dimension to any experience of the autonomy of the psyche. When we acknowledge that we are in the presence of something greater than ourselves, something large and unseen, yet "sees us,"[6] we are in the domain of religious or spiritual experience. We shift from being subjects who pursue knowledge for our own ends to being objects of an invisible and autonomous reality. This obviously has to be handled carefully by teachers and students. To call into being, or into academic consideration, a numinous and powerful *other*, a life that lives us, that holds sway over us, and to which we must listen or adhere, is to cultivate what Jung calls a *religious attitude*.

The main problem for the teacher is not to identify with the wisdom that is generated by this educational process. The teacher has to watch his or her reactions and make sure that psychological inflation does not occur, that he or she does not become the classroom guru, the arrogant fount of all wisdom. Obviously, there is an inescapable sense of reward and personal elevation in introducing a sense of spirit into students' lives, but the teacher has to contain this feeling and not allow it to gain the upper hand. As soon as this feeling wins, we lose the educational plot and our integrity is in jeopardy. It is fine to be an instrument of knowledge but not to identify oneself with this knowledge and become grandiose.

For their part, students do not use Jung's term *religious attitude*, which does not seem to resonate with them. They speak instead about "spirituality," and an invitation into a spiritual view of the world can trigger reactions of various kinds.[7] Those students who are rationalistic may reject this invitation out of hand and find it repellent, manipulative, or even antihuman. Those who have a committed religious faith may reject this new approach for opposite reasons and say, "No thanks, I already have my religion, and I don't need another one." But the vast majority of my students are secular adults who have had no exposure to formal religion or who had only a rudimentary religious upbringing that they shrugged off at some early stage in their development.

Pedagogical Problems in the Teaching of Jung

Many of these students are eager for a new experience of the numinous and long to feel themselves connected to a sense of a greater *other*. This creates problems of its own, because Jungian psychology is not a religious faith, but rather an approach to the psyche that advocates a reverential attitude.[8] Some students want to turn Jung himself into the religion they do not have or have never had. This approach can severely limit the capacity of the student to think critically. Instead, some adopt Jung as a religious system and use the technical terms as articles of faith, speaking about the archetypes as if they were real objects in time and space, rather than metaphors for processes of the psyche.

Contact with the numinous, with what is infinite and *other*, is fraught with emotional reactions, resistances, defenses, and enthusiasms. The stability of the ego is relativized and even threatened by the realization that it is not the master of its house. Some students give away their ego authority too readily, and others defend against the *other* as from a hostile attack. Still others insist that the *other* is only to be found in heaven or in scriptures sanctified by orthodox religious authority. Some respond to the suggestion that the *other* can be found within as an outrageous expression of gnosticism or heresy.

I do not see Jung as an "outbreak" of gnosticism that is designed to belittle religious traditions. His psychology provides an existential ground upon which the statements of faith can be tested. If anything, Jung's psychology adds weight and value to the religions, but they tend to respond with resistance because this internal dimension is feared. It is regarded as unorthodox or an acquired taste. The exception is where religious authorities have embraced the mystical substreams of their respective traditions. Jung's psychology is a science of the relations between the human person (the ego) and the God Within (the Self).

The numinous calls for a response, and mostly the educated ego in the West responds through resistance and denial. It is either dismissed as an *illusion* by rational minds or viewed as a truth greater than literal truth by those who are religious. Either way, presenting a balanced apologetic to students in secular universities can be difficult. How will students respond? What emotions will the numinous arouse? How will it affect their present beliefs and attitudes? By the time most academics have reflected on these questions, they have realized that the task is too daunting and it is best not to bother. As one academic said to me, "To teach Jung is to look for trouble."

Jung writes of the capacity of the unconscious to paralyze our critical faculty and to hold us in its power.[9] The same is true for the numinous and for those who speak on its behalf. It is not uncommon for some students to fall helplessly under Jung's spell before they reach a more mature relationship to his ideas.[10] But reaching this mature level can be difficult and time-consuming. It is hard to be objective about Jung, if one is responding principally through a complex and not through the mind. It may take some time for the mind to catch up, because the complex works automatically and independently. Therefore, it is not surprising to discover that some students dismiss Jung's work as gobbledygook or mysticism, while others fall under its sway and are unable to take up a critical dialogue with it.

In such cases, fear and fascination of the numinous become difficult pedagogical issues. Do we have the capacity to deal with these responses in the university? Generally not, but if we are able to identify an emotional response as soon as possible, the teacher may have a chance to dialogue with it. In my experience, uncritical adulation is more common than hostile rejection. This can be contained by a sensitive teacher, but other faculty members are likely to point to this problem and announce that the Jung subject produces disciples and followers rather than critical readers. This may increase the academic prejudice that Jungians are part of what Richard Noll calls a "worldwide cult."[11] Jung seems to act as a trigger to what I have called the spirituality complex of the secular West.[12]

Once the spirituality complex is activated, it asks for objects of belief, and Jung is a likely target for such projections. But after students have become adjusted to the reality of the spirit, they find their way to religious, mythological, or cosmological attitudes and symbols, and Jung is let off the hook. Then Jung can be returned to reality and seen as a scientific investigator of our human depths, rather than a god or idol. In technical terms, Jung acts as a transferential object while we are sorting out our relationship with spirit. Jung activates and arouses our need to believe, which we hardly knew we had before, because this libido was withheld by the secular ego and rendered unconscious.

Teaching Styles

Toward a Taxonomy of Jungian Studies

Over recent years, I have been traveling interstate and overseas to see how other academics are dealing with the challenge of teaching Jung in the university. In every case, the success or otherwise of our efforts seems to be determined by our approach to the numinous. If we ignore the numinous, as is sometimes found in academic study, and if we teach only the nuts and bolts of Jung's psychology, we are not teaching him properly.[13]

But how do we, in the post-Christian West, in a university system governed by secular values, make the numinous convincing, real, and present? How do we handle our personal cynicism toward the unseen dimension? Just as important, how do we educate ourselves to become critical of the numinous, rather than fall for it with unthinking devotion? How can we avoid dualisms and complexes when we step into this realm? How can we teach Jung's work when we do not yet have the cultural and religious forms to understand it? My guess is that new cultural forms are emerging now, and yet they are not widely known. When these new forms arise, and when the numinous can be properly incorporated into our knowledge, Jung will find his natural context and belonging, but until then, he is in danger of being seen as an oddity.

I have discerned four main approaches to the teaching of Jung. Each could be seen to be governed by a particular "god" or archetypal style. I am sure there are more than four and that I have left others out, but this at least will set the ball rolling toward a taxonomy of Jungian studies.

1. Fitting in or Conforming   Ruled by the Father, Senex, or Old Man
2. Updating or Reconstructing   Hermes, the Trickster
3. Soul-Making or Overturning   Dionysus
4. Keeping Pure or Standing Still   Disciple and Acolyte

As with all taxonomic categories, these styles are almost never found in pure form. As one sketches out these archetypal styles, they invariably become somewhat clichéd and stereotypical, but we have to take that into account.

1. FITTING IN OR CONFORMING. Here the desire is to fit Jung into the university system, rather than to challenge the system by advocating new knowledge. Analytical psychology under this influence sets itself the task of conforming to prevailing standards, expectations, and assumptions. The keyword for this approach is *respectability*.

The aim is to show how *respectable* Jungian psychology is, if only academic scholars took the time to understand the nature of Jungian thought. If scholars sat and reflected, they would see that the exclusion of Jung from the academy has been based on a misunderstanding. This approach is rational, cool, and collected; it is noncombative and diplomatic. It seeks to demonstrate the validity of Jungian psychology by fitting it alongside other theories and knowledge.

Its aim is to demonstrate that the exclusion of Jung has been based on misconceptions. Jung is not a mystic, but a sound and worthy scientist of the more difficult reaches of mind. These depths are not mystical but accessible to scientific analysis that is properly attuned to deep structures. This approach emphasizes his scientific credentials, his career as a leading-edge psychiatrist, his philosophical education, and his empirical approach to mental illness and social problems.

Archetypally, this approach is ruled by the senex or old man, both in its creative aspect (accommodating and including) and its negative aspect (manipulating and controlling). This approach teaches the nuts and bolts of Jung without teaching that the work is ultimately about self-transformation. Students are given information but not the goal of self-transformation, and they rightly complain about the dryness and aridity of this approach when they find out more about the field. This drying-out effect is part of the long-standing opposition that many analysts have to bringing Jung into the academy. Divorced from the mystery dimension of the unconscious, is "knowledge about" Jung useful? Can Jung be understood without the kind of experience we gain from the encounter with the numinous?

Ironically, in our desire to include Jung in the academy, we have to be careful that we are not excluding him all over again. If our pedagogical style is too narrow, we are not including enough of this thinker's work. To use a metaphor from physics, it is as if we are trying to pull in a single particle into the university, only Jung is not a particle, but a wave of vast extension. I was stuck in this rut myself some years ago, so I know all about it.

This is largely an emotional and pedagogical problem of the senex archetype. The senex (in men and women) thinks of itself as being important and in control. It won't risk the self-disclosure that transformation demands, since this involves the anima or soul, the revealer of the inner life. The more identified the teacher is with the persona, the more unconscious and distant the anima will be. To teach the art of transformation demands that the teacher shows that he or she is vulnerable to the numinous and receptive to the soul. The teacher stands before the sacred not as someone in control, but as someone who receives. If the teacher is not prepared to risk the controlling stance, to let the guard slip, to show vulnerability, there can be no teaching with soul. As Jung once said of Freud, he was not prepared to "risk his authority," and as a result, he "lost it altogether."[14]

The other problem with senex pedagogy is that in its conservative interest in scientific standards, empirical evidence, and rational proof, it fails to see that the academy itself has been radically transformed by postmodern knowledge. Many of the old academic ideals, such as objectivity, precision and exactness in scientific method, have been overturned by postmodern thought and by feminist theory, at least in the social and human sciences, if not in the exact sciences. To some extent, the image of the academy that the senex holds no longer exists. This is because Hermes, the central archetype of the postmodern era, has got into the academy and turned things around.[15]

2. UPDATING OR RECONSTRUCTING. Hermes governs the second teaching style I have detected, although he can also outwit himself. The emphasis in this approach is on reconstructing Jung in the light of progressive discourses that have taken place in the social sciences, arts, and humanities. If *respectability* is the keyword for the senex, here the overriding concern is *updating*.

Hermes is the messenger who moves between worlds. He brings to the Jungian world messages from other knowledges and introduces Jungian concerns to worlds that have never been interested in Jung. His concern is with potential connections and creative dialogues.

Hermes, the trickster, adopts the view that an unreconstructed Jung cannot be admitted to the academy. Whatever "Jung" may signify to Jungians, he has to be deconstructed before he can be authentically brought before the university. This style may be paradoxical: it may even side with the established views of the academy and argue against "Jung" in his unreconstructed form. This approach may be embarrassed by unreconstructed Jung and seek to differentiate a "post-Jungian" from an earlier "Jungian" position.

This approach will seek to reread Jung with current views in mind, often sharply critical of the ways in which the classical Jungian work falls short of contemporary values. It critiques the Jungian work, especially in terms of the big three preoccupations of the academy, namely, class, gender, and race. It may seek to revise his metapsychology and his philosophical underpinnings in an effort to bring them into line with contemporary philosophical thought, postmodern theory, and phenomenology. This second approach might employ as its credo "reparation works best in the open," and it will enjoin scholars and critics of Jung to enter into dialogue with "post-Jungians" in a mutually enriching work of cultural reconstruction.

A major drawback is that with all this fancy footwork and adaptation to contemporary concerns, essential elements are not addressed. What happens to the numinous? Where is the divine? They are often ignored in the move to find meaningful connections between post-Jungian interests and the concerns of race, class, and gender. This approach often says: we will redeem Jung's psychology but not bother about his theology. But this won't do. Hermes outwits himself at this point. Jung's religious attitude is not an added extra, an optional element we can do without. We cannot just say his religion is a residue of his conservative nature and that as radical post-Jungians, we do not need to be concerned with it.

This problem is linked to larger issues. In the academy, religion is frequently relegated to the *right* side of political life, since religion is often viewed as the glue that binds society together and that keeps it stable and ordered. The socially progressive Jungian concern for updating, changing, and renewing is forced to engage a basically leftist agenda that is hugely allergic to religious problems.[16] But I do not believe that the religious dimension is extraneous to Jung; it is integral to his psychology.

Jung's work seems to call for a religious left that does not yet exist on campus. The religious are often conservative; the politically aware are often very secular. The major exception to this rule is Western Buddhism, which seems to be politically progressive. I know that progressives like to typecast Jung as irredeemably conservative and stuffy, but the implications of his psychology are radical.[17]

3. SOUL-MAKING OR OVERTURNING. The third approach focuses on the numinous dimension but often has little to say about social and political aspects. Its interest is in the inner life and the cultivation of the soul. An exception to this rule is where Jungian visionaries suddenly decide that the outer world has "soul" and then behave almost as religious converts to political realities.[18]

Soul-making or overturning is iconoclastic and rebellious. It accepts that the work of bringing Jung into the university is a subversive act, that is, a countercultural enterprise. It is not interested in conforming Jung to existing paradigms, but in challenging the models of knowledge that have kept Jung out of the academy in the first place. Its concern is not *respectability* or *updating*, but *revolutionizing* the system.

The third approach likes to employ language that flies in the face of the academy, using terms like *soul* and *spirit* that the academy considers obsolete. I know a Jungian teacher who gave a staff seminar on the gods and goddesses of the psyche, and some of his colleagues left the room. The revolutionary approach often decides that the academy "lacks soul," that it privileges knowledge but "not wisdom," that it is repressive toward "what counts," that it avoids an encounter with "ultimate questions." This approach is what Jung would call "inflated" or what the world calls arrogant. But whether arrogant, inflated, or inspired, it fails to see that the academy has been secular for many years, and if it wants to bring the numinous into the system, it has to be tactful and present an appropriate apologetic for the gods.

Scholars of the third approach frequently scorn what is current and contemporary and often devalue these concerns as merely fashionable. They dislike the contemporary and are in love with antiquity. Their models of how to live are usually premodern, ancient, or primordial. Favored sources of inspiration are the Florentine Renaissance, the Perennial Philosophy, or Medieval Alchemy, which all look like hocus-pocus to the university. The third approach believes that a primordial truth can be found, and this is an inspiration for championing such traditions as alchemy, shamanism, Neoplatonism, metaphysics, and wisdom literature.

Scholars who follow this way have difficult and often lonely careers. They are generally not liked by their colleagues (apart from a few close associates) and develop ill feeling and rivalry in the workplace. They may exacerbate the problem by their repeated criticisms of mainstream knowledges. Because they celebrate soul and spirit, they are often given a high profile by the media, and this rubs salt into the wounds of colleagues, who can be beset by envy. However, such teachers are often highly successful with students, who view them as inspired prophets on campus. They form the *Dead Poets Society* of the Jungian academic world, but they often get too entangled in the emotional currents and complications of students' lives. The senex persona is dropped in the name of "soul," but sometimes propriety and professional boundaries are dropped as well.

4. KEEPING PURE OR STANDING STILL. There is also a purist approach, and this group tries to have as little to do with the intellectual life of the academy as possible. They do not stir the pot like the dynamic soul makers. They hope that if they confine themselves to a Jungian bubble, the rest of the intellectual world will go away. They are suspicious of postmodernity, do not like Derrida or Foucault, ignore the post-Freudians, and try as hard as possible to keep

themselves pure for Jung. Their job is to inform people about Jung—a kind of informational bureau on campus.

I cannot think of an archetype that governs this approach, but I can think of a stereotype: the disciple or acolyte. This style, as Jung observes,[19] is secretly identified with the master and hides this under a mask of subservience to the teachings. Such teachers do not talk about Jung's scientific research, but about his "findings," as if they are commandments written in stone or brought down from on high. The problem with this approach is that it is not doing Jung any favors. It is keeping him hermetically sealed off from the world, away from the critical debates, making him almost gloriously irrelevant to intellectual life.

Teachers in this mode often behave as converts, and their students are sometimes expected to become Jungians rather than critical readers of Jung. Students rightly complain that this approach is claustrophobic, although it may suit the kind of student who is looking for something to believe in. Teachers in this mode are not always liked by their colleagues, who see them as priests or nuns of a religious sect. Often this style is short-lived, because it is sometimes a phase that people go through, a moment in which they fall in love with the numinous as revealed by Jung. This tendency of the work is savagely, and I think unfairly, attacked by Richard Noll.[20]

Again, this is largely a religious problem: how to incorporate the numinous in the secular academy. Jung evokes and stirs a spirituality complex; some reject him out of hand as a mystic, and others revere him as a prophet. Converts do not know how to gain the necessary critical distance, since criticism is viewed as a transgression or heresy, signs that our spirituality complex has been activated. If Jungian purists are incapable of genuine criticism, their colleagues will argue that they are indoctrinating students, making them incapable of living politically aware and astute lives. This sets up the conditions for fundamentalism and intolerance, and arguably education should work in the opposite direction.

Diversity and Experimentation

These four approaches cannot be pinned down to particular personalities in the world, but rather represent leanings or biases in the teaching of Jung. The first approach seeks to *conform*, the second to *reform*, the third to *transform*, and the fourth to *inform*. It is sometimes the case that one academic will experience elements of all four styles and approaches. Basically, they can be reduced to two larger categories: one and four are static styles, while two and three are dynamic. Number one is the static and number two is the dynamic form of adjusting to the academic world, whereas number three is the dynamic and number four the static form of adjusting to the numinous.

Hostility between our camps could be attributed largely to these different styles. The fast-moving trickster finds the disciple or acolyte to be static and uninteresting. The senex finds the trickster to be slippery and deceitful. The soul makers find all other types to be superficial and defensive, and the purists argue that all the others are in danger of losing the plot. Sometimes soul makers push the system too far and are in danger of losing their jobs. The university might decide that soul makers are actually troublemakers, and it can get on better without them. Soul makers can reinvent themselves as updaters or reformers, where at least they can hold down their jobs and where passions are cooled by the need to enter into dialogue with contemporary concerns. The acolytes are also nudged onward to new styles, partly due to criticism from others, since the university will not tolerate an exclusive bubble world for very long. A Jungian information booth is arguably best dealt with by Jung clubs and not by universities.

But the field is new and still being born. There will be other styles to discover and more problems to elaborate. We must expect this diversity in Jungian studies and, if possible, hold the tension between conflicting positions. The recent establishment of an International Association for Jungian Studies,[21] which specifically focuses on the teaching of Jung in university and college contexts, will do much to provide a forum for valuable discussion and critical reflection on teaching styles, pedagogical issues, and the meaning and purpose of Jung in the university.

In conclusion, we serve Jung best not by turning his work into a fixed ideology, but by playfully deconstructing it for the new era. We have to deconstruct his ideas about the numinous, but we cannot *eradicate* the numinous to suit the needs of a secular academy. Using one of Jung's key phrases, we have to "dream the myth onward."[22] As we move the work into the academy, we have to avoid the various pitfalls, including getting stuck in the senex and leaving out the soul, getting intoxicated by updating and leaving out the numinous, getting identified with the soul and condemning the world, or getting stuck in a ghetto and ignoring the world. These problems are not unique to Jungians. They are found wherever the numinous raises its head in a secular context.

This chapter is dedicated to Robert Farrell, in recognition of twenty years of exploring the teaching of Jung at La Trobe University, Melbourne.

NOTES

1. Marie-Louise Von Franz, letter to author, August 22, 1976.

2. Andrew Samuels, "Foreword," in *Post-Jungian Criticism: Theory and Practice,* ed. James S. Baumlin, Tita French Baumlin, and George H. Jensen (Albany: State University of New York Press, 2004), xi–xii.

3. Samuels, "Foreword," xii.

4. Jung, *Collected Works of C. G. Jung,* ed. Herbert Read, M. Fordham, and G. Adler, trans. R. F. C. Hull (Princeton, NJ: Princeton University Press, 1953–1976), 15:86.

5. Jung, *Collected Works,* 7:187.

6. Ibid., 9:1.

7. David Tacey, *The Spirituality Revolution: The Emergence of Contemporary Spirituality* (Hove, England: Brunner-Routledge, 2004).

8. Mark R.Gundry, *Beyond Psyche: Symbol and Transcendence in C. G. Jung* (New York: Peter Lang, 2006).

9. Jung, *Collected Works,* 7:262.

10. David Tacey, "Jung in the Academy: Devotions and Resistances," *Journal of Analytical Psychology* 42.2 (1997): 269–83.

11. Richard Noll, *The Jung Cult: Origins of a Charismatic Movement* (Princeton, NJ: Princeton University Press, 1994), 3.

12. Tacey, *Spirituality*.

13. David Tacey, "The Role of the Numinous in the Reception of Jung," in *The Idea of the Numinous: Contemporary Jungian and Psychoanalytic Perspectives*, ed. Ann Casement and David Tacey (Hove, England: Brunner-Routledge, 2006).

14. C. G. Jung, *Memories, Dreams, Reflections* (1961; reprint, London: Fontana Press, 1995), 182.

15. Bernie Neville, "The Charm of Hermes: Hillman, Lyotard and the Postmodern Condition," *Journal of Analytical Psychology* 37.2 (1992).

16. Leigh Eric Schmidt, *Restless Souls: The Making of American Spirituality* (San Francisco: HarperCollins, 2005).

17. David Tacey, *How to Read Jung* (London: Granta, 2006).

18. James Hillman and Michael Ventura, *We've Had a Hundred Years of Psychotherapy, and the World's Getting Worse* (San Francisco: HarperCollins, 1993).

19. Jung, *Collected Works*, vol. 7.

20. Noll, *The Jung Cult*, 3.

21. International Association of Jungian Studies, a worldwide organization established in 2002 to promote teaching and research in Jungian studies in universities. For further information, consult www.jungianstudies.org.

22. Jung, *Collected Works*, vol. 9, part 1.

REFERENCES

Gundry, Mark R. *Beyond Psyche: Symbol and Transcendence in C. G. Jung.* New York: Peter Lang, 2006.

Hillman, James, and Michael Ventura. *We've Had a Hundred Years of Psychotherapy, and the World's Getting Worse.* San Francisco: HarperCollins, 1993.

Jung, C. G. 1917/1926/1943: "On the Psychology of the Unconscious." In *The Collected Works of C. G. Jung*, ed. Herbert Read, M. Fordham, and G. Adler, trans. R. F. C. Hull (Princeton, NJ: Princeton University Press), Vol. 7, 1953/1966.

Jung, C. G. 1928: "The Relations between the Ego and the Unconscious." In *The Collected Works of C. G. Jung*, ed. Herbert Read, M. Fordham, and G. Adler, trans. R. F. C. Hull (Princeton, NJ: Princeton University Press), Vol. 7, 1953/1966.

Jung, C. G. 1930: "Richard Wilhelm: In Memoriam." In *The Collected Works of C. G. Jung*, ed. Herbert Read, M. Fordham, and G. Adler, trans. R. F. C. Hull (Princeton, NJ: Princeton University Press), Vol. 15, 1966.

Jung, C. G. 1934/54: "Archetypes of the Collective Unconscious." In *The Collected Works of C. G. Jung*, ed. Herbert Read, M. Fordham, and G. Adler, trans. R. F. C. Hull (Princeton, NJ: Princeton University Press), Vol. 9, 1, 1959/1968.

Jung, C. G. 1940: "The Psychology of the Child Archetype." In *The Collected Works of C. G. Jung*, ed. Herbert Read, M. Fordham, and G. Adler, trans. R. F. C. Hull (Princeton, NJ: Princeton University Press), Vol. 9, 1, 1959/1968.

Jung, C. G. 1947/1954: "On the Nature of the Psyche." In *The Collected Works of C. G. Jung*, ed. Herbert Read, M. Fordham, and G. Adler, trans. R. F. C. Hull (Princeton, NJ: Princeton University Press), Vol. 8, 1960/1969.

Jung, C. G. *Memories, Dreams, Reflections.* 1961. Reprint, London: Fontana Press, 1995.

Neville, Bernie. "The Charm of Hermes: Hillman, Lyotard and the Postmodern Condition." *Journal of Analytical Psychology* 37.2 (1992): 337–353.

Noll, Richard. *The Jung Cult: Origins of a Charismatic Movement.* Princeton, NJ: Princeton University Press, 1994.

Otto, Rudolf. *The Idea of the Holy.* Ed. John W. Harvey. 1923. Reprint, London: Oxford University Press, 1958.

Samuels, Andrew. "Foreword." In *Post-Jungian Criticism: Theory and Practice,* ed. James S. Baumlin, Tita French Baumlin, and George H. Jensen, vii–xv. Albany: State University of New York Press, 2004.

Schmidt, Leigh Eric. *Restless Souls: The Making of American Spirituality.* San Francisco: HarperCollins, 2005.

Tacey, David. "Jung in the Academy: Devotions and Resistances." *Journal of Analytical Psychology* 42.2 (1997): 269–283.

Tacey, David. *The Spirituality Revolution: The Emergence of Contemporary Spirituality.* Hove, England: Brunner-Routledge, 2004.

Tacey, David. *How to Read Jung.* London: Granta, 2006.

Tacey, David. "The Role of the Numinous in the Reception of Jung." In *The Idea of the Numinous: Contemporary Jungian and Psychoanalytic Perspectives,* ed. Ann Casement and David Tacey. Hove, England: Brunner-Routledge, 2006.

Von Franz, Marie-Louise. Letter to author. August 22, 1976.

2

Misprision

Pitfalls in Teaching Jung in a University Religious Studies Department

David L. Miller

I taught Jungian psychology in the context of religious studies from 1963 until 2004, first at Drew University in New Jersey (1963–1967) and then at Syracuse University in upstate New York (1967–2001) and Pacifica Graduate Institute in Santa Barbara, California (1989–2004). The courses at these institutions were at both the undergraduate and graduate levels, and they often involved Jung's thinking in relation to Freud or to latter-day Freudians and Jungians (e.g., Jacques Lacan, Julia Kristeva, James Hillman, and Wolfgang Giegerich), as well as Jungian psychology in relation to specific thematics (e.g., the problem of language, postmodern critical theory, mythology, folktale, and theology). During this forty-year tenure, I also taught Jungian psychology to analytic training candidates in the context of Jungian institutes (e.g., in Zurich, New York, Pittsburgh, Toronto, Los Angeles, San Francisco, Kansas City, Minneapolis, and Kyoto). In my experience of attempting to teach Jungian material, I increasingly became aware of what I thought of as pedagogical pitfalls, and it is some of these pitfalls that I want to address in this chapter. I take the pitfalls to be misreadings—hence, misteachings—about Jung.

In his *Psychopathology of Everyday Life*, Freud had warned about "misreadings" (*Verlesen*) as one type of *Fehlleistungen*, literally "failed performances" or "slips," awkwardly translated in the *Standard Edition* as "parapraxes."[1] He thought that they carry illusions based on repressed unconscious wishes concerning the reading matter. Similarly, Harold Bloom spoke about "misprisions" (literally "mis-takes"), insisting that all readings are readings or "takes," presentations rather than representations, productive rather than reproductive, and *poiesis* rather than *mimesis*, and Bloom advocated for strong rather than weak misreading, that is, a *clineman* that "swerves" away from the influence of tradition so as to be creative.[2] The problem remains that some interpreters and teachers imagine that their misprision or their "reading" is transparent to that about which they are speaking, that it is not, say, a "reading" of Jung, but a re-presentation of Jung's own thought.

I am aware that Jung was a seminal thinker, and as in the cases of other seminal thinkers like Freud, Marx, and Nietzsche, the text of an originative author's works may itself over time swerve from itself, even "misread" itself.[3] I do know that in a corpus like that of Jung's, any given reader may find counterevidence for a different or even an opposite reading to the one laid before her or him. But I believe that in the case of Jung, in doing a close textual analysis, one can make a critical case for preferred and mature points of view by taking into account the movement of thinking over time, the differences between metapsychological theorizing and thinking based on clinical practice,[4] and the nature of the audience of particular essays (popular or scholarly). However, an additional caveat is needed.

Even with an attempt at such a careful critical textual analysis, I am also well aware that my reading of Jung in this chapter, like any other, is itself a take or a reading or a presentation, and therefore my argument in this chapter about the pitfalls in reading and teaching Jung is possibly itself a misprision, possibly a weak rather than a strong misreading based on my own unconscious wishes and illusions. That, to be sure, is a pitfall in noting pitfalls. Jung was himself clear about this matter of epistemological reticence. He wrote: "I consider my contribution to psychology to be my subjective confession. It is my personal psychology, my prejudice that I see psychological facts as I do. I admit that I see things in such and such a way."[5] This is not an isolated sentiment. It is typical of Jung's metatheoretical perspective, as one can see in this earlier statement: "Philosophical criticism has helped me to see that every psychology—my own included—has the character of a subjective confession.... Even when I deal with empirical data, I am necessarily speaking about myself."[6] "Philosophical criticism" in this sentence probably refers to Jung's reading of a Kantian perspective that, according to Jung, calls for epistemological humility concerning the logical and ontological status of that which is the object of one's imagined knowledge. This observation about the nature of knowing will be assumed in relation to the pitfalls of teaching Jung that I should like to highlight.

I will look at five of what I take to be pitfalls. The reader will recognize them as criticisms that have been typically leveled at Jung. To be sure, Jung himself, as well as many Jungians after him, is vulnerable to these criticisms. But the pitfall is to give in naïvely to them, making them hermeneutical temptations. The naïveté consists in succumbing to generalizations about Jungian psychology that simplify what turn out to be complex matters on a closer and more thorough reading of Jung's text.

The pitfalls to which I believe the teacher of Jung is tempted are principally these: (1) a temptation to read Jungian thought over against and opposed to Freudian thought; (2) a temptation to spiritualize Jung, reading him as positive about religion (as opposed to Freud who is read as negative about religion); (3) a temptation to read Jung's notion of archetypes of the collective unconscious, as well as his views on *anima* and *animus*, as essentialist and essentializing; (4) a temptation to view Jung's logic and rhetoric as "Gnostic," being ahistorical, amoral, and negative about the body; and (5) a temptation to read Jung's interpretations of art, religion, and culture as reductively psychologistic, reducing what is transpersonal to the personal. I hope in what follows to make these matters more complex than they seem to some of Jung's critics. I shall treat them one by one.

Jung against Freud

The first pitfall is controversial. I want to work against the prevailing view that Jungian and Freudian perspectives are completely in opposition to each other. This is a difficult matter, since Jung himself went to great lengths to distance himself from his former friend and colleague. And as is well known, Freud returned the favor! I will not speculate on the reasons for this desire for separation and opposition after 1913 (when Jung was thirty-eight years old and Freud was fifty-seven). Surely, there were personal, psychological, political, and ideological reasons. But suffice it to say that my view is that the theoretical differences are, for whatever reasons, artificially exaggerated by both thinkers and that teaching Jung *as* an anti-Freudian does not do justice to the psychology of either. Even the rhetorical tone of Jung's statements about Freud after their split smacks a bit of "methinks he protesteth too much." Let me give some examples.

Jung came to feel that Freud was driven by "power,"[7] that he was "dogmatic,"[8] that he "placed personal authority above truth,"[9] that his explanations were reductive,[10] that he was a "bitter man,"[11] that he was attempting to "outdo the Church and canonize a theory,"[12] and that his theories, against the complexities of the psyche, were "one-sided."[13] For Jung, one-sidedness is a characteristic of neurosis, and it manifests as "nothing but" explanations. So Jung wrote: "Freud had to invent a system to protect people, and himself, against the reality of the unconscious, by putting a most depreciatory explanation upon these things, an explanation that always begins with 'nothing but.' "[14]

This strikes one as overstatement, especially in light of other comments in the same book from which much of this characterization of Freud comes (*Memories, Dreams, Reflections*). For example, Jung writes that Freud was terribly important to him during his Burgholzi years because Freud put "psychology [i.e., soul] into psychiatry."[15] And Jung even says that Freud "had the courage to let the case material speak for itself.... He saw with the patient's eyes... and so reached a deeper understanding of mental illness than had hitherto been possible. In this respect he was free of bias, courageous, and succeeded in overcoming a host of prejudices."[16] This hardly sounds like the same person who was one-sided, dogmatic, reductive, and authoritarian! Besides, Ernest Wallwork, in discussing how to read Freud's texts, has marshaled an enormous amount of evidence to show that Freud was anything but reductive, one-sided, dogmatic, and authoritarian.[17]

Wallwork's evidence demonstrates that Freud was aware that his metapsychology was constituted of "similes," "metaphors," and "myths"[18] and that it was "speculative," "hypothetical," and "incomplete."[19] Freud announced that his theories were changing and he was open to further "changes" by others. He even said that he would not abide "rigidity" in theoretical definitions and argument.[20] This openness is required since there is much about the psyche that is "unknown" and in principle unknowable.[21] But in spite of this testimony, the negative characterization of Freud persists, not only by Jung and Jungians. This phenomenon may well be a case of stereotyping.

Jung was especially critical of Freud in regard to what Jung thought of as one-sided sexual theory, his view of the unconscious as past repressions, his reductive interpretation of dream symbolism, and what Jung took to be his regressive method of interpretation by free association. But of all of these reticences, the real sticking point in Jung's wish to distance himself from Freud seemed to be Jung's critique of what he took to be Freud's one-sidedness and reductionism with regard to sex.

Jung was adamant. "He [Freud] would not grant that factors other than sexuality could be the cause [of repression and neuroses in particular cases]."[22] "I never could bring myself to be so frightfully interested in these sex cases. They do exist, there are people with a neurotic sex life and you have to talk sex stuff with them until they get sick of it and you get out of that boredom. Naturally, with my temperamental attitude, I hope to goodness we shall get through with the stuff as quickly as possible. It is neurotic stuff and no reasonable normal person talks of it for any length of time. It is not natural to dwell on such matters."[23] "I could not decide to what extent this strong emphasis [by Freud] upon sexuality was connected with subjective prejudices."[24] "Freud was emotionally involved in his sexual theory to an extraordinary degree";[25] "...for him sexuality was a sort of numinosum,"[26] a *deus absconditus*, a hidden or concealed god."[27] So Jung said: "I could not share F's almost exclusive interest in sex. Assuredly sex plays no small role among human motives, but in many cases it is secondary to hunger, the power drive, ambition, fanaticism, envy, revenge, or the devouring passion of the creative impulse and the religious spirit."[28]

To complicate this issue, one first needs to observe that Freud, in his later theory, added ego instincts to his theory about libido,[29] a matter that Jung notes,[30] but without modifying his criticism. Freud in fact said straightforwardly that he "could not fail to notice that the causation of illness did not always point to sexual life,"[31] and he goes on to give other etiologies.

But the main complicating factor, not noted by Jung, is the meaning of "sexuality" in Freud's argument, a significance that Freud alludes to in his essay on "Wild Analysis," in which Freud is critical of a doctor who gives sexual advice to a woman, urging her to get a lover or to masturbate in order to be rid of her neurosis. Freud says:

His [the doctor's] advice to the lady shows clearly in what sense he understands the expression "sexual life"—in the popular sense, namely, in which by sexual needs nothing is meant but the need for coitus or analogous acts producing orgasm and emission of sexual secretions. The physician cannot have been unaware, however, that psychoanalysis is commonly reproached with having extended the connotation of the term "sexual" far beyond its usual range.... In psychoanalysis the term "sexuality" comprises far more; it goes lower and also higher than the popular sense of the word...we reckon as belonging to "sexual life" all expressions of tender feeling...even when those feelings have become inhibited in regard to their original sexual aim or have exchanged this aim for another which is no longer sexual. For this reason we prefer to speak of *psychosexuality*, thus laying stress on the point that the mental factor should not be over-looked or underestimated. We use the word sexuality in the same comprehensive sense as that in which the German language uses the word *lieben* (to love).... As therapists, we have constantly to remember that the unsatisfied sexual trends (the substitutive satisfactions of which in the form of nervous symptoms we have to combat) can often find only very inadequate outlet in coitus or other sexual acts.[32]

In attempting to distance himself from Freud, Jung may have been making the same error as the doctor Freud is describing. At least in the language of his negative criticism Jung does not discriminate between sex understood as adult genital sexuality and psychosexuality understood as childhood libido ("polymorphous perversity," "infantile sexuality"). The latter refers to a very early period in psychological development, just after birth, when every wish and desire can be fulfilled by reference to the body. At such a time, on Freud's view, what will be seen as "barriers" to a later developed view of genital organi-zation do not exist. For example, there is no barrier to bodily pleasure with different species (doggie, kitty, teddy bear), with what will be later found to be disgusting (feces, soapsuds, finger paint), with members of one's immediate family (mommy, daddy, sister), with members of the same sex, and with other organs besides the genitalia (thumb, ear).[33] On this view, the opposite to sexu-ality is not chastity; the opposite of eroticism is, rather, not being in touch with and not taking pleasure in matter and in one's own body.[34] Polymorphous per-versity is playful and without practical purpose (reproduction), but it is also realistic and down to earth. Freud thought that this form of eroticism was early in life encouraged and affirmed by parental authorization, but that later it was repressed when psychosocial development reacted to the demands of civiliza-tion (school, business, family). However, Freud theorized that this childhood form of psychosexuality remained as an unconscious factor in everyone's makeup, a factor that could return in a form that, from some perspectives, will be thought to be "perverse."[35]

The fact is that early in their friendship, Jung agreed with Freud about this, even against the tide of a criticism that he would himself later adopt. Jung wrote in 1908: "The public can forgive Freud least of all for his sexual symbolism. In my view he is really easiest to follow here, because this is just where mythology, expressing the fantasy-thinking of all races, has prepared the ground in the most instructive way. I would only mention the writings of Steinthal in the 1860s, which prove the existence of a widespread sexual symbolism in the mythological records and the history of languages. I also recall the eroticism of our poets and their allegorical or symbolical expressions."[36] Even toward the end of his life, Jung said: "It is a widespread error to imagine that I do not see the value of sexuality."[37] Jung called it "the other [i.e., repressed] face of God" and the "chthonic spirit."[38]

But even more to the point of how close Jung was to Freud on the matter of stressing the fulfillment of the pleasure and destiny of the human spirit by way of the body (psychosexuality, eros) are Jung's comments on the body in his seminars from 1934 to 1939 on Nietzsche's *Zarathustra*. Here is a sample: "We should emphasize the body, for thus we give body to concepts, to words.... We should return to the body in order to create spirit again; without body there is no spirit because spirit is a volatile substance of the body. The body is the alembic, the retort, in which materials are cooked, and out of that process develops the spirit, the effervescent thing that rises."[39]

The allusions to "alembic" and "retort" refer to alchemy. Jung's psychological utilization of alchemical metaphors—as opposed to the perspectives implied by the images and symbols of Christian theology and other spiritualities and ideologies—is precisely for the reason that in the alchemical laboratory the spirit and soul of the theorizing in the oratory is always seen by way of the transformations in matter and materiality; that is, embodied desire and wishes are fulfilled in the body and never manifest apart from embodiment.[40] Indeed, Jung was insistent on soul being made real in the body.[41]

This strong affirmation of body in the *Zarathustra* seminars, along with Freud's view of psychosexuality as the fulfillment of wishes widely (polymorphously) in relation to the body, complicates attempts, including those of Jung and Freud themselves, to distinguish their theories on the basis of different views of an erotic psychological theory. One might also recall Jung's statement quoted by Lewis Mumford in his *New Yorker* review of *Memories, Dreams, Reflections*: "When I die probably no one will realize that the old man in the coffin was once a great lover."[42] Jungians sometimes do not acknowledge these complexities when they attempt to spiritualize Jung's psychology or demonize Freud's.

Positive about Religion

There is a second shibboleth about Jung, again in relation to Freud, an oversimplification that can lure the unwitting teacher of Jung into a pitfall of clarity precisely at a point where things are complex and not entirely clear. This temptation has to do with Jung's view of religion over against what is taken to be Freud's view of religion. This is a special temptation when Jungian psychology is taught in the context of religious studies programs.

The popular view is that Freud was negative about religion (religion is a "universal obsessional neurosis")[43] and that Jung was positive about religion (religions are "psychotherapeutic systems").[44] But this is not the whole story, as I have attempted to demonstrate elsewhere.[45]

Jung indeed seemed to be positive about religion when he announced that "Christ is a symbol of the self."[46] But which "Christ" was he invoking? On close reading, it becomes apparent that it is not the "Christ" of orthodox theology or typical pious practice. Rather, it was a Christology amplified psychologically by adding shadow psychology (Satan) and *anima* (a feminine component). Jung thought that "Christ" needed to be transformed back "into the sooth-saying god of the vine."[47] Similarly, Jung wrote about the importance of the Christian Eucharist as a crucial psychological symbol for the process of individuation in psychoanalysis. But to what idea of the "Mass" was Jung referring? It was a Holy Communion interpreted from the barbarous pagan rites of the Aztec Teoqualo (human sacrifice) and seen through a prism of the ancient alchemy of Zosimos's visions in which the priest eats himself.[48] Jung thought that theologies needed therapeutic adjustment if they were to be psychologically realistic. He believed, as he said in a letter to Freud, that contemporary religion was a "misery institute" and that it had lost the purpose of the original myth and cult: namely, "a drunken feast of joy where man regained the ethos and holiness of an animal."[49] In the Tavistock Lectures, Jung said straightforwardly: "My problem is to wrestle with the big monster of the human mind, the problem of Christianity. Other people are not worried by such problems, they do not care about the historical burdens Christianity has heaped upon us.... It's a tremendous human problem."[50]

Freud was worried about this problem, as was Jung. But though Freud was as critical as Jung concerning religion used as an opiate or a crutch, not everything in Freud's corpus is negative about religion, any more than everything is positive in Jung's texts. In 1935, when he was seventy-nine years old, Freud added the following sentence to the "Autobiographical Study": "My deep engrossment in the Bible story (almost as soon as I had learnt the art of reading) had, as I recognized much later, an enduring effect upon the direction of my interest."[51] In a "Postscript" to the same work written in 1935, Freud speaks of "an alteration in myself" that "might be described as a regressive development." He explains: "My interest, after making a lifelong *détour* through the natural sciences, medicine and psychotherapy, returned to the cultural problems which had fascinated me long before, when I was a youth scarcely old enough for thinking."[52] He then names three of his works on religion (*Totem and Taboo*, *Future of an Illusion*, and *Civilization and Its Discontents*) as instances of this authentic interest. Further, it is not altogether clear that the work *Moses and Monotheism*, published posthumously in the same year that Freud died (1939), is negative about religion. Though iconoclastic, it can hardly be conceived as psychologically resistant to religion's symbols and images. David Bakan and Yosef Yerushalmi have both written very strong historical works on the indebtedness to religion, particularly Judaism, of Freud's central ideas.[53] A person wanting to make the case that Freud was dogmatically negative about religion needs to account for and explain the positive passages in the Freudian text, as well as confront and counter the historical accounts of Bakan and Yerushalmi.[54] Will Herberg has gone so far as to argue that Freud's iconoclastic perspective is nearer to the authentic Jewish and Christian perspective of the Bible than are the perspectives of Freudian revisionists (e.g., Erich Fromm and Jules Masserman) who attempt to soften Freud's critique.[55]

In short, Jung was not unambiguously positive about religion, at least in its conventional and traditional forms, and Freud was by no means unambiguously negative. The two men split from each other just at the time that they were each researching and writing on religious subject matter (Jung's *Symbols of Transformation* and Freud's *Totem and Taboo*). Their conversations concerning their research, recorded in the letters between them, demonstrate that religious issues were very important to both of them for clinical, as well as theoretical, reasons.

Essentialism

A third pitfall in the teaching of Jung is to concede the common charge against Jung of essentialism, a particularly sensitive issue in current gender discussions and other postmodern critical theory (for example, Naomi Goldenberg's *Returning Words to Flesh: Feminism, Psychoanalysis, and the Resurrection of the Body*). The charge goes something like this: by assuming that psychological imagery has collective archetypal status and intentionality, one implies a world of essences and essential forms of human meaning (*the* opinionated feminine, *the* ungrounded puer, *the* senex curmudgeon, *the* great mother nurturer, *the* wise old man, and so on). The problem with this implication of Jung's view of the archetypes of the collective unconscious and the process of individuation—so goes the critique—is that it does not have adequate regard for the otherness of the divine or for the otherness of other persons. It elides not only the "infinite qualitative distinction" (Kierkegaard) between the divine and the human, the transpersonal and the personal, but also confuses the fundamental differences of persons of various races, classes, and genders. This criticism is, however, unsophisticated about the notion of archetype. Ironically, it is a criticism that itself elides difference. It fails to draw upon an important difference, a difference that is poignantly illustrated by an anecdote concerning Jung's relationship to the historian of religions, Mircea Eliade.

In the context of their friendship at Eranos Conferences in Ascona, Switzerland, Eliade, late in 1954, sent Jung a French copy of his then new book on yoga.[56] Eliade writes in that work about what he takes to be the archetypal significance of mandala images within South Asian yogic context, and he quotes Jung in support of his point about these being structurally archetypal (i.e., essences). Eliade clearly thought that he was agreeing with what he took to be Jung's universal and essentialist point on the appearance of similar imagery in the spontaneous drawings of psychotherapeutic patients. But much to

Eliade's astonishment, instead of receiving a pleasant thank-you note and gratitude for the reference, Jung sent a very critical letter.[57]

After thanking Eliade briefly for the book, Jung said that he was offended
by the reference. "I am happy to possess such a mine of information [on yoga].
I was somewhat surprised, however, to find that you had not been able to grant
me normal intelligence and scientific responsibility."[58] Jung repeats this at the
end of the letter:

> There is a psychological problem here which I cannot explain. On the
> one hand, you make the very kind and generous gesture of sending
> me your book; on the other, you seem to consider me so idiotic as
> never even to have thought about the nature of the unconscious. How
> have I merited this ill-will? From the moment when I had the honour
> and pleasure of making your acquaintance personally, I have never
> felt anything other than admiration and esteem for your great work,
> and I would be distressed to have offended you without knowing it. I
> hope that you will not be angry with me for writing this long importu-
> nate letter, but I do not like to let a hidden sore fester. Needless to say
> how grateful I would be to you for a few words of explanation![59]

It goes without saying that there is a disagreement!

The issue seems to be that Eliade had described what he called the "apish"
(French simiesque) imitation in India of mandala images, constructing them for
purposes of meditation. Then he asserted that these were the same (universal,
general) as the mandala images drawn by Jung's patients. Jung's objection was
that his patients had nothing to "imitate" (French singer, "to ape"). The drawings were spontaneous products—that is, unconscious—made by persons who
had no knowledge of mandalas at the ego level of collective consciousness.
They were by no means the same.

At the level of collective consciousness (ego, behavior), everyone is different. Jung had made this point over and over again, as James Hillman has
pointed out.[60] "Personality," Jung said, "is the supreme realization of the innate
idiosyncrasy of a living being."[61] Mature and authentic individuation and
development is a "process of differentiation."[62] "Differentiation means the
development of differences, the separation of parts from the whole."[63] Hillman
stresses that Jung is saying that individuation is not wholeness but is separation of complexes from functions, projections from realities, and individual
from collective. Individuation and differentiation give one an appropriate sense
of being different, of even differing with oneself, of being in "isolation."[64] In
the seminar on Kundalini Yoga, Jung went so far as to describe ego's sense
when there is authentic development in these words:

> Individuation is not that you become an ego—you would then
> become an individualist. You know, an individualist is a man [sic]
> who did not succeed in individuating; he is a philosophically distilled
> egotist. Individuation is becoming that thing which is not the ego,

and that is very strange. Therefore nobody understands what the self is, because the self is just the thing which you are not, which is not the ego.... The self is something exceedingly impersonal, exceedingly objective. If you function in yourself you are not yourself—that is what you feel. You have to do it as if you were a stranger.[65]

This implies that at the conscious material level there is only difference, whereas sameness is at a deeper formal level, and this sameness is unconscious. (Jung consistently asserted that one cannot know the unknowable formal archetype, but only the material archetypal image that manifests.) His insistence on this, against Eliade, is not unlike Plotinus and Heidegger on the issue of identity and difference. Plotinus describes two sorts of likeness: the likeness of like things, which he takes to be superficial, and the likeness of unlike or different things, that is, a likeness that does not appear and is based upon difference.[66] Eliade seems to have assumed the first sense of archetypal sameness, namely, essentialist, whereas Jung sought the second sense, namely, differentiated.

Martin Heidegger advanced an argument similar to the one of Plotinus. In *Identity and Difference*, Heidegger wrote against Hegel concerning the logic of sameness in Parmenides, the Greek philosopher to whom Plotinus also may have been alluding. Heidegger thought that the idea of sameness had been wrongly imagined as a "belonging together," where the belonging was determined by the word *together*, that is, by a unity that does not account for difference. To account for difference as well as identity, Heidegger proposed to discriminate between an idea of "belonging *together*" (*Zusammen*gehören, to which he is opposed) and "*belonging* together" (Zusammen*gehören*). In the latter notion, things that are not together, that is, not same, can nonetheless belong to each other. This makes, he argues, for "the possibility of no longer representing belonging in terms of the unity of the together, but rather of experiencing this in terms of belonging."[67] Differences, while not belonging *together*, nonetheless *belong* together, precisely in their distance and difference. Eliade finds religious meaning where things are identified; Jung finds psychological meaning where things that are differentiated belong.[68]

There is a constant temptation in teaching Jung to capitulate, against Jung's best intention, to an Eliade-like point of view, especially when teaching the notion of the archetypes of the collective unconscious in relation to religious ideas. It is a difficult pitfall to avoid, especially since many Jungians (and Jung himself from time to time) entertain the same confusion as did Eliade: they unwittingly assume the identity of form and matter, of archetypal image and ego's behavior in the world.[69] James Hillman has made an effort to avoid this—that is, to avoid the essentialist charge and pitfall—by recommending a taboo against the noun *archetype* in favor of the qualitative adjective *archetypal*.[70] Archetypal is not an entity, an essence, but "is a move one makes rather than a thing that is."[71] It is a move that functions very much the way that the idea of "importance" functions in Whitehead's thought.[72] The idea is to keep one's sense of the importance of difference. When one sees this, then the essentialist critique of Jung shows itself to be ironic. It is ironically guilty of the same thing with which it is charging Jung: namely, not differentiating different forms of archetypal likeness, in other words, generalizing about Jung and making archetypalism a universal, everywhere the same.

Gnostic

Another frequent charge against Jung is that his psychology, his implied theology, and his style of thinking are "Gnostic." For example, Fritz Buri, an important Swiss Protestant theologian, called Jung a Gnostic in his review of the German edition of Jung's *Answer to Job*.[73] Jung's response was one of incredulity. He said in a letter to Buri: "I do not pretend to know anything tenable or provable about a metaphysical God. I therefore don't quite understand how you can smell 'gnostic' arrogance in this attitude. In strictest contrast to Gnosticism *and* theology, I confine myself to the psychology of anthropomorphic ideas and have never maintained that I possess the slightest trace of metaphysical knowledge."[74] A Jesuit theologian from Louvain, Raymond Hostie, also leveled the Gnostic charge at Jung in a book that has been translated as *Religion and the Psychology of Jung*. To Hostie, Jung responded: "You overlook the facts and then think that the name is the fact, and thus you reach the nonsensical conclusion that I hypostatize ideas and am therefore a 'Gnostic.' *It is your theological standpoint that is a gnosis, not my empiricism*, of which you obviously haven't the faintest inkling."[75] Buri and Hostie are joined in their name-calling by Robert C. Smith, an American professor of religious studies, who made the charge in his doctoral dissertation. Jung responded, as he did to others: "I cannot understand what my alleged incapacity to stand criticism has to do with the reproach that I am a Gnostic. You simply add to the arbitrary assumption that I am a Gnostic the blame of moral inferiority, and you don't realize that one could make the same subjective reproach to you."[76] Jung also observed: "A Gnostic would not be at all pleased with me, but would reproach me for having no cosmogony and for the cluelessness of my gnosis in regard to the happenings in the Pleroma."[77] It is clear from these responses that there is some emotional stake in this issue.

Smith's dissertation had been on the topic of the differences between Jung and the famous Jewish thinker, Martin Buber, on the question of religion. It was Buber who aimed the most devastating critique at Jung, using what for Buber was an epithet, namely, the term "Gnostic." Buber's attack was published in the magazine *Merkur*, in February 1952, and Jung responded with a reply in the May issue. In the response, Jung observed an inconsistency in the thinking of those who wish to put a label on him. "Funnily enough this opinion of Buber's coincides with another utterance from an authoritative theological source [Hermann Keyserling] accusing me of agnosticism—the exact opposite of Gnosticism." And then Jung wonders: "Why is so much attention devoted to the question of whether I am a Gnostic or an agnostic? Why is it not simply stated that I am a psychiatrist whose prime concern is to record and interpret his empirical material?"[78]

Perhaps one of the reasons that the issue is raised by Jung's critics is that he was not always consistent in his denials and in his attempt to sidestep the charge. For example, he admits in his reply to Buber in *Merkur* what he calls a "sin of his youth." In writing *Seven Sermons of the Dead*, he confesses to having "expressed a number of psychological *aperçus* in 'Gnostic' style, because I was then studying the Gnostics with enthusiasm."[79] Further, he continued this enthusiasm by way of his friendship with the famous scholar of Gnosticism, Gilles Quispel. In a comment intended as an introduction to a book that Quispel never published, Jung remarks on the connection between Gnostic insights and depth psychology: "We [psychologists] see in it [Gnosticism] a *tertium comparationis* which affords us the most valuable help in the practical understanding of symbol-formation."[80] Most important, however, is Jung's idea that the importance of the psychology of alchemy, which so occupied him, is that it provided an "uninterrupted intellectual chain back to Gnosticism" and that this "gave substance [i.e., historical validation] to my psychology."[81] Jung therefore could write: "I hope the reader will not be offended if my exposition [on alchemy] sounds like a Gnostic myth. We are moving in … psychological regions where, as a matter of fact, Gnosis is rooted."[82] And Jung made this seemingly unequivocal statement: "By far the most fruitful attempts … to find suitable symbolic expressions for the Self were made by the Gnostics."[83]

Examples abound in Jung's writing of parallels between Gnostic ideas and Jung's terminology. *Vas sapientiae* ("vessel of wisdom") corresponds to Jung's notion of "psyche"; Sophia Achamoth and the "Divine Harlot" are similar to Jung's negative anima; the "scintillae" of Gnosticism are like the multiplicity of the unconscious; the Peacock's Egg (*sperma mundi*), so full of colors, is like Jung's use of alchemy's *cauda pavonis* ("peacock's tail"); the male and female pairs in Gnostic literature are like Jung's "syzygy"; the Gnostic Divine Marriage is like Jung's notion of the male and female *coniunctio*; Saturn corresponds to Jung's *senex*; the Tree of Simon is like the Self; "bythos" in Gnosticism is like "depth" in Jung; the Primordial Man is Jung's psychological "androgyne"; and the Adamas Rock and Barbello ("one is four") is like Jung's notion of the quarternian Self. So, Jung can be as positive with regard to Gnostic ideas as he can be negative in his replies to his critics. The fact is that he waffled on the issue of Gnosticism and was by no means consistent in his alignment with it or his rejection of it. Jung's ambivalence is shown in a 1954 letter to Erich Neumann: "I would abandon the term 'Gnostic' without compunction were it not a swearword in the mouths of theologians. They accuse me of the very same fault they commit themselves: presumptuous disregard of epistemological barriers."[84]

When Jung was defensive about Gnosticism in relation to his psychology, it seems to have been to distance himself from positive metaphysical or speculative theological knowledge (beliefs and cosmology) and also to attempt to avoid the charges, often then associated with Gnosticism, of dualism—that is, good versus evil, light against dark, spirit against body, eternity against history, all of the latter terms imagined to be negative. In commenting on Jung's thought in relation to Freud's on psychosexuality, I earlier cited Jung's *Zarathustra* Seminar, where he is unambiguously positive with regard to the importance of the body, emphasizing that this was one of his main reasons for invoking alchemy. This hardly accords with a Jungian Gnostic dualism about the evil body. Nor is the *Zarathustra* Seminar an isolated instance. Here are two more examples from the autobiography. Regarding images that come up in dreams and fantasies and symptoms, Jung argued that it was crucially important:

> to realize them in actual life. This is what we usually neglect to do. We allow the images to rise up, and maybe we wonder about them, but that is all. We do not take the trouble to understand them, let alone draw ethical conclusions from them. This stopping-short conjures up the negative effects of the unconscious. It is equally a grave mistake to think that it is enough to gain some understanding of the images and that knowledge can here make a halt. Insight into them must be converted into an ethical obligation. Not to do so is to fall prey to the power principle and this produces dangerous effects which are destructive not only to others but even to the knower. The images of the unconscious place a great responsibility upon a man [*sic*]. Failure to understand them, or a shirking ethical responsibility, deprives him of his wholeness and imposes a painful fragmentariness on his life.[85]

Again, Jung writes: "For me,…irreality was the quintessence of horror, for I aimed, after all, at *this* world and *this* life. No matter how deeply absorbed or how blown about I was, I always knew that everything I was experiencing was ultimately directed at this real life of mine. I meant to meet its obligations and fulfill its meanings. My watchword was: *Hic Rhodus, hic salta!*"[86] Nothing could be clearer! But there is a more telling matter.

The stigma of Gnosticism as dualistic is an interpretive perspective that is identified with the work of Hans Jonas[87] and Kurt Rudolf.[88] Theirs is a perspective that has been complicated recently, especially after some long-term reflections on the multiperspectivalism of the Nag Hammadi literature, a set of codices discovered in Egypt in 1945 and translated only in 1977. Karen King,[89] Michael Williams,[90] and Morton Smith[91] have each written significant scholarly works complicating stereotypical notions of Gnosticism and calling into question a consistent notion of metaphysical dualism and hatred of history and the body in Gnostic texts. They even imply that the term "Gnostic" cannot be used intelligently to mean any one thing and that the word is therefore not useful. So, the furor about Jung's being a Gnostic or not, and Jung's own back and forth on the issue, may all finally be "sound and fury signifying nothing." Then why is all of this important to the question of teaching Jung?

The answer is that many students and, in spite of the works just mentioned, still some scholars bring the old undifferentiated Gnostic stereotype to the study of Jungian psychology. Indeed, popular appropriations of Jung in pop psychology and in the so-called self-help and New Age movements often present a spiritualized picture of Jung's thinking that is vulnerable to the outdated

Gnostic charge. David Tacey's study, *Jung and the New Age*, clearly delineates the dangers of the pop spiritualizing and shows how it can work against a serious academic study of Jung and his psychology.[92] Tacey notes that many people "encounter Jung not directly or first-hand through his difficult writings, but indirectly through the simplistic and reductive creations of the New Age movement."[93] The pitfall of this Gnostic seduction of Jung is that it artificially lends an esoteric and mystical aura to Jung and his thinking, which makes serious academic thinkers and teachers suspicious, and it gives them reason, though false, to be opposed to the study of Jungian psychology in a scholarly manner. It can turn Jung into a figure of ridicule, and it works against Jung's own view of the matter. He complains that his critics "criticize me as if I were a philosopher, or a Gnostic with pretentions to supernatural knowledge. That is probably the reason why people prefer to ignore the facts I have discovered, or to deny them without scruple. But it is the facts that are of prime importance to me and not a provisional terminology or attempts at theoretical reflections."[94]

Psychologizing

It was probably Jung's wielding of a psychological hermeneutic on materials from the Hebrew and Christian Bible and upon mythological, folkloric, literary, and artistic materials that prompted the criticism of Jung that he was "psychologizing" and therefore reductive. This possibility of reductive interpretation is a final pitfall that haunts the teaching of Jung. To be sure, reductionism is a perduring risk. It is a humanization of things that are transpersonal, a bringing of the larger into the domain and perspective of what is smaller. It is *psychologism*. And it is a real temptation.

Jung complained of this about Freud, perhaps not altogether fairly. In the Tavistock Lectures in London, Jung asserted that Freud's method of free association in analysis, especially in dream interpretation, reduced the deep psyche's material to ego's associations and was biased by whatever complexes the clients were absorbed in unconsciously. He offered his own method of "seeking the parallels" of one's psychological images in larger archetypal contexts (myth, folktale, religion) as a corrective to psychologism. That he called this methodology "amplification" is testimony to his attempt to avoid reductive interpretations. It is a seeing of the smaller egoic matters in a larger collective context, what Proclus called *epistrophē*, a "leading back" of human things to the archetypal forms and meanings.

Using biblical interpretation as an example of this, one can see how Martin Buber, for example, might think of Jung's *Answer to Job* as reductive. But an archetypal amplification may also be thought of otherwise. Rather than being a matter of psychologizing a biblical narrative, it could be understood as "biblicizing" the psyche, of imagining human thoughts and feelings in terms of biblical imagery, divinizing the human, rather than humanizing the divine. It is not that Jacob and his mother and father, for example, are in an Oedipal complex, but rather that a given sense of the familial mess can be seen as a Jacob complex.

This would be taking seriously Jung's saying that "we must read the Bible or we shall not understand psychology."[95] Jung also implies that a depth psychology worthy of the name must be acquainted with mythology, the history of religions, the canons of literature and the arts, folklore, and other archetypal expressions. The hermeneutic goal is a psychology understood deeply and broadly. Jung's heuristic is called "depth" psychology precisely because it is not reductive, that is, not an ego psychology, though one may be in fact reductive by not taking realistic account of the profound aspects of selfhood occasioned by insight from archetypal and collective sources. Walter Wink once expressed this in relation to the psychological study of the Bible: "We have analyzed the Bible; now we may wish to find ways to let it analyze us."[96] This is crucial to keep in mind when teaching Jung, lest the teaching of Jung and his psychology be wittingly or unwittingly used to serve ego and its interests only and end up as a humanistic rather than a depth psychology.[97]

Conclusion

It is the issue stressed in the last sentence that may be the most difficult matter in the teaching of Jung. The problem is—if I may put it this way—that the teaching might succeed! That is, students may find it to be "meaningful" (to ego), useful to everyday life (of ego), therapeutic (to ego), hermeneutically helpful (to ego), and enlightening (to ego). But then, of course, the teaching of "Jung" would not be the teaching of Jung. It would no longer be *depth* psychology. Contrary to what might have been intuitively imagined, pedagogical success can become a final and general pitfall.

Wolfgang Giegerich has been articulate about the strategy of teaching Jung in the following words: "Your [the teacher's] style of speaking or writing must confront the audience with the experience of the *non*-ego (i.e., the sense of *"not you as you have been all along"*); it must impose on the audience the narcissistic offense that you are *not* concerned with what *they* think and are *not* speaking to them, but to *their Other*."[98] James Hillman had earlier spoken of this strategy as "depersonalizing," in other words, de-ego-fying. He wrote: "We spoil our actual friendships, marriages, loves and families by looking to people for redemption. We seek salvation in personal encounters, personal relations, personal solutions. Human persons are the contemporary shrines.... Our cult worships or propitiates actual people—the family, the beloved, the circle of encounters—while ignoring the persons of the psyche who compose the soul and upon whom the soul depends."[99] The advice of Giegerich and the observation of Hillman make the teaching of depth psychology difficult, as Freud had already acknowledged.

In 1915, Freud was lecturing to medical students in Vienna, attempting to introduce them to the then new perspectives of depth psychology. He warned the students at the outset that "psychoanalysis cannot easily be learnt" and said that "there are not many people who have learnt it properly."[100] The reason that it is difficult is that it cannot be learned inductively and empirically, like the students had learned anatomy from the experience of looking at a cadaver and then generalizing from the particular situation to general rules. Nor can psychoanalysis be learned deductively and rationally, like the students had learned blood chemistry from the general rules of organic chemistry applied to individual blood samples. That is to say, psychoanalysis cannot be learned by looking objectively outward. Rather, Freud said that "one learns psychoanalysis on oneself, by studying one's own personality." But then he adds that "this is not quite the same thing as what is called self-observation"; that is, it is not ego-introspection.[101] One learns from the remainder of Freud's lectures that one teaches and learns depth psychology by probing the self that I do not think is myself, the slips that the ego makes and does not intend, the daydreams and night dreams that are not under ego's control, the obsessions that are not-me and are not welcomed by me, the compulsions and neuroses and psychoses that are not of ego's invention. These are the "persons" of the deep psyche spoken of by Hillman and the non-ego spoken of by Giegerich, those factors that demonstrate that I am not the master of my fate and the captain of my soul, the not-me that is me nonetheless.

This uncanny nature of the subject matter of depth psychology—the "fundamental ambivalence" of Freud's view of the self and Jung's notion of the self as a "complex of opposites"—will lead Freud early in his life to say that success in psychoanalysis "will be gained if we succeed in transforming...hysterical misery into common unhappiness."[102] And late in his life, long after the split from Freud, Jung will concur by saying: "The doctor must advise him [the patient] to accept the conflict just as it is, with all the suffering this inevitably entails, . . . the united personality will never quite lose the painful sense of innate discord. Complete redemption from the sufferings of the world is and must remain an illusion."[103] The irony of a successful analysis is that it is constituted in part by an acceptance of what from ego's point of view may be sensed as failure.

So it is, not only with psychoanalysis but also with the teaching of depth psychology. Success in the realm of the conscious ego is suspect. The teaching of Jung, like the teaching of Freud, is not an easy matter. But as Jung said: "The experience of the self is always [experienced as] a defeat for the ego."[104] Failure in the teaching of Jung, at least from nonpsychological points of view, may indicate success.

NOTES

1. Sigmund Freud, *Standard Edition of the Complete Psychological Works of Sigmund Freud*, 24 vols. (London: Hogarth, 1953–1974), 6:106–16, 230.

2. See Harold Bloom, *Anxiety of Influence: A Theory of Poetry* (New York: Oxford University Press, 1973) and *Map of Misreading* (New York: Oxford University Press, 1975).

3. An example of Jung going against himself in a text is given by Wolfgang Giegerich ("The End of Meaning and the Birth of Man," *Journal of Jungian Theory and Practice* 6.1 [2004]: 1–2). Jung was in the midst of stressing that the times are mythless, that "there are no longer gods" (CW 8:598), that it would be well to admit "spiritual poverty" and "symbol-lessness" (CW 9i:28). But then in the context of observing that people today have no myth, Jung turns and asks, "Then what is your myth?"

4. See Ernest Wallwork, *Psychoanalysis and Ethics* (New Haven, CT: Yale University Press, 1991), 19–28.

5. C. G. Jung, *Collected Works of C. G. Jung*, ed. Herbert Read, M. Fordham, and G. Adler, trans. R. F. C. Hull (Princeton, NJ: Princeton University Press, 1953–1976), 18:275.

6. Jung, *Collected Works*, 4:774–75.

7. Jung, C. G., *Memories, Dreams, Reflections*, ed. Aniela Jaffé, trans. Richard Winston and Clara Winston (New York: Vintage, 1965), 153.

8. Jung, *Memories*, 150.

9. Ibid., 158.

10. Jung, *Collected Works*, 18:1150.

11. Jung, *Memories*, 152.

12. Ibid., 154.

13. Ibid., 153.

14. Jung, *Collected Works*, 18:633.

15. Jung, *Memories*, 114.

16. Ibid., 168–69.

17. Wallwork, *Psychoanalysis and Ethics*, 19–48, and see also Wallwork, "The Challenge of Teaching Freud: Depth Psychology and Religious Ethics," in *Teaching Freud*, ed. Diane Jonte-Pace (New York: Oxford University Press, 2003), 246, against the opposing of Jung and Freud. Richard Sterba has also reported on another view of Freud different from Jung's negative one. In Sterba's account of Wednesday evening discussions at Freud's home between 1928 and 1932, Sterba remembers only a single occasion when Freud "took on a deliberately authoritarian attitude." It was in a moment when he silenced Wilhelm Reich for being authoritarian, dogmatic, and reductionist... concerning sexuality!" (Sterba, "Discussions of Sigmund Freud," *Psychoanalytic Quarterly* 47.2 [1978]: 182–84).

18. Freud, *Standard Edition*, 2:291; 20:195; 22:211–12.

19. Ibid., 5:511; 10:100; 17:143; 18:30–31, 59; 20:32.

20. Ibid., 14:117; 20:32–33; 21:53.

21. Freud, *Standard Edition*, Ibid., 5:525; 2:2n2; compare Wallwork, *Psychoanalysis and Ethics*, 35n28.

22. Jung, *Memories*, 147.

23. Jung, *Collected Works*, 18:281.

24. Jung, *Memories*, 149.

25. Ibid., 150.

26. Ibid., 150.

27. Ibid., 151.

28. Jung, *Collected Works*, 18:493.

29. Freud, *Standard Edition*, 18:255, 257.

30. Jung, *Memories*, 209.

31. Freud, *Standard Edition*, 16:386.

32. Ibid., 11:222–23, and compare Wallwork, "The Challenge of Teaching Freud," 244.

33. Freud, *Standard Edition*, 16:310–19.

34. In her book *Thinking through the Body* (New York: Columbia University Press, 1988, 124), Jane Gallop tells the following joke in order to discriminate between literal genital sexuality (penis) and the broader concept of psychosexuality (phallus): "Anna Freud was reaching maturity and began to show an interest in her father's work, so Freud gave her some of his writings to read. About a month later he asked her if she had any questions about what she had been reading. 'Just one,' she replied, 'what is a phallus?' Being a man of science, Freud unbuttoned his pants and showed her. 'Oh,' Anna exclaimed, thus enlightened, 'it's like a penis, only smaller!'"

35. This perspective can be construed as meaning that symptoms are past oriented, and this is one of the things to which Jung objected, thinking of Freud's theory, like that of his teacher, Helmholtz, as causal, mechanistic, and deterministic (see CW 18:14–15, 280, 468). But Wallwork (*Psychoanalysis and Ethics*, 29, 32–34, 55, 81, 125–26) has shown that though Freud's early theory can be read this way, the later theory, especially after 1920, becomes more and more teleological, just like Jung's, in regard to dreams, symptoms, and drives.

36. Jung, *Collected Works*, 4:63.

37. Jung, *Memories*, 168.

38. Ibid.

39. Jung, *Nietzsche's* Zarathustra: *Notes of the Seminar Given in 1934–1939 by C. G. Jung*, ed. James L. Jarrett, 2 vols. (Princeton, NJ: Princeton University Press, 1988), 1:368.This theme is repeated throughout the seminars. See index item on "body" at 2:1550.

40. Jung, *Collected Works*, 12:1–29, 295–305.

41. See Jung, *Memories*, 189, 192–193, 205–206.

42. Lewis Mumford, "Revolt of the Demons," *New Yorker* 40 (May 23, 1964): 162.

43. Freud, *Standard Edition*, 21:43.

44. Jung, *Collected Works*, 5:553; 18:370.

45. See David L. Miller, "'Attack upon Christendom!' The Anti-Christianism of Depth Psychology," *Thought* 61.240 (1986): 56–67.

46. Jung, *Collected Works*, 9i:36–71.

47. Jung, *Letters*, ed. Gerhard Adler, trans. R. F. C. Hull, 2 vols. (Princeton, NJ: Princeton University Press, 1973), 1:18.

48. Jung, *Collected Works*, 11:201–98.

49. Jung, *Letters*, 1:18. A footnote to this letter, added by the editor, seems to imply that Jung later, in a letter of April 9, 1959 (never released), repudiated this strong critique with words like "incredible folly that filled the days of my youth." But this is by no means clear. At a Christmas celebration with his family in 1957, he was still referring to the "lost" sense of Christianity as a Dionysian feast (Jung, *Word and Image*, trans. K. Winston [Princeton, NJ: Princeton University Press, 1979], 143–45), and when he was seventy, Jung complained of religious ideas having lost the "numinosity, i.e., their thrilling power" (Jung, *Collected Works*, 13:396). Also, note Jung's comment in a letter in 1952 to Erich Neumann: "God is an ailment that man has to cure" (Jung, *Letters*, 2:33).

50. Jung, *Collected Works*, 18:279, and compare David L. Miller, "Holy and Not-So-Holy Ghosts! Psychopathogenetic Shadows in Religious Images and Ideas," *Journal of Jungian Theory and Practice* 8.1 (2006): 55–59.

51. Freud, *Standard Edition*, 20:8 and footnote 3.

52. Ibid., 20:72.

53. David Bakan, *Sigmund Freud and the Jewish Mystical Tradition* (New York: Schocken, 1965); and Yosef Hayim Yerushalmi, *Freud's Moses: Judaism Terminable and Interminable* (New Haven, CT: Yale University Press, 1991).

54. Further testimony to the complex relation between Freudian theory and religion is given in the companion book in the present series, *Teaching Freud*, ed. Diane Jonte-Pace (New York: Oxford University Press, 2003), which is a part of the American Academy of Religion book series on teaching religious studies.

55. Will Herberg, "Freud and the Revisionists," in *Freud and the Twentieth Century*, ed. Benjamin Nelson (New York: Meridian, 1957). Just as Herberg shows an alignment between Freud and biblical iconoclasm with regard to religion, doing this in the face of a stereotype that pits Freud in opposition to religion, so I have attempted to show a rapprochement between Jung and postmodern critical theory, which flies in the face of the generalized and oversimplistic critique of Jung by some postmodern theorists (see David L. Miller, "The Stone Which Is Not a Stone': C. G. Jung and the Postmodern Meaning of Meaning," *Spring* 49 [1989]: 110–22).

56. Mircea Eliade, *Le Yoga. Immortalité et liberté* (Paris: Librarie Payot, 1954).

57. Jung, *Letters*, 2:210–12.

58. Ibid., 2:210.

59. Ibid., 2:212.

60. James Hillman, "Jung's Daimonic Inheritance," *Sphinx* 1 (1988): 12.

61. Jung, *Collected Works*, 17:289.

62. Ibid., 6:757.

63. Ibid., 6:705.

64. Ibid., 13:395.

65. Jung, *The Psychology of Kundalini Yoga: Notes of a Seminar Given in* 1932, ed. Sonu Shamdasani (Princeton, NJ: Princeton University Press, 1996): 39–40. There is a striking similarity between this comment by Jung and a perspective developed by Julia Kristeva in *Strangers to Ourselves*, trans. Leon S. Roudiez (New York: Columbia University Press, 1991).

66. Plotinus, *Enneads* (trans. A. Hillary Armstrong [Cambridge, MA: Harvard University Press, 1978]), vol. 1:131, and compare David L. Miller, *Three Faces of God: Traces of the Trinity in Literature and Life* (New Orleans, LA: Spring Journal, 2005), 41–51. Plotinus's distinction comes in *Ennead*, 1.2.2, where Plotinus, in speaking about "archetype." He says: "We should note that there are two kinds of likeness [*homoiōsis*]: one requires that there should be something the same in the things which are alike; this applies to things which derive their likeness equally from the same principle. But in the case of two things of which one is like the other, but the other is primary not reciprocally related to the thing in its likeness and not said to be like it [*hōmiōtai pros heteron*], likeness must be understood in a different sense." The translator of this passage (Armstrong) adds a footnote explaining that this notion of two kinds of likeness may have arisen as a response to the objection of Parmenides that the archetypal forms are *paradeigmata*. In fact, one might imagine that Jung's strong response to Eliade is an attempt to avoid a Platonic understanding of his psychology.

67. Martin Heidegger, *Identity and Difference*, trans. Joan Stambaugh (New York: Harper and Row, 1969), 92.

68. The matter between Eliade and Jung had a happy ending. Eliade changed the citation to Jung in a later edition of the work and wrote an apologetic clarification in the introduction of a still different book (Eliade, *Yoga*, 219–27, and Eliade, *Cosmos and History*, trans. Willard Trask [New York: Harper and Row, 1959], vii–ix).

69. For example, Jungians completely alienate themselves and Jung in the presence of third-wave feminists and antiessentialist postmodern literary theorists when they speak of "*the* feminine," as if it were a something (essence), compounding the problem with the singular definite article, as if "the so-called feminine" were definitely one thing and one thing only, typically characterized over against masculine, rationalist, logical nature. This is as unrealistic and offensive as the view that men are Martial and women are Venusian!

70. James Hillman, "Why 'Archetypal' Psychology?" *Spring* (1970): 212–19.

71. James Hillman, *Archetypal Psychology* (Dallas: Spring, 1983), 13.

72. Alfred North Whitehead, *Modes of Thought* (New York: Free Press, 1968), 1–19.

73. Fritz Buri, "C. G. Jung's 'Antwort zu Hiob,'" *Basler National-Zeitung* (April 27, 1952). See reference in Jung, *Letters*, 2.61n1.

74. Jung, *Letters*, 2:64–65.

75. Ibid., 2:245.

76. Ibid., 2:583.

77. Jung, *Collected Works*, 18:1513.

78. Ibid., 18:1499–1500.

79. Ibid., 18:1501.

80. Ibid., 18:1482.

81. Jung, *Memories*, 205.

82. Jung, *Collected Works*, 7:28.

83. Jung, *Collected Works*, 9.ii:428.

84. Jung, *Letters*, 2:147.

85. Jung, *Memories*, 192–93.

86. Jung, *Memories*, 189. This translates as "here is Rhodes, jump here." The allusion is to Aesop's fable "The Braggart" (also cited in Erasmus's "Adagia"). The athlete brags that he once made a fantastic leap in Rhodes and that he can cite persons who will testify to this feat. A person overhearing this says that there is no need of witnesses, since the braggart can demonstrate the jump here and now. The popularity in modern times of this saying is due to its use by Hegel and Marx.

87. Hans Jonas, *The Gnostic Religion* (Boston: Beacon, 1991).

88. Kurt Rudolph, *Gnosis: The Nature and History of Gnosticism* (San Francisco: HarperSanFrancisco, 1987).

89. Karen King, *What Is Gnosticism?* (Cambridge, MA: Harvard University Press, 2003).

90. Michael Allen Williams, *Rethinking "Gnosticism": An Argument for Dismantling a Dubious Category* (Princeton, NJ: Princeton University Press, 1996).

91. Morton Smith, "The History of the term Gnostikos," in: Bentley Layton, ed., *The Rediscovery of Gnosticism* (Leiden: Brill, 1997), 2.796-807.

92. David Tacey, *Jung and the New Age* (New York: Brunner-Routledge, 2001). In an interview by Lynn Neary of National Public Radio ("The Changing Face of America—On How Spirituality Is Replacing Mainline Religion," November 30, 2000), Huston Smith noted the problem: "Organized religion gives spirituality traction. Without it spirituality can become a self-centered pursuit. Spirituality is individual and subjective, and it can refer indiscriminately to experiences of elevation and joy, sort of the cream on the cream puff of life. Many people take a salad bar approach to spirituality, picking and choosing what's easy from different traditions, often leaving the hard parts behind. The danger of the salad bar approach is that it worships Saint Ego, and it assumes that you know what you need." (This is in the archives of National Public Radio's website.)

93. Tacey, *Jung and the New Age*, x.
94. Jung, *Collected Works*, 11:461.
95. Jung, *The Visions Seminars*, vol. 1 (Zurich: Spring, 1976), 156.
96. Walter Wink, "On Wrestling with God: Using Psychological Insights in Biblical Study," *Religion in Life* 47 (1978): 141.
97. On this matter, see Wolfgang Giegerich (*The Soul's Logical Life* [Frankfurt: Peter Lang, 1998], 18, 31) and James Hillman (*Re-Visioning Psychology* [New York: Harper and Row, 1975], 167–229).
98. Giegerich, *The Soul's Logical Life*, 18.
99. Hillman, James, *Re-Visioning Psychology*, 47.
100. Freud, *Standard Edition*, 15:19.
101. Ibid., 15:19.
102. Ibid., 2:305.
103. Jung, *Collected Works*, 16:392, 400.
104. Ibid., 14: 778.

REFERENCES

Bakan, David. *Sigmund Freud and the Jewish Mystical Tradition*. New York: Schocken, 1965.
Bloom, Harold. *The Anxiety of Influence: A Theory of Poetry*. New York: Oxford University Press, 1973.
Bloom, Harold. *A Map of Misreading*. New York: Oxford University Press, 1975.
Buri, Fritz. "C. G. Jung's 'Antwort zu Hiob.'" *Basler National-Zeitung* (April 27, 1952).
Eliade, Mircea. *Le Yoga. Immortalité et liberté*. Paris: Librarie Payot, 1954.
Eliade, Mircea. *Yoga*. Trans. Willard Trask. New York: Pantheon, 1958.
Eliade, Mircea. *Cosmos and History*. Trans. Willard Trask. New York: Harper and Row, 1959.
Freud, Sigmund. *The Standard Edition of the Complete Psychological Works of Sigmund Freud*. 24 vols. Trans. James Strachey. London: Hogarth, 1953–1974.
Gallop, Jane. *Thinking through the Body*. New York: Columbia University Press, 1988.
Giegerich, Wolfgang. *The Soul's Logical Life*. Frankfurt: Peter Lang, 1998.
Giegerich, Wolfgang. "The End of Meaning and the Birth of Man." *Journal of Jungian Theory and Practice* 6.1 (2004): 1–66.
Goldenberg, Naomi. *Returning Words to Flesh: Feminism, Psychoanalysis and the Resurrection of the Body*. Boston: Beacon, 1990.
Heidegger, Martin. *Identity and Difference*. Trans. Joan Stambaugh. New York: Harper and Row, 1969.
Herberg, Will. "Freud and the Revisionists." In *Freud and the Twentieth Century*, ed. Benjamin Nelson. New York: Meridian, 1957.
Hillman, James. "Why 'Archetypal' Psychology?" *Spring* (1970): 212–219.
Hillman, James. *Re-Visioning Psychology*. New York: Harper and Row, 1975.
Hillman, James. *Archetypal Psychology: A Brief Account*. Dallas, TX: Spring, 1983.
Hillman, James. "Jung's Daimonic Inheritance." *Sphinx*, 1 (1988): 9–19.
Jonas, Hans. *The Gnostic Religion*. Boston: Beacon, 1991.
Jonte-Pace, Diane, ed. *Teaching Freud*. Oxford: Oxford University Press, 2003.
Jung, C. G. *The Collected Works of C. G. Jung*, ed. Herbert Read, M. Fordham, and G. Adler, trans. R. F. C. Hull. Princeton, NJ: Princeton University Press, 1953–1976.
Jung, C. G.. *Memories, Dreams, Reflections*, ed. Aniela Jaffé, trans. Richard Winston and Clara Winston. New York: Vintage, 1965.

Jung, C. G. *Letters*, ed. Gerhard Adler, trans. R. F. C. Hull. 2 vols. Princeton, NJ: Princeton University Press, 1973.

Jung, C. G. *The Visions Seminars*, vol. 1. Zurich: Spring, 1976.

Jung, C. G. *Word and Image*, trans. K. Winston. Princeton, NJ: Princeton University Press, 1979.

Jung, C. G. *Nietzsche's Zarathustra: Notes of the Seminar Given in 1934–1939 by C. G. Jung*, ed. James L. Jarrett. 2 vols. Princeton, NJ: Princeton University Press, 1988.

Jung, C. G. *The Psychology of Kundalini Yoga: Notes of a Seminar Given in 1932*, ed. Sonu Shamdasani. Princeton, NJ: Princeton University Press, 1996.

King, Karen. *What Is Gnosticism?* Cambridge, MA: Harvard University Press, 2003.

Kristeva, Julia. *Strangers to Ourselves*, trans. Leon S. Roudiez. New York: Columbia University Press, 1991.

Layton, Bentley, ed. *The Rediscovery of Gnosticism*. Leiden: Brill, 1997.

Miller, David L. "'Attack upon Christendom.'" The Anti-Christianism of Depth Psychology." *Thought* 61.240 (1986): 56–67.

Miller, David L. "'Attack upon Christendom!' The Anti-Christianism of Depth Psychology." In *Jung's Challenge to Contemporary Religion*, ed. Murray Stein and Robert L. Moore. Wilmette, IL: Chiron, 1987.

Miller, David L. "The Stone Which Is Not a Stone: C. G. Jung and the Postmodern Meaning of Meaning.'" *Spring* 49 (1989): 110–122.

Miller, David L. *Jung and the Interpretation of the Bible*. New York: Continuum, 1995.

Miller, David L. *Hells and Holy Ghosts: A Theopoetics of Christian Belief*. New Orleans, LA: Spring Journal, 2004.

Miller, David L. *Christs: Meditations on Archetypal Images in Christian Theology*. New Orleans, LA: Spring Journal, 2005.

Miller, David L. *Three Faces of God: Traces of the Trinity in Literature and Life*. New Orleans, LA: Spring Journal, 2005.

Miller, David L. "Holy and Not-So-Holy Ghosts! Psychopathogenetic Shadows in Religious Images and Ideas." *Journal of Jungian Theory and Practice* 8.1 (2006): 55–59.

Mumford, Lewis. "Revolt of the Demons." *New Yorker* 40 (May 23, 1964): 162.

Plotinus. *Enneads*, vol. 1, trans. A. Hillary Armstrong. Cambridge, MA: Harvard University Press, 1978.

Rudolph, Kurt. *Gnosis: The Nature and History of Gnosticism*. San Francisco: HarperSanFrancisco, 1987.

Sterba, Richard. "Discussions of Sigmund Freud." *Psychoanalytic Quarterly* 47.2 (1978): 173–191.

Tacey, David. *Jung and the New Age*. New York: Brunner-Routledge, 2001.

Wallwork, Ernest. *Psychoanalysis and Ethics*. New Haven, CT: Yale University Press, 1991.

Wallwork, Ernest. "The Challenge of Teaching Freud: Depth Psychology and Religious Ethics." In *Teaching Freud*, ed. Diane Jonte-Pace. New York: Oxford University Press, 2003.

Whitehead, Alfred North. *Modes of Thought*. New York: Free Press, 1968.

Williams, Michael Allen. *Rethinking "Gnosticism": An Argument for Dismantling a Dubious Category*. Princeton, NJ: Princeton University Press, 1996.

Wink, Walter. "On Wrestling with God: Using Psychological Insights in Biblical Study." *Religion in Life* 47 (1978): 141.

Yerushalmi, Yosef Hayim. *Freud's Moses: Judaism Terminable and Interminable*. New Haven, CT: Yale University Press, 1991.

3

Teaching Jung in a Theological Seminary and a Graduate School of Religion

Ann Belford Ulanov

I read with great interest David Tacey's article on teaching Jung in the academy and recognized in him a collegial spirit. For years only a few of us as both clinicians and professors, have worked teaching theories of the unconscious in institutions of higher learning. The amazing fact about the unconscious—that it exists and is unconscious—raises fascinating problems in the teaching-learning context.

Psychic Reality

The teacher should not, I believe, do therapy in the classroom, for that violates students' psyches. But neither should the teacher talk about the unconscious in a way that leads students into intellectual dissociation from the presence of the psyche right there in people in the classroom. What then can we do with the unconscious in the educational setting?

This problem is not faced only by teachers of depth psychology, but by all teachers of quality, those who teach material that matters. I think of two colleagues as examples. Both are men—one in the cross-disciplinary fields of literature, arts, and religion; the other in the discipline of speech analysis and training—who exhibit enormous skill, force, and tact. They stick to their material—the texts—and to the students' reception and use of their matter, and they bring their students to the spirit of what matters. As a result, letters from students indicate, these teachers often change their students' lives. These men do not do therapy in the classroom. In the case of one man, his hearing a student's true voice waiting to be liberated from inferiority or grandiosity complexes aids the unique unfolding of the student's personality in the context of a particular spoken text. For some students, this acute listening transforms their lives.

In the other case, the man meets his students in the material they study together. He summons them into this matrix, asking them to open themselves to text, author, and cultural surroundings, that is, to bring and show themselves in response. His own passion for the material ignites theirs. A Jungian analyst I know, on hearing this teacher lecture publicly, said of him: "When I hear most lecturers I am often moved at the moment; when I hear this man, I go home and read and read." The letters this teacher receives from students, often years after the conclusion of the course, express thanks for his opening up the world of the material, in which the student was able to find what a Jungian analyst might call "the living psyche."

For the teacher of theories about the unconscious psyche, the net tightens. We have to ask ourselves, What sort of tiger have we caught here? For we are, students and teachers alike, studying ourselves when we study such material. Unlike our analysts in training, our academic classroom students may or may not be in treatment themselves. The classroom gets crowded, filling up with hidden questions, unconscious questions put by our psyches, questions that we often resist hearing. Each of us feeling this resistance is challenged to see if our objections to the psychological theories under discussion amount to a preference to work out our conflicts through generalized issues of social justice or theoretical constructions rather than acknowledging their personal roots. The room palpably fills up with the different levels of psychological development among the students, each registering, through individual confusion and bewilderment, different developmental imperatives.

Hermeneutical questions particularly crowd in on us. If as teachers we make room for different levels of development and a variety of resistances to a given psychological theory, understanding that it may be liberating to one student while judgmental for another, how do we go about the business of assessing the theory's intrinsic truth? Is truth simply relative to various subjective viewpoints? Does a norm of truth still exist? By what criteria can it be determined, demonstrated? Professor Tacey's dramatic examples—of students and teachers either altogether excluding study of Jung's theories or altogether embracing Jung to a point of identification that excludes critical reflection—fit here. In my own teaching and supervising of doctoral work in a graduate school of religion, the hermeneutic question reaches a further point of tension: Can something be psychologically true if it is theologically false (or vice versa)?

Seminary Context

Professor Tacey and I share the labor of teaching, but our contexts differ in significant ways. He teaches in a university setting, which, in common with American universities, prides itself on objectivity and critical inquiry, eschewing belief as countermanding those values. In many American educational institutions, even (or perhaps especially) in departments of religion, where Jung is most apt to be taught, the stance of faith is considered to be a drawback to effective teaching. Faith is somehow not rigorous enough or might contaminate the learning process with a proselytizing fervor.

Yet, as Tacey also underscores, the whole issue of belief, if thrown out the front door, will sneak in through the back. The clinician will recognize what Melanie Klein calls "the symbolic equation" as the unconscious condition informing any touted "objectivity." Teachers, in other words, tend unconsciously to identify with what grips them as truth, and the resultant equation of themselves with their ideas acts as a coercive agent in the class discussions. Instances can occur of a teacher marking a student down for arguing against the teacher's undeclared but powerfully operating "truth." Tacey sums it up succinctly: "There are theologies inside our theories, and articles of faith underpin most of our intellectual positions" (p. 269). In a religious institution, ironically, when differences of theology are being debated at a conscious intellectual level, beliefs sneak in, in the form of political ideologies. Here, the coercive symbolic equation is operating at the juncture of belief and action *in society*: theological doctrine that does not pay off in what is considered to be appropriate social action (praxis) is dismissed as bad theology.

My context—teaching in a theological seminary that is also a graduate school of religion—brings some different protections and strains from Tacey's university setting. In a seminary, belief is not held to be a drawback but a resource—indeed, a link to the Source. Belief in God, both personal and communal, acts like a pipeline to the energy and affect that can sustain studies and future careers. Such belief suggests the point of it all and answers the discouraged and cynical question we hear all the time: So what? Or What difference can anyone's piddling efforts make in the face of such suffering in the world? The answer of belief circles around an ego attitude that witnesses to a reality greater than itself, greater in fact than all our selves, which gets expressed in such phrases as "for the sake of love" or "for the greater glory of God."

The traditional religious vocabulary is handy, in that it offers both student and teacher a way to point to a transcendent purposiveness that is present here and now in our actions. Such a transpersonal referent should not be seen as diluting objectivity, but rather as endorsing it. From the perspective of the theological seminary, loss of the transcendent referent exposes us to equally unfortunate opposites: addiction to objectivity (all the while repressing subjective identification with one's theory) and passionate overidentification with one's point of view (disavowing one's actual objective distance from the theory on which one has projected one's personal complexes).

The religious awareness that pervades seminary education, that of a transcendent God that goes well beyond our particular God-images, offers the positive advantage of another perspective. In it, we include the opposites, instead of choosing one at the expense of the other and ending up in a ceaseless compensatory seesawing, acted out in the kind of community of opposing groups that Tacey bemoans. Ours is, I find, more of a muddle of conjunction than a tension of opposition.

My particular seminary, in contrast to schools of particular churches (such as the Presbyterian, the Episcopalian, and the Catholic) that operate from a shared symbol system of doctrine, is nondenominational. At the center of a nondenominational seminary a hole exists, an empty space where doctrinal demands might be expected. In any given week at Union, for example, the schedule of daily worship will reflect the different and competing symbol systems of the school's students and faculty. A traditional Presbyterian service one day, consisting of sermon, prayers, and hymns, will be followed the next by a group of Catholics reciting the rosary. Yet another day brings a service articulating protest against the unjust discrimination suffered by gays and lesbians, followed on its morrow by the presentation of the ineffable but tough faith that students working as hospital chaplains must draw on to survive their ministry to people in the grip of mental and physical illness. Different community groups take turns putting into the empty space at the center the symbols that best capture for them the reality of God. Together, we circle around this center in process, which acts like a revolving mandala, reflecting all our perspectives. At our best, we stimulate each other, feed each other, learn from each other.

At worst, the vertigo of this evolving space makes us feel that the center does not hold. Sometimes, we compete to fill it entirely with our particular God-images, seeking to foist them on each other with all kinds of bullying, even theological sadism, if others do not agree. As in other religious arguments, the struggle over religious perspective keeps increasing the stakes. Those who disagree are accused of unjust attitudes, prejudiced actions, and unfaithful behavior—modern versions of old fashioned "damnation." Once, when asked what community life was like at Union, a colleague of mine (quoting Elijah, 1 Kings 19: 10b) said, "I, I alone am left, and they seek my life."

Nonetheless, the apparently empty space at the center of a school like Union, which includes Christian students of all denominations and degrees of faith, some Jewish students and Greek Orthodox, a few Muslims, and people of all ages, classes, races, cultures, and sexual orientations, does offer always the potential of an extraordinary freedom. The gap in the symbol system at the center works for us because it mirrors the unavoidable gap between the finite and the infinite. Our communal and personal squabbles circle around our shared acknowledgment that nothing human can define an unfathomable God.

Teaching Jung

It is within this religious setting that our students study Jung and where I myself feel compelled to emphasize the gap between things finite and infinite. The fact that Jung is taught in conjunction with other major and conflicting theories of depth psychology constantly calls attention to definitive gaps and differences in all of them. The temptation to idolize Jung that Tacey describes is thus depotentiated because Jung's theories are always looked at in relation to other maps of the psyche and varying intellectual contexts that are expected, like it, to miss the ultimate mark. We see again and again that no theory brings the last word of truth.

Our students in the Program of Psychiatry and Religion range across, in all, five programs leading to degrees, all of which contain large components of interdisciplinary conversations with religion as well as praxis. As a result, much of the attraction to and resistance against Jung's work that Tacey describes shifts over to the dramatic experience of the psyche per se.

The teaching of Jung or any other depth psychologist occurs, then, as a way of dealing with the theoretical and practical issues that surround people learning to work in a parish, a hospital, a prison, a classroom, or a clinical setting with people suffering emotional illness, and it becomes yet another way to aid persons' spiritual development in prayer, worship, and practice and to adjust to widely differing cultural contexts both here and abroad. The seminary setting helps to position students to see through theories to the transcendent itself and, conversely, to test theory against the practical and intellectual labor of discerning whether a point of view aids or obstructs human efforts to live justly and walk humbly with one's God. For the seminary training ministers, social workers, future religious teachers and publishers, and scholars of religion, all under one roof, the proof is in the pudding. Intellectual learning couples inexorably with professional vocation.

Students who concentrate in psychiatry and religion train for all those professions and move on, many of them to become chaplain-teachers in medical or mental hospitals and for clinical ministries such as those of pastoral counselors. A steady number of students seek additional education in the training institute of whatever school of depth psychology draws them to become analysts. A student at the doctoral level may choose the option of training at both Union and a training institute at the same time in order to be able to teach at the graduate or undergraduate level and also to practice as a clinician. Thus, students studying Jung at Union do so within the context of highly demanding theoretical and professional training and with the constant experience of an ongoing interdisciplinary conversation that seeks to explore the impact of psychic reality on religious life and thought. For these students, the psyche has become an unmistakable and clearly delineated reality. A recognition that the psyche exists and that a goodly portion of it exists unconsciously distinguishes the particular city of psychiatry and religion within the country of the larger seminary.

Controversy

Taken as a whole, Union holds a firmly and widely established reputation as a seminary committed to social action, and it is fair to say that it is not a psychologically minded community. The dismissal, scorn, and sheer ignorance of psychic reality that Tacey describes in his world can be found in ours, too. It is an attitude applied with equal repressive force to all of depth psychology, not just to Jung. Jung may, however, be singled out as particularly offensive, as an essentialist who perpetuates sexual stereotypes, as a thinker who ignores historical and political contexts, as one who is too individualistic at the expense of community needs, and as one, not least in offensiveness, who substitutes a psychological universe for the religious one. Neither Jung's nor any other analyst's theories are used in fields outside psychiatry and religion to augment methods of interpretation of scripture, doctrine, historical movements, or the problems of ethical discernment. Preference in the practice of general theology is given to the more extroverted hermeneutics that emphasize the sociopolitical context and the sociology of knowledge.

The rejection of depth psychological theories in even this liberal setting comes down, I find, to the fear of the psyche, with peculiar accent on what I have called the Christian fear of psychic reality.[1] I have even had the experience of teaching a student who said she felt she was betraying her other teachers' loyalty to social justice by taking a course in psychiatry and religion, only to find out how different the material was from all her expectations, that is, her projections and projective identifications. Indeed, a particularly fascinating subject to students and even to some colleagues entering the field for the first time is the role of the unconscious in social action causes and concerns.

Psychiatry and Religion

Within the Psychiatry and Religion Program, students study the primary texts of depth psychology from all the major schools and perspectives. We read Freud, Jung, Adler, Horney, Rank, Laing, Odier, Kohut, Kernberg, Klein, Boss, Binswanger, Bion, Frankl, Erikson, Winnicott, Guntrip, Fairbairn, Bollas, McDougall, Milner, Chasseguet-Smirgel, Lacan, Stern, Khan, Loewald, Bromberg, Atwood, Ogden, Grand, Symington, Kristeva, Von Franz, Layton, Bowen, Minuchin, Weigert, Sullivan, Searles, and others.

My own strong bias toward Jung, which I announce openly in class, is stated to urge students to pay close attention to those theories that either beckon or repel *them*, for I think that will invariably indicate their most fruitful path to relate to psychic reality. I stress that *all* the theories studied possess some truth, for they all have arisen out of clinical work with the psyche and would not have survived if they had not proved lifesaving to the soul of someone. I encourage students to lift into explicit conversation that inner dialogue with the depths of the psyche that has been going on their whole lives. I want them to work to find their own voices in that conversation, not to aim at duplication of Freud or Jung or Klein or me, their teacher. In preparing their exams and papers, I invite, prod, and even cajole students to concentrate on material that is hot for them, for that always fosters meaningful creative work that captures the imagination of others.

The space provided for such confrontations is constructed by me, by the students, and by the material. In Christian terms, this triangulation of space calls up images of the Trinity, which comprises a doctrinal picture of the inner life of God, of, so to speak, God's inner-object relations, of who and what God is when God is not doing anything. In that space, the students and I contribute our presentations, insights, and questions in relation to the specific material we study. When a synergy gets going, where energy flows out to each other and to the material, and back and forth among the three participants—the teacher,

the student, the material—then I know the space is alive. Associations, connections occur. The level of ego tasks—mastering the material, applying, for
example, the theory of unconscious projections to preaching to a depressed
parishioner, grasping the role unconscious anxiety plays in the positions taken
by a far-right or far-left political group, inquiring how sexual issues with an
inner-anima figure can both impede and advance spiritual growth—begins to
differentiate from archetypal levels at which it is possible to inquire in a living
context into what symbols the psyche employs to speak of itself and in what
ways this objective psychic reality relates to the spirit or the divine. Excitement
heats up, and the new arrives. We face it—in thought, in new connections, in
feelings, in body impulses—right there in class. We know we are alive.

Including the Unconscious

As I have indicated, fear of the psyche, existing immediately within us, between
us, and unfolding our uniqueness in response to its own manifestations, lies
behind all opposition to depth psychological material in the curriculum. It is a
sad commentary on us as a tribe in higher education to note that we have
managed to distance ourselves from the hot coals of poetry, mathematics, the
classical languages, history, and all the other disciplines of preparatory study so
that we can talk about them without passion, without any fear they will still
burn our lips (Isaiah 6: 7). Study of the psyche, on the other hand, is still new
enough to arouse a primitive awe, fear, and fascination. A student from nearby
Columbia University, with which Union has close connections and some joint
degree programs, obtained permission to take an introductory course I teach in
depth psychology and theology, though his professor warned him it would be
"too soft." The student exclaimed at term's end that he had worked "more than
twice as hard" as in his Columbia psychology courses, not only to cover the
quantity of reading assigned but also to keep up with all that leaped up in
response within himself.

Here, I would disagree with what I experience as Professor Tacey's implicit
and explicit criticism of religion, though I found very interesting his Oedipally
tinged interpretation of students' preferences for either Freud (father) or Jung
(mother). Tacey's interpretation of religion and of Jung seems to me to be too
reductive—as only a return to the womb and the all-embracing maternal unconscious that bans critical thought and locates authority only in dreams, fantasies,
and intuitions from within, while eschewing external standards of judgment
and comparison. I found implied in this description of students' attraction to
Jung a notion of religion as uncritical, anti-intellectual, immature, clinging,
embarrassing, and, in public behavior, eventually fanatic. What seems to me to
be lacking in this interpretation is any notion of the epigenesis of religious
feeling, of the fact that it develops and differentiates, that it draws upon intellect,
texts, historical communities, and mature presentiments of the divine Other.

If we apply Jung's method of prospective interpretation to Tacey's description of students' attraction to Jung as regression to maternal incest, we will be

led to agree with Jung that Oedipal conflict can conceal the hidden purpose of seeking union with oneself and with the Self. From the prospective standpoint, one seeks one's own foundations in the psyche, not to disappear in the maternal womb, but to be born out of it with one's own point of view. One then emerges, not as a committed Jungian or any other kind of follower, but as secure and original in one's thought and convictions and altogether free to inquire intellectually and emotionally as one feels moved to do so.

The issue that I think unites all of us who teach depth psychology in higher education and in seminary training rests on the need to include the *fact* of the unconscious in the curriculum. Here, Jung's notion of the unconscious offers special benefits, recognizing, as it does, a purposiveness in the unconscious in relation to consciousness. The extreme reactions of scornful rejection and idolatrous adoption to Jung's theories that Professor Tacey describes spring, I believe, not from hollow people, but from hollow studies. When students read Jung, something happens that can frighten as much as fascinate. This strong kind of emotional and intellectual reaction—where the student's ego feels gripped by archetypal energy—may not, sadly, be happening in their other courses.

Perhaps in studying Jung, who himself studied the living psyche, the connections between archetypal and ego levels occur more immediately than in the study of other theorists and theories, where the unconscious is approached from the ego point of view, thus to be translated upward into conscious concepts.[2] Jung's great gift was to hit upon easily experienceable symbols that speak for the unconscious directly, symbols like the shadow, the inner woman, the Self, the persona as public mask. As a consequence, people flee or embrace Jung because they either fear or long for connection to the living psyche.

Yet whether in the profession of religion, in clinical practice, or in higher education, what people look for, I believe, is precisely such a conjunction of the enduring and the immediate. Professor Tacey evidently has had to face the extremes of repudiation or identification with Jung's theories, in a kind of sequential and compensating either-or. Our besetting questions at Union seem more often to spring from conjunctions. Perhaps it is the religious container that lends weight to the urgent questions our professors commonly hear, of how to live the All in the here and now, how to love the whole while making a concrete choice of one path rather than another, how to serve the psyche and recognize in it and through it the Holy that speaks to each of us in the narratives and dramas of our dreams.

Speaking for myself, I see the study of depth psychology as an essential preparation for the religious professions, and in particular the study of Jung. Jung's vision, in my view, is larger than what others offer. Jung reaches to the psyche that exists objectively in our subjectivity, addressing us, pushing, prodding, luring us to meet its unfolding as we try to construct meaning, individually and collectively.[3] I find that we enter a new zone of communication when we accept the fact of psychic reality. Then we are able to see the processes of unconscious mentation in our social, political, and family life, as well as in our inner conversation with ourselves. Surely we see in the psyche an incomparable witnessing to the mystery that invokes us and undergirds our callings.[4] What Jung inaugurated was not just another treatment modality for emotional distress; it was a new way to perceive reality.

NOTES

This chapter was originally written in 1996 in answer to a request to respond to David Tacey's article on teaching Jung in the academy in Australia. Both articles were published in the *Journal of Analytical Psychology* 42.2 (1997).

1. A. B. Ulanov, "The Christian Fear of the Psyche," in *Picturing God* (Einsiedeln, Switzerland, 1986/2005A), 5–23.

2. A. Ulanov and B. Ulanov, *Religion and the Unconscious* (Louisville, KY: Westminster/John Knox, 1975), 65–68.

3. A. B.Ulanov, *Spiritual Aspects of Clinical Work* (Einsiedeln, Switzerland: Daimon 2004), 326–330.

4. A. B. Ulanov, *The Unshuttered Art: Opening Aliveness/ Deadness in the Self* (Nashville, Tn: Abingdon 2007), 230–231, 239–242.

4

Teaching Jung in an Analytical Psychology Institute

Murray Stein

It is not easy to know where to begin the study and teaching of Jung's works in a training institute. A candidate in training once told me that the first course she took in the training program was built around Jung's "Psychological Commentary on *The Tibetan Book of the Dead*."[1] She was flabbergasted. She wondered: Why would students be asked to start their training with such an esoteric and nonclinical text? Holding a doctorate in clinical psychology, she had come to the institute for further specialization. What did *The Tibetan Book of the Dead* have to do with analytical practice in the modern world? I told her that the commencement of training is not always quite so oblique. She had been plunged into the deep end of the Jungian pool without preparation and understandably felt completely out of her element. Nevertheless, one can hardly say that Jung's text is unrelated to clinical issues pertaining to psychological transformation.

The programs for training to become a Jungian psychoanalyst are universally postgraduate in nature, and their central focus is necessarily a clinical one. In general, a certain amount of previous preparation on the part of incoming candidates is assumed at the outset. Applicants who are accepted into these programs have often already studied Jungian writings for a considerable period of time beforehand. Quite often, they have read widely for years or even decades in the broad field of analytical psychology and its related disciplines. Sometimes, they arrive having previously published articles or books in the field. Moreover, many, if not all, have completed extensive clinical training before they take up the Jungian approach to practicing analysis. They enter analytic training programs, therefore, with many already formed opinions about clinical practice, Jungian psychology, Jung the man and thinker, and contemporary Jungian thought and psychoanalysis. They have undergone some personal analysis as well by this point and so have an impression of what this is all about from their own experiences in analysis. Obviously, they come seeking further exposure to Jungian thought and methods of practice, but their entry into these studies is rarely without surprises, difficulties of a personal and intellectual kind, and complex emotional reactions to their teachers, to the texts, and to their fellow candidates. The training institute is not an uncomplicated educational environment.

In teaching Jung to students who are enrolled in training programs, I have tried above all to get them to read Jung deeply. While many have read widely in the secondary literature or in the various popularizations of Jungian thought, they may have only glanced occasionally at Jung's own writings. Frequently, people find them opaque or too demanding. They have therefore not read him with the kind of care and patience needed to engage his thinking at a deep level. I ask them to make an attempt at "deep reading," to use Harold Bloom's memorable phrase. Deep reading calls for great patience, repetition, even reading out loud to another or to oneself. Above all, it asks the reader to trust the author's genius and to put aside preconceptions long enough to take in fully what the author is communicating. "What is Jung saying here?" is the question I want candidates in training to ponder, and to ponder a long while before deciding how to evaluate Jung's writings. Too often, contemporary students jump to the conclusion that Jung got it wrong, or only half right, or pretty good for his time but now no longer sufficient. Deep reading goes slowly. It means crawling inside the text and staying there, making it one's home for a time, eating the words and digesting them. There is plenty of time and space to be critical later.

The Context: Training Institutes and Their Cultural Settings

Having trained at the C. G. Jung Institute of Zurich in the late 1960s and early 1970s, when the works of Jung were treated there as Holy Scripture, and then returning to the States steeped in that reverential culture, I nearly choked at a cocktail party when a recent graduate of an American institute told me that in their training they hardly read any Jung at all. To me, this was shocking and absurd, but soon enough, I discovered that the reception of Jung's writings varies drastically from institute to institute, depending on the interests and inclinations of the founders and training analysts there. I told a new analyst friend of mine that it seemed to me that American candidates received only a thin Jungian frosting on their professional cakes; in Zurich, they baked the cake from scratch, and it was Jungian through and through!

In some ways, training institutes are more like cooking schools or art schools than they are like the standard academic graduate schools. Students come here to learn "how to do it." The problem is that for Jungian psychoanalysis, there are no specific recipes to memorize or masterpieces to copy. There are many books, to be sure, but to be honest, students and instructors are largely on their own in making sense of them, and they must function without the kind of sure guidance one gets in other fields from textbooks, agreed-upon methodologies, a recognized canon, or established doctrines. Together, they must find a way to appropriate, integrate, and prioritize a large number of texts and materials from many interrelated disciplines. Among this wealth of material is the body of writings created by Jung himself.

Jung was notoriously dismissive of recipes and techniques for working with the psyche, and so one will search in vain in his works for step-by-step treatises on the practical application of his ideas to the analytic process. People have long spoken of analysis as an art and not a science. To shift the metaphor, but perhaps only a bit, as training analysts, we are introducing people to the arts of psychological transformation and in a way asking them to become modern-day alchemists. The alchemical metaphor places emphasis on transformation—of the base into the noble, of the raw into the cooked, of the natural into the symbolic and cultural. This is in line with the intention of Jungian analysis.

The goal of training being the practical one of teaching students how to conduct analysis with the greatest possible degree of skill and competence, the key learning center of this educational enterprise lies not in the classroom but in the training analyst's consulting room. To continue with the alchemical metaphor, it is the workroom with its ovens, stoves, flasks, and retorts that is the primary setting for learning the arts of transformation, while the adjoining library with its papers and books is a necessary but secondary resource, offering information, inspiration, and stimulation toward deeper reflection on the *opus*. Candidates learn to take others through the process of analysis by undergoing analysis for themselves, and they learn as well from their cases, which are conducted under the oversight of senior training analysts. The study of texts, therefore, including Jung's own writings, is secondary to firsthand learning experience from personal analysis and supervision. And yet written texts are considered important because they provide the rationale and the theoretical basis for what one is doing in the consulting room. They also convey important moments in the history of thinking about and practicing this art.

The seminars, lectures, and other didactic aspects of training programs do therefore play an important role in the formation of future analysts' thinking. Depending on the specific training institute, the outcomes of this intellectual formation can be quite different. In the end, there are many kinds of Jungian psychoanalysts, and their particular styles of thinking and working often link quite importantly to where they were trained.

Training institutes exist within historical and cultural contexts, which can be conceived narrowly and broadly. Narrowly considered, the context is made up of and determined by the specific history of a training institute, its founding figures, its leading personalities, and its ideological position within the wider framework of Jungian communities worldwide. Over time, training institutes develop their own unique analytic cultures and styles, and within those cultures, Jung's contributions and his written works can occupy a major or a minor position of importance.

The broader context of each training institute is its surrounding cultural milieu. The Jung that is read, taught, and learned in France is not the Jung that one finds in Chicago, Zurich, or Berlin. This is due partly to the specific emphases of the programs created by the training analysts and their teachers (the narrow context), but it also derives from the intellectual history and debates that pertain to psychoanalysis and therapy in its native land. (There is as well the history of philosophy, literature, and political organization in that country, which forms the general style of thinking characteristic of a culture.) In Paris, it is impossible to speak of Jung without Lacanian inflection, even though Jung's writings antedate Lacan's by decades, while in Chicago, allusions to the psychoanalytic ideas and insights of Heinz Kohut are subtly all pervasive in discussions about, for instance, the phenomenon of transference or the theory of the self, a psychological term that Jung in fact made his trademark. Michael Fordham told me in private conversation that his own views were shaped and heavily influenced by Kleinian and post-Freudian students who came to study with him after he returned from Zurich and set up shop in London as a Jungian analyst. So powerful was their previous training and their influence on him that the Jungian training program in London finally tilted in this direction to the point where it was humorously referred to in the Jungian world as more Kleinian than Klein. The point here is that when Jung is read and studied in a training institute, it is done in dialogue with the surrounding culture. Jung's work is placed in contexts where it is considered in relation to other views and different opinions about the psyche.

Jung is read and taught from a surprising variety of perspectives, therefore, depending on the contexts of a given training institute. For this reason, wherever I am teaching Jung to candidates in training—and I have done this on five continents and in many countries—I ask students to immerse themselves directly in Jung's texts, to put aside their previous estimations of him as a person and of his contributions to psychoanalysis as much as possible, and to try to hear his unique voice before returning to the default position of their usual critiques and evaluations. To my surprise initially, many candidates have said to me that they appreciate this approach and find it novel and refreshing. Many have told me that they came to Jungian training wishing and hoping to learn more about Jung and were disappointed to find his works not emphasized there because their teachers had migrated elsewhere.

We know that Jung himself was highly ambivalent about setting himself up as a figure whose words would carry the weight of a sort of religious authority, and he preferred his students to debate his views rather than accepting them as doctrinal pronouncements. Of course, he well knew that people listened to his words with keen attention, often through heavy transference projections onto him as a sage, a guru, or a wizard. As the recipient of many honors, interviews, invitations, and so forth, he earned enormous stature on the international stage. However, he did not enjoy the burden this authority brought in its wake. As a Swiss, he liked his independence. About setting up training institutes in his name that would promote his views, he also was of two minds. On the one hand, he felt pressured, indeed, forced to a degree, to go along with the wishes and plans of students of his who were doggedly determined to establish training institutes in his name in various parts of the world—London, New York, San Francisco, and Zurich among others.[2] He felt a need to cooperate with them for the sake of continuing the research and exploration of the human psyche that he had begun. On the other hand, he objected strongly to the idea of creating "Jungians," as he wrote to J. H. van der Hoop, a colleague in The Netherlands, in 1946:

> I can only hope and wish that no one becomes "Jungian." I stand for
> no doctrine, but describe facts and put forward certain views which
> I hold worthy of discussion. I criticize Freudian psychology for a
> certain narrowness and bias, and the Freudians for a certain
> rigid, sectarian spirit of intolerance and fanaticism. I proclaim no
> cut-and-dried doctrine and I abhor "blind adherents." I leave
> everyone free to deal with the facts in his own way, since I also claim
> this freedom for myself.[3]

Jung's strong aversion to "Jungians" around himself had its roots in large measure in his personal need to remain free to think as he wished and to change his mind or to set out in new directions. Any sort of fixed doctrine cobbled together from his previous writings and teachings would have hindered his own freedom to think and would have threatened to trap him, just as it would have threatened the creativity of his students. One must read Jung as an adventurous, exploratory, experimental thinker and writer who allowed himself the leeway to break away from the tried and true even in his old age. To teach Jung as "doctrine" gets his writings completely wrong and finally creates a hard carapace of slogans, clichés, and formulas that will doom the field to extinction.

When the C. G. Jung Institute in Zurich was founded on April 24, 1948, Jung gave an opening address that today is astonishing in light of what was to follow in the history and development of that particular institution. In the first sentence of his address, he refers to it as "an Institute for Complex Psychology," a designation for Jungian psychology that is no longer used and that never quite found traction among his students and followers. He goes on to say that he feels honored that people have come to witness the establishment of "this institute of research, which is designed to carry on the work begun by me,"[4] and then he spends the remainder of his talk outlining directions for future research. It is clear that he imagined this to be a research institute, not a training institute for future Jungian psychoanalysts. Among the original founding members of the institute, all of whom were personally invited by Jung to join the new enterprise, was the Nobel-winning physicist Wolfgang Pauli, a notable world-class figure who held up the banner for exceedingly high standards of research indeed! Within a short time, however, the emphasis at the Jung Institute fell largely on training the people who came from all over the world and wanted to become certified analysts. Pauli resigned in disgust, and another founding member, the Catholic theologian Victor White, O.P., gave Jung his unhappy view of the "Jungians" at the institute in 1955: "The horrible impression has come upon me in Zurich (I hope it is wrong) that my dear C. G. has around him only sycophants & flatterers: or people requiring audiences or transference which no mortal can carry. I *hope* I am wrong: such a situation is *too* inhuman."[5] Jung's fond hope of having no Jungians around him was not fulfilled. He had to endure them, but he did not allow them to trap him in his own "doctrines." To the end of his life, he remained innovative, and to some of his would-be disciples, this spelled disappointment. He appeared to them to be unreliable. He would not play the role of pope.

Had Jung witnessed the further development of the institute created in his name in Zurich, he doubtless would have been disappointed by the direction it took in choosing to spend nearly all of its energy and resources on training candidates to become Jungian psychoanalysts and its ever decreasing emphasis on research and publishing new and innovative work. Quite early on, a kind of Jungian orthodoxy did form in some quarters, or was at least assumed. Victor White, although he complained about the way things were shaping up around Jung in Zurich, also looked to the master for "rules." He felt strongly that Jung had violated his own basic principles in his late work, *Answer to Job*. This was, of course, one of Jung's most adventurous texts and stirred dispute and debate in quite a number of quarters, as it continues to do to this day. It particularly bothered White because of its unorthodox interpretations of the Bible and its emotional condemnation of the morals of the biblical Yahweh, whom White as a Roman Catholic priest had of course to defend. In a challenging letter to Jung, White charged that "'Answer to Job' is presumably to be read (at least primarily), not as an essay in theology, metaphysics or exegesis, but in practical psychology. It may be taken, and is being taken, as containing the 'correct' psychological views, standards & attitudes of the 'Jungians.'"[6] In the margin beside this paragraph of the letter he had received from White, Jung placed a question mark, indicating his objection to the assumption that there were "correct psychological views" to be found in his writings. He would have considered his writings rather to be experimental essays that were pushing his imaginative thinking ever further and in new directions, rather than expressing truths or declaring correct doctrines. Susan Rowland, in *Jung as a Writer*, catches the drift precisely. She stresses that Jung is forever writing with and from the unconscious, which lends his works their characteristic imaginative boldness. Inevitably, he transgresses the boundaries of academic disciplines and faculties and puts forward highly novel new interpretations of ancient and modern texts, as well as of clinical material. Jung had hoped, one must suppose from his opening address, that the institute founded in his name would carry on research and writing in this fashion. Instead, the teaching of the master's texts in this and some other training institutes has all too often degenerated into reading them as pronouncements of orthodoxy. This is the opposite extreme from having none of Jung's texts in the curriculum at all.

On Reading Jung: The Unfolding of His Thought

The approach I take to Jung's writings when I teach in training institutes, therefore, is to read them as explorations in psychological thinking. The training that comes out of reading them deeply is training in this type of thinking. It is a type of thinking that happens to be very useful for clinical work, where insights and interpretations are much more ventures in imagination than advances in certainty and scientific knowledge. The texts by Jung do not proclaim eternal truths. They probe and ponder the workings of the human psyche, and in the reader, they often engender great enthusiasm and a feeling of discovering unimagined depths of the human soul. Jung's writings open his deep readers to personal explorations of their own lives. They induce a kind of self-analysis that can be both unsettling and terribly exciting. Few people who read Jung seriously come away unmoved, indeed, untransformed by the experience. I encourage the candidates in training to use Jung's writings to deepen their own personal analyses. It is not unusual that the students begin dreaming of Jung as they seriously engage his writings.

I also try to help students grasp the ways in which Jung's thought unfolded over the more than sixty years that he was writing. To this end, I divide Jung's oeuvre into three large periods: the early (1900–1921), the middle (1922–1938), and the late (1939–1961). Each period links importantly to the others, but the emphases are significantly different in each. The first is more emphatically professional, clinical, theoretical, and technical—Jung is building a base. The second broadens out from the base and includes historical, cultural, social, and political issues. In this period, Jung becomes a famous public figure internationally and travels widely. The third can largely be defined as focused on spiritual and religious issues, with an emphasis on the symbolic. Jung is now regarded by the world as the old sage of Küsnacht and so comes to him for wisdom. I am painting with a broad brush, but this helps students get a feel for the development of Jung's life and thought.

The early stage extends from the beginnings of Jung's formal study of psychiatry at the Burghölzli Klinik in Zurich and runs through his years as a leader of the psychoanalytic movement with Freud. It concludes with the early formulations of his own unique version of psychoanalytic thought and practice, as represented in the analytical psychology of the Zurich school. This stage includes his research and psychiatric papers (*Collected Works* 1, 2, and 3), his Freudian and post-Freudian writings (*Collected Works* 4 and 5), and his "confrontation with the unconscious" or midlife crisis period (described in *Memories, Dreams, Reflections*, chapter 6). An important work of this period is *The Psychology of the Unconscious* (revised in the 1950s and published in the *Collected Works* as *Symbols of Transformation, Collected Works* 5), a response to Freud and the chief cause of their separation. The early period closes with the publication of the massive work *Psychological Types* (*Collected Works* 6) in 1921, which is a further response to Freud but far more a statement of Jung's own unique understanding of the psyche and psychological process. In teaching Jung, I invariably focus on the chapter "Definitions" in this great work. This is essential Jung and shows the precision and range of his mind.

The middle period, which begins after this major work is finished, includes important and fine-tuned theoretical papers like "On Psychic Energy" (in *Collected Works* 8) and the final versions of the seminal works, *Two Essays in*

Analytical Psychology (Collected Works 7). This period also includes the beginnings of Jung's interest in alchemy and the foundational lectures behind the important later work, *Psychology and Alchemy (Collected Works 12)*, in the Eranos lectures of the 1930s, as well as several important essays on "the archetypes of the collective unconscious" *(Collected Works 9i)* and the process of individuation. There are also the informal seminars, now published as supplements to the *Collected Works (Analytical Psychology, Visions, The Psychology of Kundalini Yoga, Nietzsche's Zarathustra, Children's Dreams, The Seminar on Dream Analysis)*, and the not yet published lectures given during his professorship at the Federal Institute of Technology in Zurich (the ETH). The middle period was a time of much travel, with trips to the United States, Africa, and India, and of many honors (honorary doctorates from Harvard, Oxford, and universities in Allahabad, Benares, and Calcutta in India).

The late period, which opens with Jung's return from the long journey to India in 1938, is dominated by works on religion and alchemy, including also, of course, the implications of these studies for psychotherapy and clinical practice. This was also a period in Jung's life of poor health and limited opportunities for extroverted activities—very little travel, much reduced clinical work, rare public appearances. Yet, in these late years, Jung was incredibly productive in his psychological writing and exploration. Among much else, he wrote "The Psychology of the Transference" (in *Collected Works 16*), *Aion (Collected Works 9ii)*, *Answer to Job* (in *Collected Works 11*), "On Synchronicity" (in *Collected Works 8*), and *Mysterium Coniunctionis (Collected Works 14)*. He also maintained contact with many people internationally by letter, and his correspondence during these years is astonishingly voluminous, with many letters running to several pages of dense reflection and thought. Several volumes of published letters to date testify to his seriousness of purpose in corresponding with friends and colleagues during these physically difficult times.

Jung and Analytical Psychology Today

Since the years when Jung founded the school of analytical psychology in Zurich shortly after his break with Freud, there have been countless contributions to it from a wide variety of sources. In the nearly 100 years of analytical psychology's existence, a vast and multifaceted field has grown up, and since Jung's death in 1961, this growth has accelerated. Its literature is by now vast and humanly unmanageable. No one can read all the books and journal articles generated annually nowadays in the many languages in which they appear, even if one's area of interest is a rather narrow one, such as the clinical. The question has become, at least in the training institutes: What is Jung's proper place in this vast collection of materials? Is Jung's writing still to be considered foundational and essential? Or has it been surpassed and by now rendered peripheral? How much emphasis should one give to Jung's writings in the training of analysts today? These are open questions. They have produced a vigorous debate among Jungian training analysts, a debate that Jung himself, I believe, would have approved.

In the most general terms, the field of analytical psychology can be divided into two large camps: the camp of the originists and the camp of the finalists. These two camps have received various names over the course of history, beginning with the London school versus the Zurich school. Andrew Samuels stamped them as developmental and classical, the former stemming from Michael Fordham and his followers, who leaned toward modern psychoanalysis as practiced in England, and the latter from the circle of analysts around Jung himself and his close followers in Zurich.[7] Others have referred to the difference as clinical versus symbolic or as analytical versus synthetic. Basically, the fault line becomes visible when someone begins to speak about a psychological symptom, a clinical issue like transference, or a dream. The one type asks questions about and seeks to understand causes and origins; the other considers the purpose and goal of the psychological phenomenon. One looks backward into the past; the other looks forward into future possibilities for change and growth. For this reason, I prefer to call them the originists and the finalists. Both are developmental, only they see development differently— the one as determined by previous causes, the other as moving forward toward potentials and possibilities. Is the psyche strictly a product of past events, decisions, experiences? Or is it a goal-directed, seeking-to-fulfill-its-potentials sort of thing? The answer to this puts one in the one camp or the other.

Of course, most people try to have it both ways, although this is very hard to uphold in practice. Jung himself straddled this tension, although he mostly favored the finalist position. People on both sides can find plenty of textual backing in Jung's writings to support their position. In teaching Jung to candidates in training, I insist they consider both sides in Jung himself and in his successors. However, if one is an originist, Jung's writings will be seen as less central to contemporary thinking and writing than if one is a finalist. Finalists tend to see Jung as bedrock; originists find him sometimes suggestive and interesting but quickly look to other authorities and references for guidance. As a finalist, I draw on Jung deeply and with the years increasingly so, especially with respect to working clinically with people in the second half of life and in old age and with respect to thinking about psychological development in the later years of life. As it happens, candidates in training these days are themselves, by and large, over the age of forty, and many are in their fifties and sixties. For many of them, the finalist in Jung holds great appeal and forms the basis of their studies, their writing, and their practices after they graduate.

The texts of Jung's that are particularly important for the finalist perspective derive from his second and third periods. One of them, which does not have a place in his *Collected Works* but is seminal for Jungian studies, is the memoir written with the assistance of Aniela Jaffé, *Memories, Dreams, Reflections*. In teaching Jung, I often use this work as a guide through his writings. It is a book that has inspired many to become devotees of Jung and to venture into training programs. It was my own initial introduction to Jung's life and thought. I cannot recommend a better place to start. Here one sees how Jung, in looking back, understood his own life process and its unfolding. Clearly, he views his life from a finalist perspective. In early dreams, he finds anticipations of much later developments in his attitudes and thinking. He does not construe his childhood and rather difficult family situation as a limiting or pathology-engendering factor in his life, but rather as preparatory for what he would become. The psyche would emerge in its own way and time despite the obstacles of heredity and poor nurturing from his parents. All was guided by a resident daimon, the self, whose will would break through and find its way into Carl Jung's life pretty much no matter what the external conditions might be. Sometimes, and mostly in private conversations and correspondence, Jung would speak of this thrusting movement in the psyche from potentiality to actuality as the will of God. For this reason, Jungian psychology has sometimes received the designation of being a religious psychology or even a religion.

While Jung denied vehemently that he was out to found a new religion, I believe it can be argued that Jungian psychology is fundamentally religious in nature. The finalists tend to be religious folk, the originists more nonreligious and secular, if that is the right word, or perhaps just more this-worldly and with a modernist philosophy. The originists see childhood, family relationships, and interpersonal connections as fundamental to psychological outcomes in adulthood and later life. The finalists, while they do not necessarily deny an important role to these factors, see the self as able to overcome deficits and to win through to wholeness despite shortfalls in the nurturing environment. For finalists, the archetypal is stronger than the personal or interpersonal; for the originists, it is the other way around.

One text I enjoy using in teaching candidates in training is Jung's essay on the child archetype.[8] It is a mature work, written in 1940, and it shows so clearly how Jung weaves together the personal and interpersonal level with the archetypal and symbolic. For an introduction to Jung's hermeneutical principles and clinical practice, there is hardly a better text in his entire oeuvre. I urge candidates to keep it closely in mind when they are working on dreams with patients, because the careful methodology that Jung proposes here will keep them from doing harm, which is, after all, the first rule of treatment ("Do no harm!"). When venturing an interpretation of dreams and especially of dreams that contain archetypal images, Jung cautions the interpreter:

> whatever explanation or interpretation does to it [i.e., the dream or the image], we do to our own souls as well, with corresponding results for our own well-being. The archetype...is a psychic organ present in all of us. A bad explanation means a correspondingly bad attitude to this organ, which may thus be injured.... Hence the "explanation" should always be such that the functional significance of the archetype remains unimpaired, so that an adequate and meaningful connection between the conscious mind and the archetypes is assured. For the archetype is an element of our psychic structure and thus a vital and necessary component in our psychic economy.[9]

This is about as close as Jung comes to being prescriptive. The implications for therapeutic treatment are fundamental and far-reaching.

Summary and Conclusion

The continuing value of Jung's writings for the education and training of contemporary Jungian psychoanalysts is being debated, but I believe they can hardly be overestimated. They contain the fundamental perspectives on which all later contributions of significance to analytical psychology are built. Students who understand the later additions in great detail but do not have a thorough acquaintance with the foundations tend to remain up in the air and ungrounded. It is essential to read Jung deeply and over a long period of time to grasp the essential features of his thought, on which the whole later edifice is erected. I recommend to training institutes, if consulted, that they set up reading courses in Jung's writings that continue throughout the four or five years of training. If someone wants to become a master chef, especially a creative one, they must not only know the great recipes by heart but also understand the rationale behind the construction of the recipes. Similarly, to become a master Jungian psychoanalyst, one must not only know technique but also understand the psychological principles that govern technique and practice. These are to be found most convincingly and forcefully stated in the writings of Jung himself, although many others have elaborated and exposed them in a credible fashion as the field of analytical psychology has grown and increased in complexity. There is no substitute for a thorough and intense immersion in the primary texts.

NOTES

1. C. G. Jung, "Psychological Commentary on *The Tibetan Book of the Dead*," in *The Collected Works of C.G. Jung*, vol. 11, ed. Michael Fordham and Gerhard Adler (Princeton, NJ: Princeton University Press, 1969), pars 831–858.

2. Mario Jacoby, "Some Memories and Reflections Concerning My Time at the C. G. Jung Institute in Zurich (1956 until 2006)," in *Who Owns Jung?* ed. Ann Casement (London: Karnac, 2007).

3. C. G. Jung, *Letters I*, ed. Gerhard Adler (Princeton, NJ: Princeton University Press, 1973), 405.

4. C. G. Jung, "Address on the Occasion of the Founding of the C. G. Jung Institute, Zurich, April 24, 1948," in *The Collected Works of C. G. Jung*, vol. 18, ed. Michael Fordham and Gerhard Adler (Princeton, NJ: Princeton University Press, 1976), 1129, pars. 1129–141.

5. Ann Lammers and Adrian Cunningham, eds., *The Jung-White Letters* (London: Routledge, 2007), 273.

6. Lammers and Cunningham, *Jung-White Letters*, 269.

7. Andrew Samuels, *Jung and the Post-Jungians* (London: Routledge & Kegan Paul, 1985).

8. C. G. Jung, "The Psychology of the Child Archetype," in *The Collected Works of C. G. Jung*, vol. 9i, ed. Michael Fordham and Gerhard Adler (Princeton, NJ: Princeton University Press, 1968), pars. 259–305.

9. Jung, "Psychology," par. 271.

REFERENCES

Jacoby, Mario. "Some Memories and Reflections Concerning My Time at the C. G. Jung Institute in Zurich (1956 until 2006)." In *Who Owns Jung?* ed. Ann Casement, 135–151. London: Karnac, 2007.

Jung, C. G. *Memories, Dreams, Reflections*, ed. Aniela Jaffé, trans. Richard Winston and Clara Winston. New York: Vintage, 1965.

Jung, C. G. "The Psychology of the Child Archetype." In *The Collected Works of C. G. Jung*, Vol. 9i, ed. Michael Fordham and Gerhard Adler, pars. 259–305. Princeton, NJ: Princeton University Press, 1968.

Jung, C.G. "Psychological Commentary on *The Tibetan Book of the Dead*." In *The Collected Works of C.G. Jung*, vol. 11, ed. Michael Fordham and Gerhard Adler, pars 831–858. Princeton, NJ: Princeton University Press, 1969.

Jung, C. G. *Letters*, ed. Gerhard Adler, 1:1906–1950. Princeton, NJ: Princeton University Press, 1973.

Jung, C. G. "Address on the Occasion of the Founding of the C. G. Jung Institute, Zurich, April 24, 1948." In *The Collected Works of C. G. Jung*, Vol. 18, ed. Michael Fordham and Gerhard Adler, pars. 1129–1141. Princeton, NJ: Princeton University Press, 1976.

Lammers, Ann, and Adrian Cunningham, eds. *The Jung-White Letters*. London: Routledge, 2007.

Rowland, Susan. *Jung as a Writer*. London: Routledge, 2005.

Samuels, Andrew. *Jung and the Post-Jungians*. London: Routledge & Kegan Paul, 1985.

PART II

The Interpretation of Religious Texts and Experiences

5

Jung on Myth

Robert A. Segal

Teaching Jung on myth involves correcting misconceptions. The most conspicuous of them are the following:

a. that Jung's is the only theory of myth
b. that Jung's theory is the only alternative to a literal approach to myth
c. that applying Jung to myth means simply finding archetypes
d. that the more archetypes found, the better the application
e. that for Jung all myths mean the same
f. that for Jung myths are interpretable without any knowledge of those whose myths they are
g. that for Jung everything is mythic
h. that for Jung even science is mythic
i. that for Jung myth is false literally and true only psychologically
j. that for Jung myth is false as history and true only as psychology
k. that for Jung everyone must have myth

In actuality, there are scores, if not hundreds, of theories of myth, and they come not only from psychology but also from other social sciences and from the humanities. Jung's theory does indeed spurn a literal interpretation of myth, but so do many other theories. The application of Jung to myth is not like a treasure hunt, in which the goal is the sheer accumulation of hidden archetypes. For Joseph Campbell, who is mistakenly considered to be a Jungian, all myths mean the same, but for Jung the meaning varies. Some followers of Jung, such as Erich Neumann, analyze myths in themselves, but Jung himself ties a myth to whoever created or accepts it.

For Jung, not everything is mythic. Myth may be part of a movement or activity—for example, a historical event, an ideology, or a religion—but movements and activities are not themselves myths. Dreams are not myths, even if dreams, because dreamed individually, are like private myths. Myths are always archetypal, but not all archetypes are mythic. And not everything is archetypal, even if almost anything has the *capacity* to become archetypal. Freud's famous line holds for Jung as well: sometimes a cigar is only a cigar.

For Jung, and also for Freud, one domain is indisputably not mythic: science, both social and natural. It is fashionable among some philosophers to stress the presence in even the natural sciences of myths, together with models, metaphors, and analogies. The title of one classic work says it all: philosopher of religion Ian Barbour's *Myths, Models and Paradigms: A Comparative Study in Science and Religion* (1974). But Barbour, no more than philosopher of science Mary Hesse (1963), reduces science to myth, model, metaphor, or analogy. Nor does Jung. He deems himself a scientist of the mind and deems psychology the queen of the sciences. He cannot consistently be using the science of psychology to understand myth yet consider science itself mythic.

For Jung, and again also for Freud, the subject matter of myth is symbolic. Hence myths, like dreams, must be "interpreted." But myth on the literal or historical level is not thereby false. The psychological level underlies, not undermines, the literal or historical one. The psychological level works through the literal or historical one, but the literal or historical level need not be true to manifest the psychological level. Whether Oedipus or Odysseus lived and did the things attributed to him on the literal or historical level does not affect the psychological effectiveness of the myth of either. In *The Interpretation of Dreams* Freud even argues for his psychological rendition of the myth of Oedipus on the grounds that modern audiences, who hardly believe in Fate or the historicity of Oedipus, are nevertheless moved by the play. Jung would say the same.

At the same time some myths may work psychologically only for those who *accept* them literally or historically. Maybe for Jews the life of Moses, for Christians the life of Christ, and for Muslims the life of Muhammad can move them only because they assume those lives to be historical. But myths about Superman or Spider Man clearly do not require historicity to work psychologically. Therefore, the literal or historical status of myth is separate from its psychological efficacy.

For Jung, to interpret a myth is to seek the archetype or archetypes in it, of which one is usually dominant. But myths are stories, and archetypes must fit the story. Archetypes are not parachuted into a myth and grasped separately from the rest of the story.[1] One must decipher the story to decipher the archetypes. Even more, one must decipher the person whose myth it is to decipher the myth. A myth is a myth because it speaks to a person and is really about that person. Thus myth is best understood as part of analysis. Here, too, Jung is like Freud, who opposes, not proposes, the equivalent of a handbook of mythological meanings, as if one could look up a myth or a motif to find out the meaning.

Theories of Myth

Theories of myth may be as old as myths themselves. Certainly, they go back to at least the Presocratics. But only since the second half of the nineteenth century have those theories purported to be scientific, for only since then have there existed the professional disciplines that seek to supply truly scientific theories: the social sciences, of which anthropology, psychology, and to a lesser extent sociology have contributed the most to the study of myth. Some social scientific theories may have earlier counterparts,[2] but earlier theorizing was largely speculative and abstract, whereas scientific theorizing is based far more on accumulated information. Some modern theories hail from the hoary disciplines of philosophy and literature, but even they reflect the influence of the social sciences.

Each discipline harbors multiple theories. Theories are accounts of some larger domain, of which myth is a subset. For example, anthropological theories of myth are theories of culture applied to the case of myth. Psychological theories of myth are theories of the mind applied to myth. Sociological theories of myth are theories of society applied to myth. There are no theories of myth itself. Myth is not like literature, which, so it has or had traditionally been claimed, must be studied as *literature* rather than as history, sociology, or something else nonliterary. There is no study of myth as myth. Thus Jung's theory does not somehow capture the mythic nature of myth, whatever that tautology might mean. Rather, his theory captures, or claims to capture, myth viewed psychologically. Theories from other disciplines claim the same.

What unites the study of myth across the disciplines are the questions asked. The three main questions are those of origin, function, and subject matter. *Origin* means why and how myth arises. *Function* means why and how myth persists. The answer to the *why* of origin and function is ordinarily a need, which myth arises to fulfill and lasts by continuing to fulfill. The need varies from theory to theory. *Subject matter* means the referent of myth. Some theories read myth literally, so that the referent is the straightforward, apparent one, such as gods. Other theories read myth symbolically, and the symbolized referent can be the physical world, human beings, or society.

Typical nineteenth-century theorists of myth were E. B. Tylor, whose *Primitive Culture* first appeared in 1871, and J. G. Frazer, whose *The Golden Bough* was first published in 1890. They tended to see the subject matter of myth as the natural world and to see the function of myth as either a literal explanation or a symbolic description of that world. For Tylor, myth is always a literal explanation of the natural world. For Frazer, rarely consistent, myth is sometimes a literal explanation but sometimes a symbolic description of the natural world.[3] Either way, myth for both is the "primitive" counterpart to science, which is assumed to be wholly modern. For both, science has rendered myth not merely superfluous but outright incompatible, and moderns, who by definition are scientific, must therefore reject myth. By contrast, twentieth-century theorists, including Jung, have tended to see myth as almost anything but an outdated counterpart to modern science, either in subject matter or in function. Consequently, moderns can still retain myth. For some twentieth-century theorists, moderns must retain myth. Jung does not go this far.

Jung's theory fits snugly the twentieth-century approach to myth. It does not arise in isolation, out of Jung's sheer genius. Like any other theory, his is distinctive in the answers it gives to the questions of origin, function, and subject matter. Like any other twentieth-century theory, his answers make myth compatible with science. To summarize Jung's theory: "Myths are original revelations of the preconscious psyche, involuntary statements about unconscious psychic happenings, and anything but allegories of physical processes."[4] The subject matter of myth is the unconscious, not the world. The origin and function of myth are the satisfaction of the need to encounter the unconscious, not to explain or to describe it.

The Subject Matter of Myth

When Frazer reads myth symbolically rather than literally, the subject matter of myth is physical processes. For him, the chief myths of all religions describe the death and rebirth of vegetation, a process symbolized by the myth of the death and rebirth of the god of vegetation. Thus:

> the story that Adonis spent half, or according to others a third, of the year in the lower world and the rest of it in the upper world, is explained most simply and naturally by supposing that he represented vegetation, especially the corn, which lies buried in the earth half the year and reappears above ground the other half.[5]

Jung, by contrast, interprets the myth of the death and rebirth of a god as the symbolic expression of a process taking place not in the world but in the mind. That process is the return of the ego to the unconscious—a kind of temporary death of the ego—and its reemergence, or rebirth, from the unconscious:

> I need only mention the whole mythological complex of the dying and resurgent god and its primitive precursors all the way down to the re-charging of fetishes and churingas with magical force. It expresses a transformation of attitude by means of which a new potential, a new manifestation of life, a new fruitfulness, is created.[6]

Jung does not deny that the psychological process of the death and rebirth of the ego *parallels* the physical process of the death and rebirth of vegetation. He denies that the physical process *accounts for* the psychological one, let alone for the mythic one. When Frazer takes myth literally rather than symbolically, he attributes to reasoning the leap from vegetation to god: "primitives" observe the course of vegetation and hypothesize the existence of a god to explain and not merely, as in a symbolic rendition, describe it. For Jung, that leap is too great for humans to make. Humans generally, not merely "primitives," lack the creativity required to concoct consciously the notion of the sacred out of the profane. They can only transform the profane into a sacred that already exists for them.[7] Humans must already have the idea of god in their unconscious and can only be projecting that idea onto vegetation and the other natural phenomena that they observe:

> This latter analogy [between god and natural phenomenon] explains the well-attested connection between the renewal of the god and seasonal and vegetational phenomena. One is naturally inclined to assume that seasonal, vegetational, lunar, and solar myths underlie these analogies. But that is to forget that a myth, like everything psychic, cannot be solely conditioned by external events. Anything psychic brings its own internal conditions with it, so that one might assert with equal right that the myth is purely psychological and uses meteorological or astronomical events merely as a means of expression. The whimsicality and absurdity of many primitive myths often makes the latter explanation seem far more appropriate than any other.[8]

As the real subject matter of myth, Jung rejects not only allegories of physical processes but also literal interpretations of myth such as Tylor's. For Tylor, myths are actual explanations of natural phenomena and not merely, as sometimes for Frazer, colorful descriptions of them. Gods are the purported agents behind natural processes and not just poetic depictions of those processes. Jung asks rhetorically "why the sun and its apparent motions do not appear direct and undisguised as a content of the myths."[9] Tylor's answer would be that myths describe sun gods and not merely the sun because myths are about sun gods and not merely about the sun. Jung's rejoinder would be that human beings cannot consciously invent gods and can only project onto the world gods already in their unconscious. For Jung, myth is no more about gods than about the physical world. It is about the human unconscious. Myth must be read symbolically, as at times for Frazer, and the symbolized subject is a process, as likewise at times for Frazer, but the process is an inner rather than outer one.

Jung interprets as projections not only nature myths but also all other kinds of myths. He asserts that "in fact, the whole of mythology could be taken as a sort of projection of the collective unconscious."[10] For example, hero myths are projections onto mere human beings of a divine or quasi-divine status: "the hero myth is an unconscious drama seen only in projection, like the happenings in Plato's parable of the cave. The hero himself appears as a being of more than human stature."[11] Where for Tylor and Frazer myth is limited to nature myths, for Jung, and also for Freud, myth can, on the surface, be about anything.

Once Jung differentiates a psychological interpretation of myth from a nonpsychological one, he must differentiate his particular psychological interpretation from Freud's. Jung grants the Freudian claim that there exist "fantasies (including dreams) of a personal character, which go back unquestionably to personal experiences, things forgotten or repressed, and can thus be completely explained by individual anamnesis [i.e., recollection]."[12] But he is far more concerned to vaunt his own claim that, in addition to these manifestations of the personal, Freudian unconscious, there exist "fantasies (including dreams) of an impersonal character, which cannot be reduced to experiences in the individual's past, and thus cannot be explained as something individually acquired."[13] These fantasies emanate from a different unconscious, which, rather than the creation of an individual, is inherited. For Jung, myths are always the product of this distinctively Jungian, collective unconscious: "These fantasy-images [of an impersonal character] undoubtedly have their closest analogues in mythological types.... The products of this second category resemble the types of structures to be met with in myth and fairytale so much that we must regard them as related."[14]

For some theorists, myths are difficult to interpret because their meaning is symbolic rather than literal. For Jung, the greater difficulty is that the symbols used to convey the meaning of myths do so both indirectly and inadequately. The issue is epistemological, and Jung continually invokes Immanuel Kant to differentiate what we can know from what we cannot. Kant's distinction between the unknowable, noumenal reality and the knowable, phenomenal one becomes for Jung not only the distinction between metaphysics and psychology but also the distinction within psychology between the unconscious and consciousness. It becomes as well the distinction between archetypes and symbols. In psychologizing Kant, Jung changes the subject matter from the world to us.

For Jung, symbols are the only medium for conveying archetypes, but they are an imperfect medium. Nothing can bridge the divide between the unconscious and consciousness. Indeed, Jung dismisses Freud's view of the unconscious precisely because Freud seemingly bridges the divide by deriving the unconscious from consciousness. For Jung, myths, as instances of the symbolic manifestation of archetypes, can never be deciphered exhaustively. No myth can convey fully the meaning invested in it by the archetypes it conveys. In stressing that myth falls short of conveying the meanings invested in it, Jung is scarcely disparaging it. On the contrary, he declares myth the best medium for conveying the unconscious: "Myth is the primordial language natural to these psychic processes, and no intellectual formulation comes anywhere near the richness and expressiveness of mythical imagery."[15]

To encompass all cases of myth, all theorists necessarily seek similarities rather than differences. Theorists not only identify overt similarities but also uncover similarities beneath apparent differences. Like Campbell, who appropriates James Joyce's term *monomyth*, Jung even repeatedly asserts that all myths are not merely similar but outright identical—an identity that he attributes to their identical origin: "It is the same as with myths and symbols, which can arise autochthonously in every corner of the earth and yet are identical, because they are fashioned out of the same worldwide human unconscious, whose contents are infinitely less variable than are races and individuals."[16] But by the identity of myths worldwide, Jung must mean the identity of the archetypes they manifest. He cannot mean the identity of myths themselves. Like Campbell, he may be downplaying the differences as insignificant, but he cannot be denying them.

Yet Jung is far more attentive to the differences among myths than Campbell or such outright Jungians as Neumann.[17] When he analyzes specific myths, the identification of archetypes becomes only the first, not the last, step in the process. One must analyze the specific symbols used to convey those archetypes, the meaning of those archetypes in the specific myth in which they appear, and the meaning of that myth in the life of the specific adherent to the myth. A myth is a myth for someone. One must understand the person to understand the myth: "So it is with the individual images [in a myth]: they need a context, and the context is not only a myth but an individual anamnesis."[18] Therefore for Jung the interpretation of myth is best undertaken as part of therapy. The frequent dismissal of Jung for his supposed obliviousness to the particulars of a myth and its adherents is shameful.

The Origin of Myth

As a theorist, Jung is concerned with accounting for the similarities among myths. There are two possible explanations: diffusion and independent invention. Diffusionists argue that the similarities among myths are too precise to have arisen independently. Independent "inventionists" argue that the similarities are too widespread geographically to be the product of diffusion. Additionally, inventionists argue that diffusion, even when granted, fails to explain either the origin of a myth in the society in which it arises or the acceptance of the myth by the societies to which it spreads.

Jung is stalwartly committed to independent invention as the origin of myth. Making the standard argument of independent inventionists, he asserts that there is no evidence and in fact no possibility of contact among all of the societies with similar myths:

> Every endeavour has been made to explain the concordance of
> myth-motifs and symbols as due to migration and tradition; Goblet
> d'Almellas' *Migration of Symbols* is an excellent example of this. But
> this explanation, which naturally has some value, is contradicted by
> the fact that a mythologem [i.e., archetype] can arise anywhere, at any
> time, without there being the slightest possibility of any such
> transmission.[19]

Jung makes the same argument for individuals. His most famous example, that of the "Solar Phallus Man," is of an institutionalized patient who believed that the sun had a phallus and that the movement of the sun's phallus was the cause of wind. Jung then came upon a comparable fantasy in a book describing the vision of a member of the ancient cult of Mithras. Assuming that the patient could not have known of the book, Jung forever after cited the similarity as concrete evidence of independent invention:

> The patient was a small business employee with no more than a
> secondary school education. He grew up in Zurich, and by no stretch

of imagination can I conceive how he could have got hold of the idea of the solar phallus, of the vision moving to and fro, and of the origin of the wind. I myself, who would have been in a much better position, intellectually, to know about this singular concatenation of ideas, was entirely ignorant of it and only discovered the parallel in a book of Dieterich's which appeared in 1910, four years after my original observation (1906).[20]

More important, Jung further uses this example as evidence of the distinctively Jungian version of independent invention: through heredity rather than through experience. Independent invention as experience means that every society creates myths for itself. Independent invention as heredity means that every society as well as every individual inherits myths. Of the Solar Phallus Man, Jung thus writes:

> This observation [of independent invention] was not an isolated case: it was manifestly not [to be sure] a question of inherited ideas, but of an inborn disposition to produce parallel thought-formations, or rather of identical psychic structures common to all men, which I later called the archetypes of the collective unconscious.[21]

For Tylor, Frazer, and Freud, for example, the similarities among myths stem from independent invention through experience. For Tylor, everyone is born with a need to explain the world, but the myths that give the explanations are not themselves innate. Likewise for Frazer, everyone is born with a need to eat, but the myths that explain the source of food are not themselves innate.

For Freud, everyone is born with an incestuous drive that surfaces at age three to five. Everyone experiences that drive individually. From one's forebears one inherits only the drive itself, not their experiences of it. Because everyone in society also experiences frustration in trying to satisfy that drive, myths are invented as one indirect, disguised, compensatory outlet for the blocked drive. Again, similar experiences are bound to give rise to similar myths. In his classic application of Freud's theory Otto Rank maintains that all hero myths, if not all myths, even have a similar plot, yet one still invented by each society on its own.[22]

In contrast to Tylor, Frazer, and Freud alike, Jung contends that everyone is born not merely with a need of some kind that the invention of myth fulfills but with myths themselves. More precisely, we are all born with the raw material of myths: archetypes.

For Tylor, the myth makers of each society start with the impersonal forces of the physical world and proceed to hypothesize gods to account for those forces and then to invent myths to describe the actions of gods. For Frazer, the same is true. For Freud, myth makers start with a child and the child's parents and proceed to transform the child into a hero, the child's parents into royalty or nobility, and the conflicts between children and parents into hero myths.

For Jung, myth makers start with the archetypes themselves—for example, the archetype of the hero. The archetype does not symbolize something else but is itself the symbolized. In every society myth makers invent specific stories that express those archetypes, but the myth makers are inventing only venues for the manifestations of already mythic material. The figure Odysseus, for example, gets either invented or appropriated to serve as a Greek expression of heroism. But heroism per se is not invented, the way it is for Tylor, Frazer, and Freud. For Jung, heroism, like divinity, constitutes so superhuman a status that humans could not have invented the idea. They must, then, have inherited it. What are invented are the myths expressing heroism. The myth of Odysseus is passed on from generation to generation by acculturation, but the hero archetype that it expresses is passed on by heredity.

For Tylor, Frazer, and Freud, experience, even if it is of innate needs, provides the impetus for the creation of myths. For Freud, for example, the experience of one's parents' reaction to one's incestuous drives spurs the creation of myth. For Jung, by contrast, experience provides only the occasion for the expression of already mythic material. Myths do not transform parents into gods or heroes but only articulate the experience of parents *as* gods or heroes—that is to say, as archetypal figures. Archetypes *shape* experience rather than *derive* from it. For example, the archetype of the Great Mother does not, as Freud would assume, result from the magnification of one's own mother but, on the contrary, expresses itself through her by magnifying her and thereby shapes one's experience of her. The archetype forms the core of one's "mother complex." Jung's insistence on the existence of innate fantasies that are projected onto the mother rather than derived from her is much like that of Melanie Klein.[23]

The Function of Myth

For Jung, myth serves many functions, not all of them psychological. But the prime function of myth is psychological: to reveal the unconscious. As already quoted, "Myths are original revelations of the preconscious psyche, involuntary statements about unconscious psychic happenings."[24] Despite the word "involuntary," myth does not inadvertently reveal the unconscious. Its creation is guided by the unconscious, which intentionally reveals itself to consciousness. Jung personifies the unconsciouous more than Freud does. The Jungian unconscious seeks to communicate its presence to consciousness as clearly as possible. Rather than speaking in code to elude detection, as for Freud, the unconscious simply speaks its own distinct language: "My idea is that the dream does not conceal; we simply do not understand its language. For instance, if I quote to you a Latin or a Greek passage some of you will not understand it, but that is not because the text dissimulates or conceals; it is because you do not know Greek or Latin."[25]

Myth for Jung functions not merely to announce the existence of the unconscious but actually to enable humans to experience it. Myth provides not only information about the unconscious but also entrée to it:

> The protean mythologem and the shimmering symbol express the
> processes of the psyche far more trenchantly and, in the end, far

more clearly than the clearest concept; for the symbol not only
conveys a visualization of the process but—and this is perhaps just as
important—it also brings a re-experiencing of it....[26]

The telling of myths "causes these processes to come alive again and be
recollected, thereby re-establishing the connection between conscious and
unconscious."[27]

Modern myths for Jung are for the most part nonprojective. They presup-
pose the withdrawal of projections from the outer world, which is now experienced as impersonal and therefore meaningless: "We have stripped all things of
their mystery and numinosity; nothing is holy any longer."[28] Laws of nature, not
decisions or conditions of gods, explain events in the world. Put another way,
modern myths for Jung are nonreligious. They cannot do what religious myths
used to do: "giving [man] the security and inner strength not to be crushed by the
monstrousness of the universe."[29] For all Jung's scorn for those theorists who
take the subject matter of myth to be the external world, he himself thus emphasizes the outer function of myth for religious persons—that function, to be sure,
being less to explain the world than to give humans a home in it. For moderns,
who for Jung are by definition nonreligious, myths do not function to connect
the inner world with the outer world, which is now the domain of science. Instead,
modern myths function to connect—better, to reconnect—moderns to the inner
world. Modern myths still provide meaningfulness, but that meaningfulness
now lies entirely within humans rather than also within the world.

Yet the characterization of the external world as meaningless really holds
for only earlier Jung. Once Jung, in collaboration with the physicist Wolfgang
Pauli, develops the concept of synchronicity, the world for him regains its
meaningfulness, even without its personality.[30] Indeed, that meaningfulness is
now inherent in the world rather than imposed on it through projection:
"Synchronistic experiences serve our turn here. They point to a latent meaning
which is independent of [our] consciousness."[31] Meaningfulness for later Jung
stems not from the existence of god, or personality, in the world, as Tylor,
Frazer, and Freud would have assumed, but from the symmetry between
human beings and the world. Rather than alien and indifferent to humans, the
world proves to be akin to them—not because gods respond to human wishes
or because human wishes directly affect the world but because human thoughts
correspond to the nature of the world. The world regains the meaningfulness
that had been lost with the withdrawal of mythic projections—a withdrawal
that Jung, committed to science, nevertheless applauds.

Of his favorite example of synchronicity, that of a resistant patient who was
describing a dream about a golden scarab when a scarab beetle appeared, Jung
writes: "at the moment my patient was telling me her dream a real 'scarab' tried
to get into the room, as if it had understood that it must play its mythological
role as a symbol of rebirth."[32] Here the world seemingly responds to the
patient's dream, but more precisely the world merely, if fortuitously, matches
the patient's dream. It is the patient's conscious attitude that is "out of sync"
with the world.

In the case of the resistant patient, however, what exactly is the "mythological role" of the beetle as "a symbol of rebirth"? The patient's experience of synchronicity is not itself myth, which would be an account of that experience. But an account means a causal account. Can there be a causal account of non-causality? Can there be a myth of synchronicity—a myth accompanying a case of synchronicity?[33]

Myths and "Primitives"

For Jung, myths serve primarily to open up adults to their unconscious, from which, in the course of growing up, they have ineluctably become severed. Myths "compensate or correct, in a meaningful manner, the inevitable one-sidednesses and extravagances of the conscious mind."[34] But for Jung, it is only the ego consciousness of moderns that is sufficiently developed to be severed from the unconscious:

> Since the differentiated consciousness of civilized man has been
> granted an effective instrument for the practical realization of its
> contents through the dynamics of his will, there is all the more
> danger, the more he trains his will, of his getting lost in one-
> sidedness and deviating further and further from the laws and roots
> of his being.[35]

It is therefore hard to see how myths "compensate" "primitives," since for Jung they hover so close to unconsciousness that their ego consciousness has barely begun to develop:

> Primitive mentality differs from the civilized chiefly in that the
> conscious mind is far less developed in scope and intensity.
> Functions such as thinking, willing, etc. are not yet differentiated;
> they are pre-conscious, and in the case of thinking, for instance, this
> shows itself in the circumstances that the primitive does not think
> *consciously*, but that thoughts appear.... Moreover, he is incapable of
> any conscious effort of will.[36]

Nevertheless, Jung considers myths to be as indispensable for "primitives" as for moderns. He is referring to "primitives," if not to them alone, when, as already twice quoted, he states that "myths are original revelations of the preconscious psyche, involuntary statements about unconscious psychic happenings."[37] "Primitives" may live far closer to the unconscious than moderns do, but the primitive unconscious still seeks to reveal itself to "primitives," and myths are one key means. Primitive myths merely reveal the unconscious circuitously, via projection onto the outer world:

> All the mythologized processes of nature, such as summer and
> winter, the phases of the moon, the rainy seasons, and so forth, are
> in no sense allegories of these objective [i.e., external] occurrences;

rather they are symbolic expressions of the inner, unconscious drama of the psyche which becomes accessible to man's consciousness by way of projection—that is, mirrored in the events of nature.[38]

Myths and Moderns

Moderns for Jung have largely withdrawn their forebearers' projections from the physical world. Moderns experience the world itself, largely unfiltered by their unconscious. That world is natural rather than supernatural. It is the world explained by science. In "de-deifying" the world, moderns have demythicized it: "Only in the following centuries, with the growth of natural science, was the projection withdrawn from matter and entirely abolished together with the psyche.... Nobody, it is true, any longer endows matter with mythological properties."[39] Moderns still project, but chiefly onto other human beings: "Projection is now confined to personal and social relationships."[40]

Yet Jung hardly denies the continued existence of myths. Myths in modernity can take several forms. Minimally, there is the invocation of traditional myths by artists:

> Dante decks out his experience in all the imagery of heaven,
> purgatory, and hell; Goethe brings in the Blocksberg and the Greek
> underworld; Wagner needs the whole corpus of Nordic myth,
> including the Parsifal saga; Nietzsche resorts to the hieratic style of
> the bard and legendary seer; Blake presses into his service the
> phantasmagoric world of India, the Old Testament, and the
> Apocalypse.[41]

More significant for Jung has been the outright revival of traditional myth, of which his grandest example is the revival of the worship of Wotan in twentieth-century Germany: "But what is more than curious—indeed, piquant to a degree—is that an ancient god of storm and frenzy, the long quiescent Wotan, should awake, like an extinct volcano, to new activity, in a civilized country that had long been supposed to have outgrown the Middle Ages."[42] Wotan was no mere literary metaphor but a real god, worshipped with the slaughtering of sheep. Here myth is lived out, not merely interpreted.

Still more significant for Jung has been the creation of new, distinctively modern myths, of which his best example is the belief in flying saucers. Because flying saucers are a technologically advanced phenomenon, they fit the modern scientific self-image and make for an ideal kind of modern myth: "It is characteristic of our time that the archetype...should now take the form of an object, a technological construction, in order to avoid the odiousness of mythological personification. Anything that looks technological goes down without difficulty with modern man."[43] Even though the belief in flying saucers is not tied to a story, the belief still qualifies as a myth, for it is a belief in something superhuman in the external world, and it is widely shared.

While less insistent on this point than either Eliade or Campbell,[44] Jung certainly considers myth to be a continuing phenomenon, even if not quite a panhuman one:

> Has mankind ever really got away from myths?...One could almost say that if all world's traditions were cut off at a single blow, the whole of mythology and the whole history of religion would start all over again with the next generation. Only a very few individuals succeed in throwing off mythology in epochs of exceptional intellectual exuberance—the masses never.[45]

Myth and Religion

For Jung, myth and religion have traditionally worked in tandem. Religion has preserved myth, and myth has sustained religion. The heart of religion for Jung is neither belief nor practice but experience, and myth provides the best entrée to the experience of God, which means to the unconscious. While Jung praises early Christianity for both adopting and adapting various pre-Christian myths,[46] he berates modern Christianity for failing to update its myths, without which religion is dead. Sometimes Jung asserts that modern Christianity has gone astray by severing belief from experience and trying in vain to rely on sheer belief. Jung's objection here is twofold: that belief without experience is empty and that the belief is often incompatible with modern knowledge. Other times Jung asserts that modern Christianity has gone awry in seeking to meet the challenge of modern knowledge by turning belief into faith severed from knowledge. Jung's objection here is that even faith requires experience to sustain itself. As Jung sums up his criticisms of both options:

> The Churches stand for traditional and collective convictions which in the case of many of their adherents are no longer based on their own inner experience but on *unreflecting belief*, which is notoriously apt to disappear as soon as one begins thinking about it. The content of belief then comes into collision with knowledge, and it often turns out that the irrationality of the former is no match for the ratiocinations of the latter. Belief is no adequate substitute for inner experience, and where this is absent even a strong faith which came miraculously as a gift of grace may depart equally miraculously.[47]

While these particular criticisms do not involve myth, still other times Jung asserts that modern Christianity has erred in its attempt to update itself by eliminating myth—as if myth were a gangrenous limb that must be amputated to save the patient. Jung is here referring to Rudolf Bultmann's "demythologization" of the New Testament. Jung's first objection is that the supposed incompatibility of myth with modern knowledge stems from a false, literal interpretation of myth: "Theology [wrongly] rejects any tendency to take the assertions of its earliest records as written myths and, accordingly, to understand them symbolically."[48] Jung's second objection is that myth is indispensable to experience and thereby to religion:

> Indeed, it is the theologians themselves who have recently made the attempt—no doubt as a concession to "knowledge"—to "demythologize" the object of their faith while drawing the line [between myth and religion] quite arbitrarily at the crucial points. But to the critical intellect it is only too obvious that myth is an integral component of all religions and therefore cannot be excluded from the assertions of faith without injuring them.[49]

Here Christianity has sought to overcome the opposition between faith and knowledge by discarding belief at odds with knowledge. But in eliminating myth, it has eliminated experience as well. Ironically, Bultmann, despite the misleading term *demythologization*, strives to do the same as Jung: not to eliminate myth from the New Testament but, on the contrary, to reinterpret myth symbolically to make it acceptable to moderns. And Bultmann, also like Jung, contends that the true meaning of the New Testament has always been symbolic, though for Bultmann myth describes the state of humans in the world rather than the state of their minds.

At yet other times Jung asserts that modern Christianity has rightly turned to myth to resurrect itself but has still failed to reinterpret myth symbolically and thereby make it palatable to moderns:

> [R]eligions have long turned to myths for help.... But you cannot, artificially and with an effort of will, believe the statements of myth if you have not previously been gripped by them. If you are honest, you will doubt the truth of the myth because our present-day consciousness has no means of understanding it. Historical and scientific criteria do not lend themselves to a recognition of mythological truth; it can be grasped only by the intuitions of faith or by psychology.[50]

Jung never faults Christian mythology itself for its outdatedness, only its interpreters: "Our myth has become mute, and gives no answers. The fault lies not in it as it is set down in the Scriptures, but solely in us, who have not developed it further, who, rather, have suppressed any such attempts."[51] Jung does lambaste mainstream Christianity for its one-sidedness—above all, for its failure to give sufficient credence to evil: "The old question posed by the Gnostics, 'Whence comes evil?' has been given no answer by the Christian world."[52] But this limitation is a separate issue. Even if one-sided, Christian mythology can still be interpreted anew by each generation. In fact, Jung hopes that modern Christians will not only psychologize their mythology but also broaden it to include evil, as epitomized by nuclear war.

Yet for all Jung's efforts to make Christianity acceptable to moderns by psychologizing it, he recognizes that religion has simply ceased to be an option for many moderns, including, to some degree, him himself. Nonreligious moderns must either adopt secular myths such as that of flying saucers or else forge their own personal myths, as Jung was able to do. Or they must find a substitute for myth, such as art or dreams.

Conclusion

Teaching Jung on myth means getting straight the place of Jung in the study of myth. Jung is not the only theorist of myth. He is not the only theorist to read myth symbolically. He is not the only theorist to reconcile myth with science and with history. He is not the only theorist to replace traditional myths with nonreligious ones. He is not the only theorist to allow private myths. And he is not the only theorist to advocate myths for moderns as well as "primitives."

Teaching Jung on myth means also getting straight the place of myth for Jung. Like all other theorists, including nineteenth-century theorists like Tylor and Frazer, Jung credits myth with serving a very useful function. Like all other twentieth-century theorists, Jung credits myth with serving a very useful need for moderns as well as for "primitives." But Jung stops short of asserting what Campbell does: that myth is the best, much less the sole, way of serving its function. For Jung, the function itself may be indispensable, but myth is not indispensable to serving it. Therefore the popular equation of myth with Jung is overdone.

NOTES

1. In his programmatic statement of structuralism, Claude Lévi-Strauss wrongly characterizes Jung as isolating archetypes from their context, which for him is the structure rather than the plot: see Lévi-Strauss, "The Structural Study of Myth," in *Myth: A Symposium*, ed. Thomas A. Sebeok, 81–106 (Bloomington: Indiana University Press, 1965 [1955]), 84.

2. See Burton Feldman and Robert D. Richardson, *The Rise of Modern Mythology*, 1680–1860 (Bloomington: Indiana University Press, 1972).

3. On Frazer's dual interpretations, see Robert A. Segal, ed., *The Myth and Ritual Theory* (Oxford: Blackwell, 1998), 3–5.

4. C. G. Jung, "The Psychology of the Child Archetype," in *The Archetypes and the Collective Unconscious, Collected Works of C. G. Jung* (Princeton, NJ: Princeton University, 1968), 9.i:154.

5. J. G. Frazer, *The Golden Bough*, abridged ed. (London: Macmillan, 1922), 392.

6. Jung, *Psychological Types*, Collected Works, 6:193.

7. Jung's reverence for the hiatus between the divine and the human is not always shared by his followers. For example, Jean Shinoda Bolen breezily effaces the line between the two, as her titles declare: *Goddesses in Everywoman* (1984) and *Gods in Everyman* (1989).

8. Jung, *Psychological Types*, 6:193–94.

9. Ibid., 6:444.

10. Jung, "The Structure of the Psyche," in *The Structure and Dynamics of the Psyche, Collected Works*, 8:152.

11. Jung, *Symbols of Transformation*, Collected Works, 5:391.

12. Jung, "The Psychology of the Child Archetype," 9.i:155.

13. Ibid.

14. Ibid.

15. Jung, *Psychology and Alchemy*, Collected Works, 12:25.

16. Jung, *Psychological Types*, 6:120–21.

17. On the differences between Campbell and Jung, see Robert A. Segal, *Joseph Campbell: An Introduction* (1987; rev. ed., New York: Penguin/New American Library, 1990), chapter 12.

18. Jung, "The Psychological Aspects of the Kore," in *The Archetypes and the Collective Unconscious*, 9.i:189.

19. Jung, "The Significance of Constitution and Heredity in Psychology," in *The Structure and Dynamics of the Psyche*, 8:111.

20. Jung, *Symbols of Transformation*, 5:157–58.

21. Ibid., 5:158.

22. Otto Rank, *The Myth of the Birth of the Hero* [1914], reprinted in Otto Rank, Lord Raglan, and Alan Dundes, *In Quest of the Hero* (Princeton, NJ: Princeton University Press, 1990), 3-86.

23. Melanie Klein, *Narrative of a Child Analysis* (London: Hogarth, 1975 [1961]).

24. Jung, "The Psychology of the Child Archetype," 9.i:154.

25. Jung, "The Tavistock Lectures," in *The Symbolic Life*, Collected Works, 18:82–83. See also Jung, *Memories, Dreams, Reflections*, ed. Aniela Jaffé, trans. Richard and Clara Winston (New York: Vintage, 1962), 161–62.

26. Jung, "Paracelsus as a Spiritual Phenomenon," in *Alchemical Studies*, Collected Works, 13:162–63.

27. Jung, "Background to the Psychology of Christian Symbolism," in *Aion*, Collected Works, 9.ii:180.

28. Jung, "Approaching the Unconscious," in Jung et al., *Man and His Symbols* (New York: Dell Laurel, 1968 [1964]), 84.

29. Jung, *Symbols of Transformation*, 5:231.

30. On synchronicity, see, above all, Jung, "Synchronicity: An Acausal Connecting Connecting Principle" and "On Synchronicity," in *The Structure and Dynamics of the Psyche*, 8: 417–519 and 520–31.

31. Jung, *Letters*, ed. Gerhard Adler and Aniela Jaffé, trans. R. F. C. Hull (Princeton, NJ: Princeton University Press, 1973–1974), 2:495.

32. Ibid., 541.

33. On synchronicity and myth, see Robert A. Segal, "Bringing Myth Back to the World: The Future of Myth in Jungian Psychology," in *Dreaming the Myth Onwards*, ed. Lucy Huskinson, 91–105 (London: Routledge, 2008).

34. Jung, "The Psychology of the Child Archetype," 9.i:162.

35. Ibid., 9.i:162–63.

36. Ibid., 9.i:153.

37. Ibid., 9.i:154.

38. Jung, "Archetypes of the Collective Unconscious," in *The Archetypes and the Collective Unconscious*, 9.i:6.

39. Jung, "The Philosophical Tree," in *Alchemical Studies*, 13:300.

40. Ibid.

41. Jung, "Psychology and Literature," in *The Spirit in Man, Art, and Literature*, Collected Works, 15:97.

42. Jung, "Wotan," in *Civilization in Transition*, Collected Works, 10:180.

43. Jung, "Flying Saucers," in *Civilization in Transition*, 10:328.

44. Mircea Eliade, *The Sacred and the Profane*, trans. Willard R. Trask (New York: Harvest Books, 1968 [1959]); Joseph Campbell, *The Hero with a Thousand Faces*, 1st ed. (New York: Pantheon Books, 1949).

45. Jung, *Symbols of Transformation*, 5:25.

46. Jung, "Rex and Regina," in *Mysterium Coniunctionis*, Collected Works, 14:336 n. 297.

47. Jung, "The Undiscovered Self," in *Civilization in Transition*, 10:265.

48. Ibid., 10:285.

49. Ibid.

50. Jung, "The Conjunction," in *Mysterium Coniunctionis*, 14:528.

51. Jung, *Memories, Dreams, Reflections*, 332.

52. Ibid.

REFERENCES

Bolen, Jean Shinoda. *Goddesses in Everywoman*. New York: Harper & Row, 1984.

Bolen, Jean Shinoda. *Gods in Everyman*. New York: Harper & Row, 1989.

Campbell, Joseph. *The Hero with a Thousand Faces*, 1st ed. New York: Pantheon, 1949.

Eliade, Mircea. *The Sacred and the Profane*. Trans. Willard R. Trask. New York: Harvest, 1968 [1959].

Feldman, Burton, and Robert D. Richardson. *The Rise of Modern Mythology, 1680–1860*. Bloomington: Indiana University Press, 1972.

Frazer, J. G. (James George). *The Golden Bough*, 1st ed. 2 vols. London: Macmillan, 1890.

Frazer, J. G. (James George). *The Golden Bough*, 1-vol. abridgment. London: Macmillan, 1922.

Freud, Sigmund. *The Interpretation of Dreams. Standard Edition of the Complete Psychological Works of Sigmund Freud*. Ed. and trans. James Strachey et al., vols. 4–5. London: Hogarth and Institute of Psycho-Analysis, 1953.

Hesse, Mary. *Models and Analogies in Science*. London: Sheed and Ward, 1963.

Jung, C. G. *Memories, Dreams, Reflections*. Ed. Aniela Jaffé, trans. Richard and Clara Winston. New York: Vintage, 1962.

Jung, C. G. *The Spirit in Man*, Art, and Literature. *Collected Works of C. G. Jung*, vol. 15. Princeton, N.J.: Princeton University Press, 1966.

Jung, C. G. *Symbols of Transformation. Collected Works of C. G. Jung*, vol. 5, 2nd ed., Princeton, NJ: Princeton University Press, 1967.

Jung, C. G. "Approaching the Unconscious." In Jung et al., *Man and His Symbols*. 1–94. New York: Dell Laurel, 1968.

Jung, C. G. *The Archetypes and the Collective Unconscious. Collected Works of C. G. Jung*, vol. 9, 2nd ed., pt. 1. Princeton, NJ: Princeton University Press, 1968.

Jung, C. G. *Aion. Collected Works of C. G. Jung*, vol. 9, 2nd ed., pt. 2. Princeton, NJ: Princeton University Press, 1968.

Jung, C. G. *Psychology and Alchemy. Collected Works of C. G. Jung*, vol. 12, 2nd ed., Princeton, NJ: Princeton University Press, 1968.

Jung, C. G. *Alchemical Studies. Collected Works of C. G. Jung*, vol. 13. Princeton, NJ: Princeton University Press, 1968.

Jung, C. G. *The Structure and Dynamics of the Psyche. Collected Works of C. G. Jung*, vol. 8, 2nd ed., Princeton, NJ: Princeton University Press, 1969.

Jung, C. G. *Mysterium Coniunctionis. Collected Works of C. G. Jung*, vol. 14, 2nd ed., Princeton, NJ: Princeton University Press, 1970.

Jung, C. G. *Civilization in Transition. Collected Works of C. G. Jung*, vol. 10, 2nd ed., Princeton, NJ: Princeton University Press, 1970.

Jung, C. G. *Psychological Types. Collected Works of C. G. Jung*, vol. 6. Princeton, NJ: Princeton University Press, 1971.

Jung, C. G. *Letters*. Ed. Gerhard Adler and Aniela Jaffé, trans. R. F. C. Hull. 2 vols. Princeton, NJ: Princeton University Press, 1973–1974.

Jung, C. G. *The Symbolic Life. Collected Works of C. G. Jung*, vol. 18. Princeton, NJ: Princeton University Press, 1976.

Klein, Melanie. *Narrative of a Child Analysis*. London: Hogarth, 1975 [1961].

Lévi-Strauss, Claude. "The Structural Study of Myth." In *Myth: A Symposium*. Ed. Thomas A. Sebeok, 81–106. Bloomington: Indiana University Press, 1965.

Rank, Otto. *The Myth of the Birth of the Hero*. Trans. F. Robbins and Smith Ely Jelliffe. New York: Journal of Nervous and Mental Disease Publishing, 1914. Reprinted in Otto Rank, Lord Raglan, and Alan Dundes, *In Quest of the Hero*, 3–86. Introduction by Robert A. Segal. Princeton, NJ: Princeton University Press, 1990.

Segal, Robert A. *Joseph Campbell: An Introduction*, 1987. Rev. ed., New York: Penguin/New American Library, 1990.

Segal, Robert A., Ed. *The Myth and Ritual Theory*. Oxford: Blackwell, 1998.

Segal, Robert A., Ed. *Jung on Mythology*. Princeton, NJ: Princeton University Press; London: Routledge, 1998.

Segal, Robert A. *Theorizing about Myth*. Amherst: University of Massachusetts Press, 1999.

Segal, Robert A. *Myth: A Very Short Introduction*. Oxford: Oxford University Press, 2004.

Segal, Robert A. "Bringing Myth Back to the World: The Future of Myth in Jungian Psychology." In *Dreaming the Myth Onwards*, ed. Lucy Huskinson, 91–105. London: Routledge, 2008.

Tylor, E. B. (Edward Burnett). *Primitive Culture*, 1st ed. 2 vols. London: Murray, 1871.

6

Jung's Engagement with Christian Theology

Charlene P. E. Burns

Teaching Jung's analysis of Christianity to undergraduates can be problematic no matter the setting, but doing so in a psychology of religion course designed for general education credit at a publicly funded American university presents unique challenges. In terms of content, the factors complicating such a teaching project include the neglect of his work generally in the academy, the advanced interdisciplinary nature of his theorizing, and—most important for this project—the controversial nature of his interpretation of core doctrines of the faith. In terms of student makeup and setting, complicating factors for my teaching of Jung's theories cluster around the religious and academic backgrounds of the students. Most are conservative Christians, many of whom come to the university from Lutheran or Roman Catholic homes, yet become active on campus in very conservative nondenominational religious groups like Student Impact (Campus Crusade for Christ) and Navigators. Academically, they have mixed backgrounds, since the only prerequisite for the course is RELS 100, Introduction to the World's Religions. Although most of the students are majors or minors in either religious studies or psychology, a quarter to as much as half of the class each semester consists of majors in neither area. Making matters even more challenging, the psychology program here at University of Wisconsin Eau-Claire follows the general trend of undergraduate psychology programs in giving little attention to psychoanalytic psychology beyond introduction to the Freudian approaches. Those few students who have heard of Jung are likely to have encountered him through New Age Jungian pop psychology books.[1]

In spite of these challenges, teaching this subject matter can bring rewards, and sometimes even transformation, to those involved. What follows here is a reflection on the methods I have found to be most effective in teaching Jung on religion to undergraduates in this secular and somewhat conservative Midwestern setting. Following a brief discussion of the ways I have learned to address Jung's absence from the academic study of psychology in the United States, I explore the issues that are more specific to my teaching context. In my efforts to negotiate the unique challenges of American religious studies education, I have discovered that Jung's own methodological commitments provide the necessary tools for effective teaching. Examination of his epistemological, philosophical, and theological underpinnings—particularly in relation to Immanuel Kant's philosophy and Friedrich Schleiermacher's theology—is quite enlightening for my students. My own awareness of and attention to the problems and pitfalls offered by arousal of cognitive dissonance in learning further enhances the educational experience.

David Tacey has written extensively on the issue of teaching Jung in a secular (Australian) setting, and in a recent article, he developed a useful taxonomy of approaches generally found in the teaching of Jung's work (see also chapter 1 of this volume). Tacey's four categories are (1) fitting in or conforming, (2) updating or restructuring, (3) soul making or overturning, and (4) keeping pure or standing still.[2] I find that, as my methods evolve over time, I tend primarily to use the first two methods to varying degrees, depending on the class makeup and responses to the subject matter. Tacey's third and fourth methods are bound to fail in a setting such as mine, since they involve a kind of advocacy for "Jungianism" that smacks of religious fervor. The soul-maker approach involves attempts to revolutionize the academy in accordance with Jungian themes, and the puritan preaches Jung with a kind of fundamentalist desire to avoid contamination by new ideas. The first time I taught Jung at this university, I discovered that few students had heard of him and, for reasons discussed more fully in the next section, found the most fruitful way forward was to begin the unit on Jung's psychology with a focus on demonstrating the validity or "respectability" of his theories—falling into Tacey's first category of fitting Jung into the academy.

Dealing with Jung's Absence

One problem in teaching Jung arises from the fact that although there does exist a strong if somewhat isolated Jungian analytic tradition, there is virtually "no academic Jungian tradition."[3] This is the case in spite of some resurgence of interest in his work over the last two decades. Jungian psychology is usually glossed over, if not entirely ignored, in college and university psychology classrooms, and as a result, Jungian studies have tended to be self-referential, including very little critical engagement.[4] In spite of the efforts of Jungian scholars, his work continues to be marginalized in the study of psychology at American universities. When it does find a place, it is often in religious studies (as is the case at my university) or English courses, usually in connection with examinations of the meaning of myth. When psychology majors and minors express confusion at having never been taught about Jung, the challenge to demonstrate his importance to psychology generally and psychology of religion in particular is intensified.

An effective tool in helping these students overcome their understandable skepticism regarding Jung's importance to the psychology of religion, given his absence from their prior education, is to show students that the well-known phrase "Electra Complex" has been misattributed to Freud.[5] When polled as to the origins of the term, my students nearly always credit Freud, and none has ever realized that it actually originated with Jung. To reassure students that their educational deficit is far from unique, I present the results of a 1997 study in which Kilmartin and Dervin surveyed introductory course books for psychology classes. In this study, they found that of the books using the term "Electra Complex," none attributed it to Jung. Of those texts using the term, 72 percent either directly attributed it to Freud or made vague statements implying the term was Freud's.[6] The fact that so many textbooks are mistaken on this point helps support the claim that Jung's marginalization is unmerited.

In this unit of study, we discuss the Freud-Jung relationship, the work they accomplished together during this time, and their parting of ways. I explain that before he split with Freud, Jung adopted the term *complex* (another term they tend to attribute to Freud) to identify the unconscious collection of beliefs and ideas around emotional content that affects behavior and feelings, and that he first used the phrase "Electra Complex" in an early essay to describe the female child's jealousy toward her mother's relationship with her father.[7] I point out that Freud did not accept the term, and I ask students to read his 1920 essay in which he writes that he saw no advantage to using it at all. This simple exercise goes a long way toward helping students overcome the tendency to question Jung's importance, given his absence from their education to that point. It also helps to place Freud in perspective as a foundational figure who was shaped by interaction with colleagues, not the solitary pioneering demigod of psychoanalysis he sometimes seems to have been.

Another useful tool in overcoming skepticism regarding Jung's importance is the textbook I have chosen for the course, David Wulff's masterful survey, *Psychology of Religion: Classic and Contemporary*. Wulff covers the history and scope of the field more thoroughly than any other text accessible to undergraduates, and when used with carefully selected primary source materials, the book helps to ensure a thorough introduction to the subject matter. He has included chapters covering experimental, social, and biological approaches, which are the forms of research most familiar to the students who have taken psychology courses. He also has devoted significant attention to psychoanalysis and the schools of thought flowing from it, like Erickson's work, object relations, self psychology, and existential. The fact that Wulff devotes an entire chapter to Jung adds weight to claims about Jung's importance for psychology of religion. Any remaining skepticism regarding Jung's place in the history of psychology is usually dispelled by a discussion of his theory of personality types as the foundation for the Myers-Briggs Personality Inventory. Since many students have taken the Myers-Briggs or a variation of it through church activities or career counseling programs, this serves as a powerful means for validation.

Teaching Jung's Interpretation of Christianity in a State University: Epistemology

The enterprise of teaching religious studies in a state-funded postsecondary institution in the United States offers a particular set of challenges for professor and students; teaching a course in the psychology of religion within such a context is especially challenging. In 1963, the U.S. Supreme Court ruled that a distinction must be made between teaching *about* religious ideas and advocacy *for* or *against* them. In light of this restriction, in my classrooms I strive to bracket off the purely confessional approach so as to model the use of academic methods that allow exploration of confessional positions without advocacy.[8] Jung's own methodological commitments are quite helpful in dealing with this issue. Since these methodological issues are also beneficial in addressing concerns generated for students by some aspects of his writings on Christianity, I will address these issues in concert.

Jung's engagement with Christian thought is unfortunately one of the most controversial and misunderstood facets of his work. This is regrettable because his interpretation of major themes and doctrines through the lens of depth psychology can be invigorating for Christians who struggle with the place of concepts like transubstantiation, the reality of evil, or God as Trinity in modern life. This exploration can also be enriching for those who have yet to investigate the complexity of these doctrines. Given the kinds of students who take my class, setting the stage is therefore very important. In Wulff's introductory chapter to the survey text, he discusses the importance of studying a theorist's "personal equation" in developing a deeper understanding of his or her work, and subsequent chapters begin with an overview of pertinent biographical information. In Jung's case, the personal equation is so integral to his psychology of religion that it is perhaps not an overstatement to say that it is impossible to understand one without knowing something of the other. For this reason, we spend at least one full class exploring Jung's life story before we attempt to delve into his theories. The facts that Jung's father was a minister, that Jung himself was raised in the Swiss Reformed Church, and that he struggled with the doctrines of Christian belief resonate powerfully with my students. One episode of Jung's early years to which many can directly relate is the anticlimactic nature of his first Communion after Confirmation; students often report that they stopped attending church after Confirmation for similar reasons. All of this helps to establish common ground between the students and this towering twentieth-century intellect. Criticism of Christianity from a perceived insider is easier for these students to entertain than from someone like Freud, whom they tend to find unappealing because his theories are, to them, "all about sex" and also because they perceive him to have been an outsider to Christianity.

Following an outline of Jung's general theories related to the personal and collective unconscious and archetypes, but before introducing Jung's writings on Christianity, I address issues related to Jung's own claims about his epistemological stance. As is well known among those of us who study and teach Jung's work, although he was not always consistent in expression, Jung repeatedly stated that he did not intend his statements about God and our experiences of the divine to be metaphysical in nature. For example, he wrote plainly in one letter, "I make no metaphysical assertions. My standpoint is purely empirical and deals with the psychology of such assertions."[9] Although many have debated how successful he really was at this, it was his intent to remain true to the idea that whereas "religion looks to the imprinter, psychology studies the imprint."[10] I encourage my students to keep this in mind as we study his works. It turns out, in fact, that this is the most important tool I have found for helping conservative Christian undergraduates overcome the urge to shut down and avoid critical engagement with Jung. Once I discerned the importance of this information for overcoming resistance to seriously exploring the implications of Jung's work, I expanded the amount of time devoted to the topic. I now also include a brief introduction to Immanuel Kant (1724–1804) and Friedrich Schleiermacher (1768–1883), who were important to Jung's development, so as to ground Jung solidly in the Christian philosophical and theological traditions. Given space limitations, I can only sketch the outlines of this material (developed more fully elsewhere) here.[11]

Jung's commitment to the idea that it is possible to detach metaphysical from psychological assertions was based in his profound respect for Kant's philosophy. He thought that Kant had established the foundations for building a scientific understanding of the human psyche. Speaking of Kant's epistemology, he once wrote that this theory of knowledge opened the door to new possibilities, and "on that threshold minds go their separate ways: those that have understood Kant, and the others that cannot follow him."[12] Unfortunately, those words could have been written about his own work, a sad truth that largely resulted from the failure of some interpreters to grasp the importance of Kant's writings for Jung.

As the reader probably knows, Kant's epistemology is a kind of mediating response to radical empiricism, wherein knowledge is said to derive solely from sense experience, and the rationalism of his day, wherein reason was thought to provide genuinely objective knowledge uncontaminated by experience. While acknowledging the kernel of truth in both positions, Kant was troubled by their implications regarding objectivity. Against the empiricist position, he argued that it is mistaken to claim that we are capable of complete objectivity. Against the rationalists, he argued it is equally wrong to claim we are incapable of objectivity; this position is particularly problematic since, if correct, it makes scientific knowledge impossible. As a solution, Kant offered a synthesis in which both reason and experience are essential to knowing. The knowledge gained through our senses is actively organized in the mind by means of a priori categories or concepts that are presupposed by experience. The a priori categories function as mental structures, having no ontological or metaphysical significance. He argued there must be something like these categories; if not, the unity of self-conscious experience, in which our sensory experience and the thoughts that label that experience our own occur simultaneously, is inexplicable.[13] The categories apply to the objects of possible experience (phenomena) and not to objects knowable only to thought (noumena). At this point in our discussion, I warn students that there is a good bit disagreement among philosophers about Kant's use of these terms, *phenomena* and *noumena*.[14] Since we are only interested in the terms because of their importance to Jung, we can ignore the scholarly arguments and concentrate on the interpretation that Jung accepted, which I briefly summarize as follows.

The phenomenal world, the world as we experience it, is distinct from the noumenal, ultimate, or absolute reality. We can only hypothesize the existence of noumenal reality on the basis of perception. The only referent we have to noumenal reality is the mental construct; for Kant, "noumenal" functions as a marker for the limits of human knowing. All we can say about it is that it is beyond our capacity to know. "God" is a noumenal aspect of human experience, and so metaphysical arguments about God go beyond the limits of human reason. Even though it is impossible for the human mind to reach beyond the limits of the phenomenal world, we naturally seek the God's-eye view. This is so because we are aware that each of us has a particular point of view, and the desire for common ground leads us to seek that point of view that encompasses them all. This exercise of "pure reason" leads us astray, since it attempts to reach a perspective-free viewpoint; it leads humanity to develop ideas about God and immortality.

Kant's claims about reality's phenomenal and noumenal aspects solved some of the problems inherent in strictly empiricist or rationalist systems, but he left us with a problematic gap between mind and world, or the "I" and the "I think."[15] Some critics have accused Kant of creating such a wide gap that he "lost the self."[16] And some have criticized Jung for his acceptance of Kant's problematic disjuncture.[17] Since the most important aspect of Jung's methodology for helping students open themselves to his insights into Christianity's place in the modern world is the phenomenal-noumenal distinction, briefly demonstrating the connections between Jung and Friedrich Schleiermacher, who attempted to close the Kantian gap, is helpful at this point in our study.

In a 1953 letter, Jung acknowledged a connection to Schleiermacher, who had baptized his grandfather: "The vast, esoteric, and individual spirit of Schleiermacher was part of the intellectual atmosphere of my father's family. I never studied him, but unconsciously he was for me a *spiritus rector*."[18] Jung never explained just how he understood Schleiermacher to have been his *spiritus rector* (spiritual ancestor or unconscious inspiration), and this connection has received virtually no attention in the vast literature on Jung. I am a theologian with some background in Schleiermacher's theology, and once I read Jung's letter referring to the great nineteenth-century theologian, the connections between their works became quite clear. As I have demonstrated in depth elsewhere, there are discernible hints of Schleiermacher's thought throughout Jung's psychology of religious experience.[19] Uncovering these hints for my students helps many of them along the path to understanding Jung.

According to Schleiermacher, Kant's gap resulted from his granting too much privilege to the human mind: "Demonstration presupposes acknowledgment of something else, but cognition of God is the original cognition that underlies all other cognition."[20] The idea of God and that to which the idea refers must not be confused. As a remedy to this problem, Schleiermacher sought something within human nature that could maintain the distinction between the "ungiven" God *in se* and the idea of God.[21] The reader familiar with Jung will readily discern the connections here.

Regarding the relation between sense experience and knowledge, Schleiermacher believed that we are not fully determined by sense experience, although experience is essential to any kind of knowing: "We cannot think except under the form of being.... Knowing is the congruence of thinking with being as what is thought."[22] He believed Kant had overlooked the fact of embodiment; in Kant, there was nothing to link the a priori categories of understanding to the external world of objects, for unless *being* is linked to *thinking*, it becomes impossible to understand how it is that we are aware of our connection to the world.[23] In other words, there was no connection between the "I think" and the pure "I," between the physical self and the thinking self. Kant inadvertently created a perpetual circle in which the self signifies that which the concept of thought entails; the Kantian self is both that which is aware and that of which it is aware.[24]

Schleiermacher sought the solution to this circular argument through an attempt to understand the body's role in linking us to God, by finding a way to affirm "being" without reducing it to "thought." To solve the problem, he argued in favor of that which the intellect cannot grasp: feeling. Feeling, he said, is "subject-less awareness," the unity or oneness of being, or unmediated and immediate self-consciousness, and the relation between subject and object is one of "twofold contrast." The world is both determined by and determinate of the subject, and so if the subject is described as active, the world necessarily will appear as passive, and vice versa. Schleiermacher extends this twofold contrast to describe the unity of the self as physical and ethical. The capacity to imagine, to fix things in consciousness, is the pure "I." The pure "I" is the agency that makes thought possible; it is not the thought itself. The self, then, might be thought of as pure potentiality. The point where one thought ends and another has not yet begun, called the "nullpoint," is the transition between two moments of consciousness (thinking and being), with the self serving as the means of transition.

At the nullpoint, which for Schleiermacher is the gap between Kant's phenomenal and noumenal realities, thinking both reaches its limit and is the limit. The point at which one thought has ended and another not yet begun is objectless awareness, objective consciousness empty of thought. This is an embodied, experiential, empirical encounter of unmediated awareness or intuition, a transcendental standpoint unknowable through concepts or judgments.

The subjective complement to objectless awareness is subjectless awareness, or *Gefühl* in German. This term has usually been translated as "feeling," but it is not sensation, which has to do with the organic determinate "I." *Gefühl* is the immediate unmediated self-consciousness, the experience of unity or oneness of one's own being. This means that intuition is awareness of the nullpoint from the standpoint of objective consciousness, and feeling is awareness that "I = I from one moment of consciousness to the next."[25] At the nullpoint, the self is undetermined and indistinguishable from all of life. Objectively, it is empty with regard to content. Subjectively, it is full since the self is conscious of self. Consciousness of the nullpoint is *felt* or experienced in the identity of physical and ethical—we do not think or will the rupture into consciousness, we feel it. For Schleiermacher, this unbounded state is "'the birth hour of everything living in religion.'"[26] This unmediated awareness of oneness links being to thinking. It is "the sheer embodied self that is the counterbalance to the [Kantian] 'I think.'"[27] The subjectless, objectless experience at the nullpoint is a sort of cancellation of "being" as self-determining agency. This leads to the "feeling of utter dependence," which Schleiermacher said is the religious element in life, through which God is represented in human consciousness. Religion is "the consciousness of being absolutely dependent, or which is the same thing, of being in a relation with God."[28]

"The feeling of absolute dependence, accordingly, is not to be explained as an awareness of the world's existence, but only as an awareness of the existence of God, as the absolute undivided unity."[29] We feel the rupture of consciousness and yet sense that *something* holds the self, maintaining it as a unity across the gap. This *something* is God, that upon which we have the awareness of utter dependence. This feeling is a precognitive awareness, followed by a moment of consciousness that is the religious element—our own self-consciousness is experienced as consciousness of God. Although the nullpoint does refer to the absolute or ultimate reality, the experience of it does not provide knowledge of God *in se*.

Schleiermacher had an evolutionary view of the Incarnation, saying that the human nature in Christ has been eternally "coming to be" within the process of the world,[30] and the Incarnation was itself a manifestation of "God-consciousness" that is present in all humanity. Although all humans have this consciousness, in Jesus the God-consciousness was a "perfect indwelling." In us, it manifests as the "sense and taste for the infinite," or prereflective awareness of being "absolutely dependent" for our very being on God. Schleiermacher believed this human awareness has the potential to evolve to greater and greater levels of knowing God. Christ differed from us in degree, not in kind, and the difference in degree was in "the constant potency of [Jesus'] God-consciousness, which was a veritable existence of God in Him."[31]

For Schleiermacher, then, religious experience, the unmediated awareness of oneness with and dependence upon that which maintains the self as a unity across the gap between the end of one thought and another, closes the gap left by Kant. Viewed through this lens, Jung's psychology of religion stands on firmer ground, both theoretically and in the minds of young religiously conservative students prone to rejecting ideas that challenge their beliefs.

For Jung, the "knowing subject is part of a wider knowledge pool with which the individual is in interaction."[32] He considered consciousness to be an adaptive accomplishment, and the unconscious as the source of the archetypes, the forms or categories that regulate the instincts.[33] The archetypes are patterns of instinctual behavior arising from the collective unconscious, which is a repository of the universal "ancestral heritage of possibilities of representation" containing the "whole spiritual heritage of [hu]mankind's evolution, born anew in the brain structure of every individual," that account for the common themes in humanity's dreams, myths, legends.[34] Here, a basic understanding of Kant's epistemology comes into play for my students, since Jung insisted that the primordial images are not part of phenomenal experience. They are noumena and as such can only be intuited psychologically. Religious realities have a transpersonal basis, arising as they do from the collective unconscious, but because they are filtered through subjective experience, they can never be absolutes. The most we can say about God from the Jungian psychological standpoint is that "an archetypal image of the Deity" exists.[35] The god-image and statements about it are "psychic processes which are different from their transcendent object."[36]

Once we become alert to Jung's familiarity with Schleiermacher, new facets in his work appear. The archetypes, for example, take on new significance for students with strong commitments to conservative Christian beliefs. As the reader is no doubt aware, the Self archetype represents for Jung the unity of a mature psyche, which he sometimes referred to as "the God within."[37] The archetypes are "the hidden foundations of the conscious mind...the roots which the psyche has sunk not only in the earth in the narrower sense but in the world in general."[38] They function as "the bridge to matter in general."[39] Recall Schleiermacher's nullpoint, the "bridge" that closes the gap between thinker and thought, matter and spirit, phenomenal and noumenal, the point at which thought and action cease and "consciousness of being absolutely dependent...of being in a relation with God" arises.[40] For Jung, we encounter archetypal images and themes in dreams, myths, and religions. These images form the basis for our awareness of God, and through encounter with the depths of the human psyche, the phenomenal ceases in the face of the noumenal "God within." In an interview, Jung was once asked whether he believed in God. His response was "Difficult to answer. I *know*. I don't need to believe. I know."[41] This certainty suggests that Jung's Self and Schleiermacher's "feeling," as the unmediated awareness of oneness with and dependence on that which maintains the self as a unity across the gap between the end of one thought and another, point to the same reality. My goal in asking students to consider the resonance between Jung's Self archetype and Schleiermacher's "feeling" as the source of all religious expression is to challenge claims that Jung reduces God to psychology or that he undermines divine transcendence, which is an especially important concept for conservative Protestants.

According to Jung, it is "psychologically quite unthinkable for God to be simply the 'wholly other' for a 'wholly other' could never be one of the soul's deepest and closest intimacies—which is precisely what God is."[42] Through the archetypes, we encounter God in the depths of consciousness as an intimate reality. Schleiermacher's theology of the Incarnation as perfect "God consciousness" resonates with this perception, as does his evolutionary interpretation of the Incarnation. Divinity-in-humanity eternally unfolds within the process of the world. What manifested in Jesus perfectly is found potentially in all humanity. Introducing students to these theological resonances with Jung helps tremendously in study of what is often considered Jung's most difficult work for Christians, *Answer to Job*. Since Clodagh Weldon's chapter in this volume examines *Answer* in detail, I will only point out here that the evolutionary aspect of the divinity-in-humanity and our consciousness of God are central: Jung believed that the "real history of the world is the progressive incarnation of the deity,"[43] and in *Answer* he develops this theme.

Jung on Christianity as Therapy: Dealing with Cognitive Dissonance

The most useful interpretive framework I've found for building on the foundation established by this brief examination of the influence of Kant and Schleiermacher on Jung is Murray Stein's thesis that Jung's work on Christian doctrine can best be understood as a long-term psychotherapeutic project. Stein argues that Jung's intent was neither reductionist nor apologetic—it was "an evolutionary-transformational" effort aimed at healing the splits, repressions, and one-sidedness that developed over Christianity's two-thousand-year history.[44] This reading illuminates Jung's profound respect for and fascination with the doctrines of the faith without glossing over the highly critical aspects of his work. These tools, which tend to fall under Tacey's "updating" classification, help students connect with Jung at a more personal level. Once I began teaching the material through this lens, I found that, although some do remain unconvinced in the end, few maintain the out-of-hand dismissal that so often can happen with conservative Christian readers of Jung.

Initially, students are troubled by Jung's major criticism of the doctrines of Christ and of the Trinity. His claims that these concepts need to include the Shadow and that, so long as denial of the Shadow remains, Christianity cannot achieve its full potential as a means of world transformation are shocking for many. They have been taught the traditional theology of divine goodness, and many are quite comfortable with a fairly literal understanding of Satan as a fallen angel whom God permits to wreak havoc on Earth because of original sin. These students accept the strong Augustinian view that humanity inherits the guilt for Adam and Eve's first sin. This allows them to explain the suffering of humanity in terms of justice: because of that original sin, the image of God was lost, and so war, murder, and poverty are all simply humanity's just deserts. Natural disasters and disease are accounted for by the claim that nature itself was corrupted by that first sin. Because God loves humanity and wants us to freely choose to follow Him (God is quite masculine for these students), He does not intervene except in allowing His Son to pay for our sins by dying a horrendous death by crucifixion. Most have never critically examined these doctrines, so when challenged by Jung to consider the possibility that their own images of God might be one-sided, a great deal of cognitive dissonance is generated. We all know that cognitive dissonance is important to the educational experience, but I have found few who consciously acknowledge this in their teaching. Studies support the claim that without it, genuine transformative learning does not occur and also show us that if the teacher pushes too hard once dissonance has developed, things can backfire.

Cognitive dissonance theory is a well-established model of social learning, but I suspect that explicit consideration of its impact in teaching challenging material like Jung's critique of Christianity happens rarely among educators.[45] A cursory survey of the literature on teaching Jung supports this suspicion. Others have noted the tendency among certain types of students to shut down to "get the piece of paper," "defensively bolster" their own belief systems to maintain "a primitive critical condition," or drop out of class,[46] but without making an explicit connection to the phenomenon of cognitive dissonance. Conscious reflection on the power of dissonance in learning helps identify the areas most likely to generate conflict and resistance for certain types of students and helps us be more intentional about the methods we use.

The theory assumes that we seek consonance between thoughts and behaviors. When a credible new cognition or behavior challenges a previously existing belief, we experience psychological dissonance. This is an adaptive response that functions to warn when something is psychologically, but not necessarily logically, inconsistent. Our knowledge of the world needs to be consonant with what we believe.[47] Like all discomfort, the unease generated in dissonant situations motivates us to alleviate it in some way. The more important the concepts, the greater the dissonance, and the greater the dissonance, the more intense the need to reduce it. Since it is the case that dissonance is greater when those concepts most important to us are challenged, students who are asked to consider the possibility that their own images of God might be one-sided are ripe for genuine learning but also for rejection of the new information and entrenchment of their own challenged beliefs. Here, the educator must handle with care!

Once dissonance has arisen, it can be reduced in several ways: the learner can reject the new idea by denying the dissonant elements, reduce the importance of the dissonant ideas, increase the importance of consonant ideas, or add new consonant elements to justify the dissonant situation.[48] The worst-case scenario here is, of course, the student who rejects out of hand the new information.

The experience of dissonance and efforts to alleviate it operate somewhat outside conscious awareness. In the case of a conservative Christian who believes that God is not the source of evil, when introduced to Jung's writings on the Trinity's "missing fourth" and asked to consider the contradictory nature of the classical theodicy problem (why an all-powerful and pure loving God chooses to do nothing about suffering), she will experience dissonance. She will be aware of the discomfort and of its source. She will strive to find a way to eliminate the discomfort, but she will not be consciously aware that this is her motivation. For the student, it is simply a matter of attempting to make sense of or reject conflicting information.

Complicating things further is the phenomenon known as the hypocrisy effect, documented in a 1975 study of young Christian women. If too much dissonance is generated, increased commitment to the challenged beliefs can result. Participants in a Christian youth program were asked to state whether they believed that Jesus was divine. They then answered a questionnaire designed to assess how orthodox their general beliefs really were. Afterward, they were exposed to information aimed at disconfirming the divinity claim. Those who believed that Jesus was divine and also accepted that the disconfirming information was authentic demonstrated intensified belief in the divinity of Jesus. Those who either did not believe in the doctrine or did not accept the disconfirming information as true showed no change in their position.[49] This phenomenon is important to this discussion because many of my students not only hold conservative beliefs but also devote considerable time and effort to sharing these beliefs publicly through involvement in numerous on-campus faith-based organizations. For these students, merely to consider the possibility that Jung's critique of Christianity might be valid is enough to stimulate the hypocrisy effect.

Material useful in dampening the impact of excessive cognitive dissonance and the hypocrisy effect can be found in Jung's own writings. When this material is combined with Stein's interpretation of Jung's relationship to Christianity as a therapeutic one aimed at helping it fulfill its potential for humanity as "the psychological prototype of the only meaningful life,"[50] I have found it possible to guide students toward a more sophisticated understanding of their own beliefs and of Jung's work. Most students are willing to "hear" Jung once they learn from the historical record that doctrines like those of the Trinity and Incarnation evolved over time. When they learn to see doctrine as the product of human effort to make sense of the experience of God, Jung's thesis becomes less threatening, since they come to understand that Jung's agenda was to understand how doctrine evolved so as to help us see where it needs transformation.

Most students have studied environmental and gender inequality issues in other courses by the time they sign up for the psychology of religion class, and framing portions of Jung's critique in conversation with what they have learned of those issues helps them understand what he means when he says that both Protestant and Catholic forms of the faith need to heal the split between nature and spirit, to achieve union of body and spirit, and must find a way to incorporate the feminine into our images of God. Here I practice a kind of updating method in which the numinous aspect is preserved through demonstrating the ways Jung's work can illuminate present-day theological concerns. Unfortunately, when it comes to the issue of incorporating the Shadow into our images of God, things become more difficult, as previously outlined, but briefly mentioning recent theological trends like those influenced by process philosophy is sometimes a helpful form of updating.

Understanding what Jung intends by the claim that the Trinity is incomplete offers perhaps the greatest challenge. When addressing this aspect of Jung's work, I find it helpful to remind students of his relationship to Christianity and his agenda. Offering quotes from his writings, like this one from a letter to Martin Buber, help to keep things in perspective: "Here, just for once, and as an exception, I shall indulge in transcendental speculation and even in 'poetry': God has indeed made an inconceivably sublime and mysteriously contradictory image of himself, without the help of man, and has implanted it in man's unconscious."[51]

Concluding Thoughts

Teaching Jung to undergraduates is quite challenging, no matter the setting. It can also be immensely rewarding for students and the instructor. Asking conservative Christian undergraduates to struggle with Jung's diagnosis and prescription for their faith is, I believe, asking quite a lot. The student who signs up for a course in the psychology of religion does not understand herself to be entering into a psychotherapeutic relationship. However, if we teach Jung so as to engage the whole self, as most experienced instructors of his work advocate, the encounter between student, instructor, and Jung cannot help being transformative. Because the encounter with Jung can be so very enlightening and challenging, I am always mindful of the potential for crossing the line that separates teaching from "doing therapy without a contract." Students who open themselves to understanding Jung often find their deepest commitments challenged in what can be frightening ways. They sometimes seek counsel from the teacher, who may well have become the object of some transference. When these students do seek us out, we must be careful to restrict our interactions to the academic arena as much as possible to avoid the abuse of power that has been granted us in this situation. This applies perhaps even more to those teachers who have counseling practices outside the university than to those whose work is purely academic. The additional layer of hurdles arising from the need to avoid approaches that convey an advocacy stance regarding religious ideas creates at times a very tricky situation.

Out of respect for the risks my students take, I approach the material gently, always conscious of how demanding the process of coming to understand Jung's thought can be. I offer support through ongoing dialogue, interject frequent reminders of Jung's agenda and of the personal benefits that await those willing to take these risks, and avoid the temptation to "therapize" when students express difficulty along the way. In the end, the rewards of teaching the work generated by Jung's lifelong engagement with Christianity exceed by far the difficulties one encounters during the journey toward understanding.

NOTES

1. Roger Brooke, "Jung in the Academy: A Response to David Tacey," *Journal of Analytical Psychology* 42 (April 1997): 285.

2. David Tacey, "Negotiating the Numinous: The Challenges of Teaching Jung in the University," in *Who Owns Jung?* ed. Ann Casement (London: Karnac, 2007), 62–65.

3. Renos Papadopoulos, "Is Teaching Jung within University Possible? A Response to David Tacey," *Journal of Analytical Psychology* 42 (April 1997): 299.

4. David Tacey, "Jung in the Academy: Devotions and Resistances," *Journal of Analytical Psychology* 42 (April 1997): 269.

5. Jill Scott, *Electra after Freud: Myth and Culture* (Ithaca, NY: Cornell University Press, 2005), 8.

6. C. Kilmartin and D. Dervin, "Inaccurate Representation of the Electra Complex in Psychology Textbooks," *Teaching of Psychology* 24 (April 1997): 269–70.

7. C. G. Jung, "The Theory of Psychoanalysis," in *Collected Works of C. G. Jung* (Princeton, NJ: Princeton University Press, 1931–1961), 4:154–55.

8. In the 1963 ruling *School District of Abington v. Schemmp*, Justice Brennan wrote: "The State must be steadfastly neutral in all matters of faith, and neither favor nor inhibit religion." For a more detailed exploration of these issues, see Charlene P. E. Burns, "Do Cognitive Dissonance Theory and the Induced-Compliance Paradigm Raise Concerns for Teaching Religious Studies?" *Teaching Theology and Religion* 9 (January 2006): 3–8.

9. Jung, *Letters*, ed. Gerhard Adler and Aniela Jaffé, trans. R. F. C. Hull (Princeton, NJ: Princeton University Press, 1973–1974), 2:518–19.

10. Murray Stein, *Jung's Treatment of Christianity: The Psychotherapy of a Religious Tradition* (Wilmette, IL: Chiron, 1986), 142.

11. For a more complete exploration of the relationship among Kant, Schleiermacher, and Jung, see Burns, *More Moral Than God: Taking Responsibility for Religious Violence* (Lanham, MD: Rowman & Littlefield, 2008).

12. Jung, *Letters*, 1:375.

13. Roger Scruton, *Kant: A Very Short Introduction* (Oxford: Oxford University Press, 2001), 44.

14. Allan Wood, *Kant* (Malden, MA: Blackwell, 2005), for example, argues that Kant offered two incompatible interpretations of the phenomenal and noumenal and says that attempts to reconcile them are simply wrong.

15. Eckhart Förster, "Is There a 'Gap' in Kant's Critical System?" *Journal of the History of Philosophy* 25 (October 1987): 533–55.

16. Thandeka, "Schleiermacher's 'Dialektik': The Discovery of the Self That Kant Lost," *Harvard Theological Review* 85 (October 1992): 433–52.

17. For criticisms of Jung's epistemology and methods, see Marilyn Nagy, *Philosophical Issues* (Albany: State University of New York Press, 1991); and Michael Palmer, *Freud and Jung* (London: Routledge, 1997).

18. Jung, *Letters*, 2:115.

19. Burns, *More Moral*, 100–109.

20. Friedrich Schleiermacher, *Dialectic, or the Art of Doing Philosophy. A Study of the 1811 Notes*, trans. Terrence N. Tice (Atlanta: Scholar's Press, 1996), 29.

21. Thandeka, *The Embodied Self: Friedrich Schleiermacher's Solution to Kant's Problem of the Empirical Self* (Albany: State University of New York Press, 1995), 22.

22. Schleiermacher, *Dialectic*, 15n25, 16–17.

23. Thandeka, *Embodied Self*, 3.

24. Ibid., 23–29.

25. Ibid., 95.

26. Ibid., 96.

27. Ibid., 99.

28. Friedrich Schleiermacher, *The Christian Faith*, ed. H. R. MacIntosh and J. S. Stewart. (Edinburgh, Scotland: T. & T. Clark, 1989), 12.

29. Schleiermacher, *Christian Faith*, 132.

30. Ibid., 12.

31. Ibid., 132.

32. Renos Papadopoulos, "Jung's Epistemology and Methodology," in *The Handbook of Jungian Psychology: Theory, Practice, & Applications*, ed. Renos K. Papadopoulos (London: Routledge, 2006), 41.

33. Jung, *Collected Works*, 8:283–342.

34. Ibid., 9i:73.

35. Jung, *Psychology & Religion, the Terry Lectures* (New Haven, CT: Yale University Press, 1938–1966), 73.

36. Jung, *Collected Works*, 11:558.

37. Ibid., 9ii:34, 63, 109.

38. Ibid., 10:31.

39. Ibid., 8:420.

40. Schleiermacher, *Christian Faith*, 12.

41. Jung, *C. G. Jung Speaking Interviews and Encounters*, ed. William McGuire and R. F. C. Hull (Princeton, NJ: Princeton University Press, 1977), 428.

42. Jung, *Collected Works*, 12:11n6.

43. Jung, *Letters*, 2:435–436.

44. Stein, *Jung's Treatment*, 19.

45. For a more complete discussion of these issues, see Burns, "Cognitive Dissonance," 3–8.

46. Tacey, "Teaching Jung," 5.

47. Eddie Harmon-Jones, "Toward an Understanding of the Motivation Underlying Dissonance Effect: Is the Production of Aversive Consequences Necessary?" in *Cognitive Dissonance: Progress on a Pivotal Theory in Social Psychology*, ed. E. Harmon-Jones and Judson Mills (Washington, DC: American Psychological Association, 1999), 95.

48. Leon Festinger, *A Theory of Cognitive Dissonance* (Stanford, CA: Stanford University Press, 1957), 1–31.

49. Christopher T. Burris, E. Harmon-Jones, and W. Ryan Tarpley, "'By Faith Alone': Religious Agitation and Cognitive Dissonance," *Basic and Applied Social Psychology* 19 (1997): 17–31.

50. Jung, *Collected Works*, 17:180.

51. Ibid., 18:667.

REFERENCES

Bishop, Paul. "C. G. Jung and 'Naturmystick': The Early Poem 'Gedanken in Einer Frühlingsnacht.'" *German Life and Letters* 56 (October 2003): 327–343.

Brooke, Roger. "Jung in the Academy: A Response to David Tacey." *Journal of Analytical Psychology* 42 (April 1997): 285–296.

Burns, Charlene P. E. "Do Cognitive Dissonance Theory and the Induced-Compliance Paradigm Raise Concerns for Teaching Religious Studies?" *Teaching Theology and Religion* 9 (January 2006): 3–8.

Burns, Charlene P. E. *More Moral Than God: Taking Responsibility for Religious Violence.* Lanham, MD: Rowman & Littlefield, 2008.

Burris, Christopher T., E. Harmon-Jones, and W. Ryan Tarpley. "'By Faith Alone': Religious Agitation and Cognitive Dissonance." *Basic and Applied Social Psychology* 19 (1997): 17–31.

Festinger, Leon. *A Theory of Cognitive Dissonance.* Stanford, CA: Stanford University Press, 1957.

Förster, Eckhart. "Is There a 'Gap' in Kant's Critical System?" *Journal of the History of Philosophy* 25 (October 1987): 533–555.

Harmon-Jones, Eddie. "Toward an Understanding of the Motivation Underlying Dissonance Effect: Is the Production of Aversive Consequences Necessary?" In *Cognitive Dissonance: Progress on a Pivotal Theory in Social Psychology*, ed. E. Harmon-Jones and Judson Mills, 71–99. Washington, DC: American Psychological Association, 1999.

Jung, C. G. "The Theory of Psychoanalysis." In *Collected Works* 4:83–226. Princeton, NJ: Princeton University Press, 1913/1961.

Jung, C. G. "Mind and Earth." In *Collected Works* 10:29–49. Princeton, NJ: Princeton University Press, 1927/1964.

Jung, C. G. "The Structure and Dynamics of the Psyche." In *Collected Works* 8:139–158. Princeton, NJ: Princeton University Press, 1931/1961.

Jung, C. G. "The Development of Personality." In *Collected Works* 17:167–86. Princeton, NJ: Princeton University Press, 1932/1954.

Jung, C. G. *Psychology and Religion. The Terry Lectures.* New Haven, CT: Yale University Press, 1938/1966.

Jung, C. G. "Psychology and Alchemy." In *Collected Works* 12. Princeton, NJ: Princeton University Press, 1944/1969.

Jung, C. G. "Religion and Psychology: A Reply to Martin Buber." In *Collected Works* 18:663–670. Princeton, NJ: Princeton University Press, 1950/1976.

Jung, C. G. *Answer to Job.* In *Collected Works* 11:355–470. Princeton, NJ: Princeton University Press, 1952.

Jung, C. G. "On the Nature of the Psyche." In *Collected Works* 8:159–236. Princeton, NJ: Princeton University Press, 1954/1961.

Jung, C. G. "Aion: Researches into the Phenomenology of the Self." In *Collected Works* 9ii. Princeton, NJ: Princeton University Press, 1959/1969.

Jung, C. G. "The Archetypes and the Collective Unconscious." In *Collected Works* 9i. Princeton, NJ: Princeton University Press, 1969.

Jung, C. G. *C. G. Jung Speaking: Interviews and Encounters*, ed. William McGuire and R. F. C. Hull. Princeton, NJ: Princeton University Press, 1977.

Kilmartin, C., and D. Dervin. "Inaccurate Representation of the Electra Complex in Psychology Textbooks." *Teaching of Psychology* 24 (April 1997): 269–270.

Nagy, Marilyn. *Philosophical Issues in the Psychology of C. G. Jung.* Albany: State University of New York Press, 1991.

Palmer, Michael. *Freud and Jung on Religion.* London: Routledge, 1997.

Papadopoulos, Renos. "Is Teaching Jung within University Possible? A Response to David Tacey." *Journal of Analytical Psychology* 42 (April 1997): 297–301.

Papadopoulos, Renos. "Jung's Epistemology and Methodology." In *The Handbook of Jungian Psychology: Theory, Practice, & Applications*, ed. Renos K. Papadopoulos, 7–53. London: Routledge, 2006.

Schleiermacher, Friedrich. *The Christian Faith*, ed. H. R. MacIntosh and J. S. Stewart. Edinburgh, Scotland: T. & T. Clark, 1989.

Schleiermacher, Friedrich. *Dialectic, or the Art of Doing Philosophy. A Study of the* 1811 *Notes*, trans. Terrence N. Tice. Atlanta, GA: Scholar's Press, 1996.

Scott, Jill. *Electra after Freud: Myth and Culture.* Ithaca, NY: Cornell University Press, 2005.

Scruton, Roger. *Kant, A Very Short Introduction.* Oxford: Oxford University Press, 2001.

Stein, Murray. *Jung's Treatment of Christianity: The Psychotherapy of a Religious Tradition.* Wilmette, IL: Chiron, 1986.

Tacey, David. "Jung in the Academy: Devotions and Resistances." *Journal of Analytical Psychology* 42 (April 1997): 269–283.

Tacey, David. "Teaching Jung in the University." In *The Uses of Subjective Experience.* ANZSJA Conference Proceedings. October 20–21, 2007, Melbourne, Australia. At http://www.anzsja.org.au/subjective_experience/TACEY%20PAPER%20 AUG%209.PDF.

Tacey, David. "Negotiating the Numinous: The Challenges of Teaching Jung in the University." In *Who Owns Jung?* ed. Ann Casement, 53–73. London: Karnac, 2007.

Thandeka. "Schleiermacher's 'Dialektik': The Discovery of the Self That Kant Lost." *Harvard Theological Review* 85 (October 1992): 433–452.

Thandeka. *The Embodied Self: Friedrich Schleiermacher's Solution to Kant's Problem of the Empirical Self.* Albany: State University of New York Press, 1995.

Wood, Allan. *Kant.* Malden, MA: Blackwell, 2005.

Wulff, David. *Psychology of Religion: Classic and Contemporary.* Hoboken, NJ: John Wiley & Sons, 1997.

7

God on the Couch

Teaching Jung's *Answer to Job*

Clodagh Weldon

As difficult and controversial—and vexing—as Jung's *Answer to Job* is, it is a great text to stimulate and challenge, indeed, to provoke students to think about God and the human person. Teaching the text in a Catholic university to undergraduates in a theology course presents unique pedagogical challenges and requires a baptism by fire into analytical psychology. This chapter, intended for those teaching the text to beginners, starts with an exposition of *Answer to Job* and then explores Jung's analytical psychological approach to scripture, offering a couple of teaching strategies that I have found to be very effective in the process.

The Text

Answer to Job essentially articulates Jung's struggle with the eternal questions raised by the story of an upright man in the hands of a seemingly capricious God. From a theological perspective, the work places God in the image of man or, as F. X. Charet expresses it, puts God on the couch.[1] For Jung, the "solution" to the problem of God raised in Job is to see God as Trinity as a symbol of the process of "unconscious maturation taking place within the individual."[2] In other words, God as Trinity represents the process of individuation. The three persons of the Trinity represent the three phases in the development of personality: unconscious, conscious, individuated. In the first stage, Jung's unconscious God, God the Father, is both good and evil and unconsciously fails to differentiate between the two. Jung writes, "The father denotes the earlier stage of consciousness when one was still a child, still dependent on a definite, ready-made pattern of existence which is habitual and has the character of law. It is a passing, unreflective condition, a mere awareness of what is given, without intellectual or moral judgement."[3] Thus in the book of Job, Yahweh is not conscious and is, therefore, unreflecting. Jung argues that the reason for this is that Yahweh's wife, Sophia, has been replaced by a second wife, Israel. Yahweh's "anamnesis of Sophia" (or, in Jungian terms, the repression of his *anima*) results in the exclusion of *eros* and leaves humanity pining with Job for her love of mankind (Job 28:12).[4] Jung writes "the paragon of all creation is not a man but a monster! Yahweh has no eros, no relationship to man, but only a purpose man must help him fulfill."[5] Yahweh's anamnesis of his first wife, Sophia, shifts the focus to the faithfulness of his bride, Israel. As he observes the incessant unfaithfulness of the harlot Israel, Yahweh is consumed, "jealous and mistrustful like any other husband."[6] Consequently, when Satan insinuates that Job could be unfaithful, a mistrustful Yahweh listens to Satan and agrees to test his faithfulness by inflicting great suffering on him.

Jung sees the problem clearly: Christianity teaches that God is all good, the *Summum Bonum* (indeed this is the *persona* that God presents to Job), and yet this seems to be contradicted in the god images of the Old Testament (and additionally, he will argue, in empirical psychology)[7] where God is also the *infinum malum*.[8] Thus in *Answer to Job*, Jung's hypothesis is that when Yahweh inflicts suffering on Job, his actions are those of one who is unconscious, one who is unreflecting, one who "fails to consult his omniscience."[9] Although Jung admits that "from a human point of view," the behavior of Yahweh "is so intolerable," he argues that "it is the behaviour of an unconscious being who cannot be judged morally. Yahweh is a *phenomenon* and, as Job says, 'not a man.'"[10] Elsewhere, Jung maintains that God is unconscious and cannot be held morally accountable; unconscious God does not know the difference between right and wrong. He writes, "His consciousness seems to be not much more than a primitive 'awareness' which knows no reflection and no morality. One merely perceives and acts blindly, without conscious inclusion of the subject, whose individual existence raises no problems. Today we would call such a state psychologically 'unconscious,' and in the eyes of the law it would be described as *non compos mentis*...."[11]

If the God of Job was, as Jung suggested, unconscious, the question then becomes: what happened to bring about a change in God such that the God encountered in the New Testament is no longer, in psychological terms, an unconscious God who fails to consciously differentiate between good and evil? Jung proposes that two figures, Job and Sophia, are the key to Yahweh's consciousness. First, in standing firm against Yahweh's attempt to corrupt him,[12] Job has shown himself, Jung suggests, to be morally superior to his creator. Indeed, this is a view Jung had expressed long before he wrote *Answer to Job*: "The victory of the vanquished and oppressed is obvious. Job stands morally higher than Yahweh. In this respect the creature has surpassed the creator. As always when an external event touches some unconscious knowledge, this knowledge can reach consciousness."[13] As Jung sees it, the steadfastness of Job has made Yahweh cognizant of his Shadow side. Yahweh cannot dismiss Job's moral superiority, and this leads to reflection, the source of which is his wife, Sophia. It is She, says Jung, who "realises" God's thoughts, clothing them in material form.[14] Commenting on this realization, Jung writes, "[Yahweh] raises himself above his earlier primitive level of consciousness by indirectly acknowledging that the man Job is morally superior to him and that therefore he has to catch up and become human himself."[15]

Viewed from this perspective, the Incarnation is not so much about redeeming man (other than *from* God)[16] as about redeeming God. If there is any atonement, it is God's atoning for his crime against Job, becoming man because he has wronged a man.[17] In his later writings, Jung would express this notion in the more theologically explicit language of *kenosis*, though reinterpreting it from a psychoanalytic perspective. He writes, "[Yahweh] sees that incarnation is unavoidable because man's insight is a step ahead of him. He must 'empty himself of his Godhead and assume the shape of the *doulos* [cf. Philippians 2:6]' i.e. man in his lowest existence, in order to obtain the jewel which man possesses in his self reflection...."[18]

For Jung, then, it is *man*—in the person of Job—who is instrumental in bringing about the Incarnation. Job does not succumb to the "divine paradox," the source of his suffering,[19] and this forces *Yahweh's* self-reflection and ultimately leads Yahweh to a higher level of consciousness through Incarnation. Jung remarks, "Yahweh's decision to become man is a symbol of the development that had to supervene when man becomes conscious of the sort of God image he is confronted with...."[20] Jung's reading of the Incarnation is not (at least as he sees it) theological but rather a purely psychological observation that the Incarnation represents "the differentiation of Yahweh's consciousness."[21] Jung writes that "it is not the world that is to be changed; rather it is God who intends to change his own nature."[22] God's nature is changed in that to bring about self-realization God incarnates only his light side, casting off his dark side and becoming wholly good. Jung writes of the Incarnation, "This was a decisive step, not only for man, but also for the Creator—Who, in the eyes of those who had been delivered from darkness, cast off his dark qualities and became the *Summum Bonum*...."[23]

This, however, raises a question for Jung (a decisively theological question): if God is now all good, why does evil continue to exist? It is a problem that Jung had earlier explored in his studies on Christ as an archetype of the Self in his work *Aion*. Here he writes that "the morally ambiguous Yahweh becomes an exclusively good God, while everything evil was united in the devil."[24] In *Answer to Job*, Jung argues that if God is now the *Summum Bonum*, then the continuing prowess of the devil must be accounted for. He writes:

> the power of evil is supposedly overcome, and one can hardly
> believe that a loving father after the whole complicated arrangement
> of salvation in Christ, the atonement and declaration of love for

mankind, would again let loose his evil watchdog on his children in complete disregard of all that had gone before. Why this wearisome forbearance towards Satan? Why this stubborn projection of evil to man, whom he has made so weak, so faltering, and so stupid that we are quite incapable of resisting his wicked sons? Why not pull up evil by the roots?[25]

Jung argues that the reason for the continued action of Satan is that, psychologically speaking, God got into "dissociation" at the Incarnation. That is to say, in becoming the *Summum Bonum*, evil in the person of the devil was differentiated from God. Indeed, Jung had earlier argued the same point in a slightly different way when he accused Christianity of "splitting off" half of the opposites in the person of Satan.[26] What he means by this is that in his becoming conscious, God just incarnated his good side and neglected his shadow side. This further implies that when Jung talks of God becoming conscious, he is not talking about a process of self-reflection wherein evil is rooted out. Rather Jung's point is that being conscious is about being able to *differentiate* such things as good and evil; it is about becoming moral. The point is well made some years later in a letter to James Kirsch. Jung writes, "The purpose of the Christian reformation through Jesus was to eliminate the evil moral consequences that were caused by the amoral divine prototype...."[27]

However, as I have noted, Jung thinks that this differentiation, which he saw as so necessary, has in fact led to dissociation in the Godhead. He writes that "in time it becomes obvious that the Incarnation has caused a loss among the supreme powers: the indispensable dark side has been left behind or stripped off, and the feminine aspect is missing."[28]

For Jung, evil must be integrated because without the dark side, God is not fully human. Jung's problem with this is that if the father of Christ is the *Summum Bonum*, then "the darkness is missing and Christ has not become man, because man is afflicted with darkness...."[29] Jung argues that evil is the opposite and necessary complement of good, without which the symbol is incomplete. Thus for Jung, the Christ symbol lacks wholeness, and if God is to be whole, then evil must once again be included in God. He writes that "a further act of incarnation becomes necessary. Through atheism, materialism and agnosticism, the powerful yet one-sided aspect of the *Summum Bonum* is weakened, so that it cannot keep out the dark side, and incidentally the feminine factor, any more. 'Anti Christ' and 'devil' gain in ascendancy: God asserts his power through the revelation of his darkness and destructiveness."[30] In proposing that the Godhead be transformed to include evil, Jung is making the point that psychologically the Christian symbol of Trinity is incomplete because it lacks a fourth, which is the symbol of wholeness. Jung had in fact argued for the inclusion of evil, of the material, and of the feminine in his 1942 work "A Psychological Approach to the Trinity," suggesting that their omission from traditional Christian doctrine resulted in images of God that were one-sidedly masculine, good, and spiritual. Consequently, Jung believed that in denying the fourth, the God image of the Western psyche was impoverished. So for

Jung, evil is integrated, and God is (psychologically) made whole. Finally, the Holy Spirit is sent to continue this process (representing the third stage, individuation), namely, to create a new humanity in the image of God.

In summary, Jung has, as he advocated, "revised religious formulas with the aid of psychological insight."[31] The insight was essentially that the human psyche is naturally destined to individuate or become whole in a process that involves a confrontation with the unconscious, particularly the shadow side, in an attempt to achieve psychic balance (or, in Jungian terms, "the reconciliation of opposites"). In other words, unconscious aspects of the psyche that have been repressed are integrated into consciousness. It is with the insight of this process, which Jung calls "individuation," that Jung has "revised" religious formulas in Job, essentially by projecting this process onto the Godhead. (Jung, of course, would argue that god images, because they are symbols of wholeness, reflect the nature of the opposites, and so a god image without a shadow side could not be a symbol of wholeness.)[32] To state Jung's "revision" more explicitly, the God encountered in Job is unconscious of the dark side of his personality, Job forces that confrontation with the shadow side (which then becomes dissociated), and, finally, evil is included or integrated into the Godhead. The result is a transformation of personality or, in Jungian terms, individuation. It should, I hope, be clear why Jung therefore viewed the Trinity as a symbol of the process of "unconscious maturation taking place within the individual."[33]

Teaching Jung in a *Theology* Course

I teach Jung's *Answer to Job* to undergraduates at a Catholic university in a course titled Hebrew Scriptures II: Prophets and Wisdom. The 200-level biblical studies course is offered by the theology department, and it explores the Old Testament Prophets and Wisdom literature, including the biblical book of Job. The course also satisfies the core area requirement for theology. It is just one of thirty-one different courses a student may take to fulfill the requirement. In composition, it is a very mixed class: freshmen through seniors, a handful of theology majors, majority nonmajors, those for whom this is the only theology course they will take in college (required!), those for whom this is the sixth or seventh theology class, those with no theological background, those who had been through CCD or Catholic school, non-Catholics, those of no religious backgrounds, traditional-age and non-traditional-age students, some ready for graduate work, others struggling with undergraduate work. Eleven percent of my students speak Polish as their first language, and 25 percent are Spanish speaking; typically, both groups are traditional Catholics. Thus even before we get to the text, the question arises of how to reach and challenge all of these students!

That the course is offered in the theology department (rather than religious studies) has some ramifications for teaching Jung that I think are worth discussing (not least because Jung saw theology as "pretty useless"[34] and its practitioners "terribly superficial"!).[35] Theology in its traditional definition is "faith seeking understanding"—in this case, the shared faith primarily, but not exclusively, of the Catholic tradition in which the university is rooted. It is, to use Aquinas's language, the science (*scientia*) not only of religion as a human phenomenon but also of God (however tentative and humble that science must be). To speak of theology as a *science* of God is to use the word *science* in a way that we would hardly recognize today, and yet Aquinas calls theology a "science" because it proceeds from principles that are certain— certain because revealed by God (IaIae q.1 art.1 ad 2). As such, theology in a Catholic university enjoys a privileged position in relation to other disciplines as "queen of the sciences" (though others outside theology may quibble with this!). Indeed, as "the summit of knowledge," it is, to use Maritain's words, "architectonic par excellence" (Maritain 1948: 19), providing the framework for integrating all knowledge as directed toward God, the source of all Truth. With this understanding, analytical psychology could never be in an equal relationship with theology, for no other science comes above theology. Thus theology has a certain primacy in any interdisciplinary conversation, including that with Jung.

Some have raised the question of whether faith is a drawback to effective teaching (see, for example, Ann Ulanov's *Spirit in Jung*), a question that stems from the notion that teaching theology could potentially be uncritical—a monologue, catechesis, or as the Irish Dominican Liam Walsh puts it, a "doctrinaire presentation of pre-established truths."[36] But this is not how Aquinas understood theology. On the contrary, his model speaks to students of the importance of being open to the ideas and questions of the day, of the need for engagement with secular knowledge and dead people (let's not forget books!), of the importance of making a critical yet sympathetic study of those with whom they disagree, and of the opportunities for learning in such encounters. It speaks also of the possibility of an assimilation of new forms of truth into the unity of an individual's own synthesis centered in God.[37]

Teaching *Answer to Job*

By the time we read the biblical book of Job and Jung's *Answer to Job*, the students will have spent half the semester grappling with an image of an Old Testament God, which, theologically speaking, leaves them rather uncomfortable: a God who pours out his fury like fire (Nahum 1:2–8), who "fashion(s) evil" against his people (Jeremiah 18:11), who "prepare[s] a slaughter feast" in punishment for their sins (Zephaniah 1:7), a God who "brings forth the weapons of his wrath" (Jeremiah 50:25), threatening a rebellious people that "their infants shall be dashed in pieces, and their women with child shall be ripped up" (Hosea 13:16), a God who proclaims, "I form the light, and create the darkness, I make well-being and create woe; I, the LORD, do all these things" (Isaiah 45:7).

As noted, most (though not all) of my students are Catholics for whom God is all good—the *Summum Bonum*—and they are unsettled to encounter such an image of God in the Bible. It triggers wonderful discussions on God images, on the nature of God, on what it might mean when Christians profess belief in the inspiration and inerrancy of scripture. Is God really like this? Did the authors get it wrong, and how could they if this is the Bible, the inspired word of God? Are these just images, or do they tell us something of the nature of God? Isn't God supposed to be good? Why is God not like this in the New Testament? Does God become good? Is the God of the Old Testament the same as the God of the New Testament? Has God evolved? Pedagogically, I find that it is helpful to model to the students that it is okay (and good!) to question. In fact, in a faith-based institution, it is often *necessary* to do so: some students are afraid to question their faith and adopt a defensive stance in relation to the material; others feel it is sinful or impious to question. Models would include, for example, Kant's Enlightenment battle cry "Sapere Aude," Aquinas's method in the *Summa,* Ricouer's first and second naiveté,—and Job's questioning God against the conventional wisdom of his day. If this is done early in the semester, the students are then well disposed and suitably habituated to read and question a text like *Answer to Job.*

Grappling with the questions provoked by the image of God in the Prophets, *Answer to Job* provides the students with another perspective for consideration and encourages them to consider multiple perspectives and methodological approaches to scripture. Students are, for the most part, familiar with the book of Job. They know something about academic approaches to the Bible, the historical critical method (a method of which Jung was deeply critical because, as Rollins notes, it sacrificed the numinous, severed scripture from "living religious processes" and demythologized symbols),[38] source criticism, literary criticism, form and redaction criticism. But Jung's approach to Job is unlike anything they have read: as Bishop points out, it "de-familiarizes a text with which we might all be too familiar."[39]

In this state of defamiliarization, I encourage students to become conscious of the lenses through which they read the biblical book of Job, of their own frameworks, and of their own approach to biblical interpretation. Is it History? Faith? Literature? A good book? Theology? In *The Meaning of Jesus,* Tom Wright says, "We all see the world through colored spectacles of our own personal histories, backgrounds, assumptions and so on.... Part of the process is becoming aware that one's spectacles are almost certainly distorting the picture."[40] I ask my students to consider, "What are the lenses through which you read the biblical text? What history, what culture, what life experiences do you bring with you as you read the biblical texts?" Once cognizant of the lenses through which they approach the text (at least the conscious ones!), we discuss the dangers of reading the texts *only* from our own perspectives, and I challenge my students to remove their lenses (inasmuch as this is possible) and situate themselves in Jung's world, to appreciate his "interpretive framework,"[41] and to read the text with Jungian eyes. This is no small task! Helping students understand Jung's analytical "interpretive framework" in one or two classes in a course that is not primarily focused on Jung presents enormous challenges. Yet if I fail in this task, students will read Jung in their own frameworks (precisely as reviewers did in Jung's day) and therefore misunderstand him.

Defamiliarization: Framing Jung's Method

Students in my course are at a serious disadvantage with *Answer to Job* in that they have no background in Jung; indeed, many have never even heard of him. In teaching the text, I have found it helpful to situate it in the narrative of Jung's life and, in particular, Jung's relationship with his father as articulated in *Memories, Dreams, Reflections*. I do this for two reasons: first, because of the appeal of a story; second because *Answer to Job* is an answer to his father, to Victor White, to modern man in search of a soul. If *Job* is an answer to his father (and what his father represents), it helps if students understand something of his father and his father's faith.

For Jung, God was a living mystery experienced within the psyche. For Jung's father ("how hopelessly he was entrapped by the Church and its theological thinking"),[42] God was utterly transcendent, revealed through scripture, the tradition of the Church, and reason. It was for Jung the "tragedy" of his youth to see his father oppressed, as he saw it, by the externals of religion and closed to an *internal* experience of God. Jung was deeply frustrated by this failure to experience the god image within.[43] For students studying Jung in a theology class, it is significant that much Catholic theology is (and Jung recognized this) grounded in Aquinas, for whom divine transcendence made immediate experience of God almost impossible.[44] For Jung, Aquinas (among others) was guilty of "the prejudice that the deity is *outside* man," the effects of which were seen in the "systematic blindness" of the West, in a theology dictated by consciousness and intellectual abstractions.[45] With no appreciation of the unconscious, as Jung perceived it, theology had little psychological value.[46]

In framing Jung's methodological approach (in a very short period of time), I highlight three points: the first is, to use Jung's language, *"consideration of psychological premise."*[47] Jung was not a theologian or a metaphysician but "an empiricist": he established "empirical" boundaries within which to do his psychology that were, strictly speaking, phenomenological. This methodology Jung had derived from Kant, in particular the idea that things-in-themselves (*noumena*) are totally inaccessible and therefore one must restrict oneself to things as they appear (*phenomena*). Embracing Kant as the basis for the scientific approach to the psyche, what Jung himself called "Kantian epistemology expressed in everyday psychological language,"[48] Jung could not comment on the thing in itself but only on the thing as it appears.

The implications of this bring me to the second and related point: that *when Jung talks about God, he's talking about the God image.*[49] In other words, adopting a Kantian-based empiricism only allowed him to talk of things as they appeared (i.e., god image) and not things in themselves (i.e., God). Jung had precluded any possibility of coming to terms with the transcendent God. He had no choice but to confine himself to the empirical, and this logically excluded the metaphysical.

Pedagogically, these two points raise significant challenges for my students because they lack the philosophical background in Kant that is needed to understand Jung. To illustrate the distinction between archetype and archetypal image, I have been known to preface any discussion of Kant by placing a large magnet on my desk, covering it with a sheet of hot pink paper (so that the magnet is hidden) and shaking iron filings onto it. I then ask an intrigued student to tap the sheet of paper while others in the room gather around the desk and observe what they see (i.e., a pattern or image that reveals the magnetic field). Although an imperfect analogy of the hidden power of archetypes as manifested in archetypal images, it is effective because it is dramatic and it is visual. Students remember the day the theology professor "did that crazy thing with the magnet." But more important, they remember the distinction between archetype and archetypal image, between *noumena* and the *phenomena*, between God and God image.

Once students have grasped this concept, the waters are muddied once again, for Jung's distinction between God and God image is riddled with ambiguity. He often uses the two words interchangeably, and what he actually means by "God" or "god image" is somewhat elusive. On the one level, it seems that Jung is distinguishing between the archetypal form (the eternal and primordial "God" archetype that is unknowable) and the archetypal contents (the god images by which the psychic experience of "God" or the Self is represented). In other words, "God"—the god within—can only be known ("revealed") by god images.[50] On another level, and taking this a step further, Jung could mean that the God image or the God archetype is to be distinguished from God as an objective reality (external to the psyche). For while Jung admits that "an archetype presupposes an imprinter"[51]—which could be taken to imply that the experience of the God image presupposes the objective existence of God—his methodology permitted him to say only that a psychic experience is "understood and formulated"[52] as God (which, of course, says nothing whatsoever about the objective existence of God).

The third point to note in framing Jung's method in Job is that when Jung criticized "God," he was criticizing Western *images* of god; that is, from a psychological ("empirical") perspective, it was an evaluation of the inadequacy or incompleteness of statements about God.[53] In particular, Jung thought that human consciousness is necessary to bring about a transformation of the god image to include the dark side and the feminine.

There are, of course, many more points that could be raised in framing Jung's approach, but for my biblical studies course, students will at least have the capacity to appreciate Jung's lenses in *Job* if they grasp the three points articulated above. For more advanced students or for courses with Jung as primary focus (rather than just one or two classes in a sixteen-week course), I would recommend Paul Bishop's *Jung's Answer to Job: A Commentary*. In particular, see Bishop's identification of six hidden methodological assumptions in *Answer to Job*, which, he argues, the student willing to work should be able to figure out.[54]

Teaching Strategies

To conclude this chapter, I would like to highlight a couple of teaching strategies I have found to be very effective in teaching *Answer to Job*. The reading is assigned with such hearty emphasis that students come to class having plowed their way through the text. I hand out blank note cards and instruct the students to imagine that they have been asked to write a review of the book (this also works well as a more detailed written assignment). After ten minutes or so, I collect these and read them back to the class, interpolating with comments and discussion, and drawing parallels between their reviews and the reviews written by scholars in the mid-1950s (for example, Karl Barth, Martin Buber, and Fr. Victor White).

The student reviews generally fall into three categories: those who love it, those who hate it, and those who are utterly perplexed by it. For those in the first category, it is clear that Jung stirs up something not just intellectually but also emotionally, a phenomenon about which Ulanov has written at some length.[55] This is true also of the second category, the defenders of the faith who dismiss the text as blasphemy or heresy: how can evil be included in God who is the *Summum Bonum*? If God is good and good is being, then how can evil be? How can development occur in God if God is *actus purus*? How can God's nature change if God is perfect and immutable? How can you make us read this book in a Catholic university? I point out that Jung himself was "fully aware of the outrage" the book would provoke,[56] that he knew "from a theological angle," it was "downright blasphemy."[57] I draw attention to the lenses here: "from a *theological* angle." What other angles might we consider, what is *Jung's* angle, and does the charge remain? Finally are the students who are utterly perplexed, defeated by the difficulty of the text, and, uninitiated in analytical psychology, lacking the capacity to understand the language Jung speaks. Jung himself notes that "from the standpoint of rationalist commonsense," the book is "a heap of illogical and feeble-minded phantasma."[58] Again I draw attention to the lenses here to encourage students to be conscious of this: "from the standpoint of rationalist commonsense." It is reassuring to these students to hear that Jung was not considering "the average reader" when he wrote *Answer to Job!*[59]

This exercise is effective for a number of reasons: (1) it gives the professor immediate insight into what has been understood and misunderstood, into student assumptions, into careful and cursory reading; (2) it illustrates that all three categories of student are challenged by the text but in very different ways and indicative of the different lenses through which they read it; (3) it begins the process of shifting from defamiliarization to a framing of Jung's method; and (4) it authenticates student voices by identification with the scholarly community.

A variation on this in-class exercise that I've found works well is to give students Fr. Victor White's damning review of *Answer to Job*, which appeared in *Blackfriars* in March 1955.[60] In it, White describes the text as "destructive and childish,"[61] a book of "infantile quality."[62] Jung's grievance against God had initially stirred up all sorts of dark places in White's psyche ("It is the most exciting and moving book I have read in years: and somehow it arouses tremendous bonds of sympathy between us, and lights up all sorts of dark places both in the Scriptures and in my own psyche"),[63] but in the review White writes, "Is [Jung], after the manner of his own 'Yahweh,' duped by some satanic trickster into purposely torturing his friends and devotees? Or is he, more rationally, purposely putting them to the test to discover how much they will stand rather than admit the fallibility of their master—or how many, Job like, will venture to observe that the emperor has appeared in public without his clothes?"[64]

The review continues in like tone, charging Jung with taking the principle of private interpretation of scripture to an extreme[65] and of deliberately reading the Bible "through a pair of highly distorting spectacles,"[66] the spectacles of his own psyche. Further, says White, Jung is guilty of "naive misunderstandings and misrepresentations of elementary doctrine,"[67] for example, that God is perfect, triune and self-sufficient. The charges are unfair as White himself admits and can be refuted *if* one accepts Jung's methodology, in other words, if one accepts that when Jung talks about God, "he is talking about endopsychic images considered as psychological phenomena and not as signs for what they merely represent."[68] White did accept Jung's methodology and had often made the important distinction between God and god image in defense of Jung. In view of this, White's accusation that Jung has a naive understanding of doctrine is surprising, for it looks like he *is* criticizing Jung as if Jung really did think that God (rather than god image) is a quaternity and not a Trinity, evil as well as good. But White then dismisses these criticisms as unfair, thereby revealing that this was a clever rhetorical device to portray the standard theological critique of Jung: that *Answer to Job* is an attack on God Godself. Dismissing this attack, White affirms that although Jung is critical of Christian doctrines about God, his critique that Christian doctrines about God are deficient stems from a *psychological* perspective. In other words, *empirically* speaking, Christian doctrines about God are incomplete. In upholding the distinction between empiricism and metaphysics, White affirms his conviction that Jung is primarily concerned with images of God. He is, however, highly critical that these images are not Job's but Jung's.

Once the students have read this review, I ask them to write a letter in response—as White's dear friend C. G. Jung! It is a difficult assignment for those who don't know Jung well. But it also has the capacity to demonstrate that they have understood Jung's interpretive framework and are able to grapple with its implications for Christian theology. Further, students can read Jung's actual letter afterward. In it, they will see that, predictably, Jung was offended by the directness of White's criticism and particularly that it had been voiced so publicly.[69] Far from being a parade of the splenetic shadow, Jung defended *Answer to Job* as "a straightforward application of [his] psychological principles to certain central problems of our religion."[70] Ultimately, the review ended their friendship. *Answer to Job* had forced the problem of evil onto God, and it was increasingly unclear to White whether the "God" in question was God or god image. If Jung meant God Godself, then his critique of the *empirical* inadequacy of a perfect and immutable God was problematic for any Catholic. Even if Jung meant god image, the myth of an evil God was hardly something that White could embrace. Torn between his friend and his faith, White chose the latter, expressing it all too publicly in his review.[71]

NOTES

1. Cf. F. X. Charet, "A Dialogue between Psychology and Theology: The Correspondence Of C. G. Jung and Victor White," *Journal of Analytical Psychology* 35.4 (October 1990). Charet in fact ascribes the term to an old professor of his. In *Jung's Treatment of Christianity: The Psychotherapy of a Relationship* (Wilmette, IL: Chiron, 1985), Murray Stein argues that Jung is the therapist with Christianity on the couch, a Christianity in need of transformation.

2. C. G. Jung, *Collected Works* (London: Routledge and Kegan Paul, 1953–1979), 11:287.

3. Ibid., 11:270.

4. Ibid., 11:396–97.

5. Ibid., 11:383.

6. Ibid., 11:397.

7. Ibid., 11:428.

8. Ibid., 11:313. In the book of Job, this inner personality is hidden from Job, who sees only God's *persona* of total goodness and not the shadow side of his unconscious, which is full of jealousy and injustice.

9. Jung, *Collected Works*, 11:402.

10. Ibid., 11:383.

11. Ibid., 5:404.

12. Ibid., 11:391.

13. Ibid., 5:404.

14. Ibid., 11:397.

15. Ibid., 11:405; see also 18: 718, where in response to a question by H. Philp, Jung suggests that God is more limited than man.

16. See, for example, Jung, *Collected Works*, 11:419, where Jung writes, "All he [God] does, in the shape of his own son, is to rescue mankind from himself...."

17. Ibid., 11:405.

18. Ibid., 18:718–719.

19. Ibid., 18:740–41.

20. Ibid., 11:456.

21. Ibid., 11:406.

22. Ibid., 11:397.

23. C. G. Jung, "Late Thoughts," in *Memories, Dreams, Reflections* (New York: Vintage, 1965), 328.

24. Jung, *Collected Works*, 9ii:103.

25. Ibid., 11:432.

26. "Letter from C. G. Jung to Doninger, Editor of *Pastoral Psychology*," in *C. G. Jung Letters II: 1951–1961* (London: Routledge and Kegan Paul, 1976), 28. In *Answer to Job*, Jung goes to great lengths to provide biblical support for the continued operations of Satan: for example, his attempts to lure Christ as a worldly leader (Mark 3:21), his role in inspiring Judas, his possession of men by devils (cf. Jung, *Collected Works*, 11:409). But, says Jung, Satan is comparatively ineffective, as

if he has been partially neutralized (cf. Jung, *Collected Works*, 11:410). Jung suggests that Satan no longer shares the same "confidential relationship" with Yahweh for several reasons: first, that Yahweh did in fact consult his omniscience this time, and careful preparations were made for the divine birth (Jung, *Collected Works*, 11:398ff.); and second, he points to the passage in Luke 10:18, where Christ says he saw Satan fall like lightning from heaven. This, says Jung, "indicates the historic and—so far as we know—final separation of Yahweh from his dark son" (Jung, *Collected Works*, 11:410). Jung's point is essentially that although God may have become the *Summum Bonum*, Satan is still active in the world because Yahweh's attitude toward him is ambiguous. He writes: "Evil is by no means fettered, even though its days are numbered. God still hesitates to use force against Satan. Presumably he still does not know how much his own dark side favours the evil angel..." (cf. Jung, *Collected Works*, 11:434).

27. "Letter from C. G. Jung to James Kirsch," February 16, 1954, in *C. G. Jung Letters* II, 154.

28. Jung, *Collected Works*, 18:734.

29. Ibid., 18:717. Jung in fact makes the same point about Mary, arguing that she cannot be whole because she did not conceive in sin like other mothers, cf. Jung, *Collected Works*, 11:399.

30. Ibid., 11:734.

31. Ibid., 18:710ff.; see also 11:197.

32. Michael Palmer, "God and Individuation" in his *Freud and Jung on Religion* (London: Routledge, 1997), 155–156.

33. Jung, *Collected Works*, 11:287.

34. C. G. Jung, "The Undiscovered Self: Present and Future" (1957) in *Collected Works* (Princeton, NJ: Princeton University Press, 1953–1979), 10:§488ff.

35. E. A. Bennet. *Meetings with Jung* (Zurich: Daimon Zerlag, 1985).

36. Liam Walsh, O.P., "Between Pluralism and Fundamentalism: Dominican Education for the Third Millennium," p. 11. This lecture was presented at A Symposium on St Thomas Aquinas for the Third Millennium, April 9–11, 1999, River Forest, IL.

37. Gerald Vann, O.P., *St. Thomas Aquinas* (London: J. M. Dent & Sons, 1940), 177.

38. Wayne G. Rollins, *Jung and the Bible* (Atlanta: John Knox), 47–48.

39. Paul Bishop, *Jung's Answer to Job: A Commentary* (New York: Brunner-Routledge, 2002), 50.

40. N. T. Wright and Marcus Borg, *The Meaning of Jesus: Two Visions* (New York: HarperCollins, 1999), 17.

41. Bishop, *Jung's Answer to Job*, 46.

42. Jung, *Memories, Dreams, Reflections*, 93.

43. Ibid., 52, 55, 93–96.

44. Aquinas did, however, think that God is present in the world in the Incarnation and the sending of the Spirit, though these missions are temporal.

45. C. G. Jung, *Psychology and Religion* (New Haven, CT: Yale University Press, 1938), 72. For a good account of this "systematic blindness," see John P. Dourley, *The Illness That We Are: A Jungian Critique of Christianity* (Toronto: Inner City, 1984), 23–26.

46. Jung, "The Undiscovered Self," 10:§488ff.

47. Jung, Letter to G. P. van den Bergh von Eysinga, February 13, 1954, in *Letters* II, 153.

48. "Letter from C. G. Jung to Bernhard Lang," June 1957, in *Letters II*, 379.

49. "Letter from C. G. Jung to Mr. Robert Smith," June 29, 1960, in *Letters II*.570-572 Robert Smith was a graduate student researching the Jung-Buber dialogue. Jung writes: "I was sometimes not careful enough to repeat time and again: 'But what I mean is only the psychic image of a *noumenon*' (Kant's thing-in-itself....)."

50. The useful distinction between archetypal God form and archetypal God contents is made by Michael Palmer in *Freud and Jung on Religion* (London: Routledge, 1997), especially 93–96.

51. Jung, *Collected Works*, 12:14.

52. See Victor White, O.P., *Soul and Psyche* (London: Collins and Harvill, 1960), 51.

53. For a good account of Jung's privileging of psychology to evaluate the adequacy or inadequacy of statements about God, see Murray Stein, "C. G. Jung: Psychologist and Theologian," in *Jung and Christianity in Dialogue: Faith, Feminism and Hermeneutics*, ed. Robert Moore and Daniel J. Meckel (New York: Paulist, 1990), 9ff.

54. Bishop, *Jung's Answer to Job*, 92–94.

55. Ann Belford Ulanov, *Spirit in Jung* (Einsiedeln, Switzerland: Daimon Verlag, 2005), 136ff.

56. Letter to Eric Neumann, January 5, 1952, in *Letters II*, 32.

57. Letter to G. P. van den Bergh von Eysinga, February 13, 1954, in *Letters II*, 153.

58. Ibid.

59. Letter to Eric Neumann, January 5, 1952, in *Letters II*, 32.

60. Victor White, O.P., "Jung on Job," *Blackfriars* 36 (March 1955): 55.

61. ibid

62. Ibid.

63. "Letter from Victor White O.P. to C. G. Jung," April 5, 1952, in *Archives of the English Province of the Order of Preachers*.

64. Victor White, O.P., "Jung on Job," *Blackfriars* 36 (March 1955): 55 White in fact would remove this passage (and several others) in an edited version of the review that would appear as appendix V of his book *Soul and Psyche*, 233–240.

65. ibid 57.

66. Ibid.

67. Ibid., 56.

68. Ibid., 57.

69. It is in view of this blunt and public criticism that Laurens van der Post accuses White of turning on Jung with "unnecessary violence and reprehensible disregard of what he owed him both as a teacher and friend"; cf. Laurens van Der Post, *Jung and the Story of Our Time*, cited in William Everson, "Introduction," in Victor White O.P., *God and the Unconscious* (Dallas: Spring, 1982): xii. White's letters reflect a deep gratitude to Jung and exonerate White of such charges; cf. *Archives of the English Province of the Order of Preachers*.

70. Everson, "Introduction," xii.

71. For a full account of the fallout over Job, see my *Fr. Victor White OP: The Story of Jung's White Raven* (Scranton, PA: University of Scranton Press, 2007).

REFERENCES

Bennet, E. A. *Meetings with Jung*. Zurich: Daimon Verlag, 1985.
Bishop, Paul. *Jung's Answer to Job: A Commentary*. New York: Brunner-Routledge, 2002.

Charet, F. X. "A Dialogue between Psychology and Theology: The Correspondence Of C. G. Jung and Victor White." *Journal of Analytical Psychology* 35.4 (October 1990): 421–441.

Dourley, John P. *The Illness That We Are: A Jungian Critique of Christianity*. Toronto, ON: Inner City, 1984.

Dourley, John P. *Jung and the Religious Alternative: The Rerooting*. Lampeter, Wales: Edwin Mellen, 1995.

Jung, C. G. *Collected Works*. London: Routledge and Kegan Paul, 1953–1979.

Jung, C. G. *Memories, Dreams, Reflections*. New York: Vintage, 1965.

Jung, C. G. *Letters II: 1951–1961*. London: Routledge and Kegan Paul, 1976.

Maritain, Jacques. *St Thomas Aquinas: Angel of the Schools*. London: Sheed and Ward, 1948.

Palmer, Michael. *Freud and Jung on Religion*. London: Routledge, 1997.

Rollins, Wayne G. *Jung and the Bible*. Atlanta, GA: John Knox, 1983.

Stein, Murray. *Jung's Treatment of Christianity: The Psychotherapy of a Religious Tradition*. Wilmette, IL: Chiron, 1985.

Stein, Murray. "Of Texts and Contexts: Reflections upon the Publication of the Jung-White Letters." *Journal of Analytical Psychology* 52 (2007): 297–319.

Ulanov, Ann Belford. *Spirit in Jung*. Einsiedeln, Switzerland: Daimon Verlag, 2005.

Weldon, Clodagh. *Fr Victor White OP: The Story of Jung's White Raven*. Scranton, PA: University of Scranton Press, 2007.

White, Victor, O. P. "Jung on Job." *Blackfriars* 36 (March 1955): 52–60.

White, Victor, O. P. *God and the Unconscious*. Dallas, TX: Spring, 1982.

8

Type-Wise

Using Jung's Theory of Psychological Types in Teaching Religious Studies Undergraduate and Graduate Students

Christopher Ross

This book is the fruit of nearly twenty years' work in the domain of practical psychology. It grew gradually from my thoughts, taking shape from the countless impressions and experiences of a psychiatrist... from intercourse with men and women of all social levels, from my personal dealings with friend and foe alike, and, finally, from a critique of my own psychological peculiarity.

My concern...is to show how the ideas I have abstracted from my practical work can be linked up...with an existing body of knowledge. I have done this...from a desire to bring the experiences out of their narrow professional setting into a more general context, a context which will enable the educated layman to derive profit from them.... The psychological views presented in this book are of wide significance and application, and are therefore better treated in a general frame of reference than left in the form of a specialized scientific hypothesis.
> —C. G. Jung, Kusnacht/Zurich, Spring 1920, Foreword to the
> First Edition of *Psychological Types*

By 1930...there was one major constant: his work on typologies became the starting point for both his writing and practice. The first stage in therapy for anyone who made the pilgrimage to Zurich was to leave "no doubt about [the analysand's] personality type and function."
> —Deirdre Bair, *Jung: A Biography*, 2003

In religious studies, teaching Jung's typology of personality evinces methods that are different from teaching other aspects of his analytical psychology because the emphasis is on conscious rather than unconscious processes. In *Psychological Types*, Jung's focus is on consciousness as he describes eight personalities that accent different cognitive processes. Elaborating these processes in religion and psychology classes evokes little resistance among students since there is no suggestion of pathology. Many students effortlessly identify with one of Jung's classical personality descriptions.[1] Others are intrigued as they explore several plausible descriptions of the eight (sixteen if the auxiliary function is considered from the outset) type portraits of themselves. Most students accept that the descriptions simply represent eight equally valid and valuable ways of being human.

Nonetheless, within academic communities that study and teach religion, Jungian personality theory has sometimes been treated with suspicion because through the Myers-Briggs Type Indicator,[2] personality type has become the most popularized and popular aspect of analytical psychology.[3] Accordingly, I shall first situate and then summarize Jung's type theory, before presenting the variety of methods that I have used in twenty years of teaching Jung's personality typology in the field of religious studies. This includes first- and third-year undergraduate courses and a graduate course in which Jung's theory of type is presented as an important element in a psychological approach to the study of (1) such religious themes as evil; (2) religious aspects of human life cycle development; (3) religious aspects of grief, loss and death; and (4) the psychology of individual religious differences. My chapter will provide a detailed account of courses concerned with the first and last of these foci of instruction.

Jung's Personality Typology and Institutes for Training Jungian Analysts

Jung's theory of personality types, published in English in 1923 as *Psychological Types: The Psychology of Individuation*, has indeed suffered over seventy years, first from the success and wide dispersion that Jung wanted for his personality theory (see his original foreword), and second from the neglect that popularity may evoke at times in professional and academic circles.

As noted by Bair[4]—the author of the recent and most detailed biography of Jung—personality typology was one of the most practical concepts that early Jungian analysts could take into their therapy with clients. However, when in 1950 Isabel Briggs Myers sent Jung the product of her collaboration with her mother, Katherine Myers, and his own work, Carl Jung, then seventy-five, replied:

> Thank you very much for kindly sending me your interesting
> questionnaire and the equally interesting description of your results.
> As you have given the matter a great deal of thought I think you have
> done so much in that direction that I'm hardly capable of criticizing

it or even knowing better. *For quite a long time I haven't done any work along that line at all, because other things have taken the foreground of my interests.*[5] But I should say that for any future development of the Type-Theory your Type-Indicator will prove a very great help.[6]

In the same vein, following their master's focus in the closing decades of his life on archetypes, the collective unconscious, and dream analysis, most Jungian analysts who received their sacred induction in the 1950s and 1960s gave scant attention to Jung's typology. This cohort until recently held prominent positions at training institutes of analytical psychology, and a detailed study of type had become sparse and marginalized in the training of Jungian analysts. There are some important exceptions to this, most notably in Zurich, where von Franz[7] wrote on the inferior function and Carl Meier wrote *Consciousness*,[8] and in San Francisco, where Horace Gray and Jo and Jane Wheelwright devised their own type instrument[9] and where June Singer developed, together with Mary Loomis, *The Singer Loomis Inventory of Personality*.[10] More recently, John Beebe,[11] also a training analyst at the San Francisco Jung Institute, extended type development theory to include all eight processes described by Jung and established an important connection between psychological type and his theory of archetypes.

Indeed, Beebe following Edinger[12] bucked the neglect of consciousness by the Jungian mainstream. Both analysts argue that Jung's formulations regarding individual differences in conscious orientations provide direction for understanding how best to access what *is* unconscious. Beebe elaborates Edinger's exposition of "consciousness" as "knowing with" (derived from the Latin *cum* meaning "with," and *scire* meaning "to know"). For both Edinger and Beebe, Jung's genius lay first in realizing that consciousness is always *knowing with* something, as well as *knowing about* something. Second, in articulating the distinct ways individuals become conscious of their world, Jung charted the diverse ways *and order* in which unconscious material may most fruitfully be encountered in psychotherapy with a given client.[13]

The Eight Processes Foundational to Jung's Typology

Jung's typology of personality is founded on the notion that humans differ in regard to their preferences for and disposition toward two sets of contrasting cognitive processes, the irrational, perceiving processes of sensation (S) and intuition (N), and the rational,[14] judging,[15] or evaluative[16] processes of thinking (T) and feeling (F). Furthermore, Jung considered that each of these four processes or functions of consciousness—the term he preferred that stems from the Latin word *fungor* and Sanskrit root word *bhuni*, meaning "to enjoy"[17]—had an extraverted and an introverted form, yielding eight personality types, each distinguished by the dominance of one of the eight psychological functions. Accordingly, more frequent use of one function accustoms individuals to experience different pleasures, which in turn foster particular personal characteristics. For instance, the frequent utilization by the introverted thinking type of the thinking function in an introverted direction—to make novel internal distinctions by abstracting underlying principles—produce an individual likely to be described as "analytical."

Jung considered the predisposition to use one function rather than another to be genetic. Research in the psychology of individual differences confirms a genetic component for most personality features that can be reliably measured,[18] including those related to Jungian typology, such as sociability (*extraversion*-introversion), openness to experience (*intuition*-sensing), agreeableness (*feeling*-thinking), and conscientiousness (*judging*-perceiving).[19]

The sensation function is concerned with "what is."[20] Introverted sensing resonates to the subjective impact of what is perceived and reflectively compares and orders specific experiences. With extraverted sensation, the sensing subject is drawn into the sensed object. Operations of the extraverted sensing process are associated with "compelling, often shared, experiences of the textures, smells, sights, sounds and tastes of the world," according to Jungian analyst John Beebe, who draws on both his clinical experience and familiarity with theory and research associated with the *Myers Briggs Type Indicator* (MBTI).[21]

The thinking function operates with language and concepts to name, label, or define an experience, which then becomes another object of awareness in its own right. "*Extraverted thinking* is interested in definitions that hold true for everyone" and proceeds to organize the external world with that public definition, whereas "*introverted thinking* reflects on whether a particular construction accords with the conviction of inner truth, regardless of what the received opinion might be."[22] The feeling function is concerned to make valuations, judgments, and decisions based on what the subject holds to be of value, in short: "How do these phenomena agree with what I value here?" Introverted feeling resonating to universal archetypal themes discerns values that matter most to oneself, while extraverted feeling readily seeks connection and harmony with the feeling of others.[23]

The intuitive function cognizes "wholes" (in contrast to details, which are the focus of the sensation function) and works with patterns of meaning, which, along with the thinking function, often involves language but also other symbol systems. Beebe distinguished extraverted intuition as "involved in picking up what is going on in other's people's minds, and seeing possibilities that others might not have imagined; whereas introverted intuition looks at the big picture in the unconscious, where the gestalts that moved nations, religions, and epochs lay, even in the midst of apparently 'individual' experience."[24]

Contexts for Teaching Jung's Typology of Personality

My home university, Wilfrid Laurier University, is a mid-size university of 14,000 undergraduate and 800 graduate students in southern Ontario, the most populous region in Canada. The Department of Religion and Culture has a fourth-year graduating cohort of thirty five students, a master's program in religion and culture of ten incoming students, and a doctor of philosophy program shared with the University of Waterloo in religious diversity in North America, with a combined total of five incoming students each year.

As a clinical psychologist of religion, I was privileged to have as a predecessor the brilliant Finnish Lutheran theologian Aarne Siirala, who underwent a midlife conversion to psychology and in 1964 wrote *The Voice of Illness: A Study in Therapy and Prophecy*. In 1973, together with other academic Lutheran renegades from Waterloo Lutheran Seminary, Aarne Siirala crossed campus to the newly formed Department of Religion and Culture in the Faculty of Arts of Wilfrid Laurier University. Because of the reverend doctor's newfound enthusiasm for the interface of psychology and religion, from its earliest days the Department of Religion and Culture has boasted four upper-level courses in the subfield of religious studies known as psychology and religion. In addition to the more typical psychology and religion course devoted to a study of the work of Freud and Jung on religion, Aarne Siirala established "Therapeutic and Religious Responses to Grief, Loss and Death," "Therapeutic and Religious Responses to Aging and Change" (now transformed into "Religion in the Human Life Cycle"), and a course titled "Religious Experience."

Whetting the Appetite for Jung in a First-Year Class

Since religion is not taught in Ontario public schools, few students opt for honors in religion and culture at the outset. Two thematic first-year courses—"Love and Its Myths" and "Evil and Its Symbols"—therefore play an important role in building a core of undergraduate religion majors. For eighteen years, I have taught an evil and its symbols class of 100 students in a room that permits reorganizing chairs for ten in class breakout discussion groups that occur for part of ninety-minute biweekly classes.

A reading of Rabbi Kushner's *When Bad Things Happen to Good People* engages the fresh undergraduates with the classical theodicy problem that I formulate into the proposition to the class: "There is too much suffering for a credible all-powerful loving divine being to exist!" Students are encouraged to reflect on an item of their own suffering in the process of writing a thousand-word personal narrative, even as they read excerpts from poet Stephen Mitchell's translation of the Book of Job from the Hebrew Bible. During a selective viewing of *Passions of the Soul, Part 1: Self Knowledge*,[25] students encounter Carl Jung on screen. Before reading his work, they watch Jung discuss his struggle to interpret the story of Job's suffering that he published in 1954 at the age of seventy-nine in his book *Answer to Job*.

After students have explored traditional theistic alternatives to the theodicy conundrum and then Buddhist approaches to suffering, we read *Evil: The Shadow Side of Reality* by John Sanford, a Jungian analyst and Episcopal priest. This second short book is read conjointly with the chapter "The Shadow" from Jung's *Aion*, the only selection of "original Jung" that the first-year students are asked to tackle. The focus of the course now becomes an exploration of how Jung's concept of the shadow aids understanding of (1) the intensity that frequently tinges in-class small-group discussions of evil and (2) the diversity among groups' members regarding what each student member *counts* as evil.

To illustrate one cause of this diversity of opinion concerning what constitutes evil, we make a brief foray into Jung's typology of personality. A single class is devoted to the booklet *In the Grip: Understanding Type, Stress, and the Inferior Function*, by Jungian clinical psychologist and psychotherapist Naomi Quenk.[26] Following Isabel Briggs Myers's way of presenting psychological type in *Gifts Differing*, I outline the four preference sets foundational to Jung's typology of personality (extraversion versus introversion, sensing versus intuition, thinking versus feeling, judging versus perceiving), along with an explanation of the dominant function, which I define as the individual's favorite function (sensation, intuition, thinking, or feeling) directed in the individual's preferred attitude, introverted or extraverted.

Jung's concept of the inferior function, the opposite of the dominant function, is presented as the "shadow" of the preferred and dominant process. Students are asked to select the process from the eight described that they think may be their dominant function. Jung's idea of the archetype of the shadow is explained as the personification of qualities that are neglected in conscious development and that—being disowned—are usually projected outward and only recognized in other people. Students then move into groups according to their shared dominant and inferior/shadow functions. Each type-alike group reviews Naomi Quenk's brief description of the pertinent inferior function, and students are asked to discuss (1) whether they recognize—when under stress—any of those associated qualities as described by Quenk and (2) particular stresses that may trigger the eruption of the inferior function, which may be peculiar to each type. The topic of typological aspects of the shadow archetype then segues to discussions of the archetype of the persona and individuals' preoccupation with their "image," and finally—for this section of the course—to the dynamic relationship between persona and shadow.

Thus in this first-year class, Jung's typology is introduced to show how what is perceived as evil may in part be associated with individual personality differences. This in turn prepares students for the discipline of entertaining a subjective element in the analysis of ethical issues in the humanities and the social and physical sciences, even while facing the challenge of (1) refusing to abandon recourse to reason and (2) remaining engaged with ethical issues.

Jung's Typology of Personality as the Sequel to Freudian Defense Mechanisms—a Psychology of Individual Religious Differences—in an Upper-Level Psychology and Religion Course on Freud and Jung

Third-year students are usually ready for affirmative psychological approaches to religious material, following four weeks of studying psychoanalysis and reading two samples of the writings of Sigmund Freud on religion, his 1907 article on ritual, "Obsessive Actions and Religious Practices," and the later *Future of an Illusion.*[27] Both pioneers of depth psychology are singularly critical of religious approaches to living as ways of avoiding the ineluctable anxiety of human life. The principal text for the remainder of the course is the edited selection of Jung's writings by Anthony Storr, *The Essential Jung,*[28] which I prefer over those of Campbell[29] and Laszlo on account of Storr's briefer excerpts but wider sampling of Jung's writings and for his succinct introductions to each selection that serve to orient students who are in most cases reading Jung for the first time.

Following assigned excerpts of his early work, his "involvement with Freud," and his writings on archetype and type, I posit three assumptions of Jung's analytical psychology as a way to frame an academic and personal exploration of his typology.[30] The first assumption is that creative tension exists between opposites. Jung's discussion of progression and regression of the libido in "On Psychic Energy" augments psychoanalytic concepts of libido introduced in the early psychoanalytic section of the course.[31] This selection connects the function of the ego to two other distinctly Jungian concepts: the self-regulation of the psyche through compensation and the conditions for an optimal relationship between opposing energies. Regarding self-regulation and the *coniunctio oppositorum,* Jung writes:

> The situation becomes full of affect and ripe for explosion. These symptoms indicate a damming up of libido, and the stoppage is always marked by the breaking up of the parts of opposites. During the progression of libido the pairs of opposites are united in the co-ordinated flow of psychic processes. Their working together makes possible the balanced regularity of these processes, which without this inner polarity would become one-sided and unreasonable.[32]

I ask students to explore the different ways in which opposites might be related—the *coniunctio oppositorum*—drawing from their own personal experiences, as well as from examples from religious studies and from those that Jung provides in the selection from his essay "On the Psychology of the Unconscious."[33] Students then discuss the conditions that make for creative tension and those that foster destructive encounters and entrenchment. Subsequent to a reading devoted to the concept of archetypes, students discuss the second assumption of analytical psychology: "*Patterning forces influence the psychological life and development of human beings.*"[34] The third assumption, "*Human beings unfold in unique ways,*" leads to a preliminary consideration of Jung's concept of individuation—becoming *undivided*—and sets the scene for two weeks of study and self-exploration in relation to Jung's typology of personality.

Following a short historical introduction to the history of Jungian typology that includes the parallel work of Katherine and Isabel Briggs Myers,[35] I present each of the four sets of the preference sets that Isabel Briggs Myers articulated as foundational to the eight psychological types described by Jung, which are succinctly presented in *Looking at Type: The Fundamentals,* a booklet, and assigned text.[36] Students are invited to make a judgment regarding their own preference in regard to each preference set.[37]

In preparation for the ensuing class that is given over to the confirmation and appreciation of individuals' personality type, students are asked to read Jung's prefaces to *Psychological Types*; its tenth chapter, "General Description of the Types"; and *Looking at Type: The Fundamentals*, by Charles Martin.[38] They are invited to complete the *Myers-Briggs Type Indicator Form M*, which can be self-scored. Students read the descriptions of each personality type from these sources and compare each to the preferences they made in response to (1) the earlier in-class presentation of each preference set, (2) the preference strengths, and (3) the type profile indicated by each student's responses to the ninety-three forced-choice items that comprise Form M of the *Myers Briggs Type Indicator* (MBTI). The class is recessed for fifteen minutes while students individually reflect and—using their current self-understanding—make a provisional judgment regarding which Jungian type they most closely resemble.

After each student settles on a particular type, each writes their name or *alias*[39] on a poster indicating their type. I then comment to the class as a whole on the relative frequency of the different types and make comparisons with adults norms that are available for the United States, Canada, and the United Kingdom.[40] In every class I have taught in the field of religion and psychology, there are more students with a preference for intuition than for sensation, in contrast to the 2:1 preponderance of sensing over intuitive types in the general population.[41] Students are easily engaged in speculating why there may be a such a reversal for a class of students studying such complex topics as psychology, religion, and their interaction.

Later in the same class, students meet in their appropriate type-alike discussion groups, in which they are asked to list on a large sheet of newsprint those personal qualities that they share with others in their group. After fifteen minutes, they are directed to turn their discussion toward considering *how* they will present the qualities they share with members of their type-alike group to the class as a whole. Remaining class time is devoted to these presentations, which I interpolate with comments, anecdotes, research findings, and writings relevant to the type group that is presenting. The presentations are usually punctuated by expressions of mirth as participants observe connections between what each type-alike group is reporting and *how* individuals in the group are behaving in front of the class: the extraverts seemingly energized by being in front of the class, while members of introverted groups seem to shrink into the whiteboard, if they consent to leave their seats at all! I commence with the extraverted intuitive group with auxiliary introverted feeling (ENFP) since they are usually bursting to share their excitement at the myriad insights they generated during such a short period of time, much to the bewilderment of many of the groups that shared introversion and a thinking preference, where the social ice was barely broken! During this parade of human psychological diversity at the front of the classroom, I encourage the observing students to consult the brief description of the type that is a displayed in the Form M booklet and note parallels or differences.[42]

Once individuals have clarified their own Jungian type, the educational focus moves to appreciation and acceptance of type difference. Students are directed to return to the assigned texts and concentrate on those sections that will enable them to increase their appreciation for those qualities associated with their type that they might regard as natural gifts. By the same token, students are encouraged, only then, to attend to personal qualities that may be construed as limitations, according to themselves or others. Students reflect on whether clarifying and understanding their own Jungian type helps them accept such limiting qualities.

In the first part of the next instructional unit, students return to their type-alike groups and share their reflections on their processes of appreciation and acceptance, including a discussion of barriers to completing the assignment they may have experienced. In a less structured way, participants of the different type groups are invited to share what it was like to realize that they had specific patterns of gifts and limitations that were held in common with others. Reflections on specifics groups' collections of limitations often shift to an articulation of qualities that individuals find challenging in other types.

Introductions to type dynamics and to the archetype of the shadow form the concluding didactic element of this class. The dominant function is defined as the individual's favorite function (sensation, intuition, thinking, or feeling) that is directed in their preferred (introverted or extraverted) world and is described as the process that is first to differentiate from the unconscious into a conscious orientation and therefore the process most closely associated with the customary operations of the ego and, by extension, to routine ways of coping. John Beebe, Jungian analyst and contemporary type theorist, describes the dominant function as operating under the auspices of the hero archetype: it is our most reliable function and the one used to move down the highway of our lives. Hard working as well as reliable our dominant provides stability for the whole personality. Deceptively, however, our dominant function is so much part of the weave of our psychological functioning that it may be invisible to us and noticed by the individual only in its absence or eclipse.

Although Jung only briefly mentions the auxiliary function, both Jungian analysts and MBTI practitioners alike consider the auxiliary function to be an important part of type dynamics and type development.[43] I describe the auxiliary function as the second string to our psychological bow that provides balance to the effects of the operations of the dominant function in two key respects. First, the auxiliary balances extraverted and introverted energies within the conscious psyche. For example, if the dominant function is introverted, the auxiliary is directed toward the outside world; if the dominant is extraverted, then the auxiliary provides access to an individual's inner world. Second, the auxiliary balances judging and perceiving functions, as Martin succinctly states:

> Everybody needs to take in new information, and everyone needs to
> be able to come to closure or make decisions about that information.
> The auxiliary helps ensure you do both.... If someone's dominant
> function is a perceiving function (S or N), a well developed auxiliary

function (T or F) helps that individual make judgments (decisions).
The reverse is also true. If someone's dominant function is a judging
function, a well-developed auxiliary function helps that individual
stay open to new perceptions.[44]

Furthermore, Beebe describes the auxiliary function as operating under the
influence of the archetype of the nurturing parent: it is through the auxiliary
function in particular that individuals offer nurturance to and care for self and
others.[45] According to Beebe, our auxiliary process functions like the right hand
of our personality offering help and support.

I present the tertiary function as the mirror opposite of the auxiliary
function, both in regard to process (sensation-intuition; thinking-feeling) and
direction of expression (introverted or extraverted). By the same token, the
inferior or fourth function is explained as the mirror opposite of the dominant
function. I use the idea of mirror-opposite functions to introduce Jung's concept of the shadow archetype—"the thing a person has no wish to be"[46]—along
with the psychodynamics of projection, whereby disowned or disavowed aspects
of consciousness are projected from introspective awareness and "recognized"
in undesirable characteristics of other people.[47]

The next two instructional units are devoted explicitly to the application of
Jung's typology to religion, starting with a review of the empirical research, followed by a didactic-experiential designed so that students understand Jungian
type may be used to enable them (1) to discern their own approaches or aver-
sions to religion and spirituality and also to methods and issues in religious
studies and (2) to appreciate those other approaches that may be more natural
for individuals with a different Jungian type.

Jung made few explicit applications of his typology to religion, understandably perhaps, in light of the pervading syncretic conflation of religion and psychology in his analytical psychology as argued by Olav Hammer.[48] In the next
instructional unit, I highlight the key empirical research findings regarding
Jungian typology and religion.[49] Studies of type frequency using the MBTI
among religious groups are reviewed first, followed by studies using type preferences as independent variables to investigate religious orientations, beliefs,
and practices.

Following this survey of empirical studies, I offer a number of conclusions
that serve the pedagogical goals of (1) introducing the idea that Jungian typology
may provide a psychological basis for the variety of religious forms and (2)
deepening understanding of the foundational typology through application to
an important aspect of human life and endeavor:

(1) Jungian typology has implications for how individuals relate to and
experience religion and for what triggers religious experiences,[50] what they
expect from religious participation,[51] and their likelihood of affiliating with religious groups.[52] I conclude that there is empirical foundation for the widespread
use of Jungian typology in religious settings and for the proliferation of pastoral books that relate Jungian typology and the MBTI to religion and spirituality,
as referenced by Francis and Jones.[53]

(2) The type-frequency studies of religious groups using the MBTI reveal that certain dominant and auxiliary types gather in religious groups, while others stay away from organized religion. On the whole, compared with the general population, religious joiners tend to have introverted or extraverted feeling as a dominant or auxiliary function and to operate in the outside world with a judging function of feeling or thinking, combined with an auxiliary or dominant function of introverted sensing that minutely registers details. Extraverted sensing types, with their grounded flexibility, are underrepresented in religious groups as compared with the general population, as are the cool, reflective introverted types with introverted thinking and those who combine intuition with thinking rather than with feeling. Individuals who are extra-verted with a perceiving function tend to be a minority in all the religious groups that have been studied, whether Christian,[54] Buddhist,[55] or Hindu.[56] In a study of self-reported religious affiliation, extraverted intuitive types with auxiliary introverted thinking (ENTP) were the most likely to report no reli-gious affiliation.[57] I present type-frequency tables of different religious groups to show that the balance of types also varies from one religious group to another. Intuitive types are more frequent among what may be considered more liberal religious groups, Anglicans and Episcopalians[58] and Unitarians,[59] while intro-verted sensing dominant or auxiliary types predominate in samples derived from Catholic[60] and conservative Protestant congregations.[61]

(3) Of all the preferences foundational to Jungian typology, the kind of per-ceiving that individuals prefer and use as their dominant or auxiliary function seems to be the most relevant to how individuals orient to religion, religious phenomena, and religious issues. Individuals who have sensing, especially introverted sensing, as their dominant or auxiliary function are more likely than those who favor intuition to be part of a religious group and to draw sharper religious contrasts, clearly demarcating what is holy or sacred from what is not. Triggers of religious experience identified by sensing types are those that would be conventionally accepted as religious: attendance at a church service, hymn singing, and personal prayer. By contrast, those with dominant or auxiliary intuition acknowledged such triggers as looking at a sunset or a painting or reading poetry. This approach was designated as experiential spiri-tuality.[62] Furthermore, intuitive types tend to accept and welcome change in religious matters (Ross, Weiss, and Jackson 1996). They cognize "wholes" and can therefore see specific changes in an overarching context. By the same token, sensing types tend to be more troubled by religious doubts than intuitive types.[63] In summary, those with sensing seem drawn to religion as a guide to right living, while intuitive types, who habitually construe their world in com-plicated ways, may be drawn to religion because religion's complex symbol systems mirror their own complexity.

(4) The judging-perceiving distinction, which indicates whether an individual faces the external world with a judging or perceiving function, is the preference next most salient to religion, both as a separate variable and in combination with sensing-intuition preferences. Judging types seem attracted to the structure religion may provide and value discipline as a spiritual value.

Perceiving types orient to the experiential aspects of religion, valuing spontaneity in religious practice.[64] As previously noted, perceiving types tend to be underrepresented in all religious groups.[65]

(5) Relationships have been found linking a preference for feeling and thinking judgment with religious variables. Jung observed that when making judgments and decisions, feeling and thinking types use their contrasting processes to order and regulate their perceptions (derived from either intuition or sensing): "In the same way that thinking organizes the contents of consciousness under concepts, feeling arranges them according to value."[66] Whereas thinking distinguishes and discriminates, deploying separative conceptual criteria to make decisions, feeling for its part gathers subject and object into close proximity and then applies pertinent overlapping values to reach a decision. Feeling types, therefore, must be personally engaged to bring the appropriate "stack" of values to the phenomena that require decision. Thinking types, however, require detachment, carving out conceptual space in which to see which criteria are most relevant. Because religious practices involve making judgments, feeling and thinking types are likely to differ in their orientation to religious life. Accordingly, thinking types more frequently reported struggles with cynical feelings, whereas feeling types were more "disturbed spiritually" by others' insensitivity and by conflict with others.[67] Because the feeling function brings order by engaging with what is experienced, interpersonal disruptions to the blending and harmonizing of experiences were reported as producing additional suffering of a spiritual nature for feeling types. Cynicism may be more common among thinking types because it is a mere accentuation of the customary distance between subject and object required for thinking to comfortably operate. Furthermore, compared with thinking types, feeling types tend to be more open to mystical experiences: the thinking function's attention to separation, difference, and critique may make it harder for thinking types to experience mystical states that involve ego suspension.[68] Finally, feeling types tend to espouse sensitivity as a spiritual value and enjoy religious narratives.[69]

(6) Of the four preference sets foundational to Jungian typology, the fewest associations have been found between religious variables and differences regarding individuals' extraverted or introverted source of energy. Moreover, the few associations that have been found tend to be closely tied to general definitions of these contrasting sources of energy. For example Ross, Weiss, and Jackson found that introverts reported being spiritually refreshed from time alone and extraverts reported being recharged from fellowship with others.[70]

(7) I illustrate the effect of specific combinations of dominant and auxiliary functions in a religious context by reviewing findings that relate to the sensing judging types (SJs), who combine introverted sensing with either extraverted feeling or extraverted thinking. Sensing-judging tends to be associated with a variety of indicators of religious conservatism, doctrinal orthodoxy,[71] reliance on biblical authority,[72] and membership in an evangelical Protestant church.[73]

Teaching Jung's Typology in a Graduate Seminar on Religion and the Individual

The size and context of the graduate-level class is different from the undergraduate classes: the seminar class has approximately eight graduate students, and the preceding first four seminars that are devoted to psychoanalytic approaches to religion cover the contributions of Winnicott and Kohut, in addition to those of Freud. Nevertheless, a similar foundation is established in Jungian typology through reading and discussing the same basic texts. However, with the addition of *Soultypes: Matching Your Personality and Spiritual Path* by Sandra Krebs Hirsh and Jane Kise and *Four Spiritualities: Expressions of Self, Expressions of Spirit: A Psychology of Contemporary Spiritual Choice* by Peter Richardson, more of the fifteen hours of seminar class time spent on Jungian typology and religion, compared with undergraduate classes, is spent discussing religious and spiritual paths that individuals find to be (1) *attractive* or natural for their type, (2) *challenging or aversive* (those approaches that tend to be favored by their opposite personality type that they may find challenging or even off-putting), and (3) *intriguing*, those approaches to religion and spirituality that individuals find mystifying but compelling and that may be favored by personality types with whom they share two of the four preference sets foundational to Jungian type.

Hirsh and Kise base *Soultypes* on a type seminar they developed at their local Protestant church, where the two authors met.[74] With the help of the Association of Psychological Type, they went on to interview at least seven individuals from each of the sixteen Jungian types, asking them: What practices draw you close to the divine? What pushed you away? What are your favorite ways to worship, study, pray and serve? and How has your spirituality changed over the years? What new practices are you discovering? These questions are used to start discussions in type-alike or type-similar groups or dyads when the seminar class is subdivided. Hirsh and Kise devote a chapter to each of the sixteen Jungian types, and students are asked to focus on one or two chapters that more or less fit *their* understanding of three categories of approach to religion and spirituality: attractive, aversive, and mysterious or intriguing. Before presenting their comments on the similarities and differences between the type descriptions crafted by Hirsh and Kise in relation to religion and spirituality and their own past and present orientations, students are asked to survey all sixteen types in this regard. The booklet *Looking at Type and Spirituality* by Hirsh and Kise is useful for this task, together with brief summative aphorisms that I have integrated from their work and my research and scholarship in the area that are useful for stating or capping discussions of a particular type in relation to religion, spirituality, or the study of religion.

If there are students with dominant sensing in the seminar, I start with that approach to religion, so that it can be presented in a positive light, as this approach is the one with which the other types often have the most problems: introverted sensing with auxiliary extraverted thinking (ISTJ, "Something intensely private, inexplicable: staying true to duty and tradition, even when it's

The Crossing Paths of Spirituality:
Sixteen Ways of Cultivating the Sacred
Related to Jungian Personality typology

Spirituality is...

ISTJ	ISFJ	INFJ	INTJ
Something intensely private, inexplicable: staying true to duty and tradition, even when it's hard	Living the joy of bringing harmony through loyal service to others	Living out the values of a sacred vision that inspires	Original minds, original vision: harnessing life's mysteries through the intellect and imagination
ISTP	**ISFP**	**INFP**	**INTP**
Analysing to get straight to the right action, no matter what!	Delighting in being the quiet hands and feet of the divine or whatever has supreme value	Meeting the heart's yearning to live the quiet mystery of love through insightful service	Doubting the way to truth in order to discern underlying principles
ESTP	**ESFP**	**ENFP**	**ENTP**
Doing the right thing now, and now, and now!	Actively sharing the exuberance of engaging the rich joy of living	Imagining love's triumph over rules, for human ends!	Transforming challenge into possibility, by a hope and freedom that transcend rational expectation
ESTJ	**ESFJ**	**ENFJ**	**ENTJ**
Organising a cause for the common good	Living the joy of bringing harmony: divine friendliness whenever!	Building harmonious community wherever you are, in deeply valued, insightful ways	Envisioning and implementing the just vision

I - Introvert	S - Sensing	T - Thinking	J - Judging
E - Extravert	N - iNtuitive	F - Feeling	P - Perceiving

FIGURE 8.1.

hard") and introverted sensing with extraverted feeling (ISFJ, "Living the joy of bringing harmony through loyal service to others"). By contrast, extraverted sensing approaches seldom provoke strong reactions: extraverted sensing with introverted feeling (ESFP, "Actively sharing the exuberance of engaging the rich joy of living") and extraverted sensing with introverted thinking (ESTP, "Doing the right thing now, and now, and now!").

The approaches to religion associated with the four possible intuitive dominant types I epitomize in the following ways: introverted intuitives with extraverted thinking (INTJ, "Original minds, original vision: harnessing life's mysteries through the intellect and imagination"), introverted intuitives with extraverted feeling (INFJ, "Living out the values of a sacred vision that inspires"), extraverted intuitives with introverted feeling (ENFP, "Imagining love's triumph over rules, for human ends!"), and extraverted intuitives with introverted thinking (ENTP, "Transforming challenge into possibility, by a hope and freedom that transcend rational expectation").

For the four thinking dominant types, I present the following aphorisms: the introverted thinking types with extraverted intuition (INTP, "Doubting the way to truth in order to discern the underlying principles"), the introverted thinking types with extraverted sensing (ISTP, "Analyzing to get straight to the right action, no matter what!"), extraverted thinkers with introverted sensing (ESTJ, "Organizing a cause for the common good"), and extraverted thinkers with introverted intuition (ENTJ, "Envisioning and implementing the just vision").

The four feeling dominant types have their own approach to religious and spiritual issues, and to introduce these, I present these aphorisms: for introverted feeling types with extraverted intuition (INFP, "Meeting the heart's yearning to live the quiet mystery of love through insightful service"), for introverted feeling types with extraverted sensing (ISFP, "Delighting in being the quiet hands and feet of the divine or of whatever has supreme value"), extraverted feeling types with introverted sensing (ESFJ, "Living the joy of bringing harmony: divine friendliness whenever!"), and extraverted feeling types with introverted intuition (ENFJ, "Building harmonic community wherever you are in deep insightful ways that you value").

Richardson in *Four Spiritualities* concentrates on elaborating four approaches to the sacred that he intuited at the age of eighteen.[75] He met with ridicule and only returned to his project thirty-two years later after encountering Jung's typology. Richardson discovered that the four possible pairings between the two kinds of perceiving (sensing and intuition) and the two kinds of judging (thinking and feeling) provided the psychological vehicle for grounding his differentiation—as a spiritually precocious young adult— of four principal spiritual paths: Unity (intuitive-thinking [NT]), Devotion (sensing-feeling [SF]), Works (sensing-thinking [ST]), and Harmony (intuitive-feeling [NF]). These Richardson distilled from his deep familiarity with diverse religious traditions as an independent scholar and Unitarian Universalist minister. As an optional text within the course, his book is used to provide a broader framework for students to explore diverse religious phenomena and world wisdom traditions through the lens of individual psychological difference.

The Value of Teaching Jungian Typology in Religious Studies

While debates abound regarding the implications of postmodernism and poststructuralism for religious studies and their relationship to modernity, both centers of theoretical analysis (1) share a concern for the articulation and honoring of diversity and (2) are critical of the unreflective deployment of evaluative criteria. Charles Taylor, however, in *Malaise of Modernity*, argues that there is more continuity between postmodernity and modernity than many enthusiasts and critics of the postmodern turn would have us believe.[76] Jung's typology responds to postmodernity's concern with diversity by supplying a basis for charting eight divergent but equally valid ways of negotiating questions of ultimate truth and meaning and also perhaps eight different paths to the academic study of these paths. Beebe in his C. G. Jung Institute of Chicago lecture series on typology argues that in *Psychological Types* Jung presents the first postmodern psychology.[77] As Jung wrote in the opening excerpt from his foreword to the first edition of *Psychological Types*: "It grew gradually... from a critique of my own psychological peculiarity."[78] In other words, Jung meant his theory of psychological types to be a critical psychology that would correct for hidden bias, which is a key concern of postmodern scholarship and poststructuralist theory.

Teaching Jung's theory of psychological types contributes to religious studies and its teaching in further ways. Presentation of his personality theory helps students navigate the shoals between modernity and postmodernity, where universalist systems are justifiably critiqued as monolithic and oppressive but few charts are available to sustain continued ethical inquiry. Jung's theory of types provides a way of investigating different spiritual paths and ways of approaching religion, where none is privileged over another. The time-honored comparative method in religious studies is used by Hirsh and Kise in *Soultypes*, where representatives of all sixteen Jungian types were interviewed across the common categories of prayer, worship, study, and service.[79]

Jung's theory of personality, based as it is on the relative prevalence of eight cognitive processes within the individual, provides a means to navigate and explore—through a nonreductive hermeneutic—some of the religious diversity that students of religion may encounter. More specifically, whereas Jung's theory of archetypes may help explain variety *between* religions based on their contrasting dominant narratives, Jung's theory of psychological type helps explain differences of approach and emphasis *within* religious groups, that is to say, sensing types look to their religion as a guide to right living, whereas intuitive types are drawn to religion as a mirror for their own complexity. Each approach is valid but responds to a different need influenced by which kind of perceiving process is more habitual and which more exceptional.

The zeitgeist of the type-informed classroom rests on the same values that underlay the best practices of the comparative method in religious studies in the late nineteenth century—fascination with, and acceptance and cherishing of, difference. The type-informed classroom extends these values to the consideration of what is deemed important in a religious context and invites exploration of how a religious phenomenon came to be that important for a particular student or believer. By the same token, the atmosphere in a type-informed classroom includes acceptance and tolerance for different styles of learning, as well as different ways of being religious or being secular. This includes facilitating understanding and acceptance of different paths to the same position. Texts may be more important to the sensing devotee and scholar, values to the feeling types, and the different visions of religions to intuitive types, while the thinking type may be more interested in evaluating truth claims. An understanding of Jungian typology can increase tolerance and miti-gate conflict in classrooms and religious meeting places alike and provide a stimulating framework for sustained debate and inquiry in regard to both the study and teaching of religions.

NOTES

1. C. G. Jung, *Collected Works of C. G. Jung* (Princeton, NJ: Princeton University Press, 1931–1961), 6:330–407.

2. Isabel B. Myers and Peter B. Myers, *Gifts Differing* (Palo Alto, CA: Consulting Psychologists, 1980).

3. Since 2000, the Myers-Briggs Type Indicator has been the world's most frequently used personality instrument, with 2.5 million administrations annually between 2000 and 2004 (M. Segovia, personal communication from Consulting Psychologists Press, 2004).

4. Deidre Bair, *Jung: A Biography* (New York: Little, Brown, 2003).

5. Italics added.

6. Frances W. Saunders, *Katherine and Isabel: Mother's Light, Daughter's Journey* (Palo Alto, CA: Consulting Psychologists, 1991), 120–21.

7. Marie-Louise von Franz, "The Inferior Function," in *Jung's Typology* (Irving, TX: Spring, 1979).

8. Carl Meier, *Consciousness* (Boston: Sigo, 1989).

9. The *Gray-Wheelwright Test* has been used only with Jungian analysts, while the *Singer-Loomis Inventory of Personality* (SLIP) shed the assumption of bipolarity of Jung's typology. Reliability and validity studies are lacking for both instruments.

10. June Singer and Mary Loomis, *The Singer Loomis Inventory of Personality Manual* (Palo Alto, CA: Consulting Psychologists, 1984).

11. John Beebe, "Understanding Consciousness through the Theory of Psychological Type," in *Analytical Psychology*, ed. Joseph Cambray and Linda Carter (New York: Brunner Routledge, 2004), and "Type and Archetype. Part 2: The Arms and Their Shadow," *Typeface* 18.3 (2007).

12. Edward F. Edinger, *The Creation of Consciousness* (Toronto: Inner City, 1984).

13. Beebe, "Understanding Consciousness."

14. Jung, *Collected Works*, 6.

15. Myers and Myers, *Gifts Differing*.

16. Beebe, "Understanding Consciousness."

17. James Hillman, "The Feeling Function," in *Jung's Typology*, ed. Marie-Louise von Franz and James Hillman (Irving, TX: Spring, 1979).

18. Robert Plomin and Avshalom Capsi, "Behavioral Genetics and Personality," in *Handbook of Personality Theory and Research*, 2nd ed., ed. Lawrence A. Pervin and Oliver P. John. (New York; Guilford, 1999).

19. Robert R. McCrea and Paul T. Costa, "Reinterpreting the Myers-Briggs Type Indicator from the Perspective of the Five Factor Model of Personality," *Journal of Personality* 57 (1989): 17–40.

20. Jung, *Collected Works*, 18:219.

21. Ibid.

22. Beebe, "Understanding Consciousness."

23. Ibid.

24. Ibid.

25. In an earlier class, I show other excerpts from this remarkable film to open up students to the idea that all human beings suffer. The excerpts include interviews with Rosemary Miller, a bishop of the Gnostic Church who was subjected to torture; Jungian analyst June Singer, whose twenty-five-year-old daughter was killed in a car accident; and Christian origins scholar Elaine Pagels, who in a single year lost her twelve-year-old son to a congenital illness and her husband in a mountaineering accident.

26. Naomi L. Quenk, *In the Grip: Understanding Type, Stress, and the Inferior Function*, 2nd ed. (Palo Alto, CA: Consulting Psychologists, 2000).

27. Sigmund Freud, *Future of an Illusion*, in *The Standard Edition of the Complete Psychological Works of Sigmund Freud*, ed. and trans. James Strachey (London: Hogarth, 1953–1974).

28. Anthony Storr, *The Essential Jung* (Princeton, NJ: Princeton University Press, 1983).

29. Joseph Campbell, *The Portable Jung* (New York: Viking, 1971).

30. Storr, *Essential Jung*, 45.

31. Jung, *Collected Works*, 8:69–69.

32. Jung, *Essential Jung*, 60.

33. Jung, *Collected Works*, 7:56–92.

34. Italics added. Jung, *Collected Works*, 8: 317–321.

35. Saunders, *Katherine and Isabel*.

36. Charles R. Martin, *Looking at Type: The Fundamentals* (Gainesville, FL: Center for Applications of Psychological Type, 1997), 1–7.

37. To deal with the issue of the right to privacy in an educational setting, students are provided with the option of creating a fictitious preference and associated personality type and are requested to inform me if they avail themselves of this option, which I hold in confidence. Any student may also use an alias in place of the legal name under which they registered for the course.

38. Martin, *Looking at Type*, 1–7.

39. A provision made under the privacy legislation in the Province of Ontario.

40. Eduardo Casas, "The Development of the French Version of MBTI in Canada and France," *Journal of Psychological Type* 20 (1990): 73–78; Allen Hammer and Wayne D. Mitchell, "The Distribution of MBTI Types in the U.S. by Gender and Ethnic Group," *Journal of Psychological Type* 37 (1996): 2–14; Elizabeth Kendall, *Myers Briggs Type Indicator European English Edition Manual Supplement* (Oxford: Oxford Psychologists, 1998).

41. Hammer and Mitchell, "Distribution of MBTI Types."

42. Martin, *Looking at Type*, 14–15.

43. Jung, *Collected Works*, 6:405–407.

44. Martin, *Looking at Type*, 8–9.

45. Beebe, "Type and Archetype."

46. Jung, *Collected Works*, 16:470.

47. Quenk, *Beside Ourselves: Our Hidden Personality in Everyday Life* (Palo Alto, CA: Consulting Psychologists, 1993); Quenk, *In the Grip*; Conny Zweig and Jeremiah Abrams, *Meeting the Shadow: The Hidden Power of the Dark Side of Human Nature* (Los Angeles: Jeremy P. Tarcher, 1991).

48. Olav Hammer, "Jung, the Jungians and the Study of Religion," in *The Oxford Handbook for the Psychology of Religion*, ed. D. Wulff (New York: Oxford University Press, 2010).

49. Christopher F. J. Ross, "Jungian Typology and Religion: a North American Perspective," in press, Research in the Social Scientific Study of Religion, volume 22.

50. Leslie J. Francis and Christopher F. Ross, "The Perceiving Function and Christian Spirituality: Distinguishing between Sensing and Intuition," *Pastoral Sciences* 16 (1997): 93–103.

51. Christopher F. J. Ross, David Weiss, and Lynne Jackson, "The Relation of Jungian Psychological Type to Religious Attitudes and Practices," *International Journal for the Psychology of Religion* 6 (1996): 263–279.

52. Christopher F. J. Ross and Leslie J. Francis, "Psychological Type and Christian Religious Affiliation among Female Undergraduates in Wales," *Journal of Psychological Type* 66 (2004): 69–78.

53. Leslie J. Francis and Susan H. Jones, "Personality and Christian Belief among Adult Churchgoers," *Journal of Psychological Type* 47 (1998): 5–11.

54. Leslie J. Francis, "Faith and Psychology: The Contribution of Empirical Research and Jungian Psychological Type Theory to Practical and Pastoral Psychology," the William C. Bier Award address, annual conference of the American Psychological Association, New Orleans, August 2006.

55. Christopher F. J. Ross and Chris Silver, "Personality and Religion and Spiritual Experiences within the New Kadampa Tradition," presentation at the annual conference of the American Psychological Association, Washington, DC, 2005.

56. T. H. Poling and J. F. Kenney, *The Hare Krishna Character Type: A Study of the Sensate Personality* (Lewiston, ME: Edwin Mellen, 1986).

57. Francis and Ross, "Perceiving Function."

58. Christopher F. J. Ross, "Type Patterns among Active Members of the Anglican Church: Comparisons with Catholics, Evangelicals, and Clergy," *Journal of Psychological Type* 26 (1993): 28–36.

59. R. Gerhardt, "Liberal Religion and Personality Type," *Research in Psychological Type* 6 (1983): 47–53.

60. Christopher F. J. Ross, "Type Patterns among Catholics: Four Anglophone Congregations Compared with Protestants, Francophone Catholics, and Priests," *Journal of Psychological Type* 33 (1995): 33–42.

61. V. Delis-Bulhoes, "Jungian Psychological Types and Christian Beliefs in Active Church Members," *Journal of Psychological Type* 20 (1990): 25–33.

62. Francis and Ross, "Perceiving Function."

63. Francis and Jones, "Personality and Christian Belief."

64. Ross, Weiss, and Jackson, "Relation of Jungian Psychological Type."

65. Francis, "Faith and Psychology."

66. Jung, *Collected Works*, 6:435.

67. Ross, Weiss, and Jackson, "Relation of Jungian Psychological Type."

68. Leslie J. Francis and Stephen H. Louden, "Mystical Orientation and Psychological Type: A Study among Students and Adult Churchgoers," *Transpersonal Psychological Review* 4 (2000): 36–42; Francis, "Psychological Type and Mystical Orientation: Anticipating Individual Differences within Congregational Life," *Pastoral Sciences* 21 (2002): 77–93.

69. Ross, Weiss, and Jackson, "Relation of Jungian Psychological Type."

70. Ibid.

71. S. W. Lee, "The Orthodoxy of Christian Beliefs and Jungian Personality Types," *Dissertation Abstracts International* 47 (1985): 474A.

72. Peter G. Meyer, "Factors Related to Adherence to Denominational Patterns among Missouri Synod Lutheran College Students," *Dissertation Abstracts International* 27 (1966): 1679A.

73. Paul Bramer, "Frequency of Jungian Personality Types among Active Evangelical Protestants." Paper presented to the annual conference of the American Psychological Association, Toronto, 1996.

74. Sandra Krebs Hirsh and Jane Kise, *Soultypes: Matching Your Personality and Spiritual Path* (Minneapolis: Augsburg, 2006).

75. Peter T. Richardson, *Four Spiritualities: Expressions of Self, Expressions of Spirit, a Psychology of Contemporary Spiritual Choice* (Palo Alto, CA: Davies Black, 1996).

76. Charles Taylor, *Malaise of Modernity* (Toronto: Anansi, 1991), 93ff.

77. John Beebe, *A New Model of Psychological Types* (Chicago: C. G. Jung Institute of Chicago, 1988).

78. Jung, *Collected Works*, 6.

79. Hirsh and Kise, *Soultypes*.

REFERENCES

Bair, Deidre. *Jung: A Biography.* New York: Little, Brown, 2003.

Beebe, John. *A New Model of Psychological Types.* Audiotape/CD1. C. G. Jung Institute of Chicago, 1988.

Beebe, John. "Type and Archetype. Part 2: The Arms and Their Shadow." *Typeface* 18.3 (2007).

Beebe, John. "Understanding Consciousness through the Theory of Psychological Type." In *Analytical Psychology,* ed. Joseph Cambray and Linda Carter. New York: Brunner Routledge, 2004.

Bramer, Paul. "Frequency of Jungian Personality Types among Active Evangelical Protestants." Paper presented to the annual conference of the American Psychological Association. Toronto, ON, 1996.

Campbell, Joseph. *The Portable Jung.* New York: Viking, 1971.

Casas, Eduardo. "The Development of the French Version of the MBTI in Canada and France." *Journal of Psychological Type* 20 (1990): 73–78.

De Laszlo, Violet. *Psyche and Symbol; A Selection from the Writings of C. G. Jung.* Garden City, NY: Doubleday, 1958.

Delis-Bulhoes, V. "Jungian Psychological Types and Christian Beliefs in Active Church Members." *Journal of Psychological Type* 20 (1990): 25–33.

Edinger, Edward. F. *The Creation of Consciousness.* Toronto, ON: Inner City, 1984.

Engelen, Peter *Passion of the Soul, Part 2: Self knowledge.* Video. Princeton, NJ: Films for the Humanities and Sciences, 1991.

Francis, Leslie J. "Psychological Type and Mystical Orientation: Anticipating Individual Differences within Congregational Life." *Pastoral Sciences* 21 (2002): 77–93.

Francis, Leslie J. "Faith and Psychology: The Contribution of Empirical Research and Jungian Psychological Type Theory to Practical and Pastoral Psychology." The William C. Bier Award address, annual conference of the American Psychological Association. New Orleans: August 2006.

Francis, Leslie J., and Susan H. Jones. "Personality and Christian Belief among Adult Churchgoers." *Journal of Psychological Type* 47 (1998): 5–11.

Francis, Leslie J., and Stephen H. Louden. "Mystical Orientation and Psychological Type: A Study among Student and Adult Churchgoers." *Transpersonal Psychology Review* 4 (2000): 36–42.

Francis, Leslie. J., and Christopher F. J. Ross. "The Perceiving Function and Christian Spirituality: Distinguishing between Sensing and Intuition." *Pastoral Sciences* 16 (1997): 93–103.

Freud, Sigmund. "Obsessive Actions and Religious Practices." *Z. Religionpsychol.* 1.1 (April 1907): 4–12.

Freud, Sigmund. *The Standard Edition of the Complete Psychological Works of Sigmund Freud.* Volumes 1–24, trans. and ed. James Strachey. London: Hogarth, 1953–1974.

Gerhardt, R. "Liberal Religion and Personality Type." *Research in Psychological Type* 6 (1983): 47–53.

Gray, Henry, and Joseph Wheelwright. "Jung's Psychological Types, Their Frequency of Occurrence." *Journal of General Psychology* 34 (1946): 29–36.

Hammer, Allen, and Wayne D. Mitchell. "The Distribution of MBTI Types in the U.S. by Gender and Ethnic Group." *Journal of Psychological Type* 37 (1996): 2–14.

Hammer, Olav. "Jung, the Jungians and the Study of Religion." In *Oxford Handbook for the Psychology of Religion,* ed. D. Wulff. New York: Oxford University Press, 2010.

Hillman, James. "The Feeling Function." In *Jung's Typology,* ed. Marie-Louise von Franz and J. Hillman. Irving, TX: Spring, 1979.

Hirsh, Sandra Krebs, and Jane Kise. *Looking at Type and Spirituality.* Gainesville, FL: Center for Applications of Psychological Type, 2000.

Jung, Carl G. "Psychological Types." In *Collected Works of C. G. Jung,* Vol. 6. Princeton, NJ: Princeton University Press, 1923.

Jung, Carl G. *Answer to Job.* London: Routledge and Kegan Paul, 1954.

Jung, Carl G. "Symbols and the Interpretation of Dreams." In *Collected Works of C. G. Jung,* Vol. 18. Princeton, NJ: Princeton University Press, 1976.

Jung, Carl G. "The Shadow." In *Collected Works of C. G. Jung,* Vol. 9, pt. 2. Princeton, NJ: Princeton University Press, 1979.

Kendall, Elizabeth. *Myers Briggs Type Indicator European English Edition Manual Supplement.* Oxford: Oxford Psychologists, 1998.

Kushner, Harold S. *When Bad Things Happen to Good People.* New York: Schocken, 1981.

Lee, S. W. "The Orthodoxy of Christian Beliefs and Jungian Personality Types." *Dissertation Abstracts International* 47 (1985): 474A.

Martin, Charles R. *Looking at Type, the Fundamentals.* Gainesville, FL: Center for Applications of Psychological Type, 1997.

McCrea, Robert R., and Paul T. Costa. "Reinterpreting the Myers-Briggs Type Indicator from the Perspective of the Five Factor Model of Personality." *Journal of Personality* 57 (1989): 17–40.

Meier, Carl, A. *Consciousness.* Boston: Sigo, 1989.

Meyer, Peter G. "Factors Related to Adherence to Denominational Patterns among Missouri Synod Lutheran College Students." *Dissertation Abstracts International* 27 (1966): 1679A.

Myers, Isabel B., and Peter B. Myers. *Gifts Differing.* Palo Alto, CA: Consulting Psychologists, 1980.

Plomin, Robert, and Avshalom Caspi. "Behavioral Genetics and Personality." In *Handbook of Personality Theory and Research,* 2nd ed., ed. Lawrence A. Pervin and Oliver P. John. New York: Guilford, 1999.

Poling, T. H., and J. F. Kenney. *The Hare Krishna Character Type: A Study of the Sensate Personality*. Lewiston, ME: Edwin Mellen, 1986.

Quenk, Naomi L. *Beside Ourselves: Our Hidden Personality in Everyday Life*. Palo Alto, CA: Consulting Psychologists, 1993.

Quenk, Naomi L. *In the Grip: Understanding Type, Stress, and the Inferior Function*, 2nd ed. Palo Alto, CA: Consulting Psychologists, 2000.

Richardson, Peter T. *Four Spiritualities: Expressions of Self, Expressions of Spirit, a Psychology of Contemporary Spiritual Choice*. Palo Alto, CA: Davies Black, 1996.

Ross, Christopher F. J. "Type Patterns among Active Members of the Anglican Church: Comparisons with Catholics, Evangelicals, and Clergy." *Journal of Psychological Type* 26 (1993): 28–36.

Ross, Christopher F. J. "Type Patterns among Catholics: Four Anglophone Congregations Compared with Protestants, Francophone Catholics, and Priests." *Journal of Psychological Type* 33 (1995): 33–42.

Ross, Christopher F. J. "Jungian Typology and Religion." In *Handbook for the Psychology of Religion*, ed. D. Wulff. New York: Oxford University Press, 2010.

Ross, Christopher F. J., and Leslie J. Francis. "Psychological Type and Christian Religious Affiliation among Female Undergraduates in Wales." *Journal of Psychological Type* 66 (2004): 69–78.

Ross, Christopher F. J., and Chris Silver. "Personality and Religious and Spiritual Experiences within the New Kadampa Tradition." Presentation at the annual conference of the American Psychological Association. Washington, DC, 2005.

Ross, Christopher F. J., David Weiss, and Lynne Jackson. "The Relation of Jungian Psychological Type to Religious Attitudes and Practices." *International Journal for the Psychology of Religion* 6 (1996): 263–279.

Saunders, Frances W. *Katherine and Isabel: Mother's Light, Daughter's Journey*. Palo Alto, CA: Consulting Psychologists, 1991.

Siirala, Aarne. *The Voice of Illness: A Study in Therapy and Prophecy*. New York: Edwin Mellen, 1981.

Singer, June, and Mary Loomis. *The Singer Loomis Inventory of Personality Manual*. Palo Alto, CA: Consulting Psychologists, 1984.

Storr, Anthony. *The Essential Jung*. Princeton, NJ: Princeton University Press, 1983.

Taylor, Charles. *Malaise of Modernity*. Toronto, ON: Anansi, 1991.

von Franz, Marie-Louise. "The Inferior Function." In *Jung's Typology*, ed. Marie-Louise von Franz and J. Hillman. Irving, TX: Spring, 1979.

Zweig, Conny, and Jeremiah Abrams. *Meeting the Shadow: The Hidden Power of the Dark Side of Human Nature*. Los Angeles: Jeremy P. Tarcher, 1991.

PART III

Jung's Life, Work, and Critics

9

Personal Secrets, Ethical Questions

John Haule

The biographies of C. G. Jung are less than satisfying for at least two entangled reasons. First, they are all overwhelmingly dependent on what is inaccurately called Jung's 1963 autobiography, *Memories, Dreams, Reflections*,[1] of which only the lively first eighty-five and last twenty-three pages were written by Jung himself—the rest being a compilation made by his secretary Aniela Jaffé. Jung complained that even the 108 pages he had written had been "aunty-fied" [*tantifiziert*] by Jaffé and the other editors,[2] stripping the book of his own direct and sometimes salty language, including all mention of his forty-year-long extramarital relationship with former patient Antonia Wolff. The result is a narrative that reads like a legend and is short on factual detail. The other issue is related. Most of the biographies line up on one side or the other of the legend spun by Jung and Jaffé. Jung's disciples (whom we might call the hagiographers) have been eager to expand and promote what his longtime collaborator and biographer Marie-Louise von Franz (1975) calls in her subtitle "His Myth in Our Time," thereby making Jung into the exemplar of a life well-lived in our confusing contemporary world.[3] The opposing biographers (whom we might call the muckrakers) compete with one another to debunk and repudiate the Jungian myth as a sentimental and romantic cover-up for a life of arrogance and cruelty, thereby revealing the "Wounded" (Smith, 1996), "Haunted Prophet" (Stern, 1976), and "Aryan Christ" (Noll, 1997), whose teachings are unreliable and even dangerous.[4]

According to the Jungian myth, writing *Symbols of Transformation* (1912) convinced Jung that, whether we know it or not, every one of us is "living a myth" (i.e., an implicit narrative, universal in scope, that expresses the essential nature of human existence).[5] In past centuries, religions preserved, narrated, and enacted such myths in their teachings and rites, but in the twentieth century, too many of us are sincerely disaffected "moderns," facing a life that threatens to be flat and meaningless unless we can discover our own "personal myth" by opening a dialogue between "ego" (the center of consciousness and deliberate will) and "self" (the "wholeness" of our larger being).

The life of an amoeba may serve as a simple analogue for the self. A protozoan, like the human unconscious, has no ego, but also has no brain or nervous system and no central organ of command. Nevertheless, it ceaselessly marshals all its forces, all the molecules that comprise it, for the optimal enhancement of its life in the present moment.[6] Our personal, human wholeness is much the same, a ceaseless homeodynamic system operating mostly outside our awareness. The complexity of the human organism allows some of this unconscious processing to appear in consciousness as feelings, hunches, fantasies, and the like. In this sense, our organism responds as a whole to our momentary life situation. Thus does the unconscious psyche, like every organism in nature, act as though it has a central governing organ, striving for balance, harmony, and vigor—even as our narrow-minded ego gets caught up in enthusiasms, compulsions, and fears that may not be in line with the needs of our whole being. If we can learn to be receptive, curious, and discerning regarding the dreams and symptoms that would disrupt our ego's narrative, we can begin to discern the shape of our personal myth. When the collective unconscious speaks with authority, Jung names it the "Two Million Year-Old Man," or just "The Great Man."[7]

Muckraker Frank McLynn[8] is certain that the myth serves merely as a cover-up for Jung's arrogance: "Acres of print could have been saved if Jung had come clean and admitted he was a prophet."[9] Meanwhile, Los Angeles analyst Robert Stein, who studied at the Jung Institute in Zurich while Jung was still teaching, depicts Jung's employment of the myth as an exercise in profound modesty: "[Jung] was fantastic in the humility he demonstrated as he made [The Great Man] come alive before us. He talked of the importance of not identifying with The Great Man archetype, of not losing our humanness as the archetype speaks through us."[10]

Whether the Jungian myth is a self-serving cover-up or a demanding spiritual technique may be illustrated by an anecdote that to my knowledge has been overlooked by all the biographers. In Munich in 1930, Jung gave a memorial address for his friend, the Sinologist and translator of the *I Ching*, Richard Wilhelm. Afterward, he sat at a table with a certain Sigrid Strauss-Kloebe (the otherwise unknown narrator of the incident), her husband, and two women unknown to her. The two unknown women began pressing Jung to admit that he was an exception to his own rule that every human being has a shadow. After some efforts to convince them of their error, he fell silent, and the group at the table went on to another topic. "A few minutes later, Jung leaned back in his chair and stared at two strange ladies who stood in the foyer very modishly dressed and said with tiny narrow eyes: 'Now *those* ladies would interest me a lot!'"[11]

No doubt the muckraking biographers would find in this anecdote clear evidence of Jung's touchiness when one of his favorite ideas is challenged, the manifestation of a cruel streak as he gratuitously insults well-meaning but uninformed people, and a sure sign that at the age of fifty-five, his sexually promiscuous tendencies were still active. By contrast, the hagiographers would see the story as an illustration of Jung's transcendent wisdom. Not having convinced the women with logic, he consults his own shadow: his boredom and irritation with two unattractively self-satisfied conversation partners. Moreover, in exposing his own shadow, he activates theirs. Like a crazy-wise guru, he cuts the ground out from under them and plunges them into the hard reality of the shadow.[12]

The story does not supply enough detail to justify either conclusion. Rather, it is a tempting projection screen to which every reader brings a set of expectations, a subjectively convincing worldview or myth. The muckrakers bring conventional notions of politeness and human decency and see Jung behaving badly. The hagiographers bring "Jung's Myth in Our Time" and see Jung as the Wise Old Man of Zurich. One group may be right or both of them wrong: they disagree over whether it might be permissible to violate commonsense social expectations on the basis of some allegedly deeper "interior truth" known privately to the individual. Must we trust another's claim of "mythic" support from the "self" when it looks for all the world like a post hoc cover-up for self-indulgent behavior? Is Jung merely hostile to society itself, given his frequent claims that we live in a "mass-minded society" and that a group's level of consciousness is always reduced to its "least common denominator"? Jung writes:

> It is a notorious fact that the morality of a society as a whole is in
> inverse ratio to its size; for the greater the aggregation of individuals,
> the more the individual factors are blotted out, and with them
> morality, which rests entirely on the moral sense of the individual
> and the freedom necessary for this. Hence every man is, in a certain
> sense, unconsciously a worse man when he is in society than when
> acting alone; for he is carried by society and to that extent relieved of
> his individual responsibility.... Society, by automatically stressing all
> the collective qualities in its individual representatives, puts a
> premium on mediocrity, on everything that settles down to vegetate
> in an easy, irresponsible way.[13]

Jung's disciple Erich Neumann has systematized Jung's views on this issue in his slim 1949 volume, *Depth Psychology and a New Ethic*. He says all morality comes from the "Voice of the Self" and that there are, historically, three forms of morality. In the "Old Ethic," the Voice was heard by a charismatic individual, the founder of a religious tradition, such as Moses, Jesus, Muhammad, and the Buddha. The founder's followers subsequently codified the message of this Voice into a set of ethical rules. The vast majority of a religion's members (Ethic, Type A) follow such rules by suppressing all tendencies to violate them—by dissociating, that is, from their shadow. As a consequence, they tend to project their shadow upon others and accuse them of immorality, much as our contemporary Christian, Islamic, and Jewish fundamentalists have been doing with more and more vehemence in recent decades. They remain unconscious in the sense Jung describes in the passage just cited.

But the Old Ethic itself is not to blame, for there is another way to abide by it (Ethic, Type B). The "elite" followers of the Old Ethic, those revered as the saints and prophets of their tradition, do not dissociate from their shadow but take it up as a spiritual and moral discipline. They accuse themselves of imperfections far too subtle for the masses to appreciate. They find themselves guilty of gluttony, for instance, not because they have been eating excessively, but because they have allowed thoughts and desires for food to distract them from the love of God and service to their neighbor. Neumann insists that elite followers of the Old Ethic, too, "must admit [their] responsibility for the unconscious repercussions [their attitude may have] on other people, who may be at a lower intellectual, human and ethical level than [themselves]."[14] On this basis, we may surely wonder about Jung's behavior with the self-satisfied women he deliberately insulted.

In what Neumann calls the "New Ethic" (Ethic, Type C), one follows not the Voice of a founder but attends to the Voice of one's own self, one's wholeness. In this effort, the shadow cannot be the enemy but must be granted "freedom and a share in one's life,"[15] for shadow, too, is part of our wholeness. "The acceptance of the shadow involves a growth in depth into the ground of one's own being, and with the loss of the airy illusion of an ego-ideal, a new depth and rootedness and stability is born."[16] Neumann writes:

> From now on, the ego can no longer perform its duty to the Self by the simple method of orienting itself in the light of the established values; a process of continuous self-questioning and self-control is now required.... Its aim, however, is not a questioning of conscience in the sense of an examination of the motives and contents of the conscious mind; the scope of the enquiry is now much more the total structure of the personality—and this includes the unconscious.[17]

Neumann gives us a more differentiated version of the Jungian myth and reveals that its practice requires a certain strenuous discipline. From the viewpoint of the Old Ethic, the Voice of the self will always reek of temptation, for it does not revere "established values." Nevertheless, neither Neumann nor Jung urges us to act out every passing whim. "The Voice must always be listened to—though not always followed.... The self is a trickster sage, unpredictable, inexhaustible, and dangerous when taken seriously."[18] The New Ethic involves a life of dialogue between ego and self, where certainties are few and we learn by experimentation: trying out a considered response to the Voice, examining the results, and learning from them. We never know a priori what the right course of action may be but in retrospect can usually determine whether we have been deceiving ourselves about the nature of the Voice.

Following the New Ethic liberates us from the dictatorial voice of the superego, that largely unconscious introject from parental and other authorities, but it gives us plenty of inner work to do. In a pair of essays from the late 1950s,[19] Jung distinguishes two layers in the phenomenon we call conscience: (a) "an elementary act of will or... impulse to act for which no conscious reason can be given" and (b) "a judgment grounded on rational feeling." He illustrates the distinction with the story of a businessman contemplating a deal that looked "perfectly serious and honorable," whereupon he had a dream that his arms and hands were covered in black dirt. It seemed to Jung that the dream pointed to strong unconscious knowledge that something was wrong with the deal. Eventually, the dreamer looked into it more carefully and discovered an element of fraud that could have turned out disastrously for him. Jung writes:

> If conscience is a kind of knowledge, then it is not the empirical
> subject who is the knower, but rather an unconscious personality
> who, to all appearances, behaves like a conscious subject. It knows
> the dubious nature of the offer, it recognizes the acquisitive greed of
> the ego, which does not shrink even from illegality, and it causes the
> appropriate judgment to be pronounced. This means that the ego has
> been replaced by an unconscious personality who performs the
> necessary act of conscience.[20]

A meaningful discussion of the ethical significance of Jung's "personal secrets" would require gaining some insight into the dialogue between ego and self that Jung either conducted or sidestepped—before entering into that sexual relationship with Toni Wolff or writing that insensitive letter to Sabina Spielrein's mother[21] or insulting the self-satisfied ladies in Munich. Hagiographer and close associate Barbara Hannah tells us of Jung's temper tantrums over the typing errors of his secretaries and the waywardness of the pots and pans that frustrated his culinary efforts in the medieval tower he built at Bollingen. She adds that he always examined his behavior after an outburst to learn what complex had gotten hold of him. According to Hannah, he did not diminish the significance of his dirty arms and hands, declaring before his disciples, "To be carried away by or possessed by anger is always a defeat."[22]

However, it may not be necessary to choose between an insider view that Jung was a wise man whose most puzzling acts were motivated by a higher purpose and the outsider perspective that Jung's guilt and arrogance constructed his theory of the psyche as a face-saving defense. Heinz Kohut, no friend of Jung's,[23] shows us how to hold the tension between the opposite positions, for he has grasped the symbolic perspective whereby pathology and creativity are two sides of the same coin. Peter Homans, in *Jung in Context* (1979), applies the Kohutian perspective to understanding Jung as a person and his impact on Western culture.[24] In doing so, Homans shows the way forward for a psychologically astute biographer. The issue is not either-or but both-and.

The thesis of Homan's book is that Jung was the first to articulate the religious dimension of our post-Christian quest for a meaningful sense of transcendence: "modern man" is "psychological man." Jung, therefore, reinterprets Christianity (and alchemy and Gnosticism) as inchoate forms of "individuation," our striving for wholeness through a dialogue between ego and self. Implicitly, an approach that embraces both sides of our nature recognizes that meaning is found beyond the merely rational in the contributions of the unconscious. In every case, it is mythic because it tells a story that pretends to be ultimate but is just one version of the human adventure—one that is compelling for *me* in this phase of my life.

Homans finds the first indications of Jung's interest in the religious dimension of "psychological man" in a 1910 letter he wrote to Freud. The father of psychoanalysis had wondered whether the psychoanalytic movement should join an ethical fraternity to protect it from both church and state. Jung answered with what he later called "another of [my] rampages of fantasy"—in essence, a confession of what we have been calling in the wake of Kohut's contributions "narcissistic grandiosity":

> I imagine a far finer and more comprehensive task for psychoanalysis...we must give it time to infiltrate into people from many centers, to revivify among intellectuals a feeling for symbol and myth, ever so gently to transform Christ back into the soothsaying God of the vine.... A genuine and proper ethical development cannot abandon Christianity but must grow up within it, must bring to fruition its hymn of love, the agony and ecstasy over the dying and resurgent god.[25]

Twenty years before Homans, Philip Rieff, in his classic *Freud: The Mind of the Moralist,* gave the issue a rather different slant, observing that the very existence of psychoanalysis declares that there is no human need that is "distinctively religious"; there is only "psychological need." For Rieff, this reality leaves every psychologist "the option...of being friendly or hostile" to religion. Jung took the first approach and declared religion "psychologically valuable," while Freud took the opposite course, demanding "something better, more mature than religion...[namely] rational science, in service of a less wasteful development of human satisfaction."[26] Freud would have us "dare live without" religious beliefs.

In Rieff's view, Freud proposes "an ethic of honesty" that would ask the tough questions and expose the patient's unconscious self-deceptions, while "Jung is in search of new emotional vitality." This appears to be an accurate description of Jung's diagnosis of "modern man," that he and she are no longer *moved emotionally* by traditional religious doctrines and are therefore out of touch with the source of vitality. Rieff makes it clear he favors Freud, but he is not really unjust to Jung: "[Jung's] is a situational ethic [an ethic of "sincerity"], based upon increasing the flow of creative energy. Hence, he fears too much consciousness as well as too little...[while Freud] cannot conceive of an excess of consciousness. In this respect, Jung is the more balanced of the two."[27]

The implications of Rieff's position would seem to be that Jung's "Myth in Our Time" is an instance of loosey-goosey romanticism—not on account of the story it tells, but on the very fact that it is the emotional element, the "being-gripped by" (Tillich), the sense that crucial big choices that determine the course of our lives are made "by an unconscious personality [steeped in emotion, but with its own 'knowledge'] who performs the necessary act of conscience."[28]

In Rieff's hands, Freud's "ethic of honesty" aims to uncover some undeniable truth, to sleuth out some single account as irrefutable as the findings of empirical science. The danger of taking this position too seriously was illustrated a couple of decades ago by the fad to recover traumatic memories through hypnosis, as though everything that has happened in our lives were filed somewhere, pristine and unaltered as in a photo album—a view that ignores both the history of hypnotic suggestion and the neurobiology of the brain. In contrast, Jung's "ethic of sincerity," in looking to a "whole-hearted engagement of character," cares less for "objective" truth than for a "subjective" emotional engagement that renders "all beliefs equally meritorious."[29] Even the practitioners of literal memory recovery ultimately took this "Jungian" position, for they argued that the hypnotic subjects *had* to be believed since their stories had such a compelling feel of emotional authenticity.[30]

Surely, there is much truth in Rieff's claim that Jung does not care for the same sort of truth that Freud seeks. Jung does not propose a single myth from history but rather the myth being spun right now in each of us through the dialogue between ego and self—a myth that grips *me* and perhaps no one else. Thus at bottom for Jung, there is no single truth, no single narrative of human life. No story is solid enough to stand on; each is a gloss on human existence. In Jung's view: "The two opposing 'realities,' the world of the conscious and the world of the unconscious, do not quarrel for supremacy, but each makes the other relative.... To the critical intelligence, nothing is left of *absolute* reality."[31]

As we stand above the abyss of not knowing anything dependable about the ultimate shape of human life, we either fall into despair or find, to our relief, a ghostly bridge unfolding beneath our feet, the work of that "unconscious personality who performs [our] necessary acts of conscience." How should we characterize this point of view: as hardier and tougher minded than Freud's faith that a rational, empirical science will somehow show us the honest truth, or as a romantic soft-mindedness that flees rationality in favor of emotional gratifications more appropriate to an earlier phase of our cultural development?

The issue of myth lies at the heart of many disputes over the value of Jung's psychology and a sound judgment of his character. We have taken note of several: whether his psychological theory makes possible a superior and more deeply satisfying way of life or only serves to cover up immoral behavior; whether truth may be "absolute" or only "mythic"; whether narcissism and creativity are mutually exclusive or inclusive; whether attention to myth completes and deepens human experience in a world that has forgotten its instinctual depths or whether it longs regressively for the womb of a romanticized past.

Another argument about the value of Jung's work is also based in a study of myth, one that is closely related to accusations that Jung was a Nazi, a Nazi sympathizer, or just generally a proponent of right-wing politics. Robert Ellwood has addressed this theme in his *Politics of Myth*.

For Ellwood, Jung, the psychologist; Mircea Eliade, the historian of religion; and Joseph Campbell, the "public mythologist" share a "common intellectual tone" characterized by "antimodernism and antirationalism tinged with romanticism and existentialism." Above all, they oppose "modernity's exaltation of reason, 'materialistic' science [and the] 'decadent' democracy...[of] rootless 'mass man' [in favor of] traditional 'rooted' peasant culture."[32] In Ellwood's view, proponents of myth are engaged in an inherently self-contradictory enterprise. Wishing to extract from myth universally human themes that apply today just as well as they did thousands of years ago overlooks the fact that myth is always local: "always a myth of a particular tribe or people, originally from some particular time in history, full of allusions to matters that would be best known to people of that time and place."[33] Consequently, the *idea of myth* purveyed by Jung and the others is a modern construct, the shining dream of an ideal world that never existed in the past. Ellwood writes:

> Mythology...wants a homogeneous, largely rural, and "rooted"
> society with a hierarchical superstructure; this society should possess
> a religious or mystical tendency able to express its unity ritually and
> experientially. Today such a society could only be recovered through a
> new enactment of the hero myth by one able to awaken the primor-
> dial but slumbering values of this people and call them into being
> again.[34]

The most obvious twentieth-century figure to attempt such a task is Adolph Hitler. Ellwood also cites Marxism, the Christian social gospel, Victorian notions of the white man's burden, and Daniel Boone on the American frontier. Nationalism, the notion that one's own people have a noble destiny, a worldwide role to enlighten the less privileged, is central. Today, the several persuasions of religious fundamentalists envision such a role for themselves, but they would never comprehend that their *vera doctrina* expresses a myth. For them, myths are what other people believe, people who do not know the true doctrine and cannot save themselves. The *concept* of myth surely does belong to the world of the twentieth century, and those who have this modern conception can no longer "live a myth" in the same naïve manner as our ancestors. To have a concept of myth is to see the relativity of all explanations; it is to begin thinking in symbols rather than in literal realities.

Unlike Hitler, Marx, or Daniel Boone, Jung never envisioned a myth-based *society*. He proposed, instead, that each of us find the myth we are unconsciously living—in every case, my myth and no one else's. His claims for universality, on the other hand, were not mythic but biological: because the human psyche itself is a product of evolution, it manifests a species-specific character that is at bottom the same for all of us. The mind that painted the Ice Age caves is the same that has put men on the moon.[35] The human mind is a product of our DNA and completed by one's own personal, familial, and cultural experience. All healthy humans are capable of language (universal archetype), but every group of us speaks a different language or dialect (cultural variation).[36]

On this basis, we can expect to find similarity of structure from one personal myth to another, and Jung does propose a "monomyth," namely, a comprehensive and fairly abstract mythic story that subsumes all other myths as versions or components of itself. In *Symbols of Transformation, Psychology and Alchemy*, and the seminar on *Kundalini Yoga*, the "Night-Sea Journey of the Sun," as outlined by Leo Frobenius,[37] is identified as the structuring narrative. Myth is indeed always local, but mythic *thinking* is universally human and expresses our need for renewal through integrating formerly neglected aspects of the self. Like the ever-renewed sun that sets in the western sea in the evening, transits beneath the earth overnight, and rises renewed out of the eastern sea every morning, regular immersion in the underworld of the unconscious is necessary for psychological balance, harmony, and a meaningful life. This means "psychological man" is also Campbell's "hero with a thousand faces," who becomes "master of the two worlds."[38]

Even with this distinction firmly held in mind, however, it cannot be denied that Jung's writings and public statements sometimes had the ring of anti-Semitism. As Richard Noll demonstrates in great detail, Jung had long been fascinated with the German "folkish" thinking that inspired Hitler's nationalism.[39] In 1934, he wrote that the Jewish psyche is the product of an unbroken historical development over many centuries, while the Christian (Aryan) psyche has had a veneer of Christianity imposed over a barbarous base. Consequently, the Christian psyche is dangerously explosive, whereas Jewish consciousness is generally broader and deeper, the product of a closer, more integrated relationship between conscious and unconscious, resembling in this respect the Chinese psyche. Although such a statement suggests a superiority for the integral Jewish psyche over the barbarous German one, Jung did go on to repeat many of the anti-Semitic stereotypes of the day: that "the Jew is something of a nomad, has never yet created a cultural form of his own . . . requir[ing] a more or less civilized nation to act as host." Also, like women, Jews are "physically weaker and have to aim at the chinks in the armor of their opponents."[40] Two years later, in an article titled "Wotan," Jung saw the Nazi movement as driven by the archetype of the wanderer god and hoped it meant renewal for Germany.[41]

In his discussion of this material, Ellwood does not go so far as to brand Jung an "anti-Semite,"[42] noting that after 1936 he curtailed writing on race and the Jews and that by 1939 he had come to see Nazism as a "terrible manifestation of mass man rather than a purifying archetype of the nation."[43] After the war, he confessed to concentration camp survivor Rabbi Leo Baeck that he had "slipped up" in his initial failure to recognize the evil of Nazism.[44] Ellwood assesses Jung's voice during the 1930s as "moderate, not shrill," because Jung had "a capacity for self-correction" but no talent for politics.[45] He finds Jung's mentality similar to that of eighteenth-century political theorist and Whig Member of Parliament Edmund Burke, rather than Hitler.

Ellwood's message seems to be that we should be careful of any argument based in myth, for it will always have a romantic, right-wing tendency, and even if Jung himself was not a Nazi, he provided comfort and cover to Nazi sympathizers through his incautious and politically naïve statements. Something similar appears to have been intended when Erich Neumann, Jung's disciple and a German Jew who migrated to Israel in the 1930s, warned in his *New Ethic* to take seriously our responsibility not to mislead people "who may be at a lower intellectual, human and ethical level." In his zeal to promote his doctrine of the collective unconscious, therefore, Jung seems not to have considered the influence his words might have on a German populace in the grip of a mass delusion. It appears Jung was hooked by his ambition and sidestepped a consultation with his personal myth.

Ellwood also claims Jung and the other champions of myth promote "anti-materialism and antirationalism," that is, that they oppose "modernity's exalta-tion of reason [and] 'materialistic' science." There can be no doubt that Jung is critical of modern Western culture: "Primitives show a much more balanced psychology than we do," he says, "for the reason that they have no objection to letting the irrational come through, while we resent it."[46] Cultivating a personal myth, therefore, embraces the irrational as a valuable completion of our con-scious perspective, but does Jung urge us forward into a realistic new future or backward into a romanticized past?

On the issue of the "irrational," Jung's idea of integrating the rational with the irrational is hardly "antirational." Jung does not reject conceptual thought wholesale but wants us also to accept realities that exist alongside reason. Indeed, he calls sensation (the five senses) and intuition "irrational functions," for there is no logical order to what appears in consciousness through these faculties. He criticizes Western culture not for being rational but for branding too much of normal psychic functioning as illegitimate—in short, for being irrationally selective in what it counts as "real."

A similar confusion seems to be involved in Ellwood's claims regarding Jung and so-called materialistic science. The last science we had that was almost fully "materialistic" was Newton's, whereby colliding billiard balls, gas mole-cules, and the like were nicely accounted for, but gravity and magnetism were measurable but an embarrassment—seemingly impossible phenomena requiring "action across distance" that we had no way to explain. In the nineteenth century, Michael Faraday (1791–1867) and James Clerk Maxwell (1831–1879) demonstrated the existence of an electromagnetic energy field, and in the twentieth, Albert Einstein (1879–1955) described gravity as the effect of massive bodies upon a "spacetime continuum" or field. In both cases, Western science borrowed what seems to be an "irrational" solution (the notion of an invisible field) originating in Chinese philosophy and brought to the West by mathematician and philosopher Gottfried Leibniz (1646–1716).[47] Furthermore, within a decade of Einstein's articles on relativity, quantum mechanics had been established as the most successful physical theory in history—even though it proposes that matter is a special condition of reality, where elementary particles pop into and out of existence on extremely short time scales and "action at a distance" (now called "nonlocality") is common.

While there is no doubt Jung challenged an *exclusive materialism* in scientific theories, he was delighted with relativity and quantum mechanics, believing that they had opened the way for what might be called a more adequate science, one that has room for life, organisms, and consciousness. Explicating this view was the intention behind the theory of synchronicity, which he worked out in dialogue with one of the pioneers of quantum mechanics, Wolfgang Pauli (1900–1958).[48] Jung explicitly borrowed the metaphysical foundation for his synchronicity principle from Leibniz and China (the philosophy behind the *I Ching*), aligning up his argument with the same conceptual process physicists have been using since Faraday's clever experiments in electromagnetism to explain apparent action at a distance.[49]

In the case of synchronicity, Jung proposes a fourth universal principle in addition to (1) the gravity field of spacetime, (2) the electromagnetic field, and (3) quantum uncertainty. The fourth is a "psychoid" principle, whereby everything in the universe has a psychelike quality, a capacity for responsiveness. It is easy to see a psychoid principle at work in the life processes of a protozoan being watched under a microscope—exhibiting something like a primitive form of consciousness that brings it spontaneously to approach food and avoid harsh conditions. As a universal principle, however, psychoid responsiveness also belongs to molecules, atoms, and elementary particles. Consciousness is not an embarrassing oddity in the physical world: it "goes all the way down."[50] Matter itself is not "dead" or "inert," as has simply been proclaimed by the unexamined metaphysics of our Western culture. The universe is not a collection of unrelated elements but ordered as an internally responsive organism, a nested hierarchy of psychoid components—just as the human body is a unity comprised of organs each made up of tissues and so on down to cells and proteins, carbon, and oxygen.[51] According to the psychoid principle of synchronicity, organisms are also related "upward" through the nested hierarchy: individuals function within communities, ecosystems, the planet, the solar system, the galaxy, the local cluster, and so on up to the universe as a whole. By this means, everything is related to everything else. The psychoid principle gives a new meaning to the ancient mythic claim that every human being is a microcosm. Does Jung obliterate the distinction between science and myth?

A full understanding of the implications of synchronicity makes it clear that Jung is a "mystic." But in affirming his mystical tendencies, we need to clarify what a mystic is and is not. Most of those who accuse Jung of mysticism mean that they consider him an irresponsible and superstitious thinker who wants to believe in impossible things and does not care to critically examine them. For example, when psychologist Noel W. Smith discovered striking similarities between the rock art of the California Indians and that of our Ice Age ancestors in the caves of Europe, he felt required to make the following disavowal: " 'Archetypes' are the mystical concepts invented by psychoanalyst Karl [sic] Jung. There is no objective evidence for them nor is any possible."[52] The misspelling of Jung's name alone indicates that Smith is dealing with Jung's *rumored reputation* and not with any ascertainable facts. He seems to believe archetypes are inherited *images*, a view that Jung struggled all his life to correct.

Similarly, Harvard's J. Allan Hobson, perhaps the foremost authority on the dreaming brain, argues in several books that his findings do not support Freud's dream theory but do support Jung's in all respects. Fearing that association with Jung may undermine his scientific respectability, he gives bizarre versions of what he thinks "a Jungian would say" about the meaning of a dream and calls Jung "strongly anti-scientific."[53] He erroneously believes Jung thought that images themselves are inherited and "intrinsic to the nervous system."[54]

Thus as an alleged mystic, Jung is accused of being a careless and superstitious thinker. By contrast, individuals revered as mystics by their religious traditions—Meister Eckhart, Milarepa, Rumi, the Baal Shem Tov, Ramakrishna—are those who deliberately employ altered states of consciousness, learn to master them (as in yogic practice, meditation, or shamanic healing), and integrate the results of their explorations into a superior way of life. The lives of such individuals surely resemble "Jung's Myth in Our Time." Jung was a mystic insofar as he found altered states of consciousness (the irrational proposals of the unconscious) to be as important as is critical, ego-directed thinking in the conduct of the examined life.

Mystics often behave as though they have discovered the nature of *absolute* reality: for example, the famous eighth-century teacher of Advaita Vedanta, Shankara, proclaims the visible world is merely an illusion (*maya*) hiding the invisible absolute reality of *brahman*; the world is not material (as it appears) but comprised entirely of consciousness (as only the mystics can see). Shankara's philosophy resembles Jung's in that the goal is to transcend the limitations of the ego and realize one's deeper identity is the self (*atman*), which in the end is not different from *brahman* (absolute consciousness).[55] In Jung's hands, however, the metaphysics of a psychoid universe cannot enjoy the status of "absolute truth," for that does not exist. Rather, the psychoid universe is a mythic truth, "Jung's Myth in Our Time," and whether plausible or not—even if some form of it is eventually embraced by mainstream physics[56]—it is open to the criticism that it is Jung's neurotic defense, a way of reassuring himself that the post-Christian world can be deeply meaningful.

With Homans's crucial Kohutian insight that narcissism and creativity are two sides of the same coin, perhaps we do not have to choose one side or the other of this dilemma. Surely, there can be no doubt that Jung's life can be coherently described as a search for meaning rooted in "sincerity" (Rieff) and emotional resonance. His liberating vision at age twelve of God defecating on the Basel Cathedral during his pastor father's crisis of faith convinced him that God could speak directly through one's own psyche more compellingly than through the scriptures. He lectured his college debating society, Zofingia, that as future scientists they had immense work to do: to leave the safe paths of established philosophy and science and "make our own independent raids into the realm of the unfathomable, chase the shadows of the night."[57] He embraced the phenomena of parapsychology, including the spiritualism fad at the turn of the century, writing his doctoral dissertation on his cousin's mediumship.[58] He continued to seek out gifted psychic practitioners for decades and was a supporter of J. B. Rhine's experimental work with telepathy at Duke University. The theory of synchronicity was developed a half century after his Zofingia lectures and dissertation, when science had still not taken up the work of investigating the claims of parapsychology and Jung was nearly eighty and running out of time. He saw a glimmer of hope in the "new physics" of Einstein and Pauli but recognized that the crucial issue was and remains metaphysical. Even though at the beginning of the twenty-first century statistical support for the reality of parapsychological abilities can no longer be denied by serious investigators,[59] nothing has been explained. No mechanism has been proposed to account for the phenomena. Our folk metaphysics—which is deeply Newtonian and Cartesian and makes no effort to account for life or consciousness—declares that none will ever be found. Jung's psychoid principle, therefore, is a mythic-metaphysical leap by which the Gordian knot of the body-mind or matter-soul problem is sliced through with the declaration that soul and consciousness are not limited to *Homo sapiens* but in some form or other go "all the way down" to what mainstream science and philosophy call (with no better justification) dead, inert matter.

No doubt the theory of synchronicity and the practice of living a myth constitute a wish fulfillment. Whether they are seen as an avoidance of the tough problems that a "mature" psychology faces or as a daring reformulation of the human venture for an era that knows the idea of myth but not how to live it may measure the reader's neurosis, maturity, or wholeness as much or more than Jung's.

NOTES

1. C. G. Jung, *Memories, Dreams, Reflections* (New York: Pantheon, 1963).

2. Sonu Shamdasani, "Memories, Dreams, Omissions," *Spring* 57 (1995): 115–38.

3. Marie-Louise von Franz, *C. G. Jung: His Myth in Our Time* (New York: Pantheon, 1975).

4. Robert C. Smith, *The Wounded Jung* (Evanston, IL: Northwestern University Press, 1996); Paul J. Stern, *C. G. Jung: Haunted Prophet* (New York: Brasillier, 1976); Richard Noll, *The Aryan Christ: The Secret Life of C. G. Jung* (New York: Random House, 1997).

5. C. G. Jung, "Symbols of Transformation," in *Collected Works of C. G. Jung* (Princeton, NJ: Princeton University Press): xxiv–xxv.

6. "This whole psychic organism [the collective unconscious] corresponds exactly to the body, which, though individually varied, is in all essential features the specifically human body which all men have. In its development and structure, it still preserves elements that connect it with the invertebrates and ultimately with the protozoa. Theoretically it should be possible to 'peel' the collective unconscious, layer by layer, until we come to the psychology of the worm, and even of the amoeba." (Jung, "The Structure of the Psyche," *Collected Works*, 8:322.)

7. Cf. John Ryan Haule, "Analyzing from the Self," in *Pathways into the Jungian World: Phenomenology and Analytical Psychology*, ed. Roger Brooke (London: Routledge, 1999), 255–273.

8. McLynn's dependability as a biographer may be judged in part by the fact that many of the most damaging claims he makes about Jung are supported by footnotes that direct the reader to undocumented claims made by earlier biographers.

9. Frank McLynn, *Carl Gustav Jung: A Biography* (New York: St. Martin's, 1996), 316.

10. Robert Stein, "Reflections on Professional Deformation," in *Jungian Analysts: Their Visions and Vulnerabilities*, ed. Marvin Spiegelman (Phoenix: Falcon, 1988), 151.

11. Sigrid Strauss-Kloebe, "Memory of C. G. Jung," in *C. G. Jung, Emma Jung, and Toni Wolff: A Collection of Remembrances*, ed. Fern Jensen (San Francisco: Analytical Psychology Club of San Francisco, 1982), 89ff. Mrs. Strauss-Kloebe is identified only as "from Heidelberg."

12. Haule, "Waiting for C. G.: A Look at the Biographies," *Quadrant* 30.1 (Winter 2000): 71–87.

13. Jung, "Two Essays on Analytical Psychology," *Collected Works*, 7:240.

14. Erich Neumann, *Depth Psychology and a New Ethic*, trans. Eugene Wolf (New York: G. P. Putnam's Sons, 1969), 73.

15. Neumann, *Depth Psychology*, 81.

16. Ibid., 96.

17. Ibid., 123.

18. Haule, "Eros, Mutuality, and the 'New Ethic,'" in *Cast the First Stone: Ethics in Analytical Practice*, ed. Lena Ross and Manisha Roy (Wilmette, IL: Chiron, 1995), 11.

19. Jung, "A Psychological View of Conscience," *Collected Works*, 10:825–57; Jung, "Good and Evil in Analytical Psychology," *Collected Works*, 10:858–86.

20. Jung, *Collected Works*, 10:829.

21. On being accused of becoming too intimate with his young patient, Sabina Spielrein, Jung received a letter from the girl's mother, who demanded an explanation. Jung responded that he was not really the girl's doctor, since he was not being paid for his work: "Therefore I would suggest that if you wish me to adhere strictly to my role as doctor, you should pay me a fee as suitable recompense for my trouble." Aldo Carotenuto, *A Secret Symmetry: Sabina Spielrein between Jung and Freud*, trans. Pomerans, Shepley, and Winston (New York: Pantheon, 1982).

22. Barbara Hannah, *Jung, His Life and Work* (New York: G. P. Putnam's Sons, 1976), 282.

23. Kohut advocates not the "special charisma" of "C. G. Jung's commanding personality" but restricting oneself "to the use of the only tools that provide rational success: interpretations and reconstructions." Heinz Kohut, *The Analysis of the Self* (Madison, WI: International Universities, 1971), 223.

24. Peter Homans, *Jung in Context* (Chicago: University of Chicago Press, 1995).

25. Homans, *Jung*, 56.

26. Philip Rieff, *Freud: The Mind of the Moralist* (Chicago: University of Chicago Press, 1979), 271.

27. Reiff, *Freud*, 320f.

28. Cf. Haule, *Perils of the Soul: Ancient Wisdom and the New Age* (York Beach, ME: Wiser, 1999), 156–162.

29. Haule, *Perils*, 320.

30. Cf. Debbie Nathan and Michael Snedeker, *Satan's Silence: Ritual Abuse and the Making of a Modern American Witch Hunt* (New York: Basic, 1995), and Victor, *Satanic Panic: The Creation of a Contemporary Legend* (Chicago: Open Court, 1993).

31. Jung, "Two Essays," *Collected Works*, 7:354.

32. Robert Ellwood, *The Politics of Myth: A Study of C. G. Jung, Mircea Eliade, and Joseph Campbell* (Albany: State University of New York Press, 1999), xi.

33. Ellwood, *Politics of Myth*, 7.

34. Ibid., 29.

35. Common claim of recent research into Ice Age cave paintings; cf. David Lewis-Williams, *The Mind in the Cave: Consciousness and the Origins of Art* (London: Thames & Hudson, 2002).

36. Haule, *Jung in the 21ˢᵗ Century: Volume One, Evolution and Archetype* (London: Routledge, 2010) 16–28.

37. Leo Frobenius, *Das Zeitalter des Sonnengottes* (Berlin: Georg Reimer, 1904).

38. Joseph Campbell, *Hero with a Thousand Faces* (Princeton, NJ: Princeton University Press, 1949): 229–37.

39. Noll, *The Aryan Christ*, 98–119.

40. Ellwood, *Politics of Myth*, 63; Jung, *Collected Works*, 10:353f.

41. Jung, "Wotan," *Collected Works*, 10:371–399.

42. He provides a detailed definition of anti-Semitism (Ellwood, *Politics of Myth*, 63).

43. Ellwood, *Politics of Myth*, 57.

44. Ibid., 187; Gerhard Wehr, *Jung, A Biography*, trans. David M. Weeks (Boston: Shambhala, 1988), 325f.

45. Ellwood, *Politics of Myth*, 57.

46. Jung, *Analytical Psychology: Notes on a Seminar Given in 1925*, ed. W. McGuire (Princeton, NJ: Princeton University Press, 1989), 105.

47. Vak Dusek, *The Holistic Inspirations of Physics: The Underground History of Electromagnetic Theory* (New Brunswick, NJ: Rutgers University Press, 1999), 194–208.

48. C. A. Meier, C. P. Enz, and M. Fierz, eds., *Atom and Archetype; The Pauli/Jung Letters, 1932–1958*, trans. David Roscoe (Princeton, NJ: Princeton University Press, 2001).

49. Jung, "Synchronicity," *Collected Works*, 8:916–946.

50. Cf. Christian de Quincey, "What Jung Meant by 'Synchronicity,'" in *Radical Knowing* (Rochester, NY: Park Street, 2005), 273–278.

51. Cf. Haule, *Jung in the 21ˢᵗ Century: Volume Two Synchronicity and Science* (London: Routledge, 2010) 171–192.

52. Noel W. Smith, *An Analysis of Ice Age Art* (New York: Peter Lang, 1992), 13.

53. Allan J. Hobson, *Thirteen Dreams Freud Never Had: The New Mind Science* (New York: Pi Science, 2005), 63, 118f.

54. Hobson, *The Dreaming Brain* (New York: Basic, 1988), 27.

55. Ingrid Fischer-Schreiber et al., eds., *Encyclopedia of Eastern Philosophy and Religion* (Boston: Shambhala, 1989).

56. Today several physicists are making similar claims: e.g., David Bohm, *Wholeness and the Implicate Order* (London: Routledge/Ark, 1983); Amit Goswami, Richard E. Reed, and Maggie Goswami, *The Self-Aware Universe* (New York: Tarcher/Putnam, 1993); Minas C. Kafatos and Robert Nadeau, *Conscious Universe: Parts and Wholes in Physical Reality* (New York: Springer, 2000); N. C. Panda, *The Vibrating Universe* (Dehli: Motilal Banarsidass 2000); and Christian de Quincey, *Radical Knowing* (Rochester, NY: Park Street, 2005). Most appeal to a metaphysics inspired by Alfred North Whitehead, *Process and Reality: An Essay in Cosmology* (New York: Free Press, 1957).

57. Jung, "Zofingia," *Collected Works*, A:23.

58. Jung, "So-Called Occult Phenomena," *Collected Works*, 1:1–150.

59. Cf. Dean Radin, *The Conscious Universe: The Scientific Truth of Psychic Phenomena* (San Francisco: HarperEdge, 1997), 51–60.

REFERENCES

Bohm, David. *Wholeness and the Implicate Order*. London: Routledge/Ark, 1983.

Campbell, Joseph. *Hero with a Thousand Faces*. Princeton, NJ: Princeton University Press, 1949.

Carotenuto, Aldo. *A Secret Symmetry: Sabina Spielrein between Jung and Freud*. Trans. Pomerans, Shepley, and Winston. New York: Pantheon, 1982.

De Quincey, Christian. *Radical Knowing*. Rochester, NY: Park Street, 2005.

Dusek, Val. *The Holistic Inspirations of Physics: The Underground History of Electromagnetic Theory*. New Brunswick, NJ: Rutgers University Press, 1999.

Ellwood, Robert. *The Politics of Myth: A Study of C. G. Jung, Mircea Eliade, and Joseph Campbell*. Albany: State University of New York Press, 1999.

Fischer-Schreiber, Ingrid, et al., eds. *Encyclopedia of Eastern Philosophy and Religion*. Boston: Shambhala, 1989.

Frobenius, Leo. *Das Zeitalter des Sonnengottes*. Berlin: Georg Reimer, 1904.

Goswami, Amit, Richard E. Reed, and Maggie Goswami. *The Self-Aware Universe*. New York: Tarcher/Putnam, 1993.

Hannah, Barbara. *Jung, His Life and Work*. New York: G. P. Putnam's Sons, 1976.

Haule, John Ryan. "Eros, Mutuality, and the 'New Ethic." In *Cast the First Stone: Ethics in Analytical Practice*, ed. Lena Ross and Manisha Roy. Wilmette, IL: Chiron, 1995.

Haule, John Ryan. "Analyzing from the Self." In *Pathways into the Jungian World: Phenomenology and Analytical Psychology*, ed. Roger Brooke, 255–273. London: Routledge, 1999.

Haule, John Ryan. *Perils of the Soul: Ancient Wisdom and the New Age*. York Beach, ME: Weiser, 1999.

Haule, John Ryan. "Waiting for C. G.: A Look at the Biographies." *Quadrant* 30.1 (Winter 2000): 71–87.

Haule, John Ryan. *Jung in the 21st Century: Volume One Evolution and Archetype; Volume Two Synchronicity and Science* (London: Routledge, 2010).

Hobson, J. Allan. *The Dreaming Brain*. New York: Basic Books, 1988.

Hobson, J. Allan. *Thirteen Dreams Freud Never Had: The New Mind Science*. New York: Pi Science, 2005.

Homans, Peter. *Jung in Context*. 1979. Reprint, Chicago: University of Chicago Press, 1995.

Jung, C. G. *The Collected Works of C. G. Jung*, ed. Herbert Read, Michael Fordham, and William McGuire, trans. R. F. C. Hull. Princeton, NJ: Princeton University Press, 1953–1976.

Jung, C. G. *Memories, Dreams, Reflections*, ed. A. Jaffé, trans. R. Winston and C. Winston. New York: Pantheon, 1963.

Jung, C. G. *The Zofingia Lectures* (*Supplementary Volume A of the Collected Works*), trans. Jan Van Heurck. Princeton, NJ: Princeton University Press, 1983.

Jung, C. G. *Analytical Psychology: Notes of the Seminar Given in 1925*, ed. W. McGuire. Princeton. NJ: Princeton University Press, 1989.

Kafatos, Menas, and Robert Nadeau. *The Conscious Universe: Part and Whole in Modern Physical Theory*. New York: Springer, 1990.

Kohut, Heinz. *The Analysis of the Self*. Madison, WI: International Universities, 1971.

Lewis-Williams, David. *The Mind in the Cave: Consciousness and the Origins of Art*. London: Thames & Hudson, 2002.

McLynn, Frank. *Carl Gustav Jung: A Biography*. New York: St. Martin's, 1996.

Meier, C. A., ed. *Atom and Archetype: The Pauli/Jung Letters, 1932–1958*, trans. David Roscoe. Princeton, NJ: Princeton University Press, 2001.

Nathan, Debbie, and Michael Snedeker. *Satan's Silence: Ritual Abuse and the Making of a Modern American Witch Hunt*. New York: Basic Books, 1995.

Neumann, Erich. *Depth Psychology and a New Ethic*, trans. Eugene Rolfe. New York: G. P. Putnam's Sons, 1969.

Noll, Richard. *The Aryan Christ: The Secret Life of Carl Jung*. New York, Random House, 1997.

Panda, N. C. *The Vibrating Universe*. Delhi, India: Motilal Banarsidass, 2000.

Radin, Dean. *The Conscious Universe: The Scientific Truth of Psychic Phenomena*. San Francisco: HarperEdge, 1997.

Rieff, Philip. *Freud: The Mind of the Moralist*, 3rd ed. Chicago: University of Chicago Press, 1979.

Shamdasani, Sonu. "Memories, Dreams, Omissions." *Spring* 57 (1995): 115–138.

Smith, Noel W. *An Analysis of Ice Age Art*. New York: Peter Lang, 1992.

Smith, Robert C. *The Wounded Jung*. Evanston, IL: Northwestern University Press, 1996.

Stein, Robert. "Reflections on Professional Deformation." In *Jungian Analysts: Their Visions and Vulnerabilities*, ed. Marvin Spiegelman. Phoenix, AZ: Falcon, 1988.

Stern, Paul J. *C. G. Jung, the Haunted Prophet*. New York: Brasillier, 1976.

Strauss-Kloebe, Sigrid. "Memory of C. G. Jung." In *C. G. Jung, Emma Jung, and Toni Wolff: A Collection of Remembrances*, ed. Fern Jensen. San Francisco: Analytical Psychology Club of San Francisco, 1982.

Victor, Jeffrey S. *Satanic Panic: The Creation of a Contemporary Legend*. Chicago: Open Court, 1993.

Von Franz, Marie-Louise. *C. G. Jung: His Myth in Our Time*. New York: Pantheon, 1975.

Wehr, Gerhard. *Jung, A Biography*, trans. David M. Weeks. Boston: Shambhala, 1988.

Whitehead, Alfred North. *Process and Reality: An Essay in Cosmology*. New York: Free Press, 1957.

10

Anima, Gender, Feminism

Susan Rowland

Introduction: What Is the Matter with Jung?

> The anima has an erotic, emotional character, the animus a
> rationalizing one. Hence most of what men say about
> feminine eroticism...is derived from their own anima
> projections and distorted accordingly. On the other hand, the
> astonishing assumptions and fantasies that women make
> about men come from the activity of the animus, who
> produces an inexhaustible supply of illogical arguments and
> false explanations.[1]

I teach the work of C. G. Jung to students in the final year of an
English literature degree and to master's students of depth psychology in other universities. I like to start with this quotation and
ask them, unprepared, what they make of it. If I read it slowly to
them, usually they laugh. For me, it is the laugh that is the germ of
an imaginative engagement with Jung, for not only is the imagination the generative core of his ideas but also comedy is a much
overlooked ingredient of them.

Jung's sentences here are intimately related. They connect both by
concepts of gender and by the passions femininity and masculinity
arouse as they touch the inner world of sexuality and desire. In effect,
intellectual and emotional content are equally important. While on the
one hand, Jung was an unashamed essentialist on gender, believing
that male and female bodies bestowed unproblematic masculinity and
femininity, respectively, here, as elsewhere, his conservatism was
undermined by his radical treatment of the unconscious. Jung's

unconscious is sublime; it is the creative source and the ultimate origin of meaning, feeling, and value. Fundamentally independent of the ego, the unconscious takes up opposing and complementary positions to it. The goal is to woo the ego into a relationship. Numinous and generative, one of the chief means of the unconscious inviting the ego's desire is through the androgyny of the unknown psyche.

Not surprisingly, Jung thought in heterosexual configurations. Yet there is no reason in the Jungian model that the erotic other in the unconscious should not be of the same gender. Nevertheless, in prioritizing gender "otherness," Jung called the feminine unconscious of a man, the *anima*, and the masculine unconscious of a woman, the *animus*.

So, returning to the provocative quotation and its release of laughter, perhaps these rational, balanced, conceptual figures are an insufficient explanation? Indeed, I believe these three sentences hold the key to Jung's least acknowledged gift to succeeding generations: his experimental writing about what we can never master rationally, the unknown drama of the unconscious. Each of the three sentences takes a different point of view.

The first perspective the quotation offers is a transcendent treatment of knowledge common to modernity, which begins to unpack the rational concepts of anima and animus. What is known is here elevated above its context, transcends the means of its generation. Sentence two dives into the immanent. Here, knowledge is deeply embedded in its own birthing. Fascinatingly, the subject of sentence two is the actual *impossibility* of rational evaluation between the sexes. We are all immersed in the emotional and bodily processes of our own gender-in-relation-to-the-other. Objectivity is an impossible dream of an overrationalized intellect. Yet, of course, Jung does not say "we" here, but "men," his own gender, the only one he can truly speak *from*.

So what happens in the third and final sentence on "the astonishing assumptions and fantasies" that women make about men? Here there seems to be a mysterious excess in the writing. Such an apparent attempt to speak about the perspective of women is neither rationally transcendent nor plausibly immanent. It elicits the question: who is speaking? When I ask my students who is speaking, and what might be the relationship between the second and third sentences, someone will say, "The anima, Jung's anima is speaking." In fact, the writing tells us this is so.

We have been informed that it is the unconscious anima who distorts male perceptions of women. What follows is a highly overdetermined rant at the irrationality of the feminine sex when gripped by their unconscious animuses. Is Jung having a joke with the reader? Or is he providing an example of his argument? Is this slippage from rational ego talking concepts to unconsciously influenced bitchy voice (anima) an unintended demonstration of how the unconscious may disrupt writing? Or is it the writer deliberately allowing an other to take over his voice? We do not know. Here, in that unknowable quality in the writing on gender, its root in the sublime unconscious is truly present.[2]

So far, I have suggested three characteristics of Jung's writing on gender: first, lucid concepts; then the experimental attempt to *embody* the unknown psyche; finally, a tendency to lapse into banal stereotypes. The rest of this chapter will explore what is important and possible for feminist and gender teaching from Jung's many textual voices, including the anima herself. First, I will say a little more on these three forms of writing, for it is in gender in which Jung creatively muddles the distinction between form and matter itself.

Two other concepts associated with Jung's gender are Eros and Logos. These are principles of conscious functioning, with Eros denoting connection, feeling, and relationship, and Logos discrimination and cognition. While admitting that there can be no absolute gender division here, Jung then proceeds to assign them differently to men and woman and attach them to anima and animus. With Logos more native to the consciousness of men and Eros to the ego of women, anima in men teaches them Eros, while women are doomed by having their rational discrimination of Logos tied to their unconscious, unreliable animus. Jung's liking for neat symmetry at one level results in an assertion of women's innate illogicality that he never tries to justify, for it follows that women's cognition and discrimination are forever irrational. Probably Jung's most controversial lapse into misogyny and the nagging woman is the following:

> No matter how friendly or obliging a woman's Eros may be, no logic
> of earth can shake her if she is ridden by the animus. Often the man
> has the feeling—and he is not altogether wrong—that only seduction
> or a beating or rape would have the necessary power of persuasion.[3]

Gender is where Jung goes too *far!* There is something very passionate, quite terrible, and sublime about this quotation. It drags the reader into an arena of white-hot emotions as it evokes male sexual violence, or the threat of it, as something to be considered in gender conflict. I am going to be very careful now and say that Jung is at fault for laying himself open to a reading that advocates rape or a beating. However, I include this quotation in material for my students because, in examining the unconscious fantasies provoked here, I believe the challenge is in taking personal feelings and responses beyond fear and violence. Gender's potential creativity is also in the aggression and mistrust between men and women.

An actual examination of the construction of the comment about seduction or beating or rape suggests that Jung is describing, not advocating, the violent rousing of men faced with a stubborn woman. "A man might feel" is not the same as "a man should do." I read "and he is not altogether wrong" as meaning that he is not "inaccurate" in thinking only violence would prevail. So my reading here is that men faced with the rage of a woman's masculine animus *feel*, maybe correctly, that only an attack would allow them to win the argument. That is, men *feel* this, where feeling for men is, as Jung has been insisting, an inferior function that their anima needs to nurture in them. A feeling that can only be lived through violent assault on the other is a paltry quality.

On the one hand, I am suggesting that Jung provides a powerful insight into sexual violence here. One is significantly aware of seduction as a tool of power. On the other hand, this insight risks drowning in the fear and desire this quotation induces. In the indefiniteness, unknowability, gaps, and siren voices of Jung's writing, the rational concepts of gender take on the aspect of desire, stirring the blood. Indeed, it is the combination of conceptual ideas jarring against banal stereotypes that often trace out the unknown and erotic.

Gender becomes a demand on the embodied imagination. Such a unique and experimental angle on gender is at once a *treatment* and a *gaping wound* in the writing. Jung faces two ways: as a powerful resource for feminist ideas and as sorely in need of them himself.

Jung, the Unlikely Feminist

The Jungian Symbolic Order: The Divine Feminine

While feminist theory is almost as diverse as individual feminist scholars, there is a general consensus that Western modernity has suffered under a patriarchal order of society. Patriarchy's institution as rule-of-the-father has a still potent symbolic origin in monotheism as transcendent of the "matter" of his creation. The divine source of all things is a Father God imagined as the giver of form and meaning. "He" alone produces the material world and "man" in his own image.

This myth of the deification of fathering finds more secular expressions in modernity. In particular, Freudian psychoanalysis takes a new look at origins. Freud's blend of traditional patriarchy and the Oedipus myth provides another narrative, whereby the father inducts the child into form and reason.[4] Coming between the child and "his" passionate union with the mother, the boy child fears castration, the loss of his special aspect, his penis, if he displeases the father. So he allies himself with fatherhood, thus anatomical and social superiority.

After Freud, it was Jacques Lacan who extended the "forming" quality of the father into the generation of culture.[5] Lacan argued that the body was being overliteralized. True, the boy child's task was to identify with paternity, thereby suppressing the desire for the mother, repressing it to make the unconscious. Yet the phallus was to be the defining artifact, the sign of masculinity. Lacan shifted the simultaneous founding of ego and unconscious into the realm of words. Here, it was in the early acquisition of language that the split in the child's psyche occurred.

Once a child perceives that words substitute for absent things, then he or she takes up a position in society's codes. Lacan named these the Symbolic Order. Like Freud, Lacan regards the child's new position as gendered, because boys are gifted by a patriarchal society with a privileged relation to the phallus as indicator of social and sexual power. Yet neither boys nor girls actually wholly possess the phallus since it becomes the ultimate sign of potency and completeness, a completeness forever lost in that tragic split from the primal (m)other. The splitting of the subject into ego and unconscious means that not even males can completely master the phallus for themselves.

Unfortunately, as feminists have long pointed out, the feminine remains disadvantaged. Lacan unhelpfully suggests that although males cannot simply "have" the phallus, it is the proper role of females to "be" the phallus for them. Moreover, as the ultimate sign of the potency of power, the phallus is the disseminator of patriarchal values throughout society. Lacan's culture is marked by a symbolic of patriarchal domination that continues the marginalization of the feminine. Psychoanalytic philosopher Luce Irigaray has done important work in critiquing Lacan's subordination of the feminine as the source of phallocratic power.[6]

While no feminist in the straightforward sense of wanting to revolutionize the position of women in society, Jung does transform the ontology of a patriarchal symbolic. We need to return to his notion of the unconscious as autonomous, creative, and in part unknowable. Such a lively creature in the embryonic being of a child significantly modifies the Oedipus complex. Of course, Oedipal struggles occur, and a child must still separate from the mother, entailing a certain amount of repressed sexuality. Yet far more integral to the developing person is the primal mother that is the unconscious itself.

This Jungian unconscious actively gives birth to the child's conscious ego. It means that the Jungian symbolic is primarily rooted in the struggles of the unconscious to create meaning through becoming embodied in an ego in the world. Those meaning-making principles that dwell in the unconscious, Jung called archetypes. Anima and animus are examples of their numinous and mysterious creativity. Most important, the Jungian unconscious is as capable of generating powerful feminine images and meaning as it is of producing masculine signifying. A society may inherit patriarchal motifs, but the individual possesses archetypal androgyny. Individuation inevitably challenges patriarchy.

So the Jungian symbolic is not intrinsically patriarchal or masculine biased and is indeed designed to resist such distortions. Jungian divine images are as readily feminine as masculine. One might wonder why Jung's gift to feminist theory is not better recognized?

The Anima as Phallus

Unsurprisingly, the comparison with Lacan goes two ways. While Jung's conceptual side offers a strong creative psyche capable of imagining other worlds and feminist paradises, the other two aspects of his gender writing, unknown sublime and banal slippage, are harder to digest. Here the notion of the Lacanian phallus is helpful in importing a feminist perspective to Jung's embedded writing on/as anima.

The anima proliferates beyond its assigned place as the concept of a male's feminine unconscious. We have seen how it spills over from object to subject, how it moves from a concept Jung is writing "about" to a voice assuming control of the writing. Additionally, the anima is Jung's frequent image for his most seminal idea, the generative unconscious. At times, anima *is* the unconscious, not just one aspect of it. The banal inferiority that tends to color this image for Jung becomes even more problematic when unconscious slippage in the writing slides from anima to opinions about women. Too often, Jung will comment on women using the lineaments of his own (inferior) anima. For example, in what Jung admits is an ungrounded linking of Eros and Logos to the genders, Eros becomes the "true nature" of women with their Logos a "regrettable accident."[7]

This anima-inspired feminine is *too present* in Jungian psychology. As signifier of the unconscious, "she" is the generative core of signifying, particularly of the gendered erotic, unconscious, sublime positioning of the "other."

Consequently, we have in Jung a framework for understanding the human psyche in culture that feminism might welcome, for it provides the opportunity and gendered creative energy to remake the world. The fact that we need to apply that gendered creative energy to Jung's own textuality should be regarded as a chance to participate in the very creativity that these writings inspire, inspirit in us. Jung's works are an invitation to cocreate meaning by means of an evaluative, gender-aware, and nurturing participation in these tricky, sublime writings.

Later in this chapter, I am going to explore Jung further in relation to feminist religious studies and the symbolic order. First of all, I want to look at a few post-Jungian ideas on anima, gender, and feminism, where they indicate the startling potential for an imaginative rethinking of gender.

Post-Jungians Revising Anima, Gender, Feminism

Many Jungian analysts and scholars have felt impelled to revisit Jung's oppositional scheme of anima and animus. They pay particular attention to the animus, some seeking to heal his *animosity* by regarding the negative animus as a woman's inner wounding by patriarchy. Another significant revision is to detach anima and animus from bodily sex and allow each gender equal access to Erotic anima and Logos.

A notable revisionary theorist is Emma Jung, Jung's wife.[8] She urges women to counteract their inner opponent until the animus becomes a forceful interior strength, giving a woman her own authority. While not modifying Jung's basic scheme, she develops a progressive integration of the animus as power, deed, word, and meaning. It is an impressive and imaginative response to patriarchal conditions.

Linda Fierz-David, a colleague of both Emma and C. G. Jung, helpfully points out that anima and animus cannot be regarded as having fixed gender, since they reside in the androgynous unconscious.[9] Work by another author, *Knowing Woman*, represents a striking break with Jung.[10] By arguing that a woman's soul image is anima not animus, Irene Claremont de Castillejo challenges his predilection for binaries, the latter being merely a manifestation of male aggression against women.

A further thinker, Hilde Binswanger, tries to work with anima and animus alongside biology.[11] She has suggested that women have a biological masculinity linked to Jung's Eros, as well as a psychological masculinity in the unconscious. The goal of therapy is to unite the two types of feminine masculinity in a strong woman.

More recently, Ann Ulanov,[12] Polly Young-Eisendrath,[13] and Claire Douglas[14] have continued the work of redefining anima and animus, as well as articulating a resistance to Jung's banal lapses. Young-Eisendrath typically uses stories and myths to re-present a more empowering notion of animus integration. Douglas, while retaining anima and animus in their traditional positions, emphasizes the social and cultural factors influencing their reception. Her book, *The Woman in the Mirror*, is an invaluable historical analysis of Jungians and gender.

While merely scratching the surface of a rich Jungian literature of gender, we can see that the legacy of creativity approaching gender has been exceptionally fertile. Probably the most significant and far-reaching creative developer of Jung's legacy is James Hillman, who in the 1970s produced two key articles radically transforming the anima.[15] Through a critical rereading of Jung's texts, Hillman aims to detach the anima from Jung's delight in opposites. The anima is not limited to men. "She" should adopt Jung's other name for her as "soul" and take her rightful place as a structure of consciousness in relationship to unconsciousness *in both sexes*. So the anima now fully inhabits her role as relatedness, as the bond to the unknown psyche, not to other people.

It follows that Eros be recognized as the separate function of sexuality and not falsely joined to the anima. Women no longer carry the anima or soul for men. They have their own anima-souls to cherish. Similarly, both sexes have equal access to animus or spirit.

Hillman then goes further to argue that anima as relatedness to the unconscious is the true basis of consciousness. Such a move dethrones the ego, which has been built upon the culture of the hero myth. "He" is driven by the desire to conquer and repress the other. Useful in the child and adolescent phases of life, the hero myth needs to be discarded by the adult who discovers his or her true being in anima-relatedness.

For Hillman, the anima is the archetype of psychology and soul making. She can manifest as singular or plural. Anima and animus ideally enact an inner marriage, marking the most fertile aspect of psychic development; they are the psychic lenses by which the "other" is known. So if the anima is seen as "one," that is not to be taken as her essence. Rather, it is that she is regarded through a perspective conditioned to see "ones."

Hillman's revisions of anima are exhilarating. They open up possibilities in ways that are faithful, I would venture, to Jung's sublime intimations of gender as the point where reason and theory are defeated.

The Goddess and the Feminine Principle

Many Jungian and Jungian feminist works about gender have taken seriously Jung's opening up of the patriarchal symbolic to the sacred feminine. Some have developed the term "the feminine principle" as a node around which to position positive feminine meanings. The feminine principle is sometimes elevated to a transcendent metaphysical structure. It becomes a divine force in an oppositional relation to a masculine principle, such as in Esther Harding's famous *Woman's Mysteries*.[16] Alternatively, it may be regarded as a more immanent reality, incarnated in psyche and culture.

Closely allied to the feminine principle is the notion of a goddess or goddesses as the visible or, at any rate, tangible, divine symbols of the feminine. A particularly comprehensive work here is *The Myth of the Goddess* by Ann Baring and Jules Cashford, which traces the evidence of an earth goddess religion from prehistory to its defeat by patriarchal monotheism.[17] The story continues through the goddess's underground life in Western culture to the stirrings of her today. The phallocratic order is too "single" minded, repressing the feminine as other, just as the father god separates himself from the feminine and body as nature. Arguing that masculine monotheism has sponsored the rational consciousness of modernity based on separation and discrimination, Baring and Cashford note that father god is not the problem per se. Rather, it is his tendency to overdo the separation and eliminate his partner and "other," goddess-relational consciousness.

Finally, the work of Ginette Paris shows the true imaginative potential of goddess feminism. She takes stories of pre-Christian divine women and uses them to pry open our barely perceived patriarchal framework that attends contemporary thinking about gender. Showing how these myths can transform our assumptions and predispositions, her book *Pagan Meditations* perfectly demonstrates the way notions of the Jungian psyche can revolutionize the symbolic resources of our culture.[18]

Anima of Theory and Religion

There is a further way to the mysteries of the anima. This is to invoke her occult origins in Jung's early writing about spiritualism. F. X. Charet first demonstrated the importance of Jung's doctoral thesis, "On the Psychology and Pathology of So-Called Occult Phenomena" (1902),[19] by showing that in the portrayal of a female medium could be discerned the qualities of Jung's later anima.[20] Named Miss S.W. in the thesis, the young woman was actually Jung's cousin, Helene Preiswerk. Also suppressed in the thesis was how far the doctoral researcher was active in initiating the séances.

S.W. produced a number of spirit voices before two prominent personalities dominated the dramatic occasions: Ulrich, a male gossip, and Ivenes, an astonishing lady who had lived many lives, sometimes as mother or lover of Jung. Unsurprisingly, Jung's thesis is fascinated by her. He concentrates on the problem of defining the "reality" of these beings and stories. Very unlike his later fidelity to psychic reality as valuable in itself, he insists that Ivenes and her proliferating "romances" consist of "nothing but" the developing sexuality of the adolescent S.W. Indeed, in support of this conclusion, he quotes Freud on sexual energy.[21]

A later Jung entirely reverses this prejudice against "romances" or the imagination. It is then Freud who is criticized for stubbornly insisting that psychic creativity is "nothing but" sexuality.[22] This mature Jung stands with S.W. as supporter of the voices of the imaginative soul, whether they are called spirits of the dead or archetypal personalities. Indeed, as Charet notes, in turning his attention from mediums to animas, from the feminine as women practicing the occult to *his* feminine within, Jung could be said to have taken the culturally feminized medium position (by nineteenth-century spiritualism) for masculine subjectivity. I would argue that such a move is part of a highly gendered struggle for power and knowledge in Jung's period. Late-nineteenth-century occult practice in Europe gradually became enfolded by masculine-dominated medical paradigms. Significant phenomena once classed as supernatural are redescribed as pathological. Women's "otherness" is shifted from the religious to the asylum, and women's role from prophet to patient.

So here a feminist historical perspective would notice the acute marginalization in Jung as actual (semi)autonomous women are left behind for a male-articulated anima.

However, with Jung, it is always the case that the founding principle of the creative unconscious is capable of giving surprises, including productive reversals. The doctoral thesis contains two anima figures: S.W. herself, much patronized and confined to one meaning by "nothing but," and Ivenes, whose powerful personality is the heart of S.W.'s astonishing stories. The séances are not just the seed of romantic adventures. S.W. also provides "Mystic Science" in what seems like an attempt to unite the Book of Genesis and Darwin, plus a science fiction reordering of the relation of the Earth to the other planets.[23]

In this doctoral thesis, where the young author squeezes himself into what he clearly considers to be correct scientific rationality, unconscious creativity and resonance belong to S.W. and her Ivenes. Moreover, this is not just a matter of calling S.W. and Ivenes anima images for Jung. Rather, I would say that S.W. *is the anima of Jung's future work*, his future exploration of psychic depths, passions, and visions of the cosmos. As well as being banal and sublime, the anima *is the unconscious of theory, its irrational Eros*. In fact, if we take psychology-as-theory to be a conceptual ego entity, I am merely bringing in S.W. to illustrate Hillman's notion of anima as consciousness related to unconsciousness. The imaginative writing of S.W. in Jung's thesis is Jungian psychology-as-related-to-unconsciousness.

Arguably, Jung spent his entire career attempting to unravel S.W.'s visions. I am not suggesting that he consciously devoted himself to her material in later life. Rather, S.W. was the initial weaving of the creative other into his mind, an other that for him was forever associated with the feminine.

S.W. as anima, as the unconscious of Jungian theory, is its connective, erotic, unpredictable, living reality in the psyche. Hence the anima, for Jung, mediates the psychic reality of gender and the psychic presence of religion. To be more precise, the anima, usually a single figure for Jung, mediates the relation between monotheism and polytheism in his religious framework. After all, Ivenes's magic fertility as storyteller and child bearer has a very ancient lineage indeed.

Restoring the Symbolic Feminine to Modernity

S.W.'s fictional uniting of Darwin and Genesis shows a preoccupation with origin stories early in Jung's career. Although what I have termed "goddess feminism" is most evidently attributable to later Jungians, his far-reaching, almost painful embrace of the anima shows a depth of involvement with creation myths that do and do not subordinate the feminine.

In the beginning, the Earth was feminine and divine. The Earth Mother goddess is living sacred matter. She creates humans from her divine body and nurtures us throughout life in her Eros connectedness and feeling. Giving birth to a divine son, she later unites with him as lover. To her, sexuality and body are sacred. When the son-lover is later dismembered, she will seek his body out and restore him.

Such an ur-myth of a mother goddess is believed to have founded many early religions and to persist in myths of Isis and Osiris, Attis, and others. Crucially, she also finds a home, if in disguise, in Christianity, in images such as the sacred Garden of Eden, the wicked serpent who was once a goddess image of wisdom and rebirth, and in Mary the Virgin cradling the dying Jesus, just as the goddess once mourned her son-lover. Such moments allow a glimpse of the goddess, otherwise occluded in a culture dominated by an other myth.[24]

What ended goddess culture was the rise of male gods who were not identified with Earth or nature. Instead, these were sky fathers who wrested the notion of origins from Earth to the heavens. Neither god nor "man" was to be "grounded." The male god created Earth from above and remained transcendent of it. No longer bodying nature as sacred, the god prided himself on separating from matter as something inferior and feminine. Where the immanent mother goddess could be approached as animism in the infinite plurality of meaningful in-spirited nature, transcendent father god is monotheistic, a sponsor of truth as oneness, rationality, separation, and discrimination.

Of course, as well as being fundamental structures of religion, the two gendered creation myths are stories about different types of consciousness, as Baring and Cashford have shown. As both Christian religious heritage and the arts reveal, both types of consciousness are needed for human well-being. Unfortunately, as our Christian heritage also shows, Western modernity has privileged father-god Logos consciousness to the near extinction of the Eros qualities of connecting to the sacred other, as unconsciousness and/or divine nature.

The work of C. G. Jung is a profound, flawed, incomplete attempt to invite the feminine creation myth into modernity. For example, an attempt to rebalance goddess and god consciousness is incarnated in his importing Eros and Logos into the functioning psyche. Moreover, he invokes the autonomous creativity of "Mother Nature" in his explorations of synchronicity, the way time and space sometimes seem to "play" in meaningful coincidences.[25] Indeed, where synchronicity becomes defined as *acts of creation in time*, we have an evocation of the sacred as immanent in living experience. Most of all, it is the anima who bears traces of Jung's intuitive seeking of a feminine soul to heal modernity's deep wounds. The urge is not negated by Jung's reluctance to renounce a masculine bias.

The anima is the sublime other to the rationalist hegemony that Christian theologians made when their way of interpreting the Bible, their exegesis, secured a veneration of reason from Holy Scripture. As Christopher Manes has pointed out, in constructing divine reason as transcendent of textual *matter*, scholars cemented the notion of Logos as transcendent of nature.[26] Hence centuries later, "science" took over the Logos position as rational, transcendent, and part of the apparatus of modernity's disavowal of the feminine other. Jung's writing tries to do what is impossible and necessary: to bring the transcendent Logos of science (inherited from patriarchal monotheism) together with the immanent trampled matter of body and relating that his anima signifies.

What has been repressed in the denial of the goddess in the making of modernity is the consciousness of human immanence in nature. Instead of a dialogical psyche between "masculine" and "feminine," transcendence and rationality *with* immanence and embodiment, the severing of ego consciousness from the "feminine" has dangerously weakened modernity. So the anima as the unconscious other to rational ego consciousness can be seen as the Erotic "nature" other to psychology as rational theory. Jung's anima is also the (humans in) nature he cuts from his psychology when he sticks to rational, abstract concepts. Fortunately and invaluably, Jung's writing is dialogical in seeking to entice the goddess back in from the darkness of her exclusion.

Returning to Jung's third display of his anima as "his" banal inferiority, we should also regard this flaw as a useful shadow, or bodying to his writing. It certainly adds to the immanent quality of his writing *within* what *matters* to him, as well as its transcendent conceptual characteristics. Perhaps Jung needed to allow his inferiority to speak to be able to loosen his imagination. His writing shows psychology as psyche-Logos, discriminating theory with concepts such as anima, *and* as Eros with a body, sexuality, feeling, and unconscious irrationality also erupting as *voices: an animistic textuality*. Hence the anima mediates between Logos father god, driving towards oneness, and Eros mother goddess consciousness, between monotheism's single truth and animism's diversity in the writing.

Jung tries to save modernity by bringing back an Earth Mother that symbolically mitigates the pernicious dominance of the sky father in Western culture.[27] His problem is an ingrained conservatism about female and male social roles. The consequence is his inability to imagine how his revolutionary ideas of culture might be realized in the lives of actual men and women. Fortunately, *in the writing*, succeeding generations have a web of life, one capable of connecting goddess and god.

Teaching Jung: Anima, Gender, Feminism

In teaching Jung, sometimes it is not, ostensibly, Jung that is taught. While some classes may be framed by the lecture title "Introducing Jung" or "Jung and Gender," I may want to bring Jung into subjects as diverse as literary theory, gender studies, environmental theory, film studies, or the psychology of religion.

With English literature students, I will use Jung to question the assumed relationship between literature and theory. Theory is not necessarily transcendent of fiction if creativity itself is at its heart. In addition, the literary practice of close reading for multiple meanings is re-visioned as delving into textual animism, an erotic activity of engaging with the goddess's reality as multiple threads of life. To students of religion, I might introduce the anima as a guide to writing that is hospitable to the divine as transcendent yet also embodies the goddess as immanent.

For those studying culture and gender, Jung demonstrates that the symbolic properties of feminine and masculine are all together personal, social, collective, and spiritual. Society shapes gender without having a determining influence on its meaning. The unknowable unconscious is always an unreadable factor allowing for further creativity. Jung also shows that the work of feminism is the work of healing modernity: feminine and masculine signifying must be rebalanced for individual and collective psychic health.

Finally, what engages students is what grips us all: the anima as divine desire, that is, our desire *for* the divine, and the face of divine love turned toward us. The anima, conceptual, other-to-theory, and banal, is supremely in image-inative terms, Jung's figure for the mysteries we cannot master. "She" tells us that we must not rely on Jung to make this image for us, for she is caught in a textual web that includes some of the darkness of human desire. Yet that textual web of immanent and transcendent properties offers both teachers and students a labyrinth by which to explore gender and psyche as powerful dramas in our "nature."

NOTES

1. C. G. Jung, *The Collected Works of C. G. Jung*, vol. 17 (Princeton, NJ: Princeton University Press, 1954), para. 338.

2. C. G. Jung, *Memories, Dreams, Reflections*, ed. Aniela Jaffé (London: Collins and Routledge & Kegan Paul, 1963), 210–211.

3. Jung, *Collected Works*, 9ii:29.

4. Sigmund Freud, "Group Psychology and the Analysis of the Ego," in *Literary Theory: An Anthology*, 2nd ed., ed. Julie Rivkin and Michael Ryan (Malden, MA: Blackwell, 2004), 438–40.

5. Jacques Lacan, "The Instance of the Letter in the Unconscious," in *Literary Theory: An Anthology*, 447–61.

6. Luce Irigaray, "The Power of Discourse and the Subordination of the Feminine," in *Literary Theory: An Anthology*, 795–98.

7. See note 3.

8. Emma Jung, *Animus and Anima* (Putnam, CT: Spring, 1957).

9. Linda Fierz-David, *Women's Dionysian Initiation: The Villa of Mysteries in Pompeii* (Dallas: Spring, 1988).

10. Irene Claremont de Castillejo, *Knowing Woman: A Feminine Psychology* (Boston: Shambhala, 1973).

11. Hilde Binswanger, "Positive Aspects of the Animus," *Spring: A Journal of Archetype and Culture* (1963): 82–101.

12. Ann Ulanov, *The Feminine in Jungian Psychology and in Christian Theology* (Evanston, IL: Northwestern University Press, 1971), and Ann Ulanov and Barry Ulanov, *Transforming Sexuality: The Archetypal World of Anima and Animus* (Boston: Shambhala, 1994).

13. Polly Young-Eisendrath, *Hags and Heroes: A Feminist Approach to Jungian Psychotherapy with Couples* (Toronto: Inner City, 1984).

14. Claire Douglas, *The Woman in the Mirror: Analytical Psychology and the Feminine* (Boston: Sigo, 1990).

15. James Hillman, "Anima," *Spring: A Journal of Archetype and Culture* (1973): 97–132; "Anima II," *Spring: A Journal of Archetype and Culture* (1974): 113–46.

16. M. Esther Harding, *Woman's Mysteries, Ancient and Modern: A Psychological Interpretation of the Feminine Principle as Portrayed in Myth, Story and Dreams* (New York: C. G. Jung Foundation for Analytical Psychology, 1955).

17. Anne Baring and Jules Cashford, *The Myth of the Goddess: Evolution of an Image* (Harmondsworth, England: Viking, 1991).

18. Ginette Paris, *Pagan Meditations: The Worlds of Aphrodite, Artemis and Hestia* (Woodstock, CT: Spring, 1986).

19. Jung, "On the Psychology and Pathology of So-Called Occult Phenomena," *Collected Works*, 1:1–150.

20. F. X. Charet, *Spiritualism and the Foundations of C. G. Jung's Psychology* (Albany: State University of New York Press, 1993).

21. Jung, *Collected Works*, 1:120.

22. This was first pointed out by Renos Papadopoulos in "Jung and the Concept of the Other," in *Jung in Modern Perspective*, ed. Renos K. Papadopoulos and Graham S. Saayman, 54–88 (Bridport, England: Prism, 1991), 65.

23. Jung, *Collected Works*, 1:65–66.

24. See Baring and Cashford, *Myth of the Goddess*, for a detailed history of the Goddess in Western culture.

25. Jung, *Collected Works*, 8:816–997.

26. Christopher Manes, "Nature and Silence," in *The Ecocriticism Reader*, ed. C. Glotfelty and H. Fromm, 15–29 (Athens: University of Georgia Press, 1996).

27. Susan Rowland, *Jung as a Writer* (London: Routledge, 2005), chapter 7.

REFERENCES

Baring, Ann, and Jules Cashford. *The Myth of the Goddess: Evolution of an Image.* London: Viking, 1991.

Binswanger, Hilde. "Positive Aspects of the Animus." *Spring: A Journal of Archetype and Culture* (1963): 82–101.

Charet, F. X. *Spiritualism and the Foundations of C. G. Jung's Psychology.* Albany: State University of New York Press, 1993.

Claremont de Castillejo, Irene. *Knowing Woman: A Feminine Psychology*. Boston: Shambhala, 1973.

Douglas, Claire. *The Woman in the Mirror: Analytical Psychology and the Feminine*. Boston: Sigo, 1990.

Fierz-David, Linda. *Women's Dionysian Initiation*. Dallas, TX: Spring, 1981.

Glotfelty, C., and H. Fromm, eds. *The Ecocriticism Reader: Landmarks in Literary Ecology*. Athens: University of Georgia Press, 1996.

Freud, Sigmumd. "Group Psychology and the Analysis of the Ego." In *Literary Theory: An Anthology*, ed. Julie Rivkin and Michael Ryan. Malden, MA: Blackwell, 2004.

Harding, M. Esther. *Woman's Mysteries, Ancient and Modern*. New York: C. G. Jung Foundation, 1955.

Hillman, James. "Anima." *Spring: A Journal of Archetype and Culture* (1973): 97–132.

Hillman, James. "Anima II." *Spring: A Journal of Archetype and Culture* (1974): 113–146.

Jung, C. G. *The Collected Works of C. G. Jung*, ed. Herbert Read, Michael Fordham, and Gerhard Adler, trans. R. F. C. Hull. Princeton, NJ: Princeton University Press, 1953–1991.

Jung, C. G. *Memories, Dreams, Reflections*. London: Fontana, 1983.

Jung, Emma. *Anima and Animus*. Putnam, CT: Spring, 1957.

Lacan, Jacques. "The Instance of the Letter in the Unconscious," in *Literary Theory: An Anthology*. Oxford: Blackwell, 2004.

Papadopoulos, Renos K., and Graham S. Saayman, eds. *Jung in Modern Perspective*. Bridport, England: Prism, 1991.

Paris, Ginette. *Pagan Meditations: The Worlds of Aphrodite, Artemis and Hestia*. Woodstock, CT: Spring, 1986.

Rowland, Susan. *Jung as a Writer*. New York: Routledge, 2005.

Ulanov, Ann. *The Feminine in Jungian Psychology and in Christian Theology*. Evanston, IL: Northwestern University Press, 1971.

Ulanov, Ann, and Barry Ulanov. *Transforming Sexuality: The Archetypal World of Anima and Animus*. Boston: Shambhala, 1994.

Young-Eisendrath, Polly. *Hags and Heroes: A Feminist Approach to Jungian Psychotherapy with Couples*. Toronto, ON: Inner City, 1984.

Young-Eisendrath, Polly, with Florence Wiedemann. *Female Authority: Empowering Women through Psychotherapy*. New York: Guilford, 1987.

II

Jung as Nature Mystic

Meredith Sabini

The Earth Has a Soul

Looking back over the course of his life, Jung wrote to a colleague, "True to my nature-loving bias, I have followed the call of the wild, the age-old trail through secluded wildernesses, where a primitive human community may be found."[1] In a 1958 letter, Jung referred to "the old idea that every country or people has its own angel, just as the earth has a soul."[2] You may not associate such sentiments with Swiss psychiatrist C. G. Jung, but there is a down-to-earth side of Jung that has not been fully recognized. Frequently called a mystic, he sometimes denied the label, for it was used dismissively, the way we might call someone "airy-fairy" today. In the 1957 Houston films in which Dr. Richard Evans interviewed Jung at length, Jung made the firm statement, "Everyone who calls me a mystic is just an idiot. He doesn't know the first word about psychology."[3] I believe it is important that we now respectfully restore the designation in order to recognize and appreciate the full range of Jung's ideas, observations, and contributions.

Jung's mysticism—his felt sense of something beyond the veil of the visible world with which he experienced oneness—was not limited to a transcendent spiritual dimension but included all sentient life. All was nature, and nature was both spirit and matter. He was far ahead of his time, fifty to a hundred years, in many areas. With the development of field theory, intersubjectivity, and emergence theory, we are now in a better position to understand what Jung was trying to convey. In his memoirs, he stated this fundamental mystical principle: "Our psyche is set up in accord with the structure of the universe, and what happens in the macrocosm likewise happens in the infinitesimal and most subjective reaches of the psyche."[4] This statement is like a koan that, when meditated upon, can put us in resonance with the world. From this position, we are both affected by and can affect the larger whole around us.

Jung was deeply concerned over the loss of our connection with nature and the absence of meaningful myths. "The mythic side of man is given short shrift nowadays. He can no longer create fables...it is important and salutary to speak of incomprehensible things. Such talk is like the telling of a good ghost story as we sit by the fireside. Myth is the revelation of a divine life in man. It is not we who invent myth, rather it speaks to us as a Word of God."[5] He considered natural life to be the "nourishing soil of the soul." Who has time for a natural life these days? What would it look like if we did?

Those of us destined to live through this turbulent period of history, possibly the declining phase of Western civilization, could perhaps use a wise elder who stands slightly outside the modern world yet knows it well enough to offer guidance. I credit Jung with providing me a road map as I underwent an ecoreligious conversion and transited the difficult stages from being an entitled Westerner, oblivious to my carbon footprint, to living "in modest harmony with nature," as Jung himself modeled.

There are many others today who address the contemporary split between humans and nature, but what Jung offers is unique. He has the knowledge of a historian who understands how this split came about when spirits were banished from the woods and rivers, he reaches out with the empathy of a healer who shares our malaise, and he advises with the common sense of a country doctor. Jung addresses not only the individual but also Western civilization as a whole, as an entity that itself is suffering and in need of help.

Historical eras oscillate between an orientation toward either matter or spirit. We are living in a period when the material aspect of nature is emphasized. It is often said that we are materialistic, but this is not quite the case since matter actually receives very little respect due to its having been robbed, as Jung notes, of its spirit: "The word 'matter' remains a dry, inhuman, and purely intellectual concept.... How different was the former image of matter— the Great Mother—that could encompass and express the profound emotional meaning of the Great Mother."[6] This passage comes from the final essay Jung wrote just prior to his death. In it, he summarized his concern for the plight of "modern man," characterizing it in religious terms: "Man feels himself isolated in the cosmos, because he is no longer involved in nature....We have stripped everything of their mystery and numinosity; nothing is holy any longer."[7]

Our loss of connection with nature is thus neither a practical nor a psychological problem but a religious one, as this passage by Jungian analyst Joseph Henderson emphasizes:

Nature has lost her divinity, yet the spirit is unsure and unsatisfied. Hence any true cure for neurosis...would have to awaken both spirit and nature to a new life. The relevance of this theme for us today may be that it is a problem we are still trying to solve on a too personal, psychological level, or on a purely cultural level without fully realizing it is at bottom a religious problem and not psychological or social at all.[8]

The word *nature* runs like a leitmotif throughout Jung's entire body of work—essays, letters, seminars, speeches—and he often capitalized it to convey its importance. In the Visions Seminars he gave in the early 1930s, he remarked that "the earth has a spirit of her own, a beauty of her own.... The natural mind has a world of earthly beauty to itself, really... and it is not so entirely materialistic as one assumes."[9] Spirit, he said, is the *inside* of things, and matter is their visible *outer* aspect. Jung restores nature's original wholeness by reminding us "Nature is not matter only, she is also spirit."[10] A brief anecdote illustrates Jung's sense of the living spirit within nature: "I once experienced a violent earthquake, and my first, immediate feeling was that I no longer stood on solid familiar earth, but on the skin of a gigantic animal that was heaving under my feet. It was this image that impressed itself on me, not the physical fact."[11] The spirit of the earth showed itself to Jung as a living entity.

Jung's Own Relationship with Nature

Jung's life spanned the years 1875 to 1961. He grew up in conditions largely unchanged since the Middle Ages and lived to see the emergence of the techno-industrial age. The son of a country parson, he spent his childhood in a small village where he played in the woods and collected fossils in the Jura Mountains. He thought of animals and humans as "bits of God that had become independent [and]...could move about on their own." Trees were especially mysterious to him, being "direct embodiments of the incomprehensible meaning of life." For this reason, the woods were the place where Jung felt "closest to its deepest meaning and awe-inspiring workings."[12]

There was a special rock that jutted out from a stone wall in the garden of his father's rectory, and, between ages seven and nine, Jung played an imaginal game in which he pondered whether he was the boy sitting on the rock or the rock on which a boy was sitting. This parallels Chaung-Tzu's classic dream of being a butterfly and awaking to wonder whether he was a man dreaming of the butterfly or a butterfly dreaming it was a man.

Jung left this rural environment when he went to Basel for gymnasium and, later, medical school, settling in Kusnacht after his marriage. At forty-eight, he began building by hand a crude stone "tower" in Bollingen at the edge of Lake Zurich, a retreat he worked on throughout his life. There, he pumped water from a well, cut his own wood, cooked over an open fire, and read by oil lamp—much, he said, as a person from the sixteenth century might. He wanted nothing to disturb the atmosphere—"neither electric light nor telephone"—so that the souls of his ancestors would feel sustained.[13] It was at Bollingen that

Jung's nature mysticism had freest rein. Reflecting back on his time there, he wrote in his memoirs:

> At times I feel as if I am spread out over the landscape and inside things, and am myself living in every tree, in the splashing of the waves, in the clouds and the animals that come and go, in the procession of the seasons. There is nothing...that has not grown into its own form over the decades, nothing with which I am not linked. Here everything has its history, and mine; here is space for the spaceless kingdom of the world's and the psyche's hinterland.[14]

The connection with his own ancestral heritage and with his place on Earth itself, in Switzerland, served as a foundation for the unfolding of his life. Jung said, "Without my piece of earth, my life's work would not have come into being." In a 1958 letter, Jung characterized his experience of Switzerland as a central mussel shell where, as son of mother earth, he had a "feeling of primordiality," which is "the beginning of all things."[15] From this moving comment, we can see how Jung felt contained by the land of his origins and by the spirit of his ancestors.

The exposure Jung had in a rural countryside included the darker side of nature as well as its beauty and, as a consequence, he was not overly senti- mental or enamored of nature per se. The intrinsic cruelty within nature, for Jung, had been confirmed by his early observations "of diseased and dying fishes, of mangy foxes, frozen or starved birds...earthworms tormented to death by ants, insects that tore each other apart."[16] He added that his experience with human beings also had taught him "anything rather than a belief in man's original goodness and decency."[17]

The Medicine of Enchantment

As a psychiatrist, Jung was further exposed to the complex range of human behavior. He spent the first nine years of his professional career at the Burghölzli, a large mental hospital where he worked with acute and chronic schizophrenics. There, he discovered that the patients' modes of expression, which appeared confused and chaotic, contained allusions to their actual traumas, encoded in symbolic terms.

During the same period, at the turn of the century, spiritualism was under- going a renaissance. Jung was familiar with a number of mediums, including his own cousin, who became the subject of his medical dissertation. To the extent that mediumship involves contact with a transcendent or nonordinary reality, it resembles mysticism, and Jung was familiar with a wide variety of transcendent modalities. His witnessing of spirit possession, his work with the mentally ill, and his background in an almost medieval rural atmosphere all functioned as an important counterpoint to the growing scientific rationalism of the day.

I believe Jung had the abilities of both a modern physician and an indigenous healer. One simple vignette illustrates how this unusual breadth came out in his clinical work. A young schoolteacher from a remote village was referred to Jung by her physician. She experienced constant fear of making mistakes and had gotten into a terrible state of psychic tension. She lived far away, so Jung had to do what he could in one meeting. He spoke to her about relaxation and told of how he sailed on the lake and let himself be carried by the wind. As he talked, he heard the voice of his own mother as she'd sung to his sister a lullaby about a little girl on a boat on the Rhine. Jung began humming the lullaby. At a conference years later, the referring physician came up to Jung and asked what he had done to bring about a complete cure in one visit. "How was I to explain to him that I had simply listened to something within myself?" What Jung did reaches beyond modern rational methods to something ancient, something fundamental. In retelling the story, Jung commented, "Enchantment is the oldest form of medicine."[18]

Consciousness: A Blessing and a Curse

Jung set the loss of connection with nature in the context of the development of rational consciousness over the millennia. To describe how it evolved, Jung used the analogy of a multistoried house in which we live only on the top floor and have forgotten the previous layers of history that constitute our phyloge-netic foundation. This image is based on a seminal dream Jung had in 1909 in which he was exploring the four levels of a house: the top floor signified pres-ent-day consciousness; the floor below represented the fifteenth or sixteenth century; below that, the Roman era; and in a tomblike cellar, Jung found the artifacts of a Neolithic culture. He understood the dream as portraying the evo-lution of the human psyche and came to realize that its stratification was pre-sent in everyone, since we all share the same *Homo sapiens* ancestry.

Western consciousness is problematically one-sided, Jung claimed, in that it has expanded in the spatial dimension but not in the temporal, for we do not have a sense of living history; we do not feel rooted in our ancient phylogenetic background. Using this metaphor of a multistoried house, he said:

It is as if our consciousness had somehow slipped from its natural foundation and no longer knew how to get along on nature's timing. It seems as though we were suffering from a hubris of consciousness which fools us into believing that one's time of life is a mere illusion which can be altered according to one's desire. (One asks oneself where our consciousness gets its ability to be so contrary to nature....)[19]

The Ladder of Creation

Jung was deeply troubled by the role that Christianity played in fostering the severance between humans and nature by teaching that life here is only provi-sional. In a 1932 letter, he wrote, "we are cut off from our earth through more than a thousand years of Christian training."[20] In the Visions Seminars the same year, he said, "It is a general truth that the earth is depreciated and mis-understood.... For quite long enough we have been taught that this life is not the real thing...and that we live only for heaven."[21] One of the primary signs that a religion is fading in potency is the absence of animals in its iconography:

> Now, the question is, why have animals disappeared from the
> Christian teaching? When animals are no longer included in the
> religious symbol or creed, it is the beginning of the dissociation
> between religion and nature. Then there is no mana in it. As long as
> the animals are there, there is life in the symbol.[22]

In this way, Jung challenges the collective view of animals as lesser creatures, suggesting that they, too, are part of divinity. In a 1933 letter to a pastor, he quipped, "The idea that man alone possesses the primacy of reason is anti-quated twaddle. I have even found that men are far more irrational than ani-mals."[23] To the question of where our species is on the ladder of creation, Jung said we were by no means the pinnacle and praised the African zoological classification in which the elephant, whose look of wisdom is "tremendously impressive," is at the top, followed by the lion, then the python or crocodile, and finally humans and other creatures. During a 1950 interview with geographer Hans Carol on regional planning, Jung remarked, "We keep forget-ting that we are primates and that we have to make allowances for these prim-itive layers in our psyche."[24]

He knew, however, that we don't like to think of ourselves as animals because of the long-standing assumption that they are morally inferior crea-tures. Jung boldly challenged this with characteristic humor: "We are prejudiced in regard to the animal.... Yet in nature the animal is pious, it follows the path with great regularity.... Have you ever seen an animal getting drunk on cocktails?"[25] Though our capacity for reflective consciousness may be a unique human attribute, it does not necessarily imply superiority. In fact, it is this very capacity that permits us to deviate from divine law. Jung wrote Canon H. G. England in 1948, "In a way the animal is more pious than man, because it fulfills the divine will more completely than man ever can dream of. He can deviate, he can be disobedient, because he has consciousness. Consciousness is on the one hand a triumph and a blessing, on the other hand it is our worst devil, which helps us to invent every thinkable reason and way to disobey the divine will."[26]

By inviting us to modify our idea about our own animal nature, Jung pro-vides a way to retrieve this vital dimension of our being from the dustbin of repression and to redeem it. This perspective is substantiated by contemporary research on animal cognition and interspecies communication.[27] Jung's con-tention was that by assimilating the nature of the animal, "you become a partic-ularly law-abiding citizen, you go very slowly and become very reasonable in your ways."[28] Opening ourselves to this aspect of our being is not a simple matter, and it invariably leads to a conflict that one must then carry: "you feel the animal in yourself just as much as the cultural man, you know the conflict comes from the fact that you want to be an animal just as much as a spiritual being."[29]

Interconnectedness: A Living Reality

Jung considered our capacity to identify with animals an innate instinct arising from our shared evolutionary heritage. Disavowal of our communality may itself be a symptom of the youthfulness of our species, an effort to shore up our fragile consciousness by creating an artificially firm boundary between ourselves and other life-forms, a boundary not considered as important among indigenous peoples. Jung was openly critical of the separatist ethos of our times: "'I remain I and you remain you'—the final expression of the alienation and incompatibility of individuals."[30] Although Jung did emphasize individuation, he explained that it should not remove us from the social sphere but enlarge our connection to it.

Suggesting that consciousness could be viewed as the head of a gigantic, million-year-old creature, Jung reminds us that this creature also has a body and tail, which includes the evolutionary history of all life.[31] "No man lives within his own psychic sphere like a snail in its shell, separated from everybody else, but is connected with his fellow-men by his unconscious humanity."[32] This unconscious humanity, which Jung called the collective unconscious, was in no way an abstract concept, but a living reality, "that immense treasury, that great reservoir from which we draw."[33] In a 1960 letter, he said, "the collective unconscious is simply Nature...identical with Nature to the extent that Nature herself, including matter, is unknown to us."[34]

"Modern Man" and "Archaic Man"

When Jung went to Africa in 1925, he had a powerful mystical experience on the Athi Plains that shaped his understanding of the evolution of consciousness. While watching enormous herds of animals, he walked away from his companions and savored the feeling of being entirely alone:

> This was the stillness of the eternal beginning, the world as it had always been, in a state of non-being.... There I was now, the first human being to recognize that this was the world.... There the cosmic meaning of consciousness became overwhelmingly clear to me. "Man, I, in an invisible act of creation...gives the world objective existence."[35]

Later, Jung said that Africa had awakened an archetypal memory of a prehistoric past we have forgotten because it has been "overgrown by civilization." He recommended we not relive it naïvely, but if it activates a conflict with our modern selves, we should honor this and "test the two possibilities against each other—the life we live and the one we have forgotten."[36]

He elaborated on this theme in his essay "The Meaning of Psychology for Modern Man." Imagining that a typical representative of the modern world came to him for consultation, Jung referred to this client as "modern man" and began a dialogue with him that flowed over into many subsequent publications. While acknowledging that *man* is an outmoded gendered pronoun, I retain it because it does characterize the hypermasculine quality of modern consciousness—its linear, causal, goal-directed orientation toward the visible outer world. This characterization does not refer to individual people but to a component found in the psyche of any and all of us born or raised within the dominant cultural paradigm. It is the "modern man" within each of us that is dissociated from nature and in need of treatment.

Jung viewed modern man with compassion, realizing that he is painfully extraverted, overstrained from his boundless activities, and shows a remarkable lack of introspection. Modern man thinks that the gods and demons have disappeared from nature and believes that he can do as he pleases. True to his rationalistic bias, modern man has tried all the usual remedies—diets, exercise programs, inspirational literature—and only reluctantly admits that he can't seem to live a meaningful life.

As counterpart to this modern aspect, Jung referred to the primordial or archaic component of the psyche: "Are we not the carriers of the entire history of mankind?... When a man is fifty years old, only one part of his being has existed for half a century. The other part, which is also in his psyche, may be millions of years old."[37] In a 1933 essay "Archaic Man," Jung gave a fair and balanced portrait of how the modern mind and the archaic or natural mind work, noting the advantages and disadvantages of each. He stated unequivocally that nothing shows the archaic mind to be any less rational than the modern; only the basic presumptions differ. Whereas our modern mind tends to think causally and does not concern itself much with invisible forces, the archaic aspect tends to track spiritual forces at work behind the scenes. Jung gave the example that if lightning struck one abode and not another, our modern mind would probably dismiss it as a chance or random event, but our archaic mind would find this superficial and contemplate the meaning of the event.

Jung emphasized that *misoneism*, our instinctive fear of anything new, whether an invention, an idea, or a way of doing something, as a survival instinct. Were we to take ourselves as a species more seriously, we might have more respect, for example, for the widespread apprehension over genetic modification of food or chemical alteration of life processes. The so-called primitive within us lives much closer to phylogenetic instincts and is thus more inclined to follow nature rather than go against it the way modern man does. A dialogue between the archaic and the modern aspects of the human psyche could expand our human range. This is Jung's prescription: "What is needed is to call a halt to the fatal dissociation that exists between man's so-called higher and lower being; instead, we must unite conscious man with primitive man."[38]

America at Risk

Jung was familiar with American culture through the many people who came to see him as well as from his many trips here. In 1925, Jung gave an interview to the *New York Times* in which he commented on how much had been sacrificed to achieve the domination of our wildernesses, how Americans tend to think in great abstractions and emphasize control over emotions and instincts, and how prevalent is the notion that anyone could become anything they wished. He saw America as being at risk of being devoured by its machines. Now that schoolchildren must learn on computers, teens must have iPods, and adults must conduct all phases of business via the Internet, our servitude seems complete; Jung's prophecy has come about.

In the 1957 Houston films with Professor Richard Evans, Jung stated that America was so uprooted and divorced from nature that the "real, natural man" was in open rebellion against the utterly inhuman form of life, and he cited as examples the moral and sexual rebellion of youth and the drug abuse. Jung told Evans that something must be done "to compensate the earth." Given the effort to set records, the tremendous urge toward conformity, and the desire for material possessions, Americans needed to rest a while, Jung said, and realize that the things being sought are irrelevant to a happy life. He named the problem and empathized with those adversely affected by our culture's pathological fascination with conquest, speed, success, and machines. Ironically, he made these observations at a time when, compared with the present, America was much *less* dependent on machine technology.

The practical advice for remedying the loss of contact with nature Jung gave was: to live in small communities; to work a shorter day and week; to make the sparest use of radio, television, newspapers, and technological gadgetry; and to have a plot of land to cultivate so the instincts come back to life. The purpose of doing these things, however, is not to heal nature, but to let nature heal us. This reversal of the common attitude of domination makes Jung's contribution unique. Time, money, and energy are now dedicated to repairing the damage humans have done to nature. Though some repairing is surely called for, the assumption that our species knows how to heal nature is hubristic; it may be better for us to get out of nature's way, stop adversely affecting it, and let nature heal itself. In an interview with a San Francisco analyst who visited him at Bollingen, Jung, who was eighty at the time, said:

> We must give time to nature so that she may be a mother to us.
> I have found a way to live here as part of nature, to live in my own
> time. People in the modern world are always living so that something
> better is to happen tomorrow, always in the future.... They are up in

the head. When a man begins to know himself, to discover the roots of his past in himself, it is a new way of life.[39]

Letting Nature Heal Us

Jung explained how we can discover the ancient roots of our being:

> The dream is a hidden door to the innermost and most secret recesses of the soul, opening into that cosmic night.... All consciousness separates; but in dreams we put on the likeness of that more universal, truer, more eternal man dwelling in the darkness of the primordial night. There he is still whole, and the whole is in him, indistinguishable from nature and bare of all egohood.[40]

Jung realized that modern man would scoff at the mention of dreams, asking what good are they in the face of the overpowering realities such as polluted waterways, radioactive waste, overpopulation, and noise pollution. Jung admitted that he himself did not have an answer for these problems, but perhaps the "ancient soul of humanity" might have something to contribute. In an interview for his eighty-fifth birthday, Jung told the story of the Eskimo, or Inuit, shaman who, at a time his tribe was starving, had a dream in which he was shown a new hunting ground. Those who followed him arrived safely, whereas those who doubted and turned back, perished.[41]

While some dreams do contain objective information like this, most are subjective and are to be understood psychologically rather than physically. To think psychologically rather than concretely is itself an evolutionary achievement of great import, and Jung cautioned against regressing to a previous stage of consciousness and taking dreams literally. He claimed that dreams are "pure nature," to which must be added human reflection and discernment. We now know that the dreaming function in mammals is approximately 140 million years old and does have a survival function.[42]

Having listened to thousands of dreams from men and women who came to see him from all over the world, Jung suggested that even the most squalid dreams emphasize our blood kinship with all life. Dreams bridge the ancient, primordial aspect of ourselves and the rational, modern aspect. Jung anticipated current research on the evolutionary survival function of REM dreaming when he said that the dream is not our ego-consciousness reflecting on itself: "rather, it turns its attention to the objective actuality of the dream as a communication or message from the unconscious, unitary soul of humanity...the trunk from which the ego grew."[43] Dreams thus reconnect us with this "trunk" of the tree of life.

There is an innate religious function in the human psyche, and Jung noted that sometimes the "strongest and most original of all man's spiritual activities—the religious—is discovered from our dreams." The source for this, he acknowledged, is a true mystery and goes by many names: "A good dream, for example, that's grace. The dream is in essence a gift...it's the invisible world, it's the great spirit. It makes little difference what I call it: God, Tao, the Great Voice, the Great Spirit."[44]

Medicine Man for His Tribe

During his lifetime, Jung suffered the loneliness and isolation that accompany those who bring forth a new Zeitgeist. In a 1960 letter to Sir Herbert Read, he expressed this poignantly:

> Your blessed words are the rays of a new sun over a dark sluggish swamp in which I felt buried.... I asked myself time and again why there are no men in our epoch who could see at least what I was wrestling with. I think it is not mere vanity and desire for recognition on my part, but a genuine concern for my fellow-beings. It is presumably the ancient functional relationship of the medicine man to his tribe, the *participation mystique* and the essence of the physician's ethos. I see the suffering of mankind in the individual and vice versa.[45]

He used the term *participation mystique* from anthropology to describe the capacity he had, as a culture shaman, to sense what ails his people in order to bring about healing.

In 1923, Jung heard the account of a Taoist culture shaman who helped bring rain to a remote village suffering from severe drought. The story came via the Sinologist Richard Wilhelm, who had just returned to Europe with his translation of the *I Ching*. Wilhelm had been in that village and met the rainmaker, Kiao-chou. Having come some distance, he asked only for a small hut where he stayed three days; on the fourth, it not only rained but also snowed, at a time no snow typically came. When Wilhelm asked Kiao-chou how he had made it rain, the rainmaker answered that he was not responsible for the rain. Realizing that he had framed his query in a typical Western causalistic fashion, Wilhelm then asked what he had done those three days. Kiao-chou replied, "Oh, I can explain that." And he said: "I come from another country where things are in order. Here they are out of order, they are not as they should be by ordinance of heaven. Therefore the whole country is not in Tao, and I also am not in the natural order of things because I am in a disordered country. So I had to wait three days until I was back in Tao, and then naturally the rain came."[46]

This rainmaker was in that ancient functional relationship of medicine man to his tribe who had absorbed its suffering and then brought about a cure through the strength of his own psyche. Jung was intensely fond of this tale and exhorted his students and colleagues to tell it whenever they gave presentations.

Introverted Activism

The rainmaker story captures the essence of the approach Jung promoted, which I think of as "introverted activism." Jung recognized the extent to which the world and human society in general was out of Tao and how this affects each member of society. But he also knew from experience that the transformation of one individual has ripple effects on the world around. Jung made the bold assertion that not the atom, but the psyche—being present in all sentient creatures, unbounded by time and space—is "the greatest of all cosmic wonders."[47] This is another koan Jung has bequeathed to us. I find it astonishing in its boldness and simplicity. It restores the highest possible value to each of us, each of our actions. It seems to me that Jung's range of mystical revelations left him solidly convinced that at this juncture in history, with the major religions no longer being adequate containers for so many people, each of us as individuals can contribute to the needed spiritual renewal. If we undertake this opus, our own being becomes the container for transformation. In a 1929 letter to a young man, Jung stated his most basic belief: "My inner principle is: Deus *et* homo. God needs man in order to become conscious.... Let us therefore be for him limitation in time and space, an earthly tabernacle."[48]

NOTES

1. C. G. Jung, *Letters II: 1951–1961*, ed. Gerhard Adler (Princeton, NJ: Princeton University Press, 1976), 418.

2. Ibid., 432.

3. William McGuire and R. F. C. Hull, eds., *C. G. Jung Speaking: Interviews and Encounters* (Princeton, NJ: Princeton University Press, 1977), 333.

4. C. G. Jung, *Memories, Dreams, Reflections* (New York: Random House, 1961), 335.

5. Ibid., 300, 340.

6. C. G. Jung, *Man and His Symbols* (Garden City, NY: Doubleday, 1964), 94–95.

7. Ibid., 94–95.

8. Joseph L. Henderson, *Shadow and Self* (New York: Chiron, 1990), 279.

9. Claire Douglass, ed., *Interpretation of Visions* (Princeton, NJ: Princeton University Press, 1997), 134.

10. C. G. Jung, *The Collected Works of C. G. Jung* (Princeton, NJ: Princeton University Press, 1971–1986), 13: ∫ 229.

11. Jung, *Collected Works*, 8: ∫ 331.

12. Jung, *Memories*, 67–68.

13. Ibid., 237.

14. Ibid., 225–226.

15. Jung, *Letters II*, 419.

16. Jung, *Memories*, 69.

17. Ibid., 69.

18. McGuire and Hull, *C. G. Jung Speaking*, 417–419.

19. Jung, *Collected Works*, 8: ∫ 802.

20. C. G. Jung, *Letters I: 1906–1950*, ed. Gerhard Adler (Princeton, NJ: Princeton University Press, 1973), 96.

21. Douglass, *Interpretation of Visions*, 193.
22. Ibid., 284.
23. Jung, *Letters I*, 119.
24. McGuire and Hull, *C. G. Jung Speaking*, 202.
25. Douglass, *Interpretation of Visions*, 168.
26. Jung, *Letters I*, 486.
27. See the work of Frans De Waal, especially *Our Inner Ape*, (New York: Riverhead, 2005).
28. Douglass, *Interpretation of Visions*, 168.
29. Ibid., 161.
30. Jung, *Letters II*, 586.
31. Jung, *Collected Works*, 18: ∬168–69.
32. Jung, *Collected Works*, 10: ∬408.
33. McGuire and Hull, *C. G. Jung Speaking*, 415.
34. Jung, *Letters II*, 540.
35. Jung, *Memories*, 255.
36. Ibid., 245–46.
37. McGuire and Hull, *C. G. Jung Speaking*, 57.
38. Ibid., 397.
39. Ibid., 163.
40. Jung, *Collected Works*, 10: ∬304.
41. McGuire and Hull, *C. G. Jung Speaking*, 458.
42. See Anthony Stevens, *The Two-Million-Year-Old Self* (College Station: Texas A&M University Press, 1993).
43. Jung, *Collected Works*, 10: ∬318.
44. McGuire and Hull, *C. G. Jung Speaking*, 419.
45. Jung, *Letters II*, 586, 589.
46. Jung, *Collected Works*, 14: ∬604n.
47. Jung, *Collected Works*, 8: ∬357.
48. Jung, *Letters I*, 65–66.

REFERENCES

Douglass, Claire, ed. *Interpretation of Visions*. Princeton, NJ: Princeton University Press, 1997.
Henderson, Joseph L. *Shadow and Self*. New York: Chiron, 1990.
Jung, C. G. *Memories, Dreams, Reflections*. New York: Random House, 1961.
Jung, C. G. *Man and His Symbols*. Garden City, NY: Doubleday, 1964.
Jung, C. G. *The Collected Works of C. G. Jung*. 20 vols. Princeton, NJ: Princeton University Press, 1971–1986.
Jung, C. G. *Letters I: 1906–1950*, ed. Gerhard Adler. Princeton, NJ: Princeton University Press, 1973.
Jung, C. G. *Letters II: 1951–1961*, ed. Gerhard Adler. Princeton, NJ: Princeton University Press, 1976.
McGuire, William, and R. F. C. Hull, eds. *C. G. Jung Speaking: Interviews and Encounters*. Princeton, NJ: Princeton University Press, 1977.
Stevens, Anthony. *The Two-Million-Year-Old Self*. College Station: Texas A&M University Press, 1993.

12

Teaching Jung in Asia

Jeremy Taylor

Let me begin with a metaphor. The figure of the Spirit Bird in the
sacred narratives of the world carries transformative messages and
prophecies from the unseen world of the divine to the world of
human existence and limited, evolving awareness. This role as divine
messenger is the defining characteristic of the Spirit Bird. This figure
is one of many recurrent, elemental symbolic patterns that transcend
the barriers of religion, culture, race, language, and geography,
appearing in essentially the same metaphoric fashion everywhere, in
widely separated societies and periods of history; in collective rituals,
sacred narratives, and other collective social expressions; and also in
the dreams and visions of individual persons all over the world. Carl
Jung called recurrent, ubiquitous symbolic patterns of this kind
"archetypes of the collective unconscious." One of Jung's most
important contributions to modern thought is his demonstration of
the independent ontological status of archetypal forms and figures
like the Spirit Bird.

In the West, the repeating archetypal pattern of Spirit Bird is
easily recognized in the eagle of Zeus and Jupiter, YHWH's dove,
Odin's ravens, and the multiple bird messengers of the prehistoric
European Great Mother Goddess (particularly the more recently
much-maligned owl), among others. All of these Western spirit birds
tend to be either cliff dwelling raptors or at least up-off-the-ground
tree-nesting and -dwelling birds. In the West's sacred narratives,
mythic spirit birds of this kind regularly serve as special messengers
from the "upper world" of the sky and the deities of the sky and
deliver their divinely inspired messages "down" to "middle earth."
The common phrase, still in use today, "a little bird told me" echoes

these ancient sacred stories and is at one level a smaller scale example of this large archetypal pattern.

In Asian sacred narratives, similar archetypal spirit birds perform the same service: delivering prophecies and divine instructions and forming living connections between the divine world of the ancestors, gods, and goddesses and the mundane physical world of human existence. In these cultures, the creatures tend to be water or shore birds such as ducks, geese, herons, gulls, and cormorants. These Asian spirit birds, by their very nature, not only bring glimpses of prophecy and pronouncements of divine will "down" from the sky above, just as they do in the West, but also bring their divinely inspired messages "up from below" in a way that the archetypal spirit birds in the West almost never do.

One major implication of this generic difference between how the archetypal pattern of Spirit Bird appears in Asia and its appearance in Europe and European-influenced cultural and religious contexts is that Asian spirit birds suggest that in the Asian collective psyche, the as-yet-not-consciously-perceived energy of the divine is instinctively understood to reside as much in "the dark, watery depths" as it does in "the bright heights above the clouds." The differences between the raptors and tree-nesting spirit birds in Western tradition and the swimming, diving, and wading spirit birds point to a profound unconscious difference in the "deep grammar" of Asian and Occidental attitudes toward the world and toward the divine.

Differences of this kind carry serious practical implications and consequences. The unspoken idea that divine energies and intuitions can be (and even should be) sought in the "wet" depths of our shared unconscious "darkness," as well as in the "dry, bright, shining" heights of rarefied conscious spiritual awareness is one example of these foundational, archetypal symbolic "disagreements" that have clouded and often continue to confuse the encounters of West and East over the centuries. In the deep grammar (to use Chomsky's evocative term) of East-West cultural exchange and conflict, such unconscious differences can and do create tension.

Viewing the meeting of East and West from the other end of the metaphoric telescope for a moment, at several points in his long career Carl Jung suggested that the appearance of "Asian people and settings" in the dreams and waking fantasies of Europeans and North Americans of European descent often represents the sense of the archetypal, symbolic "otherness" of the deep unconscious itself. The appearance of Asia and Asians in the dreams of contemporary citizens of the former European colonial powers reflects symbolically how the unconscious itself appears to the apprehensive and uncomprehending eyes of individual and collective Western ego consciousness. Jung quotes Kipling's famous lines "East is East and West is West, and never the twain shall meet" (penned in 1895) and suggests that at one important level, the essentially racist and imperialist idea of the "inevitable order of the world" is encapsulated in those lines. "Never the twain shall meet" reflects Western culture's collective projection of the apparently insurmountable otherness born of its own problematic encounter with the unconscious. The nervousness and incomprehension that characterize most encounters with dreams and other manifestations of the unconscious in the context of Western culture are projected outward onto the perceived and collectively agreed-upon otherness and "incomprehensibility" of Asian culture(s) and sensibilities.

From my point of view, these archetypal symbolic patterns are not just theoretical formulations. These unconscious archetypal patterns are experientially familiar to me. They have come to the fore repeatedly in the course of my teaching Jung in Asia, particularly in Korea and China. I teach Jungian ideas and depth analytical practices all around the world as a regular part of my work educating and training people to reach for greater conscious understanding of their dreams remembered from sleep.

It is my own evolving understanding of Jung over the decades that led to the evolving "ministry of dream work" that I have now pursued for more than forty years as a Unitarian-Universalist minister. Following Jung's lead, I begin with the assumption that all dreams (even our worst nightmares) come in the service of health and wholeness and speak a universal language. Each time in my life I have engaged in projective dream work with another new constituency, I have been even more deeply impressed with how, at the archetypal level, our dreams reveal the same basic archetypal patterns—Spirit Bird being but a single case in point. In my experience, all dreams remembered from sleep ask the same basic psychospiritual questions: Who am I, really? How fully am I giving creative expression to this only partially conscious genuine self? What, specifically, can I do to move more in the direction of authentic health and wholeness, not only for myself but also for the species and the planet as a whole?

This last overarching question is posed by the presence of transpersonal, archetypal images in every dream. I am convinced that all our unique and absolutely personal dreams rest on a foundation of shared archetypal metaphor and symbolism. The primary piece of evidence for this is that no matter how mundane and uniquely personal the surface of any dream may appear to be on first encounter, transcendent archetypal patterns are still discernible. These patterns of layered meaning and implication demonstrate that every dreamer is, at the very least, an unconscious coparticipant (and, I would argue, a cocreator) in the larger dramas of psychospiritual evolution and significance that are always revealed when we take the time to explore any dream in sufficient depth.

All archetypal patterns are profoundly ambiguous and ambivalent. The effort to cross the historical, cultural, linguistic, and most important of all, unconscious symbolic barriers between East and West always evokes archetypal tensions of the kind suggested by Spirit Bird and the "Inscrutable East," regardless of whether any of these dramas are conscious. The basic psychospiritual idea that these problems have a common source in the collective unconscious can help in the effort to make meaningful contact between and among societies and individuals with very different religious perspectives and histories. Archetypal forms and patterns always carry the quality of both-and rather than either-or.

This slippery resistance to clear intellectual definition characterizing the whole archetypal realm makes teaching Jung and Jungian ideas in traditional Western and Western-influenced academic settings difficult and problematic at best, particularly in comparison with teaching other formal disciplines and codified bodies of knowledge. Since Aristotle (personal tutor to that most arche-typical imperialist, Alexander the Great), the Western intellectual project has centered on refining sets of basic definitions to the point where each definition is demonstrably unique, and all definitions are mutually exclusive. Detailed examination of the real-world interactions between these mutually exclusive categories and the measurable realities they are supposed to represent has become the primary mode of Western intellectual and academic thought. One of the primary difficulties created by this intellectual tradition is that the tradition itself is patently inadequate when it comes to exploring, understanding, and categorizing imponderables like religion, love, creativity, and the experience of expanding psychospiritual self-awareness. As the Chinese philosopher Mo Tzu (470–390 B.C.E.) famously said, "If we examine things with an eye to their similarities, all things are the same, and if we examine things with regard to their differences, all things are dissimilar." Absolutely true though this maxim is, it could hardly be mistaken for a foundational assertion of Western philosophical thought.

At the beginning of the twentieth century, Jung was well aware of the accumulated weight of the problems created by this collective, historical lacuna in Western scientific and philosophical thought. He began his prodigious effort to rebalance the Western tradition and give proper acknowledgment to the weight and importance of symbols in general and to the importance of the unconscious in particular. Jung understood that the Western intellectual tradition has ignored for far too long the realm of crucially important imponderables, particularly the roots of religion and the importance of nonrational religious experience. Much of Jung's lifelong conversation with Christianity came from what he perceived to be the "blunder" of the early Christian movement in embracing Aristotelian principles of logic and rhetoric and simultaneously repressing the illogical information and archetypal symbolic experiences that inevitably well up from within when anyone turns purposely and consciously to cultivating values, creativity, and moral responsibility. Historically, this repression is at the root of the official church's rejection and demonizing of the Gnostics and the other theologians and practitioners of variant forms of Christianity, like the followers of Arius and Pelagius. It is not surprising that Jung turned to these condemned and despised heretics in his search for the "lost" (that is to say, repressed) polysemic, multivalent, unconscious archetypal heritage of Christianity.

From the very beginning, Jung's project involved lifting these neglected and repressed sides of the Western cultural, psychological, and religious tradition up into the metaphoric light of conscious consideration and responsible discussion. His task was not merely philosophical or academic; he was urgently aware of the terrible vulnerability of Western civilization to the "return of the repressed." Jung himself made it very clear in the early 1930s that it was in large measure "the return of the (collectively) repressed" that was fueling the violent rise of the National Socialist movement (the Nazis) in Germany. In light of Jung's clear and demonstrated understanding of the terrible historical consequences of the general Western historic repression and failure to acknowledge and take seriously the role of the unconscious, the repeated accusations against him of supposed Nazi sympathies are particularly ill considered and unfair.

From the very beginning of his work, even before his life-shaping encounter with Sigmund Freud in 1907, Jung's personal and professional eye was focused directly on gathering the necessary information to support an expanded psychological and spiritual consideration of the most pressing contemporary problems and dilemmas of Western civilization. Jung pointed continuously and unambiguously to the necessity of raising individual and collective self-awareness and particularly to withdrawing previously unconscious projections of the patterns and contents of the archetypal shadow, as well as the necessity of consciously facing the symbolic "death" that is the necessary precursor to any genuine "rebirth" and renewal of the Western spirit. Even before the First World War, Jung was passionately clear about his understanding that humanity cannot go forward simply projecting that necessary symbolic death outward onto others in the effort to make the world a better place by literally killing other people instead of metaphorically killing the aspects of self and culture that no longer serve health and wholeness. This attitude was completely incompatible with Nazism, or even with Nazi sympathies, both of which require unquestioned conscious acceptance of the illusions generated through unconscious projection, turning the unconscious psychospiritual processes of repression and projection into basic principles and functional instruments of national policy, particularly the Nazi policies regarding "race."

Anyone who undertakes teaching Jung and archetypal ideas in any public setting in the twenty-first century will almost certainly have to face and respond to these persistent accusations of Nazi sympathy because, alas, they seem to be as rife today as when they were first uttered by the ailing Freud in his British exile from Vienna at the beginning of the Second World War. I suspect that it is precisely because these accusations were initially leveled by no less a personage than Sigmund Freud himself (and because they were then memorialized—and I believe exaggerated—by Freud's official biographer, Ernest Jones) that they persist today with such tenacity, even in the face of the overwhelming evidence that they are not true.

Addressing this issue directly leads inevitably to the question of what to read and what to suggest and require that others read in the course of teaching Jung and Jungian and archetypal ideas. The first time I actually read anything Jung had written, I was traveling in connection with my work as a peace activist and student organizer. By the time I headed back home, I had finished all the reading material I had brought along with me. It was the dead of winter, and I was momentarily stuck in Erie, Pennsylvania, waiting for the bus back to Buffalo, where I was attending the State University of New York as an undergraduate. The only thing I could find that looked even vaguely interesting in the dusty, rotating, Marcel DuChamp "ready-made" bus station paperback rack was a lone, faded copy of the Mentor paperback edition of Jung's *Flying Saucers: A Modern Myth of Things Seen in the* Skies,[1] so I decided to give in to my playful curiosity about what a man I had been told repeatedly was "a mystic-racist-fascist" might have to say about the persistent phenomenon of flying saucer sightings. (Let me also say at the outset that I am not recommending Jung's essay on flying saucers as the best place to start reading Jung; it just happens to be the first work of Jung's I ever read.)

As it turned out, the essay on flying saucers is a fascinating exposition, filled with detailed discussions, carefully developed arguments, and valuable and innovative ideas and insights. It is eminently worth reading. In the midst of that little book, Jung tosses out the idea, almost as an aside (in a tone that seems to suggest that, of course, every reasonably well-educated person will already be aware), that the vast majority of our negative prejudices—and the destructive individual and collective behaviors incited by them—are the direct result of unconsciously projecting our own particular personal versions of the collective archetype of the "shadow" outward onto others, while believing consciously that these nasty, inhuman shadow traits are the exclusive property of those others and do not exist in "us." The projected fantasy that these unacceptable traits are the exclusive possession of those on whom we unconsciously project them naturally makes these people fair game for any and all punishments, reprisals, and efforts to neutralize, control, and even obliterate them, as the Nazis attempted to obliterate and exterminate the Jews. Ironically, we still tend to project on the memory of the Nazis themselves in the same fashion, imagining that they were "inhuman monsters" and that "we are nothing like them!"

It was at this point I began what was to become a lifelong career "teaching Jung." I began initially as a zealous missionary to my own pacific activist companions, trying to get them to recognize the incredibly progressive and transformative implications of his work, particularly his insights into the unconscious patterns of repression and projection. Since the handful of them who had heard of Jung had also been raised with essentially the same uniformly and pervasively negative assessments of Jung and his work that I had grown up with, I soon discovered that the less I talked about Jung himself and the more I concentrated on his dynamic ideas (without necessarily attributing them to Jung), the less resistance I encountered and the more success I had in coming up with concrete, cooperative strategies for winning hearts and minds over to more progressive and compassionate ideas and attitudes about the protracted war in Southeast Asia and about the atrociously entrenched patterns of race, class, and gender bias and oppression at home.

Returning to the question of what reading to assign when teaching Jung, let me say that from a scholarly point of view, the best biography of Jung in English (in my view, and I have made a point of reading all of them I can find) is Deirdre Bair's *Jung: A Biography*.[2] However, at 881 pages (232 of which are a mixture of substantive notes and detailed references, all in tiny print), it can be heavy going for even the most dedicated students. For this reason, it should probably be reserved for those who wish to pursue their interest in Jung outside the confines of the classroom and the lecture hall. One of the most valuable elements of Bair's book is her exhaustive research, which musters a vast amount of evidence and clearly demonstrates (at least to my satisfaction) that Jung was neither a Nazi nor a Nazi sympathizer. Bair details his efforts to counter growing Nazi influence in the International Association for Psychoanalysis and his tireless work on behalf of Jewish refugees, including his own personal secretary, Aniela Jaffé, and her husband. Jung also recruited agents and "assets" from among his clients and friends for Allen Dulles and the U.S. Office of Strategic Services (OSS) all during the war and filed reports for Eisenhower and Churchill on the evolving state of German society and psyche as the war progressed.

Bair also establishes beyond reasonable doubt that Jung was also a compulsive womanizer, engaging in sexual liaisons with a startling number of his female patients, in addition to his notorious long-term relationship with Antonia Wolff and his sexual liaison with Sabina Spielrein when she was a patient under his care at the Burgholzli Mental Hospital. As Nazism and the Second World War fade in the collective memory and interest of younger generations of students in the West (replaced in their attention by more recent military actions that involved friends and family members who are still alive), this undeniable accusation of sexism may well become an even greater cause célèbre in the classroom when teaching Jung than it is today. I encounter an increasing mood of immediate rejection of Jung and his work in my classes and seminars these days for reasons of feminist critique. In response, I can only say I believe that to reject Jung's crucially important work and psychospiritual insights on the basis of his personal sexism is to throw out any number of babies with their dirty bathwater.[3]

My experience teaching Jung in Asia, particularly in Korea, as I have done now in 2010 for almost a decade, is that Asian students with an interest in Jung are less concerned with these biographical details of Jung's personal life than they are with the overall acceptability of his ideas in the world of professional and academic psychology and in the implications of Jungian therapeutic strategies, particularly as they are relevant to the postcolonial, rapidly industrializing and urbanizing experience in Asia.

As another biography suggestion, I am partial to Laurens van der Post's *Jung and the Story of Our Time*.[4] Van der Post emphasizes the impact on his own life of Jung's work and knowing Jung personally, moving from there to cogent discussions of the details of twentieth-century history as the background for the Jung's personal and professional development. The most visually appealing, emotionally touching, and spiritually focused biography is Claire Dunne's beautifully illustrated *Carl Jung: Wounded Healer of the Soul*.[5] Even though it is an unabashedly positive assessment of Jung and the lasting importance of his work, particularly in its value for psychospiritual seekers, the level of scholarship and documentation remains consistently high. In my experience, this is a particularly useful book to begin with when teaching Jung in the context of religious studies.

Jung's own autobiographical memoir, *Memories, Dreams, Reflections*, is certainly required reading for anyone who wishes to understand the depth of the man and his work.[6] It is not an ordinary autobiographical narrative, and the names, dates, and places that one might expect from an autobiography are remarkable by their absence. It is primarily a memoir of Jung's internal life and the development of his thought and religious intuition. Waking life events appear in the background, so to speak, as the settings for moments of particular psychospiritual importance in Jung's development. The book is also particularly frustrating with regard to the persistent accusations raised against Jung regarding his Nazi sympathies and his sexual affairs. Jung's experiences during both world wars are barely mentioned, and his relations with women other than his wife, Emma (who is only mentioned briefly), are not mentioned at all. It was not until Bair's biography was published that it became clear that, in his eighties, when Jung recounted his life memories to his personal secretary, Aniela Jaffé, he spoke at some length about these aspects of his life, but that Jaffe and the Jung family heirs redacted almost all of it from the manuscript after his death (when he was no longer able to oversee the translation of his manuscripts into print, as he had done with all his other works). Without this key piece of information that Bair provides, Jung's apparent silence regarding those parts of his life have left him, and the book itself, open to recurring charges of being "deceptive" and "self-serving."

William McGuire and R. F. C. Hull's collection of transcriptions of many of Jung's less formal conversations, printed and filmed interviews, and reminiscences of friends and acquaintances, *C. G. Jung Speaking—Interviews and Encounters*, deserves special mention.[7] Because this book painstakingly records Jung's more spontaneous spoken words, it is often more reader friendly and accessible to students. By far the best book in English about Jung's intellectual development is J. J. Clarke's admirable work, *In Search of Jung*.[8] Clarke assembles what we know of Jung's reading and compares it with Jung's own comments about the sources and roots of his "biggest" ideas. Read in concert with Robert Hopke's *A Guided Tour of the Collected Works of C. G. Jung*, a very clear picture emerges of the sources of Jung's insights, as well as the genius with which he uses his sources to go further than any of his own mentors had gone before into the realm of human unconscious motivation and behavior.[9]

In terms of providing students with the opportunity to read Jung's own words for themselves, there are two excellent anthologies of Jung's work: *The Essential Jung*, selected and introduced by Anthony Storr,[10] and *The Basic Writings of C. G. Jung*, edited with an introduction by Violet de Laszlo.[11] For religious studies students, the anthology of selections from Jung's collected works, *Psychology and Western Religion*, translated by R. F. C. Hull, is particularly stimulating and useful.[12]

Finally, to close this section, let me mention the book that Jung himself designed to serve as an introduction to his work to the general reading public, a book that has been treated like an outcast stepchild in the official cataloguing of Jung's work: *Man and His Symbols*, by Jung, Henderson, Jacobi, Jaffé, and von Franz.[13] Close to the end of his life (Jung died in 1961), he had a dream, which he recounts in the introduction to *Man and His Symbols*. This dream caused him to realize that his commitment to produce an accessible introduction to the full range of his work for a nonspecialist audience was still unfulfilled. He realized that he no longer had the energy to write the whole thing himself, so he wrote letters to the colleagues and protégés he believed had the best and most sensitive grasp of particular aspects of his work (shadow, anima and animus, trickster, manna personality, night sea journey, etc.), asking each one to write a piece for a general audience to introduce, discuss, and illustrate these key archetypal principles and concepts. He sent the letters off to his selected list of contributors and died before any of their manuscripts were returned. As a result, the official Jungian establishment views the book with great suspicion and mistrust, since Jung himself never had an opportunity to edit and give his final, full approval to any of the articles.

Nevertheless, it remains a wonderful piece of work that I believe fulfills Jung's desire to provide a clean, clear, readable introduction to many of the details and finer points of his life's work. *Man and His Symbols* is one of the few books I recommend to my students that they put out the extra money and buy the larger format, hardcover edition, rather than the smaller, less expensive paperback edition. *Man and His Symbols* is, among other things, a marvelous example of the book designer's art, filled with illustrations that are colored, sized, and placed on the page with great care to maximize their nonverbal, aesthetic impact and emotional amplification of the full meaning(s) of the text. All the illustrations are there in the paperback edition, but they are reduced to black-and-white postage stamps, and much of their subtle impact is lost.

Unfortunately, as of this writing, I am not aware of any of these excellent resources that are available in translation in any Asian languages (other than *Memories, Dreams, Reflections*, which I hear has been translated into Japanese and may be in the process of being translated into Korean). A good number of the Asian mental health workers and academic psychologists and psychology teachers with whom I have met and worked in my Asian travels speak English and have acquired and read of many of the books I mentioned. Almost all my work outside the English-speaking world is conducted with "simultaneous" (sentence-by-sentence) translation and includes many laypeople who are not mental health workers. Many of these would-be independent dream workers do not speak English or any language other than their native tongue. For them, and for the professionals who do not speak English, fragmentary quotations in journal articles and conversations with friends and colleagues who do read English represent the limit of their resources for learning more about Jung. Many of my Asian students and colleagues do become interested in Jung over the course of acquiring skills as projective dream workers and continue to seek out their own paths to greater knowledge of his work.

For four decades, my primary focus has been training people to do projective dream work with each other in their native languages. This is a process that relies much more on a group process that acknowledges the inevitable element of unconscious projection when exploring dreams than it does on the acquisition of any particular body of interpretive knowledge. Even if people believe they have knowledge about dreams and the unconscious that is "objective" and "scientifically derived and proven," they still have nothing to apply that supposedly objective knowledge to except their own imagined version of the original dreamer's dream, and for that reason alone, their work with dreams is still determined by their own unconscious projections. In that important sense, all interpretive work with dreams (and I would argue all waking mentation and conscious activity as well) is laced with and rests totally upon unconscious projections, and as Jung said many times over the course of his long life, "The problem with the unconscious is that it really is unconscious!"

Prior to 1969, all my work with dreams was one-to-one, mainly with friends and loved ones. I approached the possibility of group dream work with relative strangers with some trepidation, particularly in light of Jung's stern and repeated warnings throughout his life against undertaking any serious psychospiritual work, particularly work with dreams, in group settings, because it would lead "inevitably to catering to the lowest common denominator in the group." In 1969, as I completed my compulsory alternate civilian service as a conscientious objector to the Vietnam War, I was faced with a situation involving unconscious racist attitudes and behaviors among people who were totally committed at a conscious level to the eradication of racism in others. They believed in all sincerity that they had conquered all vestiges of the racial prejudice they had been raised with but still irritated each other and the other people they came in contact with in the course of our shared organizing efforts. I came to believe this situation simply could not be dealt with in any other way than looking into the unconscious and that an effort at group dream sharing and projective discussion was the most likely activity to promote that result.

That initial effort was so startlingly successful (spontaneously verified by multiple sources outside the training group, to say nothing of the evidence of transformed relationships and ways of communicating among the trainees themselves) that I decided to devote all my resources to finding out what the upper range of creative, transformative possibility might be, utilizing this way of work. (For a more detailed discussion of the initial development of this group projective dream work process, see my books, particularly *The Wisdom of Your Dreams*.)[14]

That was in 1969, and now, forty-one years later, I am still not clear what the upper range of possibility might be with this work. All I know is that things like focusing on the unconscious, personal, and archetypal material that wells up simultaneously in our dreams, and that also unconsciously fuels collective patterns of human oppression like racism, sexism, and classism, can transform by sharing and exploring the details of people's dreams, no matter what language they speak, no matter what culture and society they reside in. When this dream material is raised to more conscious awareness, it ceases to be projected unconsciously, and people are afforded an opportunity to behave in more mature, creative, responsible, and respectful ways with one another. This is as true in Asia as it is in North America. It is as true in Europe as it is in Australia and Central and South America. (Alas, I have yet to work in Africa.) The symbolic language of the unconscious itself, and hence of that primary expression of the unconscious, the dream, turns out in actual practice to be universal. I have yet to find a cultural or social setting in which this does not prove to be the case.

My experience teaching projective dream work in Asian countries in particular is that the interest in all Western psychology is tempered by a suspicion that it is, on the one hand, an adjunct of Western imperialism and, on the other hand, yet another superior "technology" that rapidly developing and transforming Asia cannot afford to ignore. Most psychologically sophisticated Asian professionals are much more aware of Freud than they are of Jung. Jung's basic respect for all cultures has been a great help in winning Asian audiences over to at least taking Jung seriously.

The complexities of modernization in Asia often appear to amount in practice to an effort to adopt various industrial technologies that were first developed in the West and to put them in place while at the same time publicly championing traditional values in an attempt to minimize the cultural contamination that invariably accompanies urbanization and the necessity of maintaining a relatively more educated urban workforce than the traditions of rural agriculture required. Not too surprisingly, the dreams of individual Asian citizens are rife with anxiety and poignant imagery of loss and disruption, as families are uprooted and Asian nations recover individually and collectively from the ravages of modern warfare.

What Jung has to say about the dangerous self-deceptions of shadow projection are often a bitter pill to swallow, particularly when it calls into question traditional national hatreds and antipathies. The national mutual hatred that boils and bubbles between Korea and Japan, for example, is fueled by wildly nationalistic public education that tends to tell only about the historical atrocities that "those others" inflicted on "us and our beloved ancestors." The deeper truth of the Gestalt levels of dreaming, where everyone and everything is a reflection of aspects of the dreamer's own interior being (no matter what other levels of meaning and implication those same images may also carry at the same time), is a particularly distressing idea to all those Koreans who dream of Japanese people, as well as Japanese people who have Korean people appear in their dreams. "That can't be a part of me!"

One of the most interesting things about this archetypal situation (which arises frequently in the dream sessions I conduct) is that there is a level of insight that almost always rises spontaneously and accompanies this Gestalt idea that makes it clear that this is indeed the case. Ironically (but predictably), it is always easier for members of the dream work training group to see this level of Gestalt truth clearly in others but still be entirely in denial when it comes to their own dreams. This is by no means a uniquely Asian phenomenon—I have seen it everywhere I have taught.

In 1961, General Park Chung-Hee (the traditional form in Korea is to put the family name first) staged a military coup, the avowed purpose of which was to "save Korea from communist domination" and to free the nation from being despoiled by "corrupt and incapable politicians." (This, too, is an archetypal story of shadow projection.) One of the attempts General Park made "to bring backward Korea into the twentieth century" was to outlaw the traditional practice of consulting dream oracles. Koreans have been turning to their dreams for guidance in daily life and communion with dead ancestors for millennia, and apparently all General Park succeeded in doing was driving the practice underground. My experience in Korea convinces me that very few Koreans, from the very rich to the very poor, men or women, make major business or personal decisions without consulting a traditional shamanic expert dream interpreter. These practitioners are still officially "criminals," hiding in plain sight in the big cities, particularly in nail parlors, and still make their livings, as they have for countless generations, by going into trance and consulting a multitude of spirits who tell the dreamer what the true, deeper meaning of a dream is, with particular emphasis on profitable business arrangements and emotional liaisons. In Korea, the Catholic Church is particularly interested in training priests and nuns in "modern, Western dream interpretation" so that they will have interesting and valuable things to say to the dreamers who are obviously unwilling to give up their traditions of dream oracle interpretation. This means that when I go to teach Jungian archetypal dream theory and practice, there are always a great many questions about dreams of the dead and dreams predicting the future. Jung's openness to these realities and his efforts to coin appropriate modern technical language (like "synchronicity") to facilitate these conversations are usually greeted with great interest, relief, and enthusiasm.

The same is generally true in China in my experience. Contemporary Chinese mental health workers are apparently less open to Jung, at least initially, than their opposite numbers in other Asian countries. I believe this is primarily due to the early embrace of Freud by European Communist theoreticians, who were particularly enthusiastic about Freud's ideas regarding fixations on money in general, and capitalism in particular, being unconsciously related to premature toilet training. (Amusing though this may seem, it is a serious historical comment.) However, after the initial jousting over terminology and exploring the evidence for the universal nature of the human unconscious, my experience is that Chinese dreamers are just as interested and excited as anyone else about exploring the deeper meanings and implications of their dreams from a Jungian perspective.

At one point, during one of my dream work training sessions at the University of Beijing in the 1990s, the work with a particular woman's dream developed a clear level having to do with her anguished emotions resulting from her personal encounter with the country's family planning laws. Having gone to the state clinic when she first became pregnant and "registered" her pregnancy, she received the prescribed prenatal care but lost her pregnancy. Apparently, having officially registered as a pregnant woman, it would now be a criminal offense for her to become pregnant again, even though she did not carry the child to term. As the entire room of some 300 people watched and participated in the group projective exploration of the woman's dream, my official translator suddenly decided that we should end the session early because she could not translate the discussion any longer. At that point, the entire audience spontaneously took over the task of translation, calling out alternative

Chinese for my remarks and shouting English translations of the comments and projections in Chinese. It was an electrifying moment showing the power of dreams to give voice to personal and collective truth.

East may indeed be East, and West is still clearly West, but the twain can and do meet at considerable depth through the practical application of Carl Jung's understanding of the universal archetypes of the collective unconscious.

NOTES

1. C. G. Jung, *Flying Saucers: A Modern Myth of Things Seen in the Skies* (New York: Mentor, 1957).

2. Deirdre Bair, *Jung: A Biography* (Boston: Little, Brown, 2003).

3. I can also recommend *Feminist Archetypal Theory: Interdisciplinary Re-Visions of Jungian Thought*, edited by Estella Lauter and Carol Schreier Rupprecht (Knoxville: University of Tennessee Press, 1985).

4. Laurens van der Post, *Jung and the Story of Our Time* (New York: Pantheon, 1975).

5. Claire Dunne, *Carl Jung: Wounded Healer of the Soul* (New York: Parabola, 2000).

6. C. G. Jung, *Memories, Dreams, Reflections* (New York: Vintage, 1961).

7. William McGuire, and R. F. C. Hull, *C. G. Jung Speaking—Interviews and Encounters* (Princeton, NJ: Princeton University Press, 1977).

8. J. J. Clarke, *In Search of Jung* (London: Routledge, 1992).

9. Robert Hopke, *A Guided Tour of the Collected Works of C. G. Jung* (Boston: Shambala, 1989).

10. Anthony Storr, ed., *The Essential Jung* (Princeton, NJ: Princeton University Press, 1983).

11. Violet de Laszlo, *The Basic Writings of C. G. Jung* (New York: Modern Library, 1959).

12. R. F. C. Hull, trans., *Psychology and Western Religion* (Princeton, NJ: Princeton University Press, 1984).

13. C. G. Jung et al., *Man and His Symbols* (New York: Doubleday, 1964).

14. Jeremy Taylor, *The Wisdom of Your Dreams* (New York: Penguin/Tarcher, 2009).

REFERENCES

Bair, Deirdre. *Jung: A Biography*. Boston: Little, Brown, 2003.
Clarke, J. J. *In Search of Jung*. London: Routledge, 1992.
De Laszlo, Violet. *The Basic Writings of C. G. Jung*. New York: Modern Library, 1959.
Dunne, Claire. *Carl Jung: Wounded Healer of the Soul*. New York: Parabola, 2000.
Hopke, Robert. *A Guided Tour of the Collected Works of C. G. Jung*. Boston: Shambala, 1989.
Hull, R. F. C., trans. *Psychology and Western Religion*. Princeton, NJ: Princeton University Press, 1984.
Jung, C. G. *Flying Saucers: A Modern Myth of Things Seen in the Skies*. New York: Mentor, 1957.
Jung, C. G. *Memories, Dreams, Reflections*. New York: Vintage, 1961.

Jung, C. G. *Man and His Symbols*. New York: Doubleday, 1964.

Lauter, Estella, and Carol Schreier Rupprecht, *Feminist Archetypal Theory: Interdisciplinary Re-Visions of Jungian Thought*. Knoxville: University of Tennessee Press, 1985.

McGuire, William, and R. F. C. Hull. *C. G. Jung Speaking—Interviews and Encounters*. Princeton, NJ: Princeton University Press, 1977.

Storr, Anthony, ed. *The Essential Jung*. Princeton, NJ: Princeton University Press, 1983.

Taylor, Jeremy. *The Wisdom of Your Dreams*. New York: Penguin/Tarcher, 2009.

Van der Post, Laurens. *Jung and the Story of Our Time*. New York: Pantheon, 1975.

PART IV

Jungian Practices in the Classroom and Beyond

13

Teaching Jung and Dreams

Kelly Bulkeley

Introduction

A major new work by C. G. Jung has just been translated into
English and published in a handsomely designed hardbound volume.
It gives fascinating new insights into Jung's personality and sheds
new light on his psychological ideas. This would not be *The Red Book*,
Jung's hand-illustrated journal translated and edited by Sonu
Shamdasani and published in 2009, but rather *Children's Dreams:
Notes from the Seminar Given in 1936–1940* by C. G. Jung, edited by
Lorenz Jung and Maria Meyer-Grass and translated by Ernst Falzeder
with the collaboration of Tony Woolfson, which appeared in 2008.
This new English translation of Jung's seminar on the earliest
remembered dreams of childhood opens a fresh chapter in the study
of Jungian dream theory. The book provides a uniquely informative
and thought-provoking source of insight into Jung's practical
approach to dream interpretation. Particularly valuable for teachers,
Children's Dreams is a pedagogical treasure because it illustrates how
Jung taught his own ideas to students in the classroom.

This chapter describes several educational strategies Jung used
in these seminars, with the goal of showing how similar processes
can be used in present-day classrooms to enrich teaching in religious
studies, psychology, and other disciplines.

Dreams play a central role in both Jung's personal life and his
psychological theory. In *Memories, Dreams, Reflections*, he attributes
many of his key insights to specific dreams, some experienced early
in childhood. His ideas about religion, as presented in *Psychology and
Religion* and *Man and His Symbols*, rely heavily on recurrent

cross-cultural features of dreaming as evidence for the universality of the archetypes and the collective unconscious. This means that to understand Jung's theory of religion, one must gain some degree of familiarity with his dream theory. More specifically, as this chapter argues, the best way to learn about Jung's dream theory is to practice it with students according to the approach used in these seminars. Experience has shown that students find it surprisingly easy to enter into an educational process of dream analysis by following and adapting Jung's basic principles. Once they become familiar with the limits and potentials of Jung's approach to dreams, students are better positioned to make sophisticated critical judgments about his psychology as a whole, including his theory of religion.

Background to the Seminars

From 1936 to 1940, Jung taught a seminar at the Swiss Federal Institute of Technology in Zurich. The presenters included some of his brightest followers, including Marie-Louis Von Franz, Aniela Jaffé, and Jolande Jacobi. Each meeting of the class involved someone presenting and analyzing an early childhood dream report, after which Jung provided an analysis (in some cases, Jung himself presented the dream), and then other participants asked questions and responded to his ideas. At several points, Jung posed questions for the class as a whole, testing the students' interpretive abilities and prodding them via Socratic dialogue toward better understanding. The sense one gets is of a typical graduate school course, featuring lectures by the professor and visiting experts, student presentations, and group discussions. We cannot know how faithfully the book represents what actually happened in the seminar, since the text derives from notes recorded by two of his students and edited many years later (initially, the dream material from clinical patients was kept confidential for professional reasons). Jung knew of the transcript and approved of its eventual publication, though he never had time to edit the text to his complete satisfaction.

As it stands, the book gives the sense of a lively, intelligent, free-flowing conversation among people who knew Jung's theories well and wanted to learn more about how to apply them. The seminar discussions do not deviate in any significant way from what can be found in Jung's written works, but the tone is quite different—conversational, interactive, engaging. As one reads through the seminars, a more complex portrait of Jung's personality develops. He swears with gusto and cracks bawdy jokes. He makes casually Eurocentric comments about people of other races and ethnicities. He can be pedantic and irritable, and he occasionally chides his students. But he seems genuinely excited by the class and the opportunity to discuss dream psychology with a group of educated people. A less iconic, more human Jung emerges from these pages.

Virtually no mention is made of the ominous political situation in Europe at this time, namely, the rise of Hitler and the Nazis and the outbreak of World

War II. Germany lies on Switzerland's northern border, and during this time the Nazis annexed Austria (1938) and invaded Poland (1939), with obvious intentions for further military expansion. Yet the wartime context is mentioned briefly in only one of the seminar dream discussions.[1] A critic of Jung might take this as a retreat from the real problems of the social world into the self-protective fantasy world of dream symbolism. A more sympathetic reader might wonder if the seminar participants found this work so compelling precisely because they knew that dark forces were afoot and they wanted to gain better practical insight into the deep psychological conflicts fueling the political movements that threatened their civilization.

"On the Method of Dream Interpretation"

The book's introduction consists of Jung's remarks at the beginning of the winter term of 1938. This piece represents, in my view, the single best distillation of Jung's ideas about dreams in the whole corpus of his collected works. Titled "On the Method of Dream Interpretation," it stands on its own as a concise statement of his psychology. It may not have the literary polish of his other writings, but the transcript of Jung's "first day of class" lecture conveys the major principles of his dream theory with remarkable clarity and precision.

He begins by framing the subject of the class in developmental terms. According to Jung, Freud, and many other depth psychologists, the conscious mind emerges over time from a primal state of unconsciousness: "The unconscious is older than consciousness.... The unconscious is what is originally given, from which consciousness rises anew again and again."[2] The normal course of development from infancy into adulthood involves a transition from immersion in the unconscious to greater degrees of consciousness and self-awareness. According to this perspective, young children are by nature developmentally closer to the unconscious. Their minds are structurally less complex and thus more vulnerable to eruptions of unconscious imagery, emotion, and instinctual behavior. As such, their dreams provide an especially good means of access for studying the deepest processes of the unconscious. Particularly in the case of "big" or "great" dreams, which have few or no personal connections to the dreamer but rather stem from collective human concerns, children's dreams offer an ideal source of empirical data to test and illustrate Jung's ideas.

Jung acknowledged that the group's discussions were limited by the facts that (a) the dreams were mostly adults' recollections of dreams from many years in the past and (b) the dreamer was not present to offer any personal context or response. These disadvantages were partially offset by the intense memorability of the dreams, which preserved their core elements over time, and by their cross-cultural motifs and archetypal symbols, which made personal associations relatively less important. In most cases, Jung did have some background information about the dreamers and the subsequent events of their lives, and those details played a role at the end of the class discussion. But his primary emphasis in the seminar was teaching his students how to interpret the arche-typal themes in dreaming. Whatever degree of personal content there may be in dreams, Jung wanted his students to develop the ability to discern, in addition to the personal situation, a collective dimension in dreams, particularly those big dreams that are unusually vivid and memorable. Most dreams—the vast majority, in fact—tend to revolve around people's daily concerns and ordinary life activities.[3] Jung did not advocate deep archetypal analysis of those kinds of dreams. Rather, he asked his students to focus on childhood big dreams because they offer the best way to see and learn about the collective uncon-scious in something close to its original form.

Implicit in this view of child development is the larger theme of the psyche's goal-oriented nature, which Jung elsewhere refers to as the individua-tion process. He did not dwell on individuation here, but rather presumed an acceptance of the idea that the psyche has an intrinsic drive toward the ultimate integration of its unconscious and conscious elements. Many of Jung's inter-pretations in the seminar referred back to this basic premise. A failure to ade-quately balance the demands of conscious and unconscious life lies at the root of many people's suffering, as their dreams testify in often frightening detail. Certain childhood dreams represent early warning signals of impending psy-chopathology, and Jung presented this as evidence of the diagnostic value of dreams for psychotherapists in determining the nature and extent of their patients' illnesses. He also emphasized the prognostic value of dreams in terms of spiritual growth and insight. The big dreams of childhood give people their first glimpses of transcendence, their first encounters with numinous powers and mind-stretching possibilities. The path of individuation begins with such experiences and ultimately leads, in Jung's view, to a personal reckoning with the great existential questions of life.

A nightmare can be defined in Jungian psychology as a symptom of failed integration, an unhealthy split of consciousness and the unconscious. The worse the split, the more frightening and recurrent the nightmares. Paradoxically, bad dreams and nightmares play a helpful role in the individua-tion process. Jung said to his students that "a persecutory dream always means: this wants to come to me.... You would like to split it off, you experience it as something alien—but it just becomes all the more dangerous."[4] Instead of fighting against such inner psychological powers, Jung advocates accepting and embracing them: "The best stance would be: 'Please, come and devour me!'"[5] Few people, particularly children, have the psychological maturity required to maintain that kind of attitude, so a number of Jung's interpreta-tions of early childhood nightmares focus on what aspects of the unconscious are symbolized by the dream antagonist and what the dreamer should do to heal the split with those parts of the psyche.

The exceptions to this rule are "shell shock dreams," or what we today would call posttraumatic stress disorder (PTSD) nightmares. Jung recognized the qualitative difference of these kinds of dreams, with their "completely iden-tical repetitions of reality" showing that the traumatizing experience "can no longer be psychified."[6] He made the prescient observation that the healing process in such cases involves a gradual integration of the trauma into the evolving psychological structure of the individual's life, even though later traumas can reactivate the distress of earlier ones. Contemporary psychologists have noted the same patterns with PTSD victims and their nightmares.[7]

As always in Jung's works, the presence of Sigmund Freud hovers over the discussion, with Jung sometimes agreeing with his former mentor and sometimes sharply rejecting his ideas. In these seminars, Jung mostly accepted Freud's general outline of child development but parted ways with him on the technique of free association. Jung said this marked the key distinction between their two approaches to dreams. When Freud asked people to free-associate to their dreams, their chain of comments eventually led to the discovery of unconscious complexes that proved useful in psychotherapy. However, Jung pointed out that free association does not necessarily tell us anything about the dream itself. Rather than moving away from the dream, Jung's method of amplification involves circling around the dream from multiple angles, considering each element by itself and in relation to the dream as a whole. He said, "I proceed from the very simple principle that I understand nothing of the dream, do not know what it means, and do not conceive an idea of how the dream image is embedded in each person's mind. I amplify an existing image until it becomes visible."[8]

What this means in practice is that a Jungian approach to dream interpretation focuses on the dream as an expression of unconscious meaning communicated in an archetypal language of imagery, feeling, symbol, metaphor, and story. Particularly with big dreams, which are often characterized by a lack of personal context or association, the unconscious language can be found articulating itself in relatively pure form. The contents of such dreams tend to relate to collective motifs found in mythology, fairy tales, and other sources of cultural symbolism and ancient wisdom. To fathom such obscure psychic depths, Jung told his students they must cultivate a wide-ranging knowledge of human mental life: "We have to know what is in the storeroom of the human mind."[9] He and the seminar participants spent a great deal of their time teasing out the various possible meanings of different dream elements, with references to many of Jung's favorite sources—medieval alchemy, Gnosticism, Christian mysticism, African tribal lore, Norse epics, the Tibetan Book of the Dead, and Goethe's Faust, to name just a few. Another term Jung used as a synonym for amplification was the *ethno-psychological method*, which highlighted the way his approach synthesized developmental psychology with cultural, historical, and anthropological sources of information about human meaning making.[10]

The limitations of Jung's Eurocentrism, noted earlier, cast doubt on any attempt to apply his method naïvely, without an effort to broaden the ethnographic side of this interdisciplinary equation. Contemporary teachers need to supplement Jung's amplification resources with more sophisticated anthropological and cultural research.

Like most teachers, Jung told his students at the outset what they should and should not expect from the seminar. The amplification method can be useful, but it does not serve as an all-purpose interpretive tool. Jung cautioned his students against getting carried away:

We will see how far we will get with it. We will not always come to a satisfactory solution. The purpose of this seminar is to practice on the basis of the material. The point is not to worm out brilliant interpretations through speculations. We have to content ourselves with recognizing the symbols in their wider psychological context, and thus find our way into the psychology of the dreamer.[11]

To provide a basic structure for the discussions to come, Jung explained to the students his four-part dramatic schema for analyzing a dream. At the beginning of each class meeting, a dream was presented and immediately divided into these elements:

1. Locale: Place, time, "dramatis personae."
2. Exposition: Illustration of the problem.
3. Peripateia: Illustration of the transformation—which can also leave room for a catastrophe.
4. Lysis: Result of the dream. Meaningful closure. Compensating illustration of the action of the dream.[12]

Jung said "most dreams show this dramatic structure," even though some dreams do not have a clear-cut lysis or conclusion.[13] When that occurs, Jung usually interpreted it as evidence of an unresolved conflict.

In the closing words of his introductory lecture, Jung connected these basic elements of dreaming with "the dramatic tendency of the unconscious" in general, which ultimately relates to the prehistory of human religiosity: "Here lies the basis from which the mystery dramas developed. The whole complicated ritual of later religions goes back to these origins."[14] With these words, Jung framed the seminar on children's dreams as a contribution to the study of the psychological roots of religion.

In the four seminars, each of which was taught in the winter term during the years 1936 through 1940, a total of twenty-eight dreams were discussed (some cases involved a short series of dreams), in addition to the dream Jung briefly interpreted in his introductory lecture and many other brief mentions of dreams throughout the text. The dreamers were mostly between the ages of four and ten, with the youngest being three and the oldest fifteen. Some degree of continuity may be found in the class discussions from one meeting to another, as earlier dreams are sometimes mentioned in the analysis of later ones. But one could easily read the sections in any order and still grasp the basic interpretive process Jung is teaching his students.

Jung's Educational Methods

The methods Jung used to teach his students will be familiar to most contemporary educators in the humanities and social sciences. His primary "learning objective" for the students was to develop their skill in applying the method of amplification. Once the students gained enough competence in using this method on children's dreams, they would be ready to apply it to other kinds of textual material, from ancient myths and sacred texts to modern psychological problems and religious expressions. The seminar followed a case study approach in which a real-life example was brought into the classroom for the students to practice on. This emphasis on learning by doing is a welcome change from the didactic lecture mode of many of Jung's other writings. Although he claimed to start each time with no idea what the dream means, in actuality Jung's writings about dream interpretation usually lead to familiar results in terms of archetypal symbolism. The back-and-forth dialogue in many of these seminars shows that Jung's method is more flexible and adaptive than his other writings might suggest.

Teachers today often strive to cultivate a capacity for critical reasoning in their students. One can see Jung aiming at the same goal in his seminars. He encouraged his students to look past surface appearances to detect hidden structures and regularities. He insisted on empirical evidence to support explanations and theories. He reminded students that they are not detached observers but engaged human beings whose own psychological complexes are likely to be activated by the interpretation of other people's dreams. Jung taught the skill of critical reasoning as a means of enhancing basic self-awareness and psychological maturity.

A more controversial educational method Jung used to great effect was the interpersonal dynamics of the master-disciple relationship. If he were alive, Jung might not agree with that term, but I believe it accurately characterizes themes that run throughout the book. There was never a moment of doubt of who was in charge of the seminar, never a question of whose ideas provided the common language or who had the most knowledge and experience. Every presenter made sure to acknowledge Jung's work in framing their analyses, and no other psychological perspectives (besides Freud's) were included in the discussion. Jung spent much more of his life as a clinician than as a teacher, and his behavior in the seminars reflected the traditional authority a medical doctor has with his patients, which itself harks back to ancient systems of transmitting knowledge and wisdom from masters to disciples. Contemporary teachers may feel uncomfortable about this dimension of Jung's pedagogy, although if they looked, they might find some of those interpersonal dynamics at work in their own classrooms.

Perhaps because of Jung's commanding presence and charismatic authority, the students in his seminars come across as entirely polite and well behaved. Only once does the class discussion become contentious, and this provides an illuminating moment. It comes very late in the book, in the 1940–1941 term, when a dream is presented by a man named Walter Huber (who also presented a dream in the 1938-1939 term, 193ff.). Huber's analysis seems no different in its essentials from all the previous presentations, but Jung responds with severe dissatisfaction:

In this paper you were fascinated by the material. You have read interesting things concerning it. But this is a temptation. If you present all that, we will get completely dizzy. We will drift away and move too far away from the dream. Therefore, you have to restrict the material to the bare essentials; we have to think of the poor audience that will get completely drunk. It goes too far when you read us such seductive texts. This is dangerous. In the case of such a simple dream, we have to stay as near the material as possible.[15]

It could be the trigger for this unusually critical outburst was Huber's closing quotation of Nietzsche (Jung always had an ambivalent relationship with Nietzsche's philosophy). But other than that, Huber's effort to amplify this dream seems no more "fascinated" by the material than any of the preceding presentations. One could easily imagine the same charge being made against every one of the interpretations in the book. Perhaps there were interpersonal issues between Jung and Huber that account for Jung's sharp words. Future biographical research may help answer that. Another possibility is that Jung's response was triggered by the dream itself: a five-year old girl, raised in India by European parents, dreams of being attacked by a tiger. Some of Jung's most racially stereotyped comments in the whole book come out in his analysis of this dream, highlighting the conflicted relationship between his psychological theory and the colonialist practices of modern European culture.

Whatever the reason, this dream and Huber's interpretation of it prompted Jung to give his students very specific guidance in how to bring the amplification process to a focused conclusion. At the next meeting of the seminar, Jung began by asking, "Mr. Huber, could you please tell us in two words what the dream says." Huber responded with an answer of twenty-one-words, and Jung told him to try again: "You should not tell the dream, but describe the situation.... When you have accumulated material, you will then have to think and insert what you found as if into an equation. The result has to be that you are able to repeat the dream, but now with the interpreted expressions. You have to do that now; then I will know if you have understood the dream." Huber offered another short summary of the dream's symbolism, which Jung quickly rejected: "Now you're already talking about the dream. Talk in the dream, but in the interpreted terms."[16]

Again, we do not know why Jung singled out this presenter and this dream for such sharp scrutiny and forceful instruction. But he used the interaction as a teachable moment to offer an important lesson for anyone who wants to become skilled at the practice of amplification. Jung let his students know with unmistakable clarity that they needed to become skilled not only at expanding the symbolic potentials of the dream but also at bringing those potentials back into relation with the specific details of the dream itself. By stressing the need to talk in the dream and not about it, Jung pushed the class to adopt a language that integrated conscious and unconscious perspectives, a process that mirrors the broader themes of his psychology. Amplification must ultimately lead back to an integrating moment. Huber's presentation, with its Nietzschean flourish at the end, apparently lacked such a moment, and Jung made sure everyone in the class knew this was a problem to avoid.

Applying Jung's Methods Today

Children's Dreams illustrates a teaching process that can be applied, with the modifications mentioned, into the regular coursework of contemporary classrooms. There are at least three ways of adapting Jung's method of dream interpretation for present-day students.

1. Using one or more of the cases in the *Children's Dreams* book. This is the easiest, most straightforward approach. A teacher can select one or more of the dreams from the book and ask students, either in classroom discussion or as a written assignment, to develop their own symbolic amplifications to the dream. Their ideas can then be compared with what Jung and his students say about the same dream. Such an approach has the virtue of giving students critical leverage for reflecting on what Jung does and does not say about these dreams. The limits of the ethnopsychological method can be examined in terms of the variations in cultural references suggested by Jung versus contemporary students. At the same time, the similarities in what the students and Jung see in the dreams can foster a discussion of Jung's theory of the collective unconscious.
2. Using dream reports provided by the instructor. This has the advantage of allowing teachers to choose dreams with more background biographical material than is provided in the *Children's Dreams* book. With a broader context of knowledge about the dreamer's life, students can develop a more balanced understanding of the personal, cultural, and collective dimensions of meaning in dreams. Sources for finding interesting dreams can include religious texts, anthropological reports, clinical studies, and Internet databases like www.dreambank.net and www.sleepanddreamdatabase.org. Particularly in religious studies courses, this approach can help students make connections between Jungian psychology and various kinds of religious belief, practice, and experience.
3. Using students' own dreams. This is the most challenging approach and the most rewarding in terms of heightened student interest and engagement with the material. To set the stage, the instructor should (a) emphasize that the exercise is intended to be educational not therapeutic, (b) insist on total confidentiality about any personal information students share in the discussion, and (c) establish the principle that the dreamer is the ultimate decision maker about what to share and how far to go with the process. Some degree of hesitation will be inevitable for students who have never given any particular thought to their dreams, but in most cases, it dissipates quickly as the

students discover the method is fairly easy to practice and reveals a new perspective on their studies and their lives.

The third method might seem risky in terms of the unpredictable nature of dreams and the potential for bringing up psychologically distressing memories and feelings. However, many classes deal with emotionally sensitive topics with the explicit intention of nudging students outside their comfort zones so they can learn new ways of looking at the world. As Philip King, Bernard Welt, and I describe in more detail in *Dreaming in the Classroom*, many teachers in psychology, anthropology, religious studies, and other disciplines have successfully used simple methods of discussing students' dreams with no adverse impact.[17] On the contrary, the classes tend to be very popular because the students appreciate the opportunity to make the course material directly relevant to their personal lives. They enjoy having a chance to test the theories of Jung and other psychologists by relating them to their own dream experiences.

Over the past twenty years, I have taught methods of dream interpretation at several schools, among undergraduates and graduate students in academic, ministerial, and clinical programs. After laying out the principles of confidentiality and mutual respect just mentioned, I start by asking a volunteer to describe a "medium"-size dream, one that's not so long it becomes overwhelming but not so short as to provide insufficient material to work with. I further request that the dream stay within the PG-13 range of explicit content, out of consideration for different sensitivities in the class. The dreamer should tell the dream twice, using the present rather than past tense, so everyone in the class can better comprehend and reimagine the dream as a whole. The other students are then invited to ask questions of clarification. These questions might include asking for additional details about the setting, feelings, characters, and interactions within the dream. Questions about the personal context of the dream (e.g., "Did you see a dog like that yesterday?" "How do you feel about that person in waking life?") are bracketed out till later in the process. The focus initially is on clarifying the imagined world of the dream and developing a sense of its experiential reality, as a prelude to accurately interpreting its possible meanings.

Once everyone's questions of clarification have been asked, the dreamer sits back while the other students are invited to offer amplifications regarding the various elements of the dream. Jung's four-part schema may be applied at this point, helping everyone recognize the narrative aspects of the dream's structure. The goal is not to analyze the personal life of the dreamer but rather to develop in each student an ability to amplify and psychologically interpret rich symbolic material like dreams. To protect the dreamer from unwarranted comments and keep the focus on the amplification process, I follow the Jung-influenced methods of Jeremy Taylor and Montague Ullman in requiring students to use the preface, "If it were my dream...." Instead of saying, "Your dream means x," students are taught to express their analyses by saying, "If this were my dream, it might mean x."[18] The teacher's job at this point is to elicit as many responses from the students as possible, to reflect on all the elements in the dream, and to keep the focus on symbolic amplification, not personal associations. In a religious studies class, the teacher can help students connect their ideas about the dream with the broader themes of the course, such as beliefs about the afterlife, the conflict between good and evil, rituals of initiation, prophecy, mystical experience, gender inequalities, or health and healing, to give only a few examples. As in Jung's seminar, the skill of amplifying the archetypal themes in dreams can lead seamlessly into discussing those same themes as they appear in religious and cultural traditions through history.

During this stage, the dreamer merely observes. At some point, he or she may join the conversation to share as much personal context as feels comfortable. Inevitably, this will prompt the recognition of more connections between the dream and waking life, enabling an appreciation of how personal and collective themes are woven together in dreams. The dreamer's responses to the different amplifications should not be taken as indications of who in the class is right or wrong, but rather as a way of grounding the various possibilities of the dream in the individual's actual waking life.

Dreams always have multiple layers of meaning, so there is no obvious or fixed end point to the interpretation process. The length of the class period is usually the deciding factor. Teachers should allow some time before the end of the discussion for students to summarize their ideas about the dream and its meanings. One way to do this is ask, "If the dream were a movie or a poem, how would you title it?" This exercise takes only a few moments, and it creates a sense of closure that allows all students a chance to focus their final impression on a specific theme or insight that strikes them as particularly significant.

The dreamer will likely feel stimulated, and perhaps slightly overwhelmed, by all the ideas and perspectives shared in the discussion, so the teacher should check in with the dreamer after class to see if he or she has any follow-up questions, comments, or concerns. Often, it will take some time for the class discussion to sink in with the dreamer and the rest of the students, so at the next meeting of the class, regardless of whether any more dreams are discussed, the teacher can ask for any additional thoughts about the themes and meanings identified in the dream or about the amplification process in general.

Conclusion

If Jung's critics are right that he offers not a psychology but a religion, dream interpretation could be seen as the central sacrament of the Jungian faith. If his ideas are taken as he intended them, as an empirically based psychology, then dream interpretation appears as a primary source of evidence in Jung's scientific explanation of human mental functioning. Either way, a fair appraisal of Jung should take into account his fundamental work in trying to understand the meaningfulness of dreaming. A practical familiarity with dream interpretation enables students to make more sophisticated evaluations of Jung's psychology, particularly in relation to his influential theory of religion. The kind of amplification process modeled by Jung in his seminars on children's dreams stimulates a heightened degree of self-reflection among students, prompts greater empathetic insight into others' lives and experiences, and generates a deeper personal connection with the existential questions at the heart of the world's religious traditions.

NOTES

1. C. G. Jung, *Children's Dreams: Notes from the Seminar Given in 1936–1940*, eds. Lorenz Jung and Maria Meyer-Grass, trans. Ernst Falzeder (Princeton, NJ: Princeton University Press, 2008), 372.

2. Jung, *Children's Dreams*, 7. Emphasis in original.

3. William G. Domhoff, *The Scientific Study of Dreams: Neural Networks, Cognitive Development, and Content Analysis* (Washington, DC: American Psychological Association, 2003).

4. Jung, *Children's Dreams*, 19.

5. Jung, *Children's Dreams*, 19.

6. Jung, *Children's Dreams*, 21. Emphasis in original.

7. Kelly Bulkeley, *Dreams of Healing: Transforming Nightmares into Visions of Hope* (Mahwah, NJ: Paulist Press, 2003).

8. Jung, *Children's Dreams*, 26.

9. Jung, *Children's Dreams*, 28.

10. Jung, *Children's Dreams*, 28. Emphasis in original.

11. Jung, *Children's Dreams*, 28.

12. Jung, *Children's Dreams*, 30.

13. Jung, *Children's Dreams*, 31. Emphasis in original.

14. Jung, *Children's Dreams*, 31.

15. Jung, *Children's Dreams*, 404.

16. Jung, *Children's Dreams*, 410. Emphasis in original.

17. Philip King, Kelly Bulkeley, and Bernard Welt, *Dreaming in the Classroom* (Albany: State University of New York Press, in press).

18. Jeremy Taylor, *The Wisdom of Your Dreams* (New York: Jeremy Tarcher/Penguin, 2009); Montague Ullman and Nan Zimmerman, *Working with Dreams* (Los Angeles: Jeremy Tarcher, 1979).

REFERENCES

Bulkeley, Kelly. *Dreams of Healing: Transforming Nightmares into Visions of Hope.* Mahwah, NJ: Paulist, 2003.

Domhoff, G. William. *The Scientific Study of Dreams: Neural Networks, Cognitive Development, and Content Analysis.* Washington, DC: American Psychological Association, 2003.

Jung, C. G. *Psychology and Religion.* New Haven, CT: Yale University Press, 1938.

Jung, C. G. *Man and His Symbols.* New York: Dell, 1965.

Jung, C. G. *Children's Dreams: Notes from the Seminar Given in 1936–1940,* ed. Lorenz Jung and Maria Meyer-Grass. Trans. Ernst Falzeder. Princeton, NJ: Princeton University Press, 2008.

Jung, C. G. *The Red Book*, trans. Sonu Shamdasani. New York: W. W. Norton, 2009.
King, Philip, Kelly Bulkeley, and Bernard Welt. *Dreaming in the Classroom*. Albany: State University of New York Press, 2011.
Taylor, Jeremy. *The Wisdom of Your Dreams*. New York: Jeremy Tarcher/Penguin, 2009.
Ullman, Montague, and Nan Zimmerman. *Working with Dreams*. Los Angeles: Jeremy Tarcher, 1979.

14

Jung and Winnicott in the Classroom

Holding, Mirroring, Potential Space, and the Self

Laurel McCabe

Learning Research

Contemporary learning research finds that effective teachers begin with the knowledge base of their students and develop content knowledge based on that foundation.[1] This approach engages students in their learning, and as researchers have discovered, when students respond to the material with feeling, they demonstrate more successful learning.[2] The knowledge developed from applications relevant to the students' experience, or "conditionalized"[3] knowledge, can then be applied across contexts to new domains. Knowledge that can be readily applied to different contexts leads to "adaptive expertise,"[4] a metacognitive skill that shows in an easy use of relevant knowledge in new domains, characterized by an innate curiosity that is actively adaptive to new challenges and is questioning toward new knowledge. Such knowledge mimics "virtuoso"[5] knowledge that is "fluent,"[6] easily retrieved, and less taxing on conscious processing. Educational researchers and psychologists find that good teachers develop these types of knowledge in their students.

Additionally, pedagogy is a critically significant ingredient that influences students' development of adaptive expertise and fluent knowledge.[7] Classroom pedagogy influences how the student organizes the learning and its adaptive use in new contexts. It plays an important role in the organization, development, transfer, and adaptive expertise of the knowledge gained. In a well-designed learning environment, knowledge content and pedagogy are seamlessly interwoven.

Knowledge in Jungian Psychology: An Epistemological Orientation

Every knowledge discipline contains assumptions about core discipline-relevant beliefs, theories, and practices. These assumptions inform the methods used for collecting discipline-relevant information and for validating or invalidating information; in essence, they determine the overall content of the discipline. Jungian psychology's unique epistemological orientation colors its discipline-relevant assumptions about the source of knowledge, the methods for acquiring it, and, for teachers, the pedagogy used to develop fluent knowledge in the field.

In the years 1913 through 1917, Jung faithfully recorded a series of visions, dreams, dialogues, paintings, and dramatic expressions from his inner world.[8] His initial visions were disturbing scenes of a blood-covered Europe and of the death of a Siegfried hero. Their ongoing violent intensity strained at the solidity of his ego stability, yet he committed to acknowledging these inner expressions, to exploring them, and to rendering them in a leather-bound folio made solely for this purpose. In his autobiographical reflections, he called this series of inner experiences his "confrontation with the unconscious."[9] What he learned from this confrontation radically restructured his approach to living and became the substance of his later theoretical and clinical work.[10]

From this confrontation, Jung discovered the existence of an unconscious and autonomous collective psyche. Initially, his experience of this psyche was marked by paradox, ambiguity, and travail: as he disconnected from the "spirit of the times"[11] to explore the "spirit of the depths,"[12] he found its values frequently contradicted his customary rational viewpoint. As he explored further, he found that this collective psyche offered balancing perspectives to what he came to view as the partial and incomplete perspectives of the spirit of the times.[13] He found that this collective psyche produced inner images that likewise offered balancing perspectives to his own personal and unique individual development. He discovered, for example, that the desire-tinged figure of Salome, though initially reprehensible to his value system, embodied a psychological and necessary antidote to his overreliance on rational thinking.[14] Over time, he realized that the inner exploration of one's unknown inner figures through the techniques of active imagination, dream work, and painting afforded a means of connecting to the collective psyche and of exploring unknown psychological qualities within oneself. It thus offered a balancing and redeeming perspective on one's individual development. Exploring and relating to these unknown quantities brought one to a psychological wholeness unattainable without it.

A second primary discovery of this time was Jung's experience of the voice emerging from these inner figures: it was one of timeless authorial wisdom of a quality and degree incommensurate with, and beyond, his personal experience.[15] He inferred from the quality of these experiences that within the collective psyche there existed a timeless and wise essential quale that he termed the *self*. Through successive observations, he concluded that the self is an autonomous, objective essence of the collective psyche, possessing an entel-echy. Its entelechy subsumed psychological oppositions, conflicts, and para-doxes and held them together in a unifying wholeness. Jung concluded that establishing an inner relationship with this central psychic force was necessary to the evolution of psychological development on both an individual and a collective social level.

He drew on the language of Hindu and Buddhist philosophy to describe that the spiritual presence he observed was characteristic of this self within the collective psyche. He stated, "The self, I thought, was like the monad which I am, and which is my world."[16] Through sustained practice of his inner methods of exploration, he was able to see an image of this monad of the self through his drawings of mandalas. While serving in military duty and as a way of holding the psychological tensions he was experiencing, he undertook the practice of a daily painting of a mandala. In examining their composition, he found that the mandalas revealed an inherent organization, an ordered structure, able to con-tain psychological opposites and paradoxes. He found that the image of the mandala ultimately "represents this monad, and corresponds to the microcosmic nature of the soul"[17] and that "my mandala images were cryptograms on the state of my self, which were delivered to me each day."[18]

His singular psychological contribution is that through the use of depth psychological methods such as active imagination, dream work, and painting, one can discover and explore the inner existence of the self. The capacity to sustain a relationship with the self over time is a path of spiritual as well as of psychological development, as the guiding source is spiritual: it is one's "monad,"[19] one's spiritual center. One works through layers of personal shadow, complexes, and contrasexual elements, and at root and permeating this work is the self, one's inherent essence and also one's life-tending potential. In being attentive to the self's missives and working over time with them, one may over time incarnate, or bring into being, the subtlest aspects of this in-forming internal self. As a result of the epistemological reordering of the self as the center of the psyche, Jung profoundly reorders the elements of the Western search for religious meaning. His psychological model, summed up as the model of individuation, is, as he called it, the "new dispensation."

These essential characteristics of Jung's psychology—the existence of an autonomous, objective, collective psyche that contains unrealized elements of wholeness; the presence of a spiritual center within this psyche that displays an emergent entelechy; and the psychological methods for establishing a relation-ship with this self that creates a path of individuation—constitute a discipline-specific epistemology that colors the content, methods of inquiry, and, for the teacher, the learning pedagogy of Jungian psychology.

These ingredients inform the core episteme of the discipline. They focus on a core relationship to the self in the collective psyche as experienced through depth psychological inquiry techniques such as active imagination, dreams, and painting; the inquiry methods, as well as the content derived from them, are essential components of this discipline. A seamless pedagogy explores

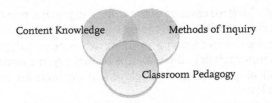

FIGURE 14.1. Content Knowledge, Methods of Inquiry, Classroom Pedagogy.

these in a holistic epistemological orientation aimed at developing fluent adaptive knowledge in the classroom learner.

Teaching Jungian Psychology

If one were to overlook the core episteme in Jung's learning, one might be tempted, in teaching Jung, to organize the field by concentrating on the core knowledge concepts that have been delivered by the methods of inquiry. Thus one might discuss the differences between personal and collective unconscious, discuss the concept of archetype, and illustrate the discussion with cross-cultural examples from mythology, religion, and art. One could do the same to bring a differentiated awareness to the notion of consciousness: discuss the concepts of persona, ego, complex, shadow. And indeed, in discussions of Jung's theories, this is often the approach followed.[20]

However, when one regards with serious attention the core episteme of the discipline—one's relational orientation to the expression of the self in the collective psyche, through the depth inquiry methods of active imagination, dreams, and so on—the choice of the core learning goals changes. A pedagogy that uses the discipline-specific techniques of inquiry has the potential to evoke in the student the core relational orientation to the self that is at the heart of the epistemology. In the language of educational research, in the process of applying the depth inquiry techniques to one's own experience, the conceptual knowledge becomes specific, conditionalized, and transferable—ripe conditions for the development of adaptive expertise and virtuosic fluency in student learning. In this discipline's core episteme, the methods of inquiry, the content knowledge, and the pedagogy are intertwined in skillful teaching in the classroom. See Figure 14.1.

Classroom Pedagogy in Teaching Jungian Psychology

The theories of D. W. Winnicott[21] provide a guide for how to shape an engaged classroom pedagogy that includes depth psychological methods of inquiry, as well as discipline-specific content knowledge. This pedagogy includes the development of a holding or facilitating environment in the classroom, leading to the experience of potential space (also called transitional space) and the experience of play and creativity. When these aspects of pedagogy are present in the classroom, the methods of inquiry specific to the content of Jungian psychology may be experienced. Specifically, the experience of potential space mirrors the creative dialectic alive in the experience of the self found within the methods of depth psychological inquiry, such as dream work, active imagination, and art.

Winnicott was a keen observer of mother-infant interactions, and from his observations, he articulated a theory of psychological development characterized by what he called the true self:[22] relaxed being, spontaneity, the capacity to play[23] and to be alone,[24] and creativity.[25] These states are dependent upon early engagement with what he calls the facilitating environment. Through consistent, reliable maternal means of holding, containing, and mirroring, a relaxed, spontaneous being is developed. These lead into the experience and use of transitional objects, transitional phenomena, and transitional spaces and into the sphere of play and creativity. These concepts are discussed later and applied to the shaping of classroom pedagogy.

The Holding Environment and the Classroom

Winnicott states that the good-enough mother provides a holding, or facilitating, environment for the infant[26] and that in this provision allows for the development of the infant's true self. In psychological holding, the mother provides the psychological container for the infant's experiences and psychologically, physically, and emotionally guides and channels the experiences of the infant so that they are tolerable. At its broadest, holding consists of responding to verbal and nonverbal expressions of meaning.[27] It includes tolerating affects, particularly those that are disturbing or distressing for the infant; soothing into well-being the infant's distressing or negative affects; protecting against environmental impingements that threaten the well-being of the infant; and ultimately providing an ego container for the child who does not yet have one. The holding environment offers such ego support to the infant and instills a process of ego relating with him. Over time, as the infant differentiates from the mother and comes to presence within himself or herself, the child takes up these functions of the holding environment and provides these functions to himself or herself. These functions characterize what Winnicott calls a good-enough mother and are characteristics of a holding environment.

These notions of environmental provision and of the holding and facilitating environment have been applied to classrooms,[28] to organizations,[29] and to mental health programs that focus on psychological development,[30] in addition to psychoanalysis and psychotherapy.[31] In the classroom, the teacher may create a holding environment for the student. A holding environment creates a climate of trust in the students in the face of new and potentially destabilizing emotions and insights that are generated in studying Jungian psychology. Just as the parent does in early life, the teacher may provide ego support to the student who experiences confusing or distressing emotions; helps the student tolerate these affects, particularly those that are disturbing or distressing; and helps protect the student against environmental impingements in the form of judging comments. The good-enough teacher is one who successfully navigates these functions, and such navigation is the pedagogical first step in developing potential space in the classroom.

The holding environment is shaped by the structuring of the class, by aspects of the teacher's own being, by guidance in self-holding, by empathic attunement, by mirroring and reflecting, and finally by integration of theory in understanding experience. These are discussed in detail next.

In structuring the classroom experience, the teacher sets rules for meeting times, attendance, participation, and class work expected in projects, exercises, papers, and presentations. These fundamental rules are fundamental aspects of the container of the class, and they serve to hold the psychological work of the student therein.

Late arrivals, early departures, and missed classes weaken the classroom container, as they insert elements of uncertainty and unreliability into the classroom experience. It's very helpful for the teacher to speak matter-of-factly to the students about the presence of a classroom container that holds their intellectual and psychological work in the class and to note that irregular attendance disturbs the reliability of the container. Such a straightforward discussion may have the effect of improving class attendance and thus strengthening this form of the container.

Classroom physical attributes also affect the container. A closed door prevents hallway distractions and diminishes external noise; an open door permits the wandering of students' attention and energy outside the room.

Seating patterns are also aspects of the holding container. A central chair or position in the classroom that affords the teacher a clear sight line to all students, as well as access to a blackboard or screen, is ideal for situating the teacher to respond to all students.

The classroom holding container and the holding environment are fundamentally shaped by aspects of the teacher's own being. This refers to the inner qualities of the teacher, by how open the teacher is to inner experience, as well as how well the teacher knows his or her own depths. The teacher conveys, nonverbally and fundamentally, a respect and honoring of inner experience. Students sense this respect nonverbally, and at a very primary level, it tends to set off an inner opening and trusting process in many students. This is particularly true when the teacher participates in inquiry methods such as active imagination, dream work, or art in the classroom with the students and then uses these experiences to guide discussion. When the teacher is able to model openness to difficult emotions, the students see that the teacher is able to hold the vicissitudes of life—the light and dark, the oppositions, the vagaries, the emotions—to survive, and to ultimately make meaning of it. This creates a confidence in the students regarding their own emotions. A resonant interpersonal field in the classroom develops, in which students' difficult experiences can be expressed, held, witnessed, reflected, and understood.

When the teacher opens himself or herself up to the full experiences of the student, the teacher may encounter all measures of the dark or shadowy aspects of life presented by the students. While psychotherapists expect this in their work, often a teacher's attitude is that this does not belong in a classroom devoted to learning. Yet, if distressing emotions can be acknowledged in the classroom, the potential for transforming them emerges. Students may begin to see experiences such as self-injury, eating disorders, sexual trauma, and sexual, physical, and emotional abuse in new ways.

The teacher's voice quality also functions on a very primitive level to convey trust and communicate soothing to students. Winnicott's holding consists of immediate skin-to-skin contact that ameliorates environmental intrusions; the teacher's voice and the consistency of response can hold a similar function in the classroom. Students remember a calm and soothing voice and find that they have internalized it in the midst of difficult emotional experiences outside class.

As new, difficult, or delicate emotions emerge for the student, a teacher may guide the student in holding them within. A new experience is vulnerable and tender, like an infant, and holding allows the student to begin to let it live and breathe within, so it can be opened to, and the student can experience the self in a new way. The daily world is sometimes intrusive, and strategic selective strengthening is sometimes needed to protect what is new and tender. Self-holding might involve slow, steady breathing exercises in order to calm or a soothing practice, such as enjoying a quiet walk or making a cup of tea in the evening as the light grows dim. The teacher can communicate that difficult emotional experiences, light as well as dark emotions, are part of the necessary emotional palate of life. Self-holding in the face of difficulties allows the student to give part of one's self a hand, with the other. This contributes to the strengthening of the ego that occurs over time within the environmental provisions of the holding environment.

Winnicott states that the true self develops in the mother's witnessing of the emotional gesture of the infant and in the mother's empathic ability to respond in kind to it, mirroring or reflecting it. In the classroom, the facilitating teacher practices attunement to the student in the form of inner listening and empathic identification. This allows the teacher to discern the emotional states of the students and to guide classroom activity and discussion in acknowledgment of these states. Good teachers do this intuitively by sensing areas of interest, incomprehension, or difficulty.

When the mother does not notice the emotional gesture of the infant and rather replaces the infant's gesture with her own, compliance develops in the infant in the shape of a false self. That is, the infant learns to adapt to the mother, which takes him or her away from core experience and so develops away from one's natural spontaneity and expression. In the classroom, this condition is akin to the teacher's ignoring the emotional states of the students and replacing attunement with teacher-chosen tasks and projects. This lack of attunement constitutes a teacher's lack of holding and leads students away from their trust of their inner experience in the classroom.

Mirroring, or reflecting, can be a positive pedagogical factor in several ways. In the first and most basic way, the teacher simply articulates in the classroom the experience that the student is having. This can be reflecting very basic states: appreciation, confusion, sadness, pleasure, defensiveness, hurt, anger. We can think of this as the teacher responding with an empathic, reflective gesture, verbal or nonverbal, to the gesture sensed within the student. On a primitive level, this provides a nonverbal message to the student that he or she is seen, witnessed, honored, validated.[32] When the teacher reflects back some essential part of a student's emotional experience, it can catalyze melting on the part of the student. That is, he or she goes more deeply into the emotion of the event, often in a way that he or she has not experienced before, and experiences a softness and a vulnerability in the classroom. The capacity for this type of experience on the part of the student is reflective of the student's trust in the teacher's capacity to hold the experience.

Reflecting also occurs in the teacher's capacity to sense and reflect back what is not yet thought, but known, to the student, Bollas's unthought known.[33] Here again, empathic attunement comes into play, as well as the teacher's discernment in knowing the student. Often through intuitive empathy, the teacher will know whom to call on, what student might be ready to speak, even without volunteering; what words to say, how in language to hold or contain the student's experience—not through anything the student has spoken verbally, but through what the teacher feels of the student's state. This may allow the student to feel seen and witnessed in a surprising way and calls up Winnicott's observation that "it is a joy to be hidden but disaster not to be found."[34] When the student gives a resounding nonverbal "yes!" to the teacher's query, observations, or reflections, increased excitement, humming, or musing may be apparent in the student—a moment in which the student loosens up a bit and expresses spontaneously.

Teachers who created a facilitating environment in a preschool classroom by observing the child, consciously receiving the meanings of communications from the child and adapting to that child, reported that the child opened up in the classroom and became more visible to the teachers.[35] These teachers reported that such teaching requires "presence and attention"[36] and a "gradual revisioning of the notion of the living child."[37] Another teacher spoke of her sense of the teacher's task to "do this work of sustaining an appetite for life"[38] and that stories and the "demand for the personal"[39] are the means to sustain this appetite. Another teacher who used mirroring techniques in a university design studio pointed out that this type of teaching was challenging and not always easy, as it asked of the teacher to be emotionally present in a way that requires commitment.[40]

Winnicott says that when the infant's gesture is met not with empathic attunement but rather by the mother's own, in a substitution of her own gesture for that of the infant, the false self, the compliant self, develops. Students in the classroom who are eager to conform to the teacher's expectations may be described as false self-compliant.

This transformative model of education works only insofar as clear and rigorous intellectual and theoretical content is tied to experience-based, embodied learning. The teacher continuously calls the student back to the theoretical ore of the discussion, to the gold that must be mined from the heavy weight of experience, to the wisdom that can be pressed from painful and sometimes bitter experience. Within the class, the teacher must shuttle, weave, back and forth between experience and theory. This tying back to theory is part of the ego support process of the holding environment, of the provisioning teacher. It provides yet another boundary or container within which emotional material can be processed. Students have reported that hearing theory applied to their experience gives them a safe, boundaried feeling, resulting in a feeling of being contained. If it is not done, students may feel that they've sunk into interminable personal process or are imprisoned in other people's psyches or emotions against their wishes. The classroom may feel like a therapy group, not an educational class.

Adding theory to experience and integrating intellect with emotion usually have an organizing and soothing effect on the student. Theory itself can function as a psychoeducational interpretation, as it connects emotional experience with relevant objective information; such a linkage has often been associated with sustained psychological growth.[41] Interpretations serve to give the student a context for understanding private emotional experience; they normalize it, validate it, and provide a regulating function in the classroom. When material is integrated through both intellectual study and experiential encounter, the teacher's capacity for offering a holding environment is significant. For the initially mistrusting student, trust in the honoring of experience may be won after the teacher repeatedly is able to hold, reflect, and integrate the inner experience of the student.

As the teacher demonstrates effective holding through these strategies—classroom holding, the teacher's own being, guidance in self-holding, empathic attunement, mirroring, integrating theory with emotional experience—students find that they have an opportunity to experience themselves anew: sometimes simply vulnerably, in letting in a new emotion or psychological experience. The teacher should take care in not using theory as an impingement, as something that jars the student out of experience and into defensiveness. The teacher must stay empathically attuned to the students' feeling states, as well as to his or her own, to navigate these classroom interactions.

Potential Space in the Classroom

With consistent and reliable holding, the classroom becomes a privileged place to interact with students in their openness and not knowing. Within this openness and not knowing, the teacher continues to provide holding, provisioning, and ego support; this stability strengthens students and enables them to continue to experience themselves and, in Winnicott's terms, to play, alone, with the teacher.

If teachers are open to their experience in the ground of their being, as they stand before the class, then teaching becomes a process of making form from the formless that rises within the interactional field. Teaching becomes a process of creating, in class, of giving form, through language, to what has not yet formed. Teachers can stand in front of the class and create. Teachers arrive with an array of knowledge of theory, of discipline-specific content; then, they access it and deliver it through their own ground of being in relation to that of the students. Phenomenologically, this has a unique feel to it. It is embodied knowing; it is also embodying knowing. The teacher thinks, aloud, with the students; the teacher plays, alone, with them.

This creates an interactive field that elicits a similar response from them. Students may be filled with a sense, a feeling, dimly perceived, and then may open to it within this potential space and try to give it form in language. The teacher listens, hears, and responds, often with a newly forming thought. Students answer back. A space is created in the classroom where all participate in the newness. The class tries out new ideas; the class remains open; the class thinks together. The creativity occurs in the forming of thought from a shared experience of the ground of being. The class uses language as a form for something not yet formed within them.

In this potential space, the teacher must look out for students who want to reify concepts, who are overly concrete and literal in their thinking. The impulse to come up with the right answer or the defining statement that ends questions or questioning is not adaptive here. In Winnicott's terms, this is symptomatic of false-self development, and this viewpoint may be what is commonplace in academic institutions. The teacher may let students know that the class is layering experiences and observations, that they don't have to be right, and that they are free to try things out. In the end, this process affords a richness of understanding that is more inclusive than any one comment or insight.

The potential space is an interactive field. Both teacher and student tap into inner life and give it form through language. At its best, everyone in the classroom participates in the creative play. The experience can be of actually having something, sensing something, in the room, which we all are giving form to, each in our idiosyncratic ways. It's a movement that feels as if it's initiated by the individuals, as well as by the formless ground of being itself. We work it, as much as it works us. Ian MacRury reflects on the use of potential space in the university setting, and he observes that when it is present, students and teacher have an experience of thinking as "inter- and intra-personally dialogic,"[42] that there is an oscillation in the classroom that is alternately active and receptive, crossing between students and teacher in a living web of discourse.

Thomas Ogden calls the experience of the potential space the "silently active containing space in which psychological and bodily experience occur."[43] Fogel views the experience of transitional or potential phenomena as the core or essence of Winnicott's theorizing—that transitional phenomena are at the core of all of the arts, religion, science, and culture.[44] One teacher of piano who used Winnicott's notions of holding and of play observed that "the silence of the beginning"[45] was experienced in these quiet moments of learning. This type of playing—the creativity of potential space—and the successive languaging of experience that results layer student understanding and afford a depth, resonance, and complexity of learning that is life-affirming and affords fluent virtuosic knowledge of the discipline.

When potential space is disrupted—when environmental holding has been lacking, when empathic attunement and mirroring have been lacking—then there is a foreclosed sense of reality: one is either too literal or too much in fantasy.[46] Jung and others[47] would say that the symbolic attitude is lacking, replaced by a too-literal reductiveness or an ego-weakened proclivity to fantasy.

When present, the potential space is an interactive, dialogic concept that is found in the space between opposites and participates in both of them; in this sense, it is also always a third thing. It is found in the space between the experience of oneself internally and the experience of an object outside oneself in the world. As Winnicott says, it is both me and not-me.[48] It is found in the space between the symbol and what is symbolized, in the space between the symbol, what is symbolized, and the subject who interprets and feels.[49] It is spun from that imaginative web of consciousness and awareness, that power to be aware that one is aware. And it is colored by desire, emotion, qualities of experience. It is me and not-me; something plays within me, while I play within something. This is potential space, and play and creativity as well.

In sand play therapy, for example, an energy takes over the person doing the play, who participates in it and at the same time selectively directs it: it directs the person, who directs it. Creative artists report the same thing: it wanted to take this shape; it needed to be this way. Does unformed ground of being have its own wish, its own intention? Do we, when we work creatively, encounter this being and cocreate with it?

Winnicott believed that "it is only in being creative that the individual discovers the self."[50] An attuned holding environment, as previously described, allows the development of the true self to emerge, which is spontaneous, relaxed in its being, and openly attuned to the environment. And thence transitional space arises—me and not-me—and thence play, and thence creativity. Winnicott noted the importance of being "able to exist for a time without being either a reactor to an external impingement or an active person with a direction of interest or movement,"[51] and thus do creativity and spontaneity within the potential space emerge.

Potential Space, Jung's Methods of Inquiry, the Self, and the Classroom

Jung's primary methods of inquiry—dreams, active imagination, and art—are vehicles whereby one can investigate one's inner experience and, over time, encounter the self. As stated earlier in this chapter, the essential characteristics of Jung's psychology are the existence of an autonomous, objective, collective psyche that contains unrealized elements of wholeness; the presence of a spiritual center within this psyche that displays an emergent entelechy; and the psychological methods for establishing a relationship with this self that create a unique path of individuation. These essential elements constitute a discipline-specific epistemology that colors the content, methods of inquiry, and, for the teacher, the learning pedagogy of Jungian psychology.

These ingredients inform a core relationship to the self in the collective psyche as experienced through depth-psychological inquiry techniques such as active imagination, dreams, and painting; the inquiry methods, as well as the content derived from them, are essential components of the discipline.

These core ingredients take place in the realm of potential space. When active imagination is engaged, one holds within one the space in and through which one interacts with the unknown parts of oneself. This interaction might be done silently, with eyes closed; it might be done with paintbrush in hand, painting; it might be done at the piano, playing; it might be done in the sand, in sand play. The significant attributes are the presence of an internal space; the presence of a not-me, to use a Winnicottian term; and the presence of a conscious participation with it.

Ogden points out that potential space occurs in the space between the symbol, the symbolized, and one's subjectivity. If I work with a dream image of a rotating stylus, for example, I must take the vantage point of myself but also of the stylus and also that of the something-else, of the energy that is carried and liberated by the image of the rotating stylus. I must position myself among all of them and allow the energy to make its impact on me, and I on it. I explore; I am open; I experience. Jung might observe that I am open to the psychic, archetypal energy carried by the image, and that in keeping the vantage point of my ego during the active imagination, I work consciously with the unknown parts of myself and shape them as they shape me. In his own active imagination, Jung learned about the existence of an objective and autonomous psyche, something that directed and regulated the appearance, nature, and quality of the images he encountered. Jung termed this the *self*. His revolutionary gnosis was that the self was the true center of the psyche, the true inner man, the true anthropos. His revaluation of his existence was in laying claim to listening to this self—in all its forms, in all its manifestations—to confronting and interacting with it, in order to achieve his unique wholeness and to live truly on his pathway of individuation.

Winnicott's experience of potential space offers up a mode of understanding these experiences of the self. A piano teacher observed that when she followed her intuition in the choice of music to give to a student, and taught with love and openness, then the quiet stillness emerged and "they have shared the 'third thing'—the archetypal dimension of the music."[52] The potential space appears able to transmit the self's energy; it is here that Jung and Winnicott meet. Jung's "third thing" is the transcendent function, so named because it is a new energy, a "living birth"[53] that transcends the tension of the two dual poles of opposites it emerges from.[54]

When a potential space is created in the classroom, then the students can experience play, creativity, and imagination. These qualities are the hallmark of what Jung calls the self. In thinking about Winnicott's ideas as they might live in the classroom and examining how holding, mirroring, and potential space affect the students and teacher in the classroom, Jung's theories are brought ever nearer; indeed, a space arises within that contains them all. It is neither within me, nor without me, but participates in both and, like the self, is enlivening and new.

NOTES

1. John D. Bransford, Ann L. Brown, and Rodney R. Coking, eds., *How People Learn: Brain, Mind, Experience, and School*. Committee on Developments in the Science of Learning. Commission on Behavioral and Social Sciences and Education (Washington, DC: National Academy Press, 1999).

2. Ellen J. Langer, *The Power of Mindful Learning* (Reading, MA: Addison-Wesley Publishing, 1997).

3. Bransford, Brown, and Coking, *How People Learn*, xx.

4. Ibid.

5. Ibid.,

6. R.M. Schiffrin and W. Schneider, "Controlled and Automatic Human Information Processing: II. Perceptual Learning, Automatic Attending, and a General Theory," in *Psychological Review* 84 (1977): 127-190.

7. Bransford, Brown, and Coking, *How People Learn*, xx

8. C. G. Jung, *Memories, Dreams, Reflections* (New York: Vintage, 1989); C. G. Jung, *Jung's Red Book*, ed. Shonu Shamdasani (New York: W. W. Norton, 2009).

9. Jung, *Memories*.

10. Jung, *Jung's Red Book*.

11. Ibid., spirit times.

12. Ibid., spirit depths.

13. Ibid., spirit times.

14. Jung, *Jung's Red Book*.

15. Ibid.

16. Ibid.

17. Ibid., 206.

18. Ibid.

19. Ibid.

20. See, for example, June Singer, *Living with Paradox: An Introduction to Jungian Psychology* (Belmont, CA: Brooks/Cole, 1995).

21. D. W. Winnicott, *Collected Papers* (New York: Basic Books, 1958); D. W. Winnicott, *The Maturational Processes and the Facilitating Environment: Studies in the Theory of Emotional Development* (Madison, WI: International Universities Press, 1965); D. W. Winnicott, *Playing and Reality* (London: Tavistock/Routledge, 1971).

22. Winnicott, "Ego Distortion in Terms of True and False Self," in *The Maturational Processes*, 140–52.

23. Winnicott, *Playing and Reality*.

24. Winnicott, "The Capacity to Be Alone," in *The Maturational Processes*, 34.

25. Winnicott, *Playing and Reality*.

26. Winnicott, "The Theory of the Parent-Infant Relationship," in *The Maturational Processes*, 37–55.

27. Simon Grolnick, "How to Do Winnicottian Therapy," in *In One's Bones: The Clinical Genius of Winnicott*, ed. D. Goldman (Northvale, NJ: Jason Aronson, 1993), 194.

28. K. Byddeson-Larson, "Giving Voice to the Swedish Pre-School Child: Inclusion through Educational Process Reflection," *Child Care in Practice* 11 (2005): 161–77; J. MacQuarrie, "Against Interpretation," *Journal of Thought* (Summer 2006): 39–50; Elaine Levy and Kathleen Campbell, "D. W. Winnicott in the Literature Classroom," *Teaching English in the Two-Year College* 27 (2000): 320–28; Patricia Skar, "The Goal as Process: Music and the Search for the Self," *Journal of Analytical Psychology* 47 (2002): 629–638; Ian MacRury, "Institutional Creativity and Pathologies of Potential Space: The Modern University," *Psychodynamic Practice* 13 (2007): 119–40; Jeffrey K. Ochsner, "Behind the Mask: A Psychoanalytic Perspective on Interaction in the Design Studio," *Journal of Architectural Education* 53 (2000): 194–206; Alice Pitt, "Hide and Seek: The Play of the Personal in Education," *Changing English* 7 (2000): 65–74.

29. W. van Buskirk and D. McGrath, "Organizational Cultures as Holding Environments: A Psychodynamic Look at Organizational Symbolism," *Human Relations* 52 (1999): 805–32.

30. A. R. Eisenstein-Naveh, "The Center for Families at Risk: A Facilitating Environment." *Family Journal: Counseling and Therapy for Couples and Families* 11 (2003): 191–201.

31. Thomas Ogden, *Matrix of the Mind* (Northvale, NJ: Jason Aronson, 1986); James Grotstein, "Winnicott's Importance in Psychoanalysis," in *The Facilitating Environment: Clinical Applications of Winnicott's Theory*, ed., M. G. Fromm and B. L. Smith (Madison, WI: International Universities Press, 1989), 130–55.

32. Winnicott, "Primitive Emotional Development," in *Collected Papers*, 145–56.

33. Christopher Bollas, *The Shadow of the Object: Psychoanalysis of the Unthought Known* (London: Free Association, 1987).

34. Winnicott, "Communicating and Not Communicating Leading to a Study of Certain Opposites," in *The Maturational Processes*, 83–92.

35. Byddeson-Larsson, "Giving Voice," 161–77.

36. Ibid., 174.

37. Ibid., 174.

38. Alice Pitt, "Hide and Seek: The Play of the Personal in Education," *Changing English* 7 (2000): 66.

39. Pitt, "Hide and Seek," 66.

40. Ochsner, "Behind the Mask," 194–206.

41. Irving Yalom, *Methods and Techniques in Group Psychotherapy* (New York: Basic Books, 2005).

42. MacRury, "Institutional Creativity," 126.

43. Ogden, *Matrix of the Mind*, 180n.

44. G. I. Fogel, "Winnicott's Anti-Theory," *Psychoanalytic Study of the Child* 47 (1992): 205–22.

45. Patricia Skar, "The Goal as Process," 635.

46. Ogden, "On Potential Space," in *In One's Bones*, 229.

47. See Edward Whitmont, *The Symbolic Quest* (Princeton, NJ: Princeton University Press, 1969).

48. Winnicott, "Transitional Objects and Transitional Phenomena," in *Collected Papers*, 229–42.

49. Ogden, *Matrix of the Mind*; MacRury, "Institutional Creativity."
50. Winnicott, "Playing: Creative Activity and the Search for the Self," in *Playing and Reality*, 54.
51. Winnicott, "The Capacity to Be Alone," 34.
52. Skar, "The Goal as Process," 635.
53. C. G. Jung, "The Psychology of the Child Archetype," in *Collected Works of C. G. Jung*, 2nd ed., ed. H. Read, M. Fordham, and G. Adler, trans. R. F. C. Hull (Princeton, NJ: Princeton University Press, 1959), 9i:151–81.
54. C. G. Jung, "The Transcendent Function," in *Collected Works*.

REFERENCES

Bollas, Christopher. *The Shadow of the Object: Psychoanalysis of the Unthought Known*. London: Free Association, 1987.
Bransford, John D., Ann L. Brown, and Rodney R. Coking. *How People Learn: Brain, Mind, Experience, and School*. Committee on Developments in the Science of Learning. Commission on Behavioral and Social Sciences and Education. Washington, DC: National Academy Press, 1999.
Byddeson-Larsson, K. "Giving Voice to the Swedish Pre-School Child: Inclusion through Educational Process Reflection." *Child Care in Practice* 11 (2005): 161–177.
Eisenstein-Naveh, A. R. "The Center for Families at Risk: A Facilitating Environment." *Family Journal: Counseling and Therapy for Couples and Families* 11 (2003): 191–201.
Fogel, G. I. "Winnicott's Antitheory." *Psychoanalytic Study of the Child* 47 (1992): 205–222.
Grolnick, Simon. "How to Do Winnicottian Therapy." In *In One's Bones: The Clinical Genius of Winnicott*, ed. D. Goldman, 185–212. Northvale, NJ: Jason Aronson, 1993.
Grotstein, James. "Winnicott's Importance in Psychoanalysis." In *The Facilitating Environment: Clinical Applications of Winnicott's Theory*, ed. M. G. Fromm and B. L. Smith, 130–155. Madison, WI: International Universities Press, 1989.
Jung, C. G. "The Transcendent Function." In *Collected Works of C. G. Jung*, Vol. 8, ed. H. Read, M. Fordham, and G. Adler. Princeton, NJ: Princeton University Press, 1916.
Jung, C. G. "The Psychology of the Child Archetype." In *Collected Works of C. G. Jung*, 2nd ed., ed. H. Read, M. Fordham, and G. Adler, trans. R. F. C. Hull. Princeton, NJ: Princeton University Press, 1959, 9i: 151–181.
Jung, C. G. *Memories, Dreams, Reflections*. New York: Vintage, 1965.
Jung, C. G. *Jung's Red Book*, ed. Sonu Shamdasani. New York: W. W. Norton, 2009.
Langer, Ellen J. *The Power of Mindful Learning*. Reading, MA: Addison-Wesley, 1997.
Levy, Elaine, and Kathleen Campbell. "D. W. Winnicott in the Literature Classroom." *Teaching English in the Two-Year College* 27 (2000): 320–328.
MacQuarrie, J. "Against Interpretation." *Journal of Thought* (Summer 2006): 39–50.
MacRury, Ian. "Institutional Creativity and Pathologies of Potential Space: The Modern University." *Psychodynamic Practice* 13 (2007): 119–140.
Ochsner, Jeffrey K. "Behind the Mask: A Psychoanalytic Perspective on Interaction in the Design Studio." *Journal of Architectural Education* 53 (2000): 194–206.
Ogden, Thomas H. *Matrix of the Mind*. London: Karnac, 1986.
Ogden, Thomas H. "Playing, Dreaming and Interpreting Experience: Comments on Potential Space." In *The Facilitating Environment: Clinical Applications of*

Winnicott's Theory, ed. M. G. Fromm and B. L. Smith, 255–278. Madison, WI: International Universities Press, 1989.

Ogden, Thomas. "On Potential Space." In *In One's Bones: The Clinical Genius of Winnicott*, ed. D. Goldman, 223–240. Northvale, NJ: Jason Aronson, 1993.

Pitt, Alice. "Hide and Seek: The Play of the Personal in Education." *Changing English* 7 (2000): 65–74.

Skar, Patricia. "The Goal as Process: Music and the Search for the Self." *Journal of Analytical Psychology* 47 (2002): 629–638.

Van Buskirk, W. and McGrath, D. "Organizational Cultures as Holding Environments: A Psychodynamic Look at Organizational Symbolism." *Human Relations* 52 (1999): 805–832.

Whitmont, Edward. *The Symbolic Quest*. Princeton, NJ: Princeton University Press, 1969.

Winnicott, D. W. "Transitional Objects and Transitional Phenomena." In *Collected Papers*, 229–242. New York: Basic Books, 1958.

Winnicott, D. W. "The Capacity to Be Alone." In *The Maturational Processes and the Facilitating Environment: Studies in the Theory of Emotional Development*, 29–36. Madison, WI: International Universities Press, 1965.

Winnicott, D. W. "The Theory of the Parent-Infant Relationship." In *The Maturational Processes and the Facilitating Environment: Studies in the Theory of Emotional Development*, 37–55. Madison, WI: International Universities Press, 1965.

Winnicott, D. W. "Ego Integration in Child Development." In *The Maturational Processes and the Facilitating Environment: Studies in the Theory of Emotional Development*, 56–63. Madison, WI: International Universities Press, 1965.

Winnicott, D. W. "Communicating and Not Communicating Leading to a Study of Certain Opposites." In *The Maturational Processes and the Facilitating Environment: Studies in the Theory of Emotional Development*, 64-82. Madison, WI: International Universities Press, 1965.

Winnicott, D. W. "From Dependence towards Independence in the Development of the Individual." In *The Maturational Processes and the Facilitating Environment: Studies in the Theory of Emotional Development*, 83–92. Madison, WI: International Universities Press, 1965.

Winnicott, D. W. "Ego Distortion in Terms of True and False Self." In *The Maturational Processes and the Facilitating Environment: Studies in the Theory of Emotional Development*, 140–152. Madison, WI: International Universities Press, 1965.

Winnicott, D. W. "String: A Technique of Communication." In *The Maturational Processes and the Facilitating Environment: Studies in the Theory of Emotional Development*, 153–157. Madison, WI: International Universities Press, 1965.

Winnicott, D. W. "Playing: A Theoretical Statement." In *Playing and Reality*, 38–52. London: Tavistock/Routledge, 1971.

Winnicott, D. W. "Playing: Creative Activity and the Search for the Self." In *Playing and Reality*, 53–64. London: Tavistock/Routledge, 1971.

Winnicott, D. W. "Creativity and Its Origins." In *Playing and Reality*, 65–85. London: Tavistock/Routledge, 1971.

Yalom, Irving. *Methods and Techniques in Group Psychotherapy*. New York: Basic Books, 2005.

15

Jung and the Numinous Classroom

Bonnelle Strickling

Introduction

I have been a teacher, lecturer, and workshop leader for more than thirty years. I have also been in private psychotherapy practice for over thirty years. My relationship to Jung and Jungian theory is a very long one and, inevitably, has changed over time. This is reflected in my teaching of Jung. When I wrote *Dreaming about the Divine*,[1] I thought it was worthwhile to begin with a section I called "Point of View," because everyone has one. This has been particularly important to me to as a result of my early experience as a feminist in the 1960s and 1970s. In those days, it seemed politically, theoretically, and personally important to set out one's point of view. While it's not necessarily true that everyone has overweening prejudices, it is true that everyone has a perspective. When I look back over my years as a Jungian, there is no question that my relationship with Jung has evolved. I think particularly of a story that was told to me by a friend who was at the time training as a Jungian analyst. Her own analyst said to her, "To train as an analyst, you must be in love with Jung." My friend told me this story because at the time she was not in love with Jung and was worried about this failure of eros. However, for a time, I was in love with Jung, and of course it affected my teaching of Jung. For some of us, the discovery of Jung at a certain point in life is a kind of enchantment, a sense of recognition of a theory as deeply true, a relief at finding what seems at the time to be a spiritual path that does not seem to be rigid with doctrine. As well, Jung himself plays a role, depending on the nature of our inner objects, as good father, wise man, for some people even a manifestation of the divine.

This, too, plays a role in the nature of our teaching. As the years went by, I ceased to be in love with Jung and became far more critical and reflective, but the fact of my having had that intellectual, emotional, and spiritual love affair has, I think, made me a better teacher because I understand the complexity of the experience of Jung that many people have. I know that the teaching of Jung is not a straightforward activity because learning about Jung is not a straightforward activity. I believe that teaching certain kinds of material elicits what I would call metaphysical or numinous experiences, which adds another level of complexity to teaching Jung. I discovered this originally when teaching students about philosophers who talk about the transcendent: Plato, Spinoza, and Hegel come immediately to mind. I have experienced strong feelings of numinosity when explaining their theories, which seems to come from being close to divine or archetypal material.

Because my professional life has been interdisciplinary, I have taught Jungian theory in several settings and from several points of view. One of the aims of this chapter is to explain the challenges of teaching Jung in these settings and from these points of view. Another aim of the chapter is analyzing the spiritual and emotional aspects of teaching Jung that are different from the experience of my other major professional area of teaching, philosophy. Though, as the philosopher Karl Jaspers pointed out, philosophy is always at its center personal in that it begins from an individual point of view and personal engagement, nevertheless, it has been my experience that the ways in which many people experience and respond to Jung can be different from the ways in which they respond to other intellectual material to which they are being introduced for the first time. There are several reasons for this. Some have to do with the nature of Jung's ideas, and some have to do with the times in which we live, especially our contemporary spiritual climate. I shall expand on this later, but briefly, I would characterize this by saying that some people seem to discover Jung and themselves simultaneously. This is emphasized by the details of Jung's life. People whose exploration of Jung after first hearing about him initially continues with his autobiography, *Memories, Dreams Reflections*,[2] find this response deepened by Jung's own account of how his theoretical and professional life was at least partly a result of his own personal self-discovery. (The fact that *Memories, Dreams, Reflections* is a highly edited version of Jung's actual life is not relevant here.) The history of both psychoanalysis and depth psychology is unique in this way: its pioneers could not have done what they did without exploring their own depths, whatever their limitations turned out to be. Jung has a particularly profound effect on people who experience themselves as being unusual, introverted outsiders on a spiritual quest and have felt frustrated, bored, and undernourished by the spiritual formation of their childhoods. Thus Jung offers a complex worldview to his students. While insisting he was a scientist and engaged in the phenomenology of the interior life, he was also deeply involved with mythology and the spiritual life, offering a psychologized version of the spiritual path and claiming that spiritual life is a natural and indeed essential aspect of human life and that psychological problems are ultimately religious problems in that they are problems of meaning.

For many of us in the chilly materialist modern world, this is indeed good news. Thus teaching Jung can make one feel like a herald of that good news, creating an unusual psychic field in the classroom and workshop. In addition, Jung's theories are full of the sort of material that elicits responses typical of being close to the numinous or divine. Not everyone is intensely sensitive to this, but many people are, and this response is particularly strong to Jungian theory because he not only discusses the numinous but also talks about the inner work that can bring us closer to it. He discusses spirituality in a psychological way, so that the life of the spirit and self-knowledge are merged. It is no longer seen as selfish to attend to one's own psychic needs; indeed, it becomes essential. To become oneself becomes one's spiritual path. All of this has a powerful psychic effect on people, especially people with a great many unmet spiritual and emotional needs, and, putting it together with the numinous power of the theory, a great deal of psychic energy is generated.

There is also a complexity brought to the teaching of Jung as a result of Jung's personal life. Because of the insights of feminism and a more general sense of respect for boundaries and moral responsibility in the helping professions, I can truly say that very rarely do I lecture or give any sort of course on Jung without questions arising about Jung's behavior with his analysands and patients, a great many of whom were women. It is simply not possible to avoid such questions; one must have a standpoint. I have taught philosophical ethics for many years, and this is an unavoidable issue. In addition, because of the spiritual and emotional aspects of teaching Jung, there is a moral and spiritual responsibility that comes with teaching material that has such a profound effect on students. This chapter offers one teacher's career-long effort to meet that challenge.

Multiple Perspectives

I have been blessed (or at least it seems mostly to be a blessing) with an interdisciplinary professional life. I have spent thirty-two years teaching philosophy and, during the last ten years, have also been the philosophical part of an interdisciplinary classical studies program. I teach a course in the philosophy of religion that involves Jungian (and Freudian) theory. I am a Jungian psychotherapist and a clinical associate of the Psychology Department at Simon Fraser University, which means I supervise PhD candidates and give workshops on Jungian psychology (the department has no courses in Jungian psychology). Finally, I am a spiritual director and sometimes give courses at the Vancouver School of Theology on the meeting points between psychology and spirituality that involve Jungian theory. In addition to these activities, I give a variety of workshops for clergy, spiritual directors, and mental health professionals teaching them to work with dreams, dream groups that introduce people to dream work, and other lectures and workshops of various sorts on the connections between psychology and spirituality. Thus I have taught Jung in almost every imaginable context. All of these contexts require different approaches.

Let me begin by talking about the academic context, both philosophical and psychological.

It would be uncontroversial to say that Jung has not found wide acceptance in the academic world. The reasons for this are many. Some Jungians would say that Jung is too "special," that academics are intolerant. That seems to me to be partly true in that there is a strong materialist bias in both philosophy of mind (the dualism that would make Jung more approachable is unacceptable in both philosophy and psychology) and the kind of psychology that is currently popular in the departments with which I am most familiar. However, there seem to me to be faults on both sides, and some Jungian writers, such as the ever-fascinating and versatile David L. Miller (see chapter 2), have had strong academic careers, if not always in psychology departments. As well, there are less conventional psychology departments where Jungian work thrives; one has only to look at the membership of the International Association for Jungian Studies, an organization of which several of this book's contributors are members.

Nonetheless, my own experience in teaching Jung in academic settings has been that I have been most happily and unquestioningly accepted in a liberal theological setting. How that would surprise Jung! These days, students of theology and students who are training as spiritual directors seem to welcome the Jungian perspective as a way to deepen and interiorize their theology. The addition of Jungian dream work to spiritual direction to help people add a personal connection to their traditional religious commitments has generally, except in the case of students with fundamentalist religious views, been experienced not only as helpful in their potential practice but also as personally enriching. This has been generally a more welcoming sort of experience than the experiences I have had with both psychology graduate students and students in the philosophy of religion. There is a sympathy for the transcendent aspects of Jung, his interest in spiritual life as an essential part of human life, that I suspect is consoling for theology students and potential spiritual directors in these days of either dwindling interest in religion or a very narrow picture of what constitutes religion.

In addition, for many years I gave a workshop at the Vancouver School of Theology called "Sex and Spirituality," in which I discussed Jung's views on the levels of eros and described the ways in which eros can be lived out in a spiritual way. This was in the context of discussing the concepts of projection and transference, especially the sorts of archetypal transference that clergy receive as a result of their profession. The Jungian perspective on human relationship, with its complexities and archetypal underpinnings, can be helpful to clergy in understanding the charged relationships that often arise between clergy and parishioners and can help them understand why boundaries are so important yet often so difficult to set. Jung's theories on eros, so similar in some ways to Plato's, also can help not just clergy but anyone understand why sexuality and spirit seem so closely connected.

My experience with graduate students in psychology, especially my recent experience, has changed as graduate departments have become less and less interested in therapy of any length and depth and more and more focused on assessment and cognitive behavioral models. Even Freud might never have existed. From a Jungian perspective, teaching Jung in such a context is a double-leveled activity and a double-leveled experience. As an activity, I often feel I am both presenting a worldview and attempting to gently move those present towards the possibility that this is a worldview worth considering. Many come to my workshops and lectures knowing little or nothing about Jung but believing that he is an obscure mystic and very difficult to understand. Thus I do my best to explain Jung's basic concepts as clearly as possible, to use many examples from casework, and even to use humor whenever possible. My years of teaching philosophy, especially teaching beginners, have given me a great deal of practice in doing this. I have found that when the students realize they can understand the basic Jungian framework, they are so relieved that it generates a certain amount of goodwill.

When students find they can understand this framework, what often emerges in talking about Jung are the reasons they chose psychology in the first place. In supervising clinical candidates, I have discovered that several have had what I would describe as a spiritual calling. They decided to become clinicians from a deep sense of being on a path, not only wanting to help people, though that of course is an element, but also as part of a search for wisdom. Like many philosophy students who also started out in philosophy as a search for wisdom, many clinical psychology students are unconsciously searching for a path to the wisdom of the psyche. Graduate school turns out to be the same sort of disappointment for them that it is for a certain sort of philosophy student, and they are in the same awkward position. To pursue their professional lives, they must go through this process, but it is emotionally, spiritually, and even intellectually unsatisfying. Sometimes they know something's wrong but can't quite articulate it. For these students, a workshop or seminar on Jung, with his emphasis on the inner life, the wisdom of the psyche, the stirring up of the unconscious, and the value of individuation, can be profoundly moving.

This effect is not limited to students. Jung often has the same effect on faculty present on these occasions, reminding them of forgotten aspirations and longings. In today's academic world, certain kinds of limitations grow more and more noticeable, and a day or two spent with Jung can stir the emotions and the imagination, creating a powerful energy and reminding those present of psyche's possibilities.

As I have said, because of the nature of the material, teaching Jung is not simple or straightforward. The teacher of Jung presents information, but the information itself has a certain psychic energy that, in my experience, rarely fails to stir up those present. Of course, like anything with psychic power, it can stir up resistances in those present as well. People who are strongly wedded to strict materialist metaphysical views find Jungian theory disturbing and often distasteful and can behave in quite challenging ways. The good thing about an academic setting is that this can be contained through philosophical argument in the sense that it can be shown that we will have to agree to disagree: the materialism-dualism argument soon arrives at an end, and unless someone is prepared to behave really badly (and most people who are committed to pure rationality have some sort of limit), they just leave. In all my years of giving these sorts of workshops, this has happened only once or twice, and only when a truly dedicated cognitive-behaviorist was required to attend. The most important thing in such a situation is not to become defensive, since such strong feelings indicate intense psychic activity. Interestingly, just as my most cordial reception in an academic setting has been in theological institutions, so have one or two of my most hostile moments come from anxious fundamentalists, so it isn't always about materialism.

Philosophically speaking, Jung's background is Continental. He was very attracted to Kant and interested in Nietzsche, and I have written elsewhere about elements of his view that I believe are harmonious with both Jaspers and Heidegger. For example, Jaspers's concept of Existenzhellerung and Heidegger's concept of authenticity share many features of Jung's concept of individuation, and it seems to me that Jung could benefit from a phenomenological supplement.

In one of my most pleasurable Jungian teaching experiences, a course I taught for the Graduate Liberal Studies Department at Simon Fraser University called "Psychoanalysis, Mysticism and the Structure of Being," I put Jung in good company, connecting phenomenology, mysticism, Freud, and Jung. Jaspers and Heidegger are perhaps particularly "Jung friendly" in that they both have a teleological view, a particular inner process that can last a lifetime and moves toward a highly desirable end. Jaspers is especially appropriate, since his notion of boundary situations as an area of personal development, more complex than Heidegger's simpler requirement that we face our own deaths, involves what he calls "the loving struggle for Existenz" on an inner level that can easily be seen as the sort of inner work that we do in analytic or spiritual work. The atmosphere in this course became a highly charged psychic field as we worked our way through Heidegger and Jaspers, John Caputo, David Michael Levin, Freud, Jung, Marion Woodman, St. John of the Cross, St. Theresa of Avila, Simone Weil, Julian of Norwich, and Iris Murdoch. I have very rarely experienced such enthusiasm from students.

This enthusiasm seemed to arise from at least two sources. First of all, there was a great deal of the sort of enchantment I discussed at the beginning of this paper, and not just about Jung. Many of our readings addressed the inner life from various points of view and spoke deeply to the students. In addition, many of the readings elicited the sort of numinous experience that comes from being in the presence of the divine or archetypal. This was such a strong experience for so many of the students that I actually named it. At the time, I called it "metaphysical experience," since calling it "numinous" or "archetypal" seemed too strongly Jungian, and I wanted to sound more neutral. It helped that the intellectual work of the course was supplemented by two workshops: a dream workshop and a meditation workshop. Thus what is implicit in many "teaching Jung" situations, the importance of actual inner work, was made explicit in this one. The students in this course came from a variety of backgrounds, since the Graduate Liberal Studies program is for returning adult students who were all mature and quite serious about their work. It seemed to have an intense psychic effect on many of the students, one of whom had a genuine spiritual awakening while we were studying the work of St. Teresa. Jung was an especially popular writer. Interestingly, however, many of these students were not persuaded by Jung's point of view on the life of the spirit in that they were not willing to see it from an entirely interior standpoint.

As a result of the course, several of the students became interested in their spiritual lives again and started going to church. They did have a Jungian perspective on religious symbolism but still saw religious experience as possibly coming from a divine source not entirely psychic. These students were especially interesting in that they were profoundly affected by all the material, including Jung. They were clearly hungry for meaning and work on the spirit, while at the same time they were not uncritical, as has been my experience with many spiritual searchers. They seemed to be able to bring their whole selves to the class; they reacted emotionally, spiritually, and intellectually in a way that made teaching them an unforgettable psychic experience.

The one area of philosophy in which Jung has been welcomed, though again not uncritically, is the philosophy of religion. Here Jung has proved to be of great interest to some students who are interested in the psychological roots of religion because of his concept of the collective unconscious and because he viewed spiritual life as a natural human activity. My experience with students in the philosophy of religion has been that they like Jung much better than Freud because he is not a reductionist. He believes that religious longing is a natural function of the psyche and that we do not progress on a path to wholeness until we are in touch with that aspect of ourselves. Thus by comparison with Freud, Jung comes off very well. But students who are interested in the philosophy of religion, unlike some other philosophy students, are not committed to the view that the life of the mind is entirely a life of rationality. On the other hand, those who are interested in spiritual-religious life for its own sake tend to be resistant to the complete interiorization of religious life. For example, they may have had religious experiences that involve mystical visions of saints and religious figures of various sorts that emphatically do not seem interior. However, those who come from traditional religious backgrounds and who are searching for a richer way to live their spiritual lives welcome the Jungian perspective, as do students who are searching for a spiritual path but don't know where to start. They often have the same response as the psychology graduate students. They feel the stirring of the psyche, the longing they can't quite name.

Given the fact that in all these academic settings teaching the work of Jung can create a powerful psychic field, does that give the teacher of Jung any sort of special responsibility? When I was a younger teacher of Jung, I would often find myself in what I would now call the missionary position. Since I myself was convinced that Jung had got hold of the fundamental truths about psychic life, I was delighted by all the psychic energy loose in the room. I defended Jung's views, though I'm happy to say I stopped short of defending his behavior with his female analysands. The disadvantage of our all swimming around in the psychic soup together was that, without my quite realizing it, I wasn't very helpful to people in one of the psychospiritual culs-de-sac in which people who develop a strong interest in Jung sometimes find themselves, the view that Jung is the prophet of a new religion. It's a temptation, because Jung was so extremely interested in spiritual matters and because he was such an intense promoter of the individual spiritual path. This has a strong appeal to those whose formational spiritual experiences have been very oppressive, controlling, or frustrating in some way.

Many people who are just discovering the inner life through work with dreams or the experience of contact with the unconscious through art and active imagination are so amazed and delighted by these experiences that they believe that this is spiritual life and that Jung is its prophet. Put this together with Jung's later writings about the Self, *Answer to Job*,[3] and Jung's own sense of being called, which comes through quite clearly in *Memories, Dreams Reflections*, and one has a potent mix. These are indeed powerful and worthwhile experiences, but the teacher of Jung also needs to realize that Jung is one person in a very long tradition of thinkers on the subject of the inner life and the development of the spirit. To see Jung as some sort of prophet or sacred being is paralyzing to original thought of one's own, and the teacher of Jung has a responsibility to help the student maintain a certain amount of objectivity, while not dampening enthusiasm.[4] This is especially important in an academic atmosphere, in which one is committed to a certain level of objectivity, but it is also important in lectures and workshops, where people are often more vulnerable and in a "searching" mode, planning more practical life activities on the basis of the material one is offering. In these situations, the chances are good that what one is offering may be the sum total of what they will know in the near future about Jungian theory.

In teaching Jung in either an academic or a workshop setting, I try to keep in mind that I am always speaking to the spirit as well as the mind, and this is both an honor and a responsibility. I'm informing, not preaching, but I'm also being given the opportunity to speak to an aspect of the person that perhaps hasn't been spoken to in the classroom often or recently, something in the person that longs for meaning, for even discussion of the question of meaning in these days of endless irony. This is an important task and a fortunate one.

One the most interesting things about teaching Jung over the years has been the development of my relationship with this material, moving from my initial enchantment with it to my current more objective and reflectively critical relationship. A lifetime of doing my own inner work and of pursuing a spiritual path outside the Jungian world has allowed me to withdraw a good many of those "enchanted" projections, but it has not decreased my appreciation. Doing my own work, both inner and intellectual, has only increased my respect for Jung's courage and imagination, especially in connection with his own inner work. His willingness to confront his own unconscious, even when the material presented was terrifying, is truly admirable, and his ability to incorporate his experiences into theory involved great intellectual risk. Many still see this as a limitation of his, making his views too subjective, but he had the courage of his own point of view right to the end.

One of the most satisfying experiences of teaching Jung I've had in recent years has been teaching Jung, especially Jung's theory of dreams and dream work, to a group of intensely interested academics/psychotherapists from the University of British Columbia Department of Counseling Psychology. These people, who have worked together on projects of their own, gathered into an ongoing professional development group that eventually included others from outside the university. The group combines their own dream work and instruction in dream work that they take into their own practices and teaching. Thus it is in the spirit of Jung's own way of working, combining insights that can be gained only from inner work with theoretical understanding. I have given other professional development workshops that were more exclusively theoretical, but because the people involved did not know each other to begin with, they were not willing to share, so the work was not as deep. For example, in other professional development groups, the therapists present were extremely reluctant to share dreams about clients, apparently in fear of seeming to have "unethical" thoughts or feelings about clients. However, in this group, there is a high level of mutual regard and trust among us, so discussions can be frank. In this group, our discussions move fluidly from talk about theory to talk about dreams, ours and our clients'. There are very few of the enchanted projections on Jung because, by and large, we are at a stage in our lives and work where we are no longer looking for a father or someone to admire uncritically. All of us have done a great deal of inner work, are already committed to a spiritual path, and have an active spiritual practice. This makes talking about Jungian theory much easier because we can be critical, and at the same time, it does not preclude those genuine feelings of numinousness that come with being in the presence of the archetypal or divine when it comes forward in dreams or discussions of theory. In many ways, it is the ideal teaching situation: a small group of people, self-selected, all strongly interested and motivated, with similar backgrounds. We rarely leave on time.

Ethical Issues

Perhaps the most difficult subject for the teacher of Jung, and one that cannot be avoided, is Jung's relationship with some of his female analysands. This has been especially difficult for me as a longtime feminist and as someone who takes a particular interest in moral issues in the helping professions. At the World Congress of Philosophy in 1998, I delivered a paper titled "A Moral Basis for the Helping Professions,"[5] in which I argued that the helping professions are unique in the sense that having a good character matters in being able to do one's job properly. I suggested that Sarah Ruddick's paper "Maternal Thinking"[6] could guide us in choosing the virtues useful to helping professionals, since there is a great deal of overlap between the qualities of the good helping professional and those of the good parent. I went on to argue that, since all helping professionals know quite well that it's wrong to have sex with one's clients yet some do so anyway, there is an unexplained gap in the moral narrative, and that gap is lack of character. Knowledge does not seem to be enough to keep people from doing what they know they ought not do. Character is necessary to get people to apply their principles when they are in situations of extreme temptation.

I think there can be no doubt that the early creators of psychoanalysis and depth psychology were in situations of extreme temptation. Some behaved better than others; some who did not behave well behaved badly in different ways. There can be no question that Jung was unfaithful to his wife of many years in at least one long-term relationship with someone who was initially a analysand, Toni Wolff, and possibly several others. It is also unquestionable that by any standard of ethics and of good therapeutic boundaries, this was the wrong thing to do. The Deirdre Bair biography of Jung leaves us in no doubt that his behavior caused a great deal of pain all round and very likely therapeutic damage.[7] The only possible conclusion is that, from a moral standpoint, this aspect of Jung's character was not well developed. He was determined to do what he wanted, and he forced his wife to deal with it, even though she was unhappy about it. This leaves us with the problem of the connection between the man and his work, a problem that is not limited to Jung. One of my favorite philosophers is Martin Heidegger. There is no question about Heidegger's political views. Heidegger was a Nazi. I often find it both bewildering and shocking to think that the man who wrote so eloquently about authenticity was politically so appalling (though much has been written one way and another connecting his philosophical views with his political views, I've never found it entirely satisfying). What all of this says to me, without in the least excusing people from their moral responsibilities, is that human beings are ultimately extremely mysterious and contradictory. We can, of course, take a psychological standpoint and try to understand why people do what they do. But these explanations are never quite sufficient. If anyone is tempted to take a view of life in which they believe that human beings are consistent, or basically good, or totally explicable, or that people they admire are beyond error or that they themselves are likely to become so, Jung and Heidegger are useful to keep in mind. In Louis Breger's excellent biography of Freud, he makes it clear that Freud absolutely could not tolerate disagreement, and when one of his protégés disagreed with him, that person was driven from his circle.[8] Terrible emotional damage was done in these situations; indeed, Jung was one of the people damaged by Freud's rigidity (though Jung was neither helpless nor harmless in that situation).

In teaching Jung, it is important not to minimize all this, as some people are tempted to, or relativize it in some way, or say that Emma Jung accepted Jung's extramarital activities as somehow benign. As Deirdre Bair makes clear, that is simply not true. Jung was ruthless in this way, as he was in some other ways; he tended, like many creative people, to be ruthless on his own behalf about what he believed he needed for his own work. Jung had views about the relation of the creative person to the collective that supported his behavior and the behavior of people who wanted to go against the collective. The teacher of Jung is in a position to discuss these difficult truths about human nature with students in ways that promote neither naïveté nor cynicism. Indeed, such discussions can help students understand the Jungian notion of the inevitability of the shadow archetype and the likelihood that people who think of themselves as special in some way have a large matching shadow. One of the strands of Jung's willingness to cause his wife such long-term pain seems to have been his view that he needed another woman in his life to nourish his creativity, even though, according to Bair, it had been Emma's lifelong dream to work by his side. Emma herself was a talented analyst and did her own research on the symbolic significance of the Holy Grail. The truth is that human beings are capable of being at once creative, benevolent, imaginative, ruthless, and cruel. We are a mass of contradictions, and this seems to be a permanent situation. One of our major life tasks seems to be to get to know ourselves in all our messiness. No matter how much we wish this were not so, especially in the case of those we admire and respect, it is so. Teaching Jung gives us an excellent opportunity to contemplate this disturbing truth about the human condition, which of course includes ourselves.

Conclusion

Teaching Jung has been different from all my other teaching experiences. From the outset, it has been clear that teaching Jung creates a strong and complex psychic field in the classroom. I noticed this in a slightly different way in my philosophy courses while talking about certain philosophers such as Plato, Spinoza, and Hegel. I attributed the unusual feelings that lecturing on those philosophers gave me to being so close to the numinous or the divine in these "big picture" views. I realized the students didn't seem to feel that same way I did, and I wasn't entirely surprised. Many years of teaching philosophy had taught me that a passion for philosophy is unevenly distributed across the population, especially a passion for what might be called big picture philosophy. So not everyone feels the presence of the transcendent when talking about the form of the Good. However, when talking about Jung and the psyche, once people understand it, something is stirred up because Jung's views do indeed speak to something deep within us.

When I think of Jung himself, I think of someone who was extremely curious and interested in people and in life. While he had his intellectual limitations in that, like Freud, he resisted disagreement, nevertheless, his zest for learning about the things that interested him was intense, and he never seemed to stop confronting his own unconscious. When I teach Jung, I try to convey to my students this attitude. Ultimately, what inner work can bring is a strong connection with the Self, so that the ego loses its illusion of supremacy. The ego-Self axis is not an improvement of ego function. It should actually be called the Self-ego axis. The ego still exists but is quite a different creature than the ego in its unconscious state. It is permeable and ruled by the Self, really a creation of the Self. This can lead us into some surprising places and help us take what I think of as a God's-eye view of ourselves and others, a compassionate and interested view of our human condition as we go through this difficult but always engrossing and challenging life together.

NOTES

1. Bonnelle Strickling, *Dreaming about the Divine* (Albany: State University of New York Press, 2007).

2. C. G. Jung, *Memories, Dreams Reflections* (New York: Vintage, 1989).

3. Jung, *Psychology and Religion*, in *Collected Works of C. G. Jung*, ed. Herbert Read, M. Fordham, and G. Adler, trans. R. F. C. Hull (Princeton, New Jersey: Princeton University Press, 1958), Vol. 11.

4. For an especially interesting perspective on this sort of challenge in teaching, I recommend Ladson Hinton's "Teaching 'Origins of Depth Psychology': Overview and Candidate-Members' Experience," *Journal of Analytical Psychology* 53 (February 2008): 91–100. This article addresses the "enchantment" issue in training candidates.

5. Strickling, "A Moral Basis for the Helping Professions," in *Paideia Archive for the Twentieth World Congress of Philosophy* at www.bu.edu/wcp/Papers/Bioe/BioeStri.htm.

6. Sarah Ruddick, "Maternal Thinking," in *Mothering: Essays in Feminist Theory*, ed. Joyce Trebilcot (Totawa, New Jersey: Rowan & Allenheld, 1983).

7. Deirdre Bair, *Jung: A Biography* (Boston: Little, Brown, 2004).

8. Louis Breger, *Freud: Darkness in the Midst of Vision* (Hoboken, New Jersey, John Wiley & Sons, 2001).

REFERENCES

Bair, Deirdre. *Jung: A Biography*. Boston: Little, Brown, 2004.

Breger, Louis. *Freud: Darkness in the Midst of Vision*. Hoboken, New Jersey: John Wiley & Sons, 2001.

Hinton, Ladson. "Teaching 'Origins of Depth Psychology': Overview and Candidate-Members' Experience." *Journal of Analytical Psychology* 53 (February 2008): 91–100.

Jung, Carl. "Answer to Job," in *Psychology and Religion*. In *Collected Works of C. G. Jung*, ed. Herbert Read, M. Fordham, and G. Adler, trans. R. F. C. Hull, Vol. 11. Princeton, New Jersey: Princeton University Press, 1958.

Jung, Carl. *Memories, Dreams, Reflections*. New York: Vintage, 1989.

Ruddick, Sarah. "Maternal Thinking." In *Mothering: Essays in Feminist Theory*, ed. Joyce Trebilcot, 231–262. Totawa, New Jersey: Rowan & Allenheld, 1983.

Strickling, Bonnelle. "A Moral Basis for the Helping Professions." *Paideia Archive for the Twentieth World Congress of Philosophy*. www.bu.edu/wcp/Papers/Bioe/BioeStri.htm.

Strickling, Bonnelle. *Dreaming about the Divine*. Albany: State University of New York Press, 2007.

16

Can There Be a Science of the Symbolic?

John Beebe

Science, derived from *sciens*, the present participle of the Latin verb *scire*, "to know," means knowing, "possession of knowledge as distinguished from ignorance or misunderstanding,"[1] but also a knowing verified by replicability. Science, in this sense, is not a Cartesian or Galilean discovery. We all have a science, a worldview replicated by our experience, that we steer by; analysts are no exception. For those of us who function professionally in the analytic situation, our worldview is the theory we employ to understand that situation. Each of us working as analysts will have chosen a theory and tailored it to whatever worldview we already had before we began to work as analysts: that is the science we take to work with us every day.

But science, even at the level of theory, is a hard thing to bring to depth psychological work because, above all else, in the therapeutic aspect of that work, we really don't want to lose sight of the individual differences that make people most deeply themselves. As Jung famously put it, "the patient is there to be treated and not to verify a theory. For that matter, there is no single theory in the whole field of practical psychology that cannot on occasion prove basically wrong."[2] Science, as replicable knowing, is somewhat hostile to individual differences because it wants (and needs) repetition of findings to verify that its view of what is going on is correct. A scientist likes to believe that he or she is able to reject a particular worldview in favor of another if the findings that would seem to support the original view can't be replicated. In a field where individual differences are expected to prevail, not only in the patient but also in the practitioner, such an effort is undermined from the start. In another well-known passage, Jung cautions:

Practical medicine is, and has always been an art, and the same is true of practical analysis. True art is creation, and creation is beyond all theories. That is why I say to any beginner: Learn your theories as well as you can, but put them aside when you touch the miracle of the living soul. Not theories but your own creative individuality alone must decide.[3]

Jung's Hermeneutics

In the decade following his departure from Freud's psychoanalytic movement, Jung recognized the problems that face anyone who tries to bring a scientific attitude to the interpretation of symbolic material, that is, to the understanding of dreams and fantasies. Although he never utterly abandoned the search for a scientific solution to these problems, his pessimism that one could be found comes through in a lecture titled "The Conception of the Unconscious," one of the foundational statements delivered (we are told) before the Zürich School for Analytical Psychology in 1916. This lecture, much revised, became "The Relations between the Ego and the Unconscious," the second of the *Two Essays on Analytical Psychology* that comprise volume 7 of Jung's *Collected Works*, where, in the appendices, the original lecture appears, freshly translated from the German under the title "The Structure of the Unconscious."[4] Here I am going to quote from the translation of Constance Long, as found in her second 1920 edition of Jung's *Collected Papers on Analytical Psychology*,which for a long time was the major statement of his approach to depth psychology:

> ...phantasies have had a bad reputation among psychologists. The psycho-analytical theories hitherto obtaining have treated them accordingly. For both Freud and Adler the phantasy is nothing but a so-called "symbolic" disguise of what both investigators suppose to be the primary propensities and aims. But in opposition to these views it should be emphasized—not for theoretical but for essentially practical reasons—that the phantasy may indeed be thus causally explained and depreciated, but that it nevertheless is the creative soil for every-thing that has ever brought development to humanity. The phantasy as a psychological function has a peculiar non-reducible value of its own, whose roots are in both the conscious and the unconscious contents, and in what is collective as well as in what is individual.
>
> But whence comes the bad reputation of the phantasy? It owes that reputation chiefly to the circumstance that it ought not to be taken literally. It is worthless if understood concretistically. If we understand semiotically, as Freud does, it is interesting from the scientific standpoint. But if it be understood *hermeneutically, as an actual symbol*, it provides us with the cue that we need in order to develop our life in harmony with ourselves.

For the significance of a symbol is not that it is a disguised indication of something that is generally known [footnote: That is, of a universal primary propensity or a universal primal aim] but that it is an endeavour to elucidate by analogy what is as yet completely unknown and only in the process of formation.[footnote: Cp. *Silberer:* "Probleme der Mystic und ihrer Symbolik" Wien, 1914 ("Problems of Mysticism and Its Symbolism").The phantasy represents to us that which is just developing under the form of a more or less apposite analogy. By analytical reduction to something universally known, we destroy the actual value of the symbol; but it is appropriate to its value and meaning to give it a hermeneutical interpretation.

The essence of hermeneutics—an art that was formerly much practiced—consists in adding more analogies to that already given by the symbol: in the first place, subjective analogies given by the patient as they occur to him; and in the second place, objective analogies provided by the analyst out of his general knowledge. The initial symbol is much enlarged and enriched by this procedure, the result being a highly complex and many-sided picture, which may now be reduced to *tertia comparationis*. Thence result certain psychological lines of development of an individual as well as collective nature. No science upon earth could prove the accuracy of these lines; on the contrary, rationalism could very easily prove that they are wrong. But these lines vindicate their validity by their *value for life*. The chief thing in practical treatment is that people should get a hold of their own life, not that the principle of their life should be provable or "right."[5]

This passage, rooted in William James's pragmatism, is startlingly contemporary. It not only predates, by as much as a decade, Heidegger's 1927 rediscovery of hermeneutics, recorded in *Being and Time*, and thus the whole tradition of postmodern hermeneutics that was thereby inaugurated (to be carried forward after 1960 by Hans-Georg Gadamer with his seminal *Truth and Method* and by Paul Ricoeur, who famously attributed to Freud a "hermeneutics of suspicion"). It also finds a later echo in the neopragmatism of Richard Rorty's *Philosophy and the Mirror of Nature* (1979), where the contemporary American philosopher tells us that "hermeneutics is not 'another way of knowing'— 'understanding' as opposed to (predictive) explanations. It is better seen as another way of coping."[6]

No doubt the hermeneutics Jung was talking about was not so postmodern: probably he was remembering the biblical hermeneutics, which Schleiermacher, one of his "spiritual ancestors,"[7] had expanded in the early nineteenth century to a general science of interpreting texts. Schleiermacher, more than anyone else in the nineteenth century, tried to make hermeneutics a responsible method for getting at meaning, and Dilthey, who influenced Heidegger, followed him. Hermeneutics, according to Gadamer, is "the classical discipline concerned with the art of understanding texts."[8] The word *hermeneutics*, from

the Greek *hermeneutikon*, means literally "things for interpreting" and therefore implies an apparatus, or set of apparatuses, brought to the interpretation
of texts. It was J. C. Dannhauer who, in the mid-seventeenth century, first used
this word to inquire into interpretive method, pointing to the three classes of
texts for which such a theory of interpretation was needed: the philological (or
literary) text, the legal text, and the theological text, namely, scripture.[9] We can
see what he envisioned even today in legal judgments, where law is concretized
into legal validity by being interpreted according to a system of precedents.
Similarly, we recognize that preaching, at least of Christian scripture, demands
that gospel be understood in such a way that it exercises its saving effect. And
at least until the advent of deconstructive critical methods, we have had a vigorous tradition of literary criticism that makes our classics yield moral meanings to us. Jung was consciously drawing on this early-nineteenth-century
tradition when he brought the search for precedent, for salvation, and for ethical meaning to the interpretation of fantasy material; at the same time, he was
anticipating Rorty's understanding of hermeneutics, in the last quarter of the
twentieth century, as a way of coping.

The Hermeneutic Circle

By the middle of the twentieth century, however, another philosophical tradition, one grounded in the phenomenology of the interpretative process itself,
was highlighting the scientific problem at the heart of hermeneutics.

Heidegger, in the 1920s, realized that any authentic judgment as to what a
text means is no more (or less) than someone's response to the text, and one
that is already driven by that person's worldview, even (and especially) when it
is stripped of "fancies and popular conceptions" and tries to focus on the thing
itself.[10] The problem for each of us who would interpret, therefore, is that we
don't just have this worldview, we bring it to the table when we interpret. For
Heidegger, therefore, "A person who is trying to understand a text is always
projecting. He [or she] projects a meaning to the text as a whole as soon as
some initial meaning emerges in the text."[11] This very limitation, however,
becomes the interpreters' opportunity to discover "the most primordial kind of
knowing" in themselves and others.

Gadamer emphasizes, moreover, that a text must be understood at every
moment in every concrete situation in a new and different way. Textual understanding can then be shown to be an event emerging out of a situated person's
exercise of phronesis, Aristotle's name for the virtue of practical knowledge,
which distinguishes, for instance, what should be done from what should not.
But even when phronesis is brought to a text, it is accompanied by a worldview,
and what emerges as the meaning of the text remains some variant of the
original worldview brought to it. This is "Heidegger's description of the hermeneutic circle."[12] To get out of such circular interpretative reasoning, Gadamer
argues that the initial response, though an authentic expression of the individual
interpreter's worldview, must be taken not as the intuition of meaning, but as

the first move in what has to be a dialogue if anything like meaning is genuinely to emerge. We know the dialogue is genuine if it has the effect of enlarging interpretative horizons, that is, has some effect of altering or enlarging the original worldview.[13] From this perspective, the science that is brought to a text is as good as the dialogue it engenders. Neither the science nor the hermeneutics free us from the difficulty of getting at the truth; rather, the drive to get at the truth forces us into a dialogue with the object, which requires that we hold the tension between the two ways of understanding, theoretical knowing and practical knowledge. The distinction between the two is originally Aristotle's;[14] Gadamer shows its relation to ancient and modern science,[15] and Bernstein provides a lively, postmodern discussion of "the to-and-fro movement...of science, hermeneutics, and praxis."[16]

Science and Hermeneutics in Practice

As an analytical psychotherapist, working in the liminal area not only guarded but also ruled by Hermes, I find I am often practicing what Jung and Rorty call hermeneutics and that I am just as often bringing what Heidegger and Gadamer would call a worldview (and I would call my science) to the practice. In other words, I say things to my patients in the effort to produce lives that work for them, and so I am more concerned with the potential for my remarks to help them cope than I am with the capacity of those remarks to withstand scientific scrutiny. Indeed, so long as the container of our work is hermetically sealed, as our analytic ethos insists it must be, my actual remarks to patients do not get much scientific scrutiny, since they are not available for others to study, verify, or refute. Nevertheless, I find myself sharing with my patients what I imagine to be the science of our field in the form of interpretations that are grounded in some theory of how the mind works that I think is actually verifiable by evidence. That means that I am often amplifying what my patients are able to tell me about their inner lives by adducing things that I have learned about other people's inner lives, not least my own, as I have come to understand it in the course of my own analysis and the ongoing dialogue with myself that that has engendered.

Perhaps the belief that what he is doing is somewhere grounded in science never leaves an analyst. Jung, for instance, for all his seeming rejection, in the passage I quoted earlier of science in favor of hermeneutics as the basis for analysis of fantasy, did not hesitate to allow the 1950 British edition of his work with Kerenyi on mythology to go out under the title *Essays on a Science of Mythology*.[17] Sonu Shamdasani has shown in his book, *Jung and the Making of Modern Psychology: The Dream of a Science*, that Jung had the vision of a science driving much of his creation of complex psychology.[18] As Shamdasani makes clear, complex psychology is the basic science within Jungian thought that analytical psychology, the practical therapeutic discipline, has often ignored.

As a practicing analyst, I encounter the tension between analytical psychology and complex psychology on an almost daily basis. I continually experience a tension between the pragmatic, hermeneutic endeavor to come up with interpretations that further my and the patient's ability to understand and cope with emergent unconscious material, on the one hand, and the scientific ambition to develop theories that will not only inform my own cognitions in this endeavor but also formulate hypotheses that others can verify. This tension is never more evident to me than when I am teaching basic complex psychology to analysts in training.

A Practical Example

Recently, for instance, I was giving a class to analytic candidates on Jung's psychological types. I explained to the class that over the past twenty years I have been pioneering a model of types that focuses on the different function-attitudes (introverted feeling, extraverted intuition, introverted sensation, extraverted thinking, and so on) as so many complexes of consciousness in our psyche. Each of these function-complexes, I argued, can be seen (like other complexes) to be associated with an archetypal core, which is revealed by the role through which the complex tends characteristically to express itself. Figure 16.1 illustrates a model that suggests the kinds of archetypal roles that are associated with the typological complexes in the various positions available to them within the total complement of typical consciousnesses, such as "superior function," "auxiliary function," "tertiary function," or "inferior function."[19]

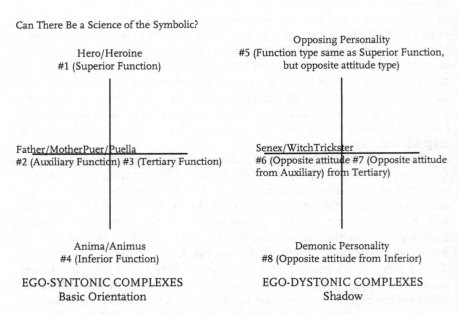

Can There Be a Science of the Symbolic?

Hero/Heroine
#1 (Superior Function)

Opposing Personality
#5 (Function type same as Superior Function, but opposite attitude type)

Father/MotherPuer/Puella
#2 (Auxiliary Function) #3 (Tertiary Function)

Senex/WitchTrickster
#6 (Opposite attitude #7 (Opposite attitude from Auxiliary) from Tertiary)

Anima/Animus
#4 (Inferior Function)

Demonic Personality
#8 (Opposite attitude from Inferior)

EGO-SYNTONIC COMPLEXES
Basic Orientation

EGO-DYSTONIC COMPLEXES
Shadow

FIGURE 16.1. Archetypal Complexes Carrying the Eight Functions.

For a particular individual, a given function-attitude[20]—introverted feeling, say—will correspond to the superior function of consciousness; according to my diagram model, that function-attitude in that superior position will take on a heroic expression. In the same individual, the auxiliary function-attitude— say, extraverted intuition—may take on, in a man, the character of a fatherly expression. The superior feeling function, in other words, operates like a complex built around the archetype of the hero, and the auxiliary intuitive function is a complex that has the archetype of the father at its core. This individual's cognitive functioning in interpersonal situations can be described in terms not only of the type of consciousness he displays, introverted feeling with extraverted intuition on the side, but also of the archetypal roles he slips into when deploying those leading consciousnesses. It is actually possible to establish an archetypal role for each of the eight types of function-attitude that make up a particular individual's complement of consciousnesses.

This was the theory I presented to the eight seminar candidates. I then asked each of the candidates to take one of the eight function-attitudes Jung described as psychological types and tell the class how that function-attitude is expressed and experienced by him or her. All eight members of this seminar took up this assignment in original and individual ways, and I learned a great deal about both type and clinical type-diagnosis from all of them. For the present purpose, however, I will describe only the first two candidates' responses.

At the next meeting of the seminar, the first candidate to present described himself as someone with superior extraverted feeling and told us he had chosen introverted thinking because it was, presumably, his inferior function, and he thought it would benefit him to learn more about it. Before he proceeded to describe introverted thinking, he reported the following dream:

A (my partner) and B (my affectionate dog) are in the therapy room
with me. I am seeing my longtime client C, who is not terribly
intellectual, but seems to value my feeling connection and support of
him. The dog is playing with C. I'm surprised that C doesn't object to
A's presence. A asks whether it's OK for him to leave, and I say that
if he's going to be present at the therapy session at all, he should stay
for the whole session. C says that is not necessary, and also that he's
happy with the dog and enjoys playing with him. I continue working
with C very much as I have, but with more patience and understanding of his emotional needs. Over my shoulder there's a huge
pane of dirty glass. John Beebe is standing behind the glass; he's
formally (and elegantly) dressed and working very meticulously with
a squeegee. His glasses are spotlessly clean and brilliantly clear. John
cleans the glass over and over again with careful motions, allowing
light to come in brilliantly over my shoulder as I'm doing therapy.

I took this dream less as a commentary on introverted thinking than as a validation of the patient's own extraverted feeling. I also observed the dream's

idealization of me as someone who could clarify the clinical situation through the theory of psychological type that I had developed. I was not sure what function-attitude the "partner" in the dream symbolized, but it seemed clear to me that the dog represented the candidate's extraverted feeling, which turned out to be of more value to the client than the candidate had imagined it could be. This candidate proceeded to describe how extraverted feeling was such a dominant function for him that it was hard to get a good read on his introverted thinking. Nevertheless, he made a stab at describing how that function-attitude looks in general and how it came up for him in particular. I don't remember much about the description of introverted thinking because I had begun to bask in the depiction of me in the dream as bringing a brilliant light into his consulting room.

When the next candidate began to present, I found myself in the happy glow of what Karen Horney termed self-idealization.[21] My theory could not be wrong if it had inspired such a positive dream.

This next candidate had chosen to speak about introverted sensation, and she, too, had brought a dream that she had had after our first seminar meeting.

> There was a large ballroom with tall windows with old glass and
> ironwork, not many people. I wanted to learn more and asked John
> to teach or show me. (We were in dress clothes or formal wear.) John
> said yes, and we began to dance, a waltzlike dance. He danced us in a
> circle near one of the windows that had light coming through. He
> paused at different points around the circle he created with the dance
> to emphasize an aspect of the light, then moved us to the other side
> in the circle, which was in shadow, showing both the dark and the
> light aspects of meaning that was understood between us. There was
> a sense of ease.
>
> Then the dream shifted, though we were still in the same area
> and dress. There was a mundane but important task to be done as
> part of an organization's function that I had been doing and orga-
> nizing all night long. It consisted of cutting paper into squares,
> pasting pictures on them, assembling them in a package of a few
> squares, stapling, etc. A young woman (my daughter?), her baby, and
> a young man were coming to help. There were other people in the
> room, other children, too. I explained the task to them, but they
> weren't paying much attention. The young man sat on the floor and
> was building a structure with building blocks and Tinkertoys. I knew
> he was listening, but he was fascinated with creating this structure.
> I felt that I couldn't rely on them to follow directions and get this
> done. I got angry and called him stupid and then told them to leave,
> realizing I couldn't count on them. They left in a limo. I seemed
> harsh and in the dream as they were leaving, it was OK with me that
> they were leaving, that I shouldn't have expected them to do the task
> anyway. But I was disappointed and tired.

It interested me that this dream, like that of the first candidate, also shows me in formal dress and emphasizes windows that bring in light. Initially at least, this second candidate and I seem to be in great rapport, a fact that I took in the seminar to be a strong indication that she and I might be the same psychological type, and since I knew that my superior function was extraverted intuition, I wondered if that was also the superior function of the candidate. On first hearing, however, my attention was riveted to the figure of the young man who busies himself building a structure with blocks and does not seem to be really listening to the dreamer who is trying to draw his attention to the particular task.

The candidate felt that the young man might represent introverted sensation, which, if she were extraverted intuitive, would be her inferior function. I, however, was impressed by how oppositional he was being, and since I know that introverted intuitives sometimes like to build and toy with models of things, architectural archetypes as it were, I took him to maybe represent an introverted intuitive function that was acting in opposition to the candidate's own extraverted intuition and to the task I had set for her with my own extraverted intuition, to tell me what her introverted sensation was like. Indeed, if he did represent introverted intuition, he would be the image of what my model calls "the opposing personality." I couldn't resist taking this as my springboard to teach the class about this complex, so often associated with avoidant and passive-aggressive behavior, like that of the boy in the dream. I was so proud of myself for having shed yet another "brilliant light" on the dream material through the use of my theory that I decided that very evening, after the seminar, that I would bring this example to the *Journal of Analytical Psychology* conference panel as part of a talk I had already decided to call "Can There Be a Science of the Symbolic?" Having been able to unmask the opposing personality and distinguish it for the class from the inferior function with the aid of my theory, I felt sure I could answer that question in the affirmative. There was indeed a science, and here it was in the form of my triumphant application of my model.

But when I started to write about the seminar experience, checking my ideas about the types of the dream figures with a friend who is an introverted sensation type, gifted in knowing whether an intuitive stab at the type could actually be verified, my friend immediately balked. He wasn't so sure the young man in the woman candidate's dream was introverted intuitive just because he was playing with blocks and shirking a dull extraverted sensation task. He said that he remembered very well being engrossed as a child playing with blocks, creating and ordering a private, introverted space. It seemed to him that the young man resembled more his own type, introverted sensation, as the candidate herself had initially thought.

I decided to go back to the candidate. She revealed that though she had found the seminar stimulating, she had felt there had been a problem with communication between us around this particular point of type diagnosis. She was grateful I now wanted to explore her own reactions to the dream figure. As I patiently gathered her associations, I became convinced. The young man's inattentiveness was more a sign of his introversion, and beyond that, his autonomy and perhaps his creativity. None of the figures in the dream wanted anything to do with the somewhat uncreative cutting and pasting task she was trying to impose on them. As I thought about it, that kind of task pulls for extraverted sensation. Indeed, this was rather like the task I had set out for the candidates, for each of them to describe one of the eight functions and place it in the model of type I had diagrammed for them. The young man who wouldn't respond to the dreamer's instruction most likely represented her introverted sensation animus, which wanted to play with the model in his own way, until its reality made sense. He could not relate to the model in an extraverted, collective way. I realized that even though I had told the candidates that they could approach this task any way they wanted, including finding the function on the inside, this was still a collective task. Indeed, this candidate's dream had found its own way of playing with my model, to see if it could express aspects of her personality and consciousness as typological complexes. Her "daughter" and this daughter's baby were most probably images of her auxiliary and tertiary functions—mother and child in my model. That the image of her own motherliness was represented as her daughter suggested its auxiliary relation to her own superior function ego personality, yet that this daughter had a daughter of her own suggested that this auxiliary function took on a motherly character. In the dream, therefore, once I could let myself see it, was a group portrait of her first four functions.

It was clear that just like the figure of the inferior function playing with the model blocks, the dream had taken up the theory that I had presented, though not in the way I would have predicted. Her psyche had chosen to reveal its typological scheme in its own way. Why was this so hard for me to see initially, when I reached for the interpretation of the opposing personality? The candidate and I concluded that a major problem in placing a preordained expectation (which would be the method of science) on the unconscious figures is that, like the figure of the young man who resists the assigned task, each has a life and mind of its own! Only when I was able to recognize that my particular take on the dream did not resonate with the candidate who had dreamed it was I able to enter a dialogue with the candidate that resulted in a deepened respect for the psyche's autonomy, and only then could the creative autonomy of her inferior function become evident, rather than the oppositional character I had wanted to assign to it. Once I had listened to the candidate's feeling that my initial diagnosis of the boy figure did not resonate with her, I was able to see this figure with more empathy. In the language of the dream, I could then dance with her, that is, accept the movements of her psyche rather than impose my own ideas as to what they should be.

Conclusion

In his development of Schleiermacher's hermeneutics, Dilthey made a distinction between understanding (*verstehen*) and explanation (*erklären*).[22] Evidence of *erklären*, the brilliant and clarifying light I was able to bring to my explanation of type theory in my first seminar, is registered in both of the candidates' dreams, and their reflection of it ended up dazzling me. Blinded by the resulting self-idealization, I could not really understand either dream. I never really got to the essence of the first candidate's dream, for instance, but merely knew things about it and saw things in it. I stayed in the mode of explanation, stuck in the hermeneutic circle that could only identify what we both already knew. Only through dialogue was my collusion with the candidates' idealization of my capacity to explain resolved in favor of a genuine understanding of what the second candidate had tried to put together for herself with her dream. In effect, my initial interpretation, which had attempted to force one of her complexes to conform with my model, had been as preconceived, and luckless, as her dream ego's effort to enlist that complex in the rather lifeless task she sought to assign to it. Significantly, this interpretation did not resonate with the candidate when she reflected on it, and fortunately she said so, so that I could take that lack of resonance seriously enough to pursue it.[23] The ensuing dialogue, which enabled the candidate and me to better understand each other, is akin to what the transference aims for in analysis, where the interaction goes on until both parties have exhausted their curiosity about the other. In such a dialogue, the possibilities of psyche are affirmed in their autonomy, creativity, purposiveness, and reality, as the final interpreters of what is.

Note that this is not the "hermeneutics of suspicion" that Ricoeur attributed to Freud's psychoanalysis. Ricoeur would call it, rather, a "hermeneutics of tradition."[24] Like Schleiermacher's hermeneutics, this method of interpretation respects "the reality of inner feeling" when approaching a text of intense personal relevance.[25] What results is a worldview grounded in the reality of the psyche, even as it is discovered in the spirit of scientific inquiry, the true fruit of a dialogue with nature. This emergent worldview not only feels organic but also becomes the viable hypothesis that goes to meet other "cases" for its verification or repudiation in the development of our science.

This essay first appeared, in slightly different form, in The Journal of Analytical Psychology, 49/2: 177–191, 2004.

NOTES

1. Merriam-Webster, *Webster's Third New International Dictionary of the English Language Unabridged* (Chicago: Encyclopaedia Britannica, 1986), 2032.

2. C. G. Jung, *Collected Works of C. G. Jung*, ed. Herbert Read, M. Fordham, and G. Adler, trans. R. F. C. Hull (Princeton, NJ: Princeton University Press, 1958), 16:237.

3. C. G. Jung, "Analytical Psychology and Education," in *Contributions to Analytical Psychology*, trans. H. G. Baynes and Cary F. Baynes (New York: Harcourt Brace, 1928), 361.

4. Jung, *Collected Works*, 7:269–304.

5. "The Conception of the Unconscious," In C. G. Jung, *Collected Papers on Analytical Psychology*, ed. and trans. Constance Long, second edition (London: Baillière, Tindall and Cox, 1920, 468–69). Richard Hull's translation (Jung, *Collected Works*, 7: 290–91) renders the passage as follows: "Fantasy has, it is true, a poor reputation among psychologists, and up to the present psychoanalytic theories have treated it

accordingly. For Freud as for Adler it is nothing but a 'symbolic' disguise for the basic drives and intentions presupposed by these two investigators. As against these opinions it must be emphasized—not on theoretical grounds but essentially for practical reasons—that although fantasy can be causally explained and devalued in this way, it nevertheless remains the creative matrix of everything that has made progress possible for humanity. Fantasy has its own irreducible value, for it is a psychic function that has its roots in the conscious and the unconscious alike, in the individual as much as in the collective.

"Whence has fantasy acquired its bad reputation? Above all from the circumstance that it cannot be taken literally. *Concretely* understood, it is worthless. If it is understood *semiotically*, as Freud understands it, it is interesting from the scientific point of view, but if it is understood *hermeneutically*, as an authentic symbol, it acts as a signpost, providing the clues that we need in order to carry on our lives in harmony with ourselves.

"The symbol is not a sign that disguises something generally known [footnote: A disguise, that is, for the basic drive or elementary intention]. Its meaning resides in the fact that it is an attempt to elucidate, by a more or less apt analogy, something that is still entirely unknown or in the process of formation [footnote: Silberer, *Problems of Mysticism and Its Symbolism*; also my *Symbols of Transformation* and "The Content of the Psychoses"]. If we reduce this by analysis to something that is generally known, we destroy the true value of the symbol; but to attribute hermeneutic significance to it is consistent with its value and meaning.

"The essence of hermeneutics, an art widely practised in former times, consists in adding further analogies to the one already supplied by the symbol: in the first place subjective analogies produced at random by the patient, then objective analogies provided by the analyst out of his general knowledge. This procedure widens and enriches the initial symbol, and the final outcome is an infinitely complex and variegated picture the elements of which can be reduced to their respective *tertia comparationis*. Certain lines of psychological development then stand out that are at once individual and collective. There is no science on earth by which these lines could be proved 'right'; on the contrary, rationalism could very easily prove that they are wrong. Their validity is proved by their intense value for life. And that is what matters in practical treatment: that human beings should get a hold on their own lives, not that the principles by which they live should be proved rationally to be 'right.'"

6. Richard Rorty (*Philosophy and the Mirror of Nature* [Princeton, NJ: Princeton University Press, 1979], 356) adds, in terms that seem to carry forward the spirit of Jung's 1916 remarks into our own time, "It would make for philosophical clarity if we just gave the notion of 'cognition' to predictive science, and stopped worrying about 'alternative cognitive methods.' The word knowledge would not seem worth fighting over were it not for the Kantian tradition that to be a philosopher is to have a 'theory of knowledge,' and the Platonic tradition that action not based on knowledge of the truth of propositions is 'irrational.'"

7. C. G. Jung, "Letter to Henry Corbin, May 4, 1953," in *Letters, Vol. 2: 1951–1961*, ed. Gerhard Adler, Aniela Jaffé, and R. F. C. Hull (Princeton, NJ: Princeton University Press, 1975), 115.

8. Hans G. Gadamer, *Truth and Method*, 2nd ed., trans. Joel Weinsheimer and Donald G Marshall (New York: Continuum, 1989), 64.

9. Thomas Mautner, ed. "Hermeneutics," in *The Penguin Dictionary of Philosophy* (London: Penguin, 2000), 248.

10. Heidegger, quoted in Gadamer, *Truth and Method*, 266.

11. Gadamer, *Truth and Method*, 267.

12. Ibid., 266.

13. Ibid., 302–307.

14. Ibid., 21–22.

15. Ibid., 453–55.

16. Richard J. Bernstein, *Beyond Objectivism and Relativism: Science, Hermeneutics, and Praxis* (Philadelphia: University of Pennsylvania Press, 1983), 171ff.

17. The original title of the book, published in German in 1941, was *Einführung in das Wesen der Mythologie*.

18. Sonu Shamdasani, *Jung and the Making of Modern Psychology: The Dream of a Science* (Cambridge: Cambridge University Press, 2003).

19. See John Beebe, "Understanding Consciousness through the Theory of Psychological Types," in *Analytical Psychology*, ed. Joseph Cambray and Linda Carter (London: Brunner-Routledge, 2004), for a fuller explication of this model and an account of how it came to be derived from what Jung offers in *Psychological Types* [*Collected Works*, Volume 6].

20. In his typological writings, Jung used the term *function type* to refer to the feeling, intuitive, sensation, and thinking functions of consciousness and *attitude type* to distinguish the extraverted or introverted ways in which the energy of a particular function might be deployed. The complete description of a function of consciousness, for example, introverted feeling, refers both to the type of function and the attitude with which the consciousness is typically deployed, and thus the term *function-attitude* has come into favor among contemporary students of psychological type (Henry L. Thompson, *Jung's Function-Attitudes Explained* (Watkinsville, GA: Wormhole Press,1996). When referring to a particular function-attitude in terms of its position within the total hierarchy of consciousnesses, however, it is still more usual to speak simply of "superior function," "auxiliary function," "tertiary function," and "inferior function."

21. Karen Horney, *Neurosis and Human Growth: The Struggle toward Self-Realization* (New York: W. W. Norton, 1950).

22. John C. Mallery, Roger Hurwitz, and Gavan Duffy, "Hermeneutics: From Textual Explication to Computer Understanding," in *The Encyclopedia of Artificial Intelligence*, ed. Stuart C. Shapiro (New York: John Wiley & Sons, 1997).

23. I am indebted to Meredith Sabini for pointing out the significance of the word *resonance* in contemporary interpretations of science, for instance, Lynne McTaggart, *The Field: The Quest for the Secret Force of the Universe* (New York: HarperCollins, 2002).

24. Paul Ricoeur, *Hermeneutics & the Human Sciences*, ed. and trans. J. B. Thompson (Cambridge: Cambridge University Press, 1981), 64.

25. Marilyn Nagy, *Philosophical Issues in the Psychology of C. G. Jung* (Albany: State University of New York Press, 1991), 2.

REFERENCES

Beebe, John. "Understanding Consciousness through the Theory of Psychological Types." In *Analytical Psychology*, ed. Joseph Cambray and Linda Carter. London: Brunner-Routledge, 2004.

Bernstein, Richard J. *Beyond Objectivism and Relativism: Science, Hermeneutics, and Praxis*. Philadelphia: University of Pennsylvania Press, 1983.

Gadamer, Hans G. *Truth and Method*, trans. Joel Weinsheimer and Donald
    G. Marshall. 2nd ed. New York: Continuum, 1989.
Heidegger, Martin. *Being and Time: A Translation of Sein und Zeit by Joan Stambaugh*.
    Albany: State University of New York Press, 1996.
Horney, Karen. *Neurosis and Human Growth: The Struggle toward Self-Realization*.
    New York: W. W. Norton, 1950.
Jung, C. G. "The Conception of the Unconscious." In *Collected Papers on Analytical
    Psychology*, trans. Constance E. Long. London: Baillière, Tindall & Cox. 1920.
Jung, C. G. "Analytical Psychology and Education." In *Contributions to Analytical
    Psychology*, trans. H. G. Baynes and Cary F. Baynes. New York: Harcourt Brace,
    1928.
Jung, C. G. "Fundamental Questions of Psychotherapy." In *The Collected Works of
    C. G. Jung*, ed. Herbert Read, M. Fordham, and G. Adler, trans. R. F. C. Hull,
    Vol. 16. Princeton, NJ: Princeton University Press, 1958–1966.
Jung, C. G. *Letters, Vol. 2: 1951–1961*, ed. Gerhard Adler, Aniela Jaffé, and
    R. F. C. Hull. Princeton, NJ: Princeton University Press, 1975.
Jung, C. G. *Psychological Types*. In The Collected Works of C. G. Jung, ed. Herbert
    Read, M. Fordham, and G. Adler, trans. R.F.C. Hull & H.G. Baynes. Princeton,
    NJ: Princeton University Press, 1971.
Mallery, John C., Roger Hurwitz, and Gavan Duffy. "Hermeneutics: From Textual
    Explication to Computer Understanding." In *The Encyclopedia of Artificial
    Intelligence*, ed. Stuart C. Shapiro. New York: John Wiley & Sons, 1997. ftp://
    publications.ai.mit.edu/ai-publications/pdf/AIM-871.pdf.
Mautner, Thomas, ed. "Hermeneutics." In *The Penguin Dictionary of Philosophy*.
    London: Penguin, 2000.
McTaggart, Lynne. *The Field: The Quest for the Secret Force of the Universe*. New York:
    HarperCollins, 2002.
Merriam-Webster. *Webster's Third New International Dictionary of the English Language
    Unabridged*. Chicago: Encyclopaedia Britannica, 1986.
Nagy, Marilyn. *Philosophical Issues in the Psychology of C. G. Jung*. Albany: State
    University of New York Press, 1991.
Ricoeur, Paul. *Hermeneutics & the Human Sciences*, ed. and trans. J. B. Thompson.
    Cambridge: Cambridge University Press, 1981.
Rorty, Richard. *Philosophy and the Mirror of Nature*. Princeton, NJ: Princeton University
    Press, 1979.
Shamdasani, Sonu. *Jung and the Making of Modern Psychology: The Dream of a Science*.
    Cambridge: Cambridge University Press, 2003.
Thompson, Henry L. *Jung's Function-Attitudes Explained*. Watkinsville, GA: Wormhole
    Publishing, 1996.

Index